Escalation and Negotiation in Internat

How can an escalation of conflict lead to negotiation. ⅄ɪ this systematic study, Zartman and Faure bring together European and American scholars to examine this important topic and to define the point where the concepts and practices of escalation and negotiation meet. Political scientists, sociologists, social psychologists, and war-making and peacemaking strategists, among others, examine the various forms escalation can take and relate them to conceptual advances in the analysis of negotiation. They argue that structures, crises, turning points, demands, readiness, and ripeness can often define the conditions where the two concepts can meet, and the authors take this opportunity to offer lessons for theory and practice. By relating negotiation to conflict escalation, two processes that have traditionally been studied separately, this book fills a significant gap in the existing knowledge and is directly relevant to the many ongoing conflict patterns in the world today.

I. William Zartman is the Jacob Blaustein Distinguished Professor of International Organization and Conflict Resolution and Director of the Conflict Management Program, the Nitze School of Advanced International Studies, at The John Hopkins University. He is the editor and author of almost 50 books.

Guy Olivier Faure is Professor of Sociology at the Sorbonne University, Paris V, Department of Social Sciences. He has authored, co-authored and edited a dozen books and over 50 articles; his works have been published in 12 different languages.

The International Institute for Applied Systems Analysis

is an interdisciplinary, nongovernmental research institution founded in 1972 by leading scientific organizations in 12 countries. Situated near Vienna, in the center of Europe, IIASA has been producing valuable scientific research on economic, technological, and environmental issues for over three decades.

IIASA was one of the first international institutes to systematically study global issues of environment, technology, and development. IIASA's Governing Council states that the Institute's goal is: *to conduct international and interdisciplinary scientific studies to provide timely and relevant information and options, addressing critical issues of global environmental, economic, and social change, for the benefit of the public, the scientific community, and national and international institutions.* Research is organized around three central themes:

– Energy and Technology
– Environment and Natural Resources
– Population and Society

The Institute now has National Member Organizations in the following countries:

Austria
The Austrian Academy of Sciences

China
National Natural Science
Foundation of China

Czech Republic
The Academy of Sciences of the
Czech Republic

Egypt
Academy of Scientific Research and
Technology (ASRT)

Estonia
Estonian Association for
Systems Analysis

Finland
The Finnish Committee for IIASA

Germany
The Association for the Advancement
of IIASA

Hungary
The Hungarian Committee for Applied
Systems Analysis

Japan
The Japan Committee for IIASA

Netherlands
The Netherlands Organization for
Scientific Research (NWO)

Norway
The Research Council of Norway

Poland
The Polish Academy of Sciences

Russian Federation
The Russian Academy of Sciences

Sweden
The Swedish Research Council for
Environment, Agricultural Sciences
and Spatial Planning (FORMAS)

Ukraine
The Ukrainian Academy of Sciences

United States of America
The National Academy of
Sciences

Escalation and Negotiation in International Conflicts

Edited by
I. William Zartman and Guy Olivier Faure

IIASA
International Institute for Applied Systems Analysis

CAMBRIDGE UNIVERSITY PRESS

Cambridge, New York, Melbourne, Madrid, Cape Town, Singapore, São Paulo

Cambridge University Press
The Edinburgh Building, Cambridge CB2 2RU, UK

Published in the United States of America by Cambridge University Press,
New York

www.cambridge.org
Information on this title: www.cambridge.org/9780521672610

© International Institute for Applied Systems Analysis 2005

First published 2005

Printed in the United Kingdom at the University Press, Cambridge

A catalogue record for this book is available from the British Library

ISBN-13 978-0-521-85664 - 5 hardback
ISBN-10 0-521-85664 - 7 hardback
ISBN-13 978-0-521-67261 - 0 paperback
ISBN-10 0-521-67261 - 9 paperback

To Francis Walder
for his exceptional illustration of what the job of a negotiator can be

and

to Christophe Dupont
for his insightful contributions to the field that we share.

Contents

Contributors

Karin Aggestam is a research fellow at the Department of Political Science, Lund University, Sweden. She has authored several articles and books on negotiation, mediation, conflict theory, and the Middle East peace process. Recent articles have been published in *International Peacekeeping* and *Civil Wars* (2003).

Rudolf Avenhaus is professor of statistics and operations research at the University of the Federal Armed Forces, Munich. Prior to his academic appointment in 1980, he was a research assistant in the Mathematical and Physical Institutes at the Universities of Karlsruhe and Geneva; a research scholar at the Nuclear Research Center, Karlsruhe; and a lecturer at the University of Mannheim. From 1973 to 1975, and again in 1980, he worked at IIASA. Professor Avenhaus has written numerous scientific publications, as well as *Material Accountability* (1977), *Safeguards Systems Analysis* (1987), and *Compliance Quantified* (together with M. Canty, 1996). In 1989 and 1990 he was chairman of his faculty; in 1993 and 1994, vice president; and in 1994, acting president of his university.

Juergen Beetz studied computer science at the University of the Federal Armed Forces, Munich, and business administration at the University of Hagen. He was a research assistant in the Faculty of Computer Science at the University of the Federal Armed Forces, Munich, from 1998 to 2000, and has been writing his PhD thesis "Game Theoretical Analysis of Arms Races." From 2000 to 2001 he worked as an executive assistant in a Bertelsman business unit, Gütersloh. Since 2001 he has been working as an IT project manager at T-Systems, Heilbronn.

Lisa J. Carlson is associate professor of political science at the University of Idaho, where she teaches international relations, American foreign policy, and political violence and revolution. Her main research interests involve the escalation and resolution of international conflicts, including international trade disputes, and, more recently, conflicts at the domestic level regarding environmental policy.

Daniel Druckman is the Vernon M. and Minnie I. Lynch Professor of Conflict Resolution at George Mason University in Fairfax, Virginia, where he has also coordinated the doctoral program at the Institute for Conflict Analysis and Resolution. He received a PhD from Northwestern University and was awarded a best-in-field prize from the American Institutes for Research for his doctoral dissertation. He has published widely on such topics as negotiating behavior, nationalism and group identity, human performance, peacekeeping, political stability, nonverbal communication, and methodology, including simulation. He received the 1995 Otto Klineberg Award for Intercultural and International Relations for his work on nationalism and a Teaching Excellence Award in 1998 from George Mason University. He is the recipient of the 2003 Lifetime Achievement Award from the International Association for Conflict Management.

Guy Olivier Faure is professor of sociology at the Sorbonne University, Paris V, Department of Social Sciences, where he teaches international negotiation. He is a member of the Steering Committee of the Processes of International Negotiation (PIN) Network at the International Institute for Applied Systems Analysis (IIASA) near Vienna, Austria. He advises enterprises, multinational companies, international organizations, and governments on international negotiations. As a practitioner, he has been involved in several types of highly conflicting negotiations in various parts of the world. His works have been published in 10 languages. He has authored, co-authored, and edited a dozen books, including *How People Negotiate: Resolving Disputes in Different Cultures* (Kluwer Academic Publishers, 2003) and *Culture and Negotiation* (Sage, 1993) with J.Z. Rubin.

D. Marc Kilgour is professor of mathematics at Wilfrid Laurier University, Waterloo, Canada; director of the Laurier Centre for Military Strategic and Disarmament Studies; and adjunct professor of systems design engineering at the University of Waterloo. His major research focus is the cross-disciplinary analysis of decisions, and he has applied game theory and related techniques in international relations, arms control, environmental management, negotiation, arbitration, voting, fair division, and coalition formation. His most recent book, co-authored with Frank Zagare, is *Perfect Deterrence* (Cambridge University Press, 2000).

Sung Hee Kim is associate professor of psychology at the University of Kentucky. She did graduate work in psychology at Seoul National University in South Korea and at the University of Illinois at Urbana-Champaign and received her PhD in psychology from Tufts University. She has received a Peace Scholar Fellowship from the United States Institute of Peace and is the co-author of the second and third editions of *Social Conflict: Escalation, Stalemate, and Settlement* (with Jeffrey Z. Rubin and Dean G. Pruitt, and with Dean G. Pruitt, respectively). Her research concerns social conflict, vengeance, and group processes.

Paul W. Meerts worked at the Universities of Groningen and Leyden as a researcher on the political elite of the Netherlands. In 1978, he became tutor of the course on international relations at the Netherlands Society of International Affairs, part of the year of training required for all young diplomats at the Netherlands Ministry of Foreign Affairs. He is currently director of the courses of the Netherlands Institute of International Relations, Clingendael. He specializes in simulation games as a tool in training diplomats and civil servants.

Patrick M. Morgan holds the Thomas and Elizabeth Tierney Chair in Peace and Conflict Studies at the University of California, Irvine. He is a specialist on national and international security as well as international relations theory, with teaching and writings on deterrence, arms control, strategic military surprise, European security and US–European relations, East Asian security, and intelligence. His latest book is *Deterrence Now* (Cambridge University Press, 2003).

Dean G. Pruitt is SUNY Distinguished Professor Emeritus in the Department of Psychology at the University at Buffalo, the State University of New York, and a visiting scholar at the Institute for Conflict Analysis and Resolution at George Mason University. He received his PhD in psychology from Yale University and did postdoctoral work in psychology at the University of Michigan and in international relations at Northwestern University. His specialties are social conflict, negotiation, and mediation. He is a fellow of the American Psychological Association and the American Psychological Society, and has received the Harold D. Lasswell Award for Distinguished Scientific Contribution to Political Psychology from the International Society of Political Psychology and the Lifetime Achievement Award from the International Association for Conflict Management. He is the author or co-author of five books: *Theory and Research on the Causes of War*; *Negotiation Behavior*; *Social Conflict: Escalation, Stalemate, and Settlement*; *Mediation Research*; and *Negotiation in Social Conflict*.

I. William Zartman is Jacob Blaustein Professor of International Organizations and Conflict Resolution at the Nitze School of Advanced International Studies of Johns Hopkins University. He is the author of *The Practical Negotiator*, *The 50% Solution*, and *Ripe for Resolution*; the editor of *The Negotiation Process* and *Positive Sum*, among other books; and the editor of *Preventive Negotiation*, the most recent book in the Processes of International Negotiation (PIN) series. He is organizer of the Washington Interest in Negotiations (WIN) Group and was distinguished fellow at the US Institute of Peace.

Part I
Introduction

Chapter 1

The Dynamics of Escalation and Negotiation

I. William Zartman and Guy Olivier Faure

Conflict is a roller coaster, with its ups and downs. The roller coaster is exhilarating because it is a simulation of danger: we have our hearts in our mouths in anticipation as we go up and a scream in our mouths in excitement as we go down. But it is only a simulation (or we would not have bought the ticket), and not an accurate one at that. While we know where the top of the roller coaster is, we do not know how extreme the conflict is going to become before it starts to decline. It is that unknown and the dynamics of getting there that make for the deadly excitement of conflict.

Escalation is the dynamics of determining where the conflict peak is and if it has been reached. The conflict occasioned by apartheid in South Africa escalated from the repression of the Defiance Campaign in 1952 through the spontaneous Sharpeville demonstrations and massacre of 1960, the Rivonia Trial of Nelson Mandela of 1963, the intensified police measures, the Black Consciousness movement, the Soweto riots of 1976, and the Umkonto we Sizwe attacks that challenged surveillance and repression through the 1980s. But it also saw the constitutional changes of 1983, followed by attempts to talk with Mandela and others of the African National Congress, until finally the apartheid policy began to crumble in 1990 and negotiations began.

When, after three decades of war, Ethiopia and Eritrea finally separated in 1991 (a separation confirmed by a referendum in 1993), their collaborative relationships immediately became strained, with expulsions in 1991 and 1992, border clashes in 1995, currency separation in 1997, and the border war in 1998, accompanied by a vicious demonization of old friends. The spiral seemed to be brought under control by a cease-fire and international mediation, but the pause only served as an occasion for both sides to launch massive armament programs and renew a war of unprecedented bloodshed in 1999, with repeated attacks and counterattacks. How long could this go on? Gradually, international efforts were able to bring the hostilities – but not the enmity – to a halt in 2000.

In the film *The Magnificent Seven*, the gunslinger and the knife thrower discuss who of the two is faster, a discussion that leads to taunts and then to a challenge for each to prove himself. Facing each other in a dry run, they both claim vindication in the contest. Where will it end? Their friends try to dissuade them, but the contest must be rerun, for real, and in the end the gunslinger crumbles with a knife in his chest.

Escalation is the mark of conflict in its dynamic form. Conflict occurs when parties who hold incompatible views seek to make their will prevail, "a situation in which the parties [holding incompatible views] are taking action against each other" (Wright 1965, pp. 434–435). Conflict actually begins when static incompatibility is turned into dynamic incompatibility. Escalation is a specific increase in conflict, a tactical step that marks a qualitative difference in conflict relations (Schelling 1960, 1966; Smoke 1977, p. 32; Rubin *et al.* 1994, p. 69).

Negotiation is a process by which the parties combine their divergent positions into a single agreed outcome (Zartman 1978, 1987; Pruitt 1981; Zartman and Berman 1982; Hopmann 1996; Faure 2003). Parties enter into a negotiation process because they believe there is a possibility of obtaining a better outcome than is offered by the status quo. Engaging oneself in a negotiation process does not imply the obligation to reach an agreement but rather the intention to aim at such a goal. It also implies that one has given up the project of subduing the other as the only way to resolve the conflict.

The negotiation activity refers to three successive phases, each with a distinct rationale (Zartman and Berman 1982). The pre-negotiation concerns the acceptance of the idea of meeting each other to discuss the issue. Such a stage can be reached, for instance, by work on reframing the problem. Even the most violent circumstances do not exclude such a possibility, as has been shown in cases of negotiation with terrorist groups (Faure 2004). The second phase consists in establishing a potential agreement formula, the overall architecture of the final package. The third stage addresses the discussion of the details and precise figures on each basic issue in order to find an acceptable balance.

Much of the study of escalation has been devoted to the ways conflict is conducted and to their implications (Kahn 1965; Smoke 1977; Zagare 1978; Brecher 1994; Geller and Singer 1998, pp. 70–92). Another important aspect of negotiation study has been the examination of mechanisms that find reconciliation points between the parties' positions, either along the flat plane of a zero-sum game through compromise, or, as more recent studies have highlighted, along a plane made convex through the search for positive-sum solutions or formulas (Iklé 1964; Walton and McKersie 1965; Young 1975; Raiffa 1982; Lax and Sebenius 1986). However, in focusing on the negotiation process – an advance over previous histories that paid attention only to outcomes – this scholarship tended to ignore the process of the conflict. Too little analysis has placed negotiation within the dynamic context of conflict and studied negotiation as an appropriate response to conflict movement.

Escalation and negotiation are not separate topics more or less artfully combined. They are conceptually and practically related through such themes as competitive behavior and commitments. Escalation is a mutually coercive mechanism embedded in a conflict perspective (Schelling 1960, 1966; Kahn 1965; Young 1968; Snyder 1972; Carlson 1995). Escalation within a conflict can produce, lead to, or provide an opportunity for negotiation under specific circumstances. These circumstances may be created by the actors involved in the situation or by a third party. One of the objectives of this book is to shed light on these contextual and structural variables. Escalation within a negotiation can be a bargaining strategy. The costs inflicted or that could be inflicted are a lever either to bring the other party back to the negotiation table or to obtain the concessions it was previously unwilling to make. Although an increasing trend of reciprocal concessions in a negotiation might also be considered a kind of "constructive escalation," the term thus used would lose its specificity and instrumentality. Structurally, negotiation is the end of escalation, even if within the negotiation process parties may still escalate. Conflict being what it is, negotiation is required to respond to dynamic conflict (Kriesberg and Thorson 1991; Kriesberg 2002). When and how to do so is what the chapters of this book seek to analyze.

To do so, the nature of escalation must first be investigated and its rationale brought to light. Then, the most appropriate times and means of negotiating its end will be determined. Parties are under pressure from the dynamics of the conflict to broaden it, moving the process from light to heavy, small to large, specific to general, few to many, winning to hurting (Rubin *et al.* 1994). These "transformations" of the conflict are part of the escalation process. Thus, parties to a conflict make a series of decisions to pursue the conflict, in response to both internal and external pressures; such decisions are imposed on them by the other party and by the conflict itself. Whether stated openly or not by the parties to the dispute, escalation as a process in itself introduces the idea of threat. The minimum threat conveyed by the escalatory mechanism is to continue with the logic of escalation, with the consequence that more resources are put into the process and/or that more costs must be paid at the end.

1.1   Dimensions and Structure

Seen as a dynamic exchange, conflict has a structure built upon escalation. Escalation is not just intensification, but a particular type of intensification by steps across time, as its very name indicates, a change in nature rather than simply a change in degree. Steps are made of a vertical and a horizontal component, and the escalatory aspect of this imaged structure is the riser, the vertical element – as distinguished from the treads, the horizontal part. To distinguish escalation from mere intensification, analysts have identified risers that cross a saliency (Schelling 1960; Smoke 1977) or have a distinct change in severity (Bonoma 1975; Brecher 1994; Rubin *et al.* 1994), although neither is always as clear and distinct as the image might suggest. On the other hand, even when conflict is characterized by gradual intensification, it is very likely that at some point "more and more" eventually (if not unequivocally) becomes "different," and thus also introduces a qualitative change.

As a result, the basic model of conflict escalation resembles two ladders with steps or treads of different heights (risers) set alongside each other, similar to the typical "life cycle of conflict" advanced by analysts (Bloomfield and Liess 1960; Lund 1996). This is admittedly a caricature and should be recognized as such, since risers and treads of different sizes and different relations between the two (or more) ladders can produce very different conflict models. Some of these are explored below. However, the duality (or plurality) of the ladders is important: conflict may escalate or be escalated unilaterally, either automatically or by decision, as discussed below, but more often it escalates as a responsive relation between the two or more parties (whether automatically or by decision). A conflict profile drawn with one line implies that the conflict rises and falls on its own, whereas a conflict profile with two lines or ladders side by side indicates a relation between the parties' separate escalations.

The ladder image is expressive in another sense, however: unlike the up side of the ladder, the down side often does not have steps. De-escalation may not be the lessening of conflict, but merely the lowering of its cost so as to prolong its duration. Negotiation can take place without de-escalation, while conflict is still high or deadlocked; de-escalation can take place without negotiation unless viewed as a tacit expression of negotiation; and both de-escalation and the lessening of conflict may or may not proceed by steps. Thus, de-escalation and negotiation are discussed later in this chapter as separate elements of the down side of the ladder.

The increase in stakes of various types through escalation takes place diachronically for each party, as well as synchronically between the two parties' positions and tactics. These dual dimensions refer to the current balance of costs in the process of escalation, but also to the anticipated balance of costs in case of compliance. The latter includes the costs of the resources required by the escalation process to induce negotiation and also the anticipated cost of concessions needed to restart the negotiation process.

Escalation, often thought of only as increases in one or two dimensions (Iklé 1971, p. 39; George *et al.* 1991, p. 388; Leatherman *et al.* 1999, pp. 74–77), can take place along many other dimensions of conflict as well, including means, ends, space, price, parties, images, risks, costs, and commitments:

- Escalation of means or increasing efforts: for instance, a party starts with demands and offers, then resorts to threats, and then goes on with a fait accompli, as in the Nazi Anschluss of Austria in 1938
- Escalation of ends, or expanding related demands to cover the initial demand: for example, a party wants grievances redressed, then wants power-sharing to ensure that grievances are removed, and then wants to take over government entirely, as in the evolution of nationalist movements (Brown 1964)
- Escalation of space, or adding unrelated issues asymmetrically: for example, hostage-takers add to their original demand to free political prisoners the additional demand for extra resources, such as money or weapons (Hayes 2001)
- Escalation of price, or increasing trade-off asymmetrically (tracking): for instance, a union on strike for a salary increase now includes the strike costs in its new requirements for a settlement (Raskin 1987)
- Escalation of parties, or adding parties to the conflict (related to means, but also to ends, space, and price): for instance, the buildup of opposing alliances before the two World Wars or in the Cold War
- Escalation of images, or demonizing: for instance, the opponent may be considered an obstacle, then an opponent, then an enemy, then a force of evil, as occurred during the Cold War, but also during the security dilemma that characterizes the escalation of ethnic conflicts (White 1984; Posen 1993)
- Escalation of risk, or increase in dangerous uncertainties: for example, increasingly conflictual actions or tactics by one party can increase the danger that the other will increase its demands, then refuse to talk or simply take unilateral action directly (Avenhaus and Sjöstedt forthcoming)
- Escalation of costs, or increasing either party's deprivations and outlays: for example, maintaining the conflict requires greater and greater expenditures and increasingly blocks other actions, as occurred in the Western Sahara where

Mauritanian participation in four years of war bankrupted the country and finally brought down the government (Zartman 1989)

- Escalation of commitment, or an increasingly firm resolution not to back down, but to continue escalating without subjecting ever-higher escalation to more and more cautious evaluations: for example, a party can consider carefully whether to embark on a course of costly competition, but then continue to raise its ante once engaged (Brockner and Rubin 1985)

In all cases, escalation raises the stakes, since more is now involved in the conflict and the parties have to climb down from a higher level to settle it. Escalation along any one of the dimensions listed above often brings escalation along other dimensions by the escalator, and invites counter-escalation by the other party along any dimension in response. "Higher" in some of these dimensions increases the risk of losing control, whereas in other dimensions – notably price, parties, risks, and costs – it decreases (or at least should decrease) that risk. In negotiating an end to the conflict, the types of escalations that characterize the pursuit of the conflict determine the types of solutions and tactics used to end it.

1.2 Nature and Causes

The previous discussion of escalation as a mutually coercive or bargaining strategy portrays escalation as a deliberate, purposeful action, but this is not the whole picture. To analyze the causes of escalation, it is necessary to distinguish between the transitive and intransitive forms of escalation, between the initiated decision and the consequential phenomenon (Smoke 1977; Rubin *et al.* 1994, p. 69; Brecher 1996). Conflict is escalated by a party, but it also escalates by itself. There is an inherent tendency for escalation to proceed on its own, dragging the parties along and making decisions for them, engulfing them in unintended and inescapable consequences. While the distinction is conceptually clear and useful, the two forms are not always easy to separate in reality; an escalation decision (transitive) is usually made under some pressure to escalate (intransitive), and conflict escalation (intransitive) results from decisions to escalate (transitive). Even when conscious decisions are involved, they are made under the pressure of stimuli and opportunities, and they tend to have unpredictable and unexpected implications. In this sense, the process itself is, indeed, coercive on both parties. Transitive escalation is powered by intransitive escalation, and vice versa. Recognizing this effect, rather than simply considering escalation as an autonomous decision out of context, enables de-escalatory or negotiation measures that counter its logic and pressures. This distinction is relevant to an understanding of escalation's causes.

Parties escalate (transitively) for various reasons, some of them rational in the sense of being appropriate to a goal, and some of them emotional or even out of control, dysfunctional in terms of the ostensible goal. These reasons do not constitute exclusive categories, but rather tend to combine in unstable mixes (Stedman 1991, pp. 18–20).

Parties escalate conflict to

- win, in order to prevail;
- not lose, so as to stay in the conflict or bring about negotiations, or speed up the negotiation process, for instance by avoiding a deadlock;
- cover investments, sunk costs, or the costs of entrapment in the conflict (and from previous escalations);
- gain support, against the opponent or simply for oneself, at home or abroad;
- seize an advantage or target of opportunity to use now or later;
- feel like a king, to reward oneself, because "I deserve it," for affective reasons; and/or
- feel like a dragon slayer, to punish the other, because "he deserves it," for affective reasons.

In between the transitive decisions and the intransitive phenomenon lies a whole minefield of "inappropriate" or "irrational" decisions fed by cognitive problems, poor information, and the like, which produces an intransitive effect, even though specific decisions are involved. Much of the literature has been devoted to the intrapersonal aspect of escalation, taking it out of the realm of mere interactive conflict behavior and in the process giving escalation a bad name. The literature on escalation highlights the driving role of cognitive factors, notably judgmental and perceptional biases (Ebbessen and Konecni 1980; Bazerman 1994; see also Iklé 1971, p. 40, for a discussion of why parties might not escalate).

Judgmental bias driven by losses from the original investment in escalation is the most common cause of further escalation. For instance, one party may believe it could recover its initial investment by mobilizing more resources. Overconfidence in the final outcome may just feed the escalation process if the other party does not behave as expected. This translates directly into entrapment, but also into related phenomena such as overcommitment, or the inability to escape from escalation because of a commitment made to followers, and lock-in, or personal overcommitment through self-fulfilling prophesies, rationalization (cognitive dissonance), demonization, and selective perception. Decision makers do not want to admit to an initial mistake or to having missed or underestimated later consequences. Pressure for consistency can be another explanatory factor of escalation, because the concern to maintain commitment and avoid indecisiveness may generate a vicious circle that leads to the opposite result of that intended (Cameron and Quinn 1988). Thus, pacifists turn into militants, and solutions become problems. Fear of failure resulting from social or psychological pressures may also explain a decision to escalate (Aronson 1968; Brockner 1992). Cognitive dissonance can produce escalation; once a course of action has been decided, negative feedback regarded as dissonant is rationalized away, and the party escalates with the thought that the next step is necessary to reach the goal and avoid the dissonance (Festinger 1957).

Perceptional biases function as a selective filter to maintain commitment to a course of action and lead the decision maker to seek out only the information that serves this commitment. Escalation is enhanced when the consequences of a decision are unclear, especially in the long term (Brockner and Rubin 1985; Bowen 1987). A related effect is impression management, which incites people to provide only information that confirms the rightness of the initial commitment. Another cause of excessive risk taking is the underestimation of some elements of the situation (Whyte 1986; Janis 1972) or the capabilities of the decision makers themselves (Schwenk 1986; Staw and Ross 1987). Escalation may also occur when an initial failure is explained by the fact that it was impossible to predict the exogenous event that was the cause of the failure.

The two types of biases combine to produce competitive irrationality, one of the phenomena most commonly associated with escalation. The parties engage in an activity that is irrational in terms of the possible outcomes, as illustrated by the dollar auction game (Shubik 1971; Rubin 1980); they keep on bidding in the hope that the other will abandon the game, an action that may be rational from the individual perspective, but that becomes irrational as soon as several people start to bid. The desire to win takes on a life of its own, functioning as an additional motivation to launch an escalation process (Bazerman *et al.* 1984). A similar effect is produced by the use of bargaining chips, tactical items of exchange value only that then take on a life of their own and so become impossible to trade, such as the Israeli-occupied territories of Palestine. Escalation may also be produced by playing out the tensions between parties, which entails a breakdown in rationality (Simonson and Staw 1992; Staw 1997). Overreaction, or responding to the other's last move in and of itself and losing sight of the goal, is a related phenomenon.

All of these elements contribute to the production of escalation (transitively or intransitively), which presumably would go on forever to the point of capitulation or elimination of one of the parties. Negotiation measures have to take into account these (and possibly other) features of intransitive conflict escalation, often before the core issues and interactions that ostensibly initiated the conflict can be tackled. Identification of the reason(s) for escalation can lead to effective measures of de-escalation and negotiation.

1.3 De-escalation and Negotiation

Escalations change the conflict situation in a way that either worsens the conflict or leads to negotiations. They can act either in prospect or in retrospect to create moments for starting the negotiation process. In prospect, impending escalation serves as a threat, working on both parties, and so can produce preemptive negotiations. Escalation in prospect – like any threat – contains an element of risk or uncertainty about its actual occurrence, and the amount of risk can be used as a tactical element (Iklé 1971, pp. 42–58; Avenhaus and Sjöstedt forthcoming). In retrospect, just-employed escalation can serve as an equalizer, a response, an assuagement, a bullying tactic, or another effect that can also be used to produce negotiations. The uncertainty inherent in the very occurrence of escalation can also be used as a tactical element.

Escalations, like negotiations, respond to a prior situation of symmetry or asymmetry. When the former obtains, a new escalation seeks to create a decisive edge for one party in order to win. In the second case, escalation can either seek to reverse the asymmetry in favor of the new escalating party (also to win) or aim to establish equality (symmetry) as a basis for negotiation. In poker terms, seeking to win can be called "escalation to raise" and equalizing can be termed "escalation to call" (Zartman and Aurik 1991). Distinguishing one from the other is key to seizing a moment for negotiation.

Like escalation, negotiation has a stepped or responsive structure. It involves the exchange of proposals with a view to arriving at a common decision from divergent positions, a process that is governed by an overarching ethos of reciprocity. As already noted, proposals can be exchanged for several purposes with regard to escalation. They can aim to confirm an asymmetrical result after several rounds of escalation, to work out an agreement that marks the predominance of one side over the other. While one party would "win" in such a situation, wins are usually not total and exchanges are made to induce the other party to accept the asymmetrical outcome (Faure 2004). Second, negotiations can also aim to halt escalation, presumably in a more symmetrical situation, to cut the costs of conflict, control its spread (further escalation), and break links between various dimensions. Such negotiations do not seek to solve the basic conflict, but merely to manage it in the hope that it will solve itself or be more amenable to resolution later on. Third, negotiations can seek solutions to the problem itself, also from a situation of escalation to symmetry. Such negotiations can bypass the conflict escalations or address them in the process of resolving the basic conflict.

A number of variables serve to dampen, interrupt, or reverse (brake or break) escalation and so allow negotiation and settlement of the dispute to take place; these are summarized here and are developed more fully in the following chapters:

1. *Fear and fatigue*: Richardson's (1960) arms-race models predict that escalation would move off the chart and into war were it not for internal (fatigue) and interactive (fear) dampening effects that provide resting points (treads) and escalation slowdown, and allow for moments of negotiation (Smoker 1964). These effects wear out the parties as they try to keep up with the race and induce them to look for alternatives, as Soviet General Secretary Mikhail Gorbachev did in meeting US President Ronald Reagan in Reykjavik in 1987.

2. *Mutually hurting stalemates*: Ripe moments for negotiation (mediated or direct) are provided by double escalations to the point where no more escalation is deemed worthwhile and the ensuing deadlock hurts both sides, the necessary if insufficient condition for negotiation (Zartman 2000a). Ripe moments can be created by escalations to call or by failed escalations to raise that end in stalemate, as happened in Angola in regard to the South West African negotiations in 1987–1988 (Crocker 1992).

3. *Changes in stakes*: New terms can be invented, so that the relationship between the parties takes a new direction, away from the items that motivate or fuel escalation of the conflict (Zartman 2001). The elements of escalation can be altered or the parties' perception of their value can be changed by reframing, as occurred in the Peru–Ecuador border negotiations in 1998 when the parties changed their focus from legal disputes over sovereign ownership to joint efforts to promote development (Simmons 1999).

4. *Changes in parties*: Internal changes in one or more parties' decision-making structures, the introduction of new parties, or the elimination of old ones can move the conflict from escalation to negotiation, as happened when Dwight D. Eisenhower succeeded Harry S. Truman as US president during the Korean War (Fan 2000), or when Joseph Kabila succeeded his father as leader of Congo in 2001.

5. *Changes in attitudes*: Escalation in the attitudes of the parties toward each other can be changed by one side's showing a willingness to negotiate, by de-demonizing, by occasions to cooperate on overarching goals, or by CSBMs [see (7) below] as second-track activities. For example, both Search for Common Ground and the Institute for Multi-Track Diplomacy have programs to accomplish in Israel, Burundi, Cyprus, and elsewhere.

6. *Disengagements and breathing space*: Truces and pauses (even rainy seasons) can allow for stocktaking and reappraisals so that the parties can cool their interaction and reevaluate their positions to see whether they are in over their heads, as occurred in Karabagh after the 1994 cease-fire or in Congo after the 1999 Lusaka Agreement. Such measures can break the momentum of escalation and push the choice between escalation and resolution toward a conscious decision (transitive) and away from the inherent dynamics (intransitive).

7. *Confidence- and security-building measures (CSBMs)*: Like periodic reappraisals, measures of transparency can remove the fear and ignorance that fuels
   escalation, contribute to accurate assessments, and create new relationships between parties, as the Stockholm Conference on Disarmament in Europe did in
   1986 (Goodby 1988).
8. *Learning processes*: Dynamic information intake or learning is necessary if
   parties are to revise their initial assessments on such aspects of the conflict as
   the way the other party sees the problem, its degree of commitment to engage
   more deeply in the conflict, and the means considered as licit to be used to
   serve the cause. Authoritative inputs of new information through fact-finding
   missions can help coordinate parties' perceptions, confirm security points, clar-
   ify commitments, introduce a more realistic understanding of risk, reduce uncertainties, and thus dampen escalation so that negotiations can begin, as has
   been attempted on numerous occasions after clashes between the Israelis and
   Palestinians. Reassessed knowledge can serve as a progressive damper on the
   conflict's escalation.
9. *Reaffirmed relationships*: Community is a particularly important form of relationship that allows parties to handle conflict within established bonds of commonality and established institutions and regimes (Zartman 2000a, Zartman
   and Kremenyuk in press). Superordinate values contribute to building a strong
   sense of community and common interest (Sherif and Sherif 1969). While it is
   difficult to create community during conflict, pre-established relationships can
   create a larger setting within which the conflict can be subsumed, which can
   provide values, interdependencies, stakes, and also procedures and mediators
   to dampen conflict (Saunders 1999).
10. *Mutually enticing opportunity (MEO)*: The prospect of future gains can be pro-
    duced by using an alternative strategy to the continuation of escalation, as was
    used in the Sant'Egidio negotiations to end the civil war between Renamo and
    Frelimo in Mozambique in 1990–1992 (Ohlson 1998).
11. *Cultural values*: Accepted notions of what is permissible and what is taboo
    with regard to the escalation process, its context, its appropriateness, and even
    morality can serve as either dampers or accelerators (Faure and Rubin 1993;
    Faure 2000, 2002). If escalation is assimilated to violence, some cultures may
    be more reluctant than others to trigger or enter an escalation process, while
    others, of course, may not countenance backing down, as explored in the cul-
    tures of negotiation in North Africa, the Horn of Africa, and Southern Africa
    (Zartman 1989).

These many mechanisms can be used or can exert themselves to provide openings
to negotiation within the escalation process. This book explores that relationship

and works through the various mechanics and dynamics of escalation to arrive at a better understanding of the appropriate times and methods of negotiation. The goals are to achieve a fuller analysis of these two important concepts and their interrelation, and to arrive at propositions for practitioners to improve their trade, focusing particularly on the subject of when parties do and should negotiate under escalation.

1.4   Themes and Chapters

The following two parts of this book seek to elucidate the relation between escalation and negotiation. The first contains chapters that address five forms and outcomes that escalation can take – deadlock, deterrence, arms races, entrapment, and vengeance. Although each is a distinct phenomenon, all are both processes and consequences in which the policy and the outcome are often referred to by the same name, and each bears some relationship to the others. Some of the outcomes are more desired than others, and some are more unintentional. Each chapter examines the hypothesis that its form of escalation can be conducive to negotiation under certain specified conditions.

Deadlock is the general outcome of conflict escalation that does not produce a winner and loser (except in the sense that each or both parties may suffer simply from the continuation of the conflict). In Chapter 2, Guy Olivier Faure addresses the question of deadlock, its forms and causes, its relation to both escalation and negotiation, and the incentives and strategies to move out of deadlock. *Deterrence* is a purposeful deadlock as a policy, the result of past escalation that leads to equality and threatened escalation that defines the future. In Chapter 3, Patrick Morgan examines the concept and practice of deterrence, showing the conditions under which it can lead to negotiation once it has been established. *Arms races* can grow out of deterrence efforts that break down, and they constitute a vicious circle of transitive and intransitive escalation with a logic that leads parties into ever-mounting conflict behaviors beyond their intended strategies. In Chapter 4, Rudolf Avenhaus, Juergen Beetz, and Marc Kilgour show how various characteristics of the escalating parties can favor stability in escalation or in accommodation. *Entrapment* also refers to an intransitive effect that carries transitive escalation beyond its intended purpose, an outbidding race that calls for strategies of closure. In Chapter 5, Paul Meerts analyzes ways to prevent entrapment from occurring, given its identifying characteristics, and shows how negotiation can provide an alternative policy, including both managing entrapment so as to bring the stronger party to negotiation and conflict management. In Chapter 6, at the end of Part II, *vengeance* is discussed as the motor of escalation, both its outcome and its motivation, the effective element behind other runaway races. Sung Hee Kim examines the dynamics of vengeance and shows how its power can be broken so as to make negotiation possible; it is not only the mechanics of the process that must be mastered, but also its emotional impulsion.

Part III of the book turns to the core of the analysis in search of answers to the question of when, in the escalation, should and do parties negotiate. Each chapter addresses the hypothesis that certain moments in escalation, defined in particular analytical terms, are amenable to negotiation and can be used for that purpose. Different dynamics of the process of escalation produce opportunities to control the process by using breaks or weak points in its logic, whether seen from the point of view of structure or actors, to produce a shift in its direction and a negotiated relationship between the parties.

Four chapters place negotiation within different conceptualizations of the escalation process to find these answers. Since escalation is a *stepped process*, one set of answers can be acquired by directing the question to the treads and risers of the process. In Chapter 7, I. William Zartman shows how parties in notable recent conflicts have negotiated immediately after risers, whether the risers have failed, as shortfalls, or succeeded, as escalations to call. The decision to negotiate also represents a *turning point* in the escalation process and can be analyzed as such. In Chapter 8, Daniel Druckman illustrates that the decision to escalate has preceded and led to a decision to negotiate in various types of conflict-management processes. *Crisis behavior* is a different form of escalation in the conduct of conflict. In Chapter 9, Lisa Carlson shows that escalation and reciprocation tend to lead to negotiation under specific structural conditions, both by imposing costs on further conflict and by checking the other party in its pursuit. *Conflict spirals* are another way to pursue escalation and can lead to their own arrest through negotiation. In Chapter 10, Marc Kilgour uses categorizations of conflict spirals to show under which conditions demand escalation can further negotiations.

Two other chapters examine the conditions under which escalating parties are ready to negotiate. In Chapter 11, Dean Pruitt introduces *communication chains and intermediaries* to move parties from escalation to negotiation, and in Chapter 12, Karin Aggestam examines the role of *substantive focal points and mediators* in keeping negotiating parties from reverting to further escalation. The examination closes with two chapters by the editors on the implications for theories of the analysis of the juncture between the two processes of negotiation and escalation, and for practice in the use of the knowledge generated to improve negotiation effectiveness.

References

Aronson E (1968). *The Social Animal*. San Francisco, CA, USA: Freeman.

Avenhaus R & Sjöstedt G (forthcoming). Negotiating Risk. Laxenburg, Austria: International Institute for Applied Systems Analysis.

Bazerman MH (1994). *Judgment in Managerial Decision Making.* New York, NY, USA: Wiley.

Bazerman MH, Giuliano T & Appelman A (1984). Escalation in individual and group decision making. *Organizational Behavior and Human Performance* **33**:141–152.

Bloomfield L & Liess A (1960). *The Course of Conflict.* New York, NY, USA: Carnegie Endowment.

Bonoma T (1975). *Conflict: Escalation and Deescalation.* Beverly Hills, CA, USA: Sage.

Bowen M (1987). The escalation phenomenon reconsidered: Decision dilemmas or decision errors? *Academy of Management Review* **12**:52–66.

Brecher M (1994). *Crises in World Politics: Theory and Reality.* Oxford, UK: Pergamon.

Brecher M (1996). Crisis escalation: Model and findings. *International Political Science Review* **17**:215–230.

Brockner J (1992). The escalation of commitment to a failing course of action. *Academy of Management Review* **17**:39–61.

Brockner J & Rubin JZ (1985). *Entrapment in Escalating Conflicts: A Social Psychological Analysis.* New York, NY, USA: Springer Verlag.

Brown LC (1964). Growth of nationalism. In *Tunisia: The Politics of Modernization*, eds. Brown LC, Micaud C & Moore CH. New York, NY, USA: Praeger.

Cameron KS & Quinn RE (1988). Organizational paradox and transformation. In *Paradox and Transformation: Toward a Theory of Change in Organization and Management*, eds. Quinn RE & Cameron KS, pp. 1–18. Cambridge, MA, USA: Ballinger.

Carlson L (1995). A theory of escalation and international conflict. *Journal of Conflict Resolution* **39**: 511–534.

Crocker CA (1992). *High Noon in Southern Africa.* New York, NY, USA: Norton.

Ebbessen EB & Konecni F (1980). Experimental research on third party intervention. *Psychological Bulletin* **86**:465–485.

Fan X (2000). US–Chinese negotiations in the Korean War. In *Power and Negotiation*, eds. Zartman IW & Rubin JZ. Ann Arbor, MI, USA: University of Michigan Press.

Faure GO, Mermet L, Touzard H & Dupont C (2000). *La négociation: Situations et problématiques.* Paris, France: Dunod.

Faure GO (2002). Negotiation: The cultural dimension. In *International Negotiations: Analysis, Approaches, Issues*, ed. Kremenyuk, V. San Francisco, CA, USA: Jossey-Bass.

Faure GO (2003). *How People Negotiate: The Resolution of Conflicts in Different Cultures.* Dordrecht, The Netherlands: Kluwer Academic Publishers.

Faure GO (2004). Negotiating with terrorists: The hostage case. *International Negotiation*, **8**(3):27-52.

Faure GO & Rubin JZ (1993). *Culture and Negotiation.* Newbury Park, CA, USA: Sage.

Festinger L (1957). *A Theory of Cognitive Dissonance.* Evanston, IL, USA: Row and Peterson.

Geller D & Singer D (1998). *Nations at War: A Scientific Study of International Conflict.* New York, NY, USA: Cambridge University Press.

George A, Hall D & Simons W (1991). *The Limits of Coercive Diplomacy.* New York, NY, USA: Little Brown.

Goodby J (1988). The Stockholm Conference. In *US–Soviet Security Cooperation*, eds. George A, Farley P & Dallin A. Boulder, CO, USA: Westview.

Hayes RP (2001). Negotiating with terrorists. In *International Negotiation*, ed. Kremenyuk V, pp. 364–376. San Francisco, CA, USA: Jossey-Bass.

Hopmann PT (1996). *The Negotiation Process and the Resolution of International Conflicts.* Columbia, SC, USA: University of South Carolina Press.

Iklé FC (1964). *How Nations Negotiate.* New York, NY, USA: Harper Row.

Iklé FC (1971). *Every War Must End.* New York, NY, USA: Columbia University Press.

Janis I (1972). *Victims of Groupthink.* Boston, MA, USA: Houghton Mifflin.

Kahn H (1965). *On Escalation: Metaphors and Scenarios.* New York, NY, USA: Praeger.

Kriesberg L (2002). *Constructive Conflicts: From Escalation to Resolution.* Lanham, MD, USA: Rowman and Littlefield.

Kriesberg L & Thorson S (1991). *Timing the De-escalation of International Conflict.* Syracuse, NY, USA: Syracuse University Press.

Lax D & Sebenius J (1986). *The Manager as Negotiator.* New York, NY, USA: Free Press.

Leatherman J, DeMars W, Gaffney P & Vyrynen R (1999). *Breaking Cycles of Violence: Conflict Prevention in Interstate Conflict.* West Hartford, CT, USA: Kumarian.

Lund M (1996). *Preventing Violent Conflicts.* Washington, DC, USA: US Institute of Peace.

Ohlson T (1998). *Power Politics and Peace Politics.* Uppsala, Sweden: University of Uppsala Department of Peace and Conflict Research.

Posen B (1993). The security dilemma and ethnic conflict. In *Ethnic Conflict and International Security*, ed. Brown M, pp. 103–124. Princeton, NJ, USA: Princeton University Press.

Pruitt DG (1981). *Negotiation Behavior.* New York, NY, USA: Academic Press.

Raiffa H (1982). *The Art and Science of Negotiation.* Cambridge, MA, USA: Harvard University Press.

Raskin AH (1987). The newspaper strike. In *The 50% Solution*, ed. Zartman IW. New Haven, CT, USA: Yale University Press.

Richardson LF (1960). *Arms and Insecurity.* London, UK: Stevens.

Rubin JZ (1980). *The Dynamics of Third Party Intervention.* New York, NY, USA: Praeger.

Rubin JZ, Pruitt DG & Kim SH (1994). *Social Conflict.* New York, NY, USA: McGraw-Hill.

Saunders H (1999). *A Public Peace Process.* New York, NY, USA: St. Martin's Press.

Schelling TC (1960). *The Strategy of Conflict.* Cambridge, MA, USA: Harvard University Press.

Schelling TC (1966). *Arms and Influence*. New Haven, CT, USA: Yale University Press.

Schwenk CR (1986). Information, cognitive biases, and commitment to a course of action. *Academy of Management Review* **11**:298–310.

Sherif M & Sherif CW (1969). *Social Psychology*. New York, NY, USA: Harper & Row.

Shubik M (1971). The dollar auction game: A paradox in noncooperative behavior and escalation. *Journal of Conflict Resolution* **15**:109–111.

Simmons B (1999). *Territorial Disputes and Their Resolution*. Washington, DC, USA: US Institute of Peace.

Simonson I & Staw BM (1992). De-escalation strategies: A comparison of techniques for reducing commitment to losing courses of action. *Journal of Applied Psychology* **77**:419–426.

Smoke R (1977). *War: Controlling Escalation*. Cambridge, MA, USA: Harvard University Press.

Smoker P (1964). Fear in the arms race. *Journal of Peace Research* **1**:55–63.

Snyder GJ (1972). Crisis bargaining. In *International Crises*, ed. Hermann CF. New York, NY, USA: Free Press.

Staw BM (1997). The escalation of commitment. In *Organizational Decision-Making*, ed. Shapira Z. New York, NY, USA: Cambridge University Press.

Staw BM & Ross J (1987). Knowing when to pull the plug. *Harvard Business Review* **65**:68–74.

Stedman SJ (1991). *Peacemaking in Civil War*. Boulder, CO, USA: Lynne Rienner.

Walton R & McKersie R (1965). *A Behavioral Theory of Labor Negotiations*. New York, NY, USA: McGraw-Hill.

White RK (1984). *Fearful Warrior: A Psychological Profile of US–Soviet Relations*. New York, NY, USA: Free Press.

Wright Q (1965). The escalation of international conflicts. *Journal of Conflict Resolution* **9**:434–459.

Whyte G (1986). Escalating commitment to a course of action: A re-interpretation. *Academy of Management Review* **11**:33–50.

Young O (1968). *The Politics of Force*. Princeton, NJ, USA: Princeton University Press.

Young O (1975). *Bargaining*. Urbana, IL, USA: University of Illinois Press.

Zagare F (1978). A game theoretic analysis of the Vietnam negotiations. In *The Negotiation Process*, ed. Zartman IW. Beverly Hills, CA, USA: Sage.

Zartman IW, ed. (1978). *The Negotiation Process*. Beverly Hills, CA, USA: Sage.

Zartman IW (1987). *The 50% Solution*. New Haven, CT, USA: Yale University Press.

Zartman IW (1989). *Ripe for Resolution*. New York, NY, USA: Oxford University Press.

Zartman IW (2000a). Ripeness: The hurting stalemate and beyond. In *International Conflict Resolution after the Cold War*, eds. Stern P & Druckman D, pp. 225–250. Washington, DC, USA: National Academy Press.

Zartman IW (2001). *Preventive Negotiation: Avoiding Conflict Escalation*. Lanham, MD, USA: Rowman and Littlefield.

Zartman IW & Aurik J (1991). Power strategies in de-escalation. In *Timing the De-escalation of International Conflicts*, eds. Kriesberg L & Thorson S, pp. 152–181. Syracuse, NY, USA: Syracuse University Press.

Zartman IW & Berman M (1982). *The Practical Negotiator*. New Haven, CT, USA: Yale University Press.

Zartman IW & Kremenyuk V (in press). *Peace versus Justice: Negotiating Forward- and Backward-Looking Outcomes*. Lanham, MD, USA: Rowman and Littlefield.

Further reading

Aggestam K & Jönsson C (1997). (Un)ending conflict: Challenges in post-war bargaining. *Millennium: Journal of International Studies* **26**:771–794.

Brams S & Kilgour D (1988). *Games and National Security*. New York, NY, USA: Basil Blackwell.

Garland HG, Sandefur CA & Rogers AC (1990). De-escalation of commitment in oil exploration; When sunk costs and negative feedback coincide. *Journal of Applied Psychology* **75**:721–727.

Jeffrey C (1992). The relation of judgment, personal involvement and experience in the audit of bank loans. *Accounting Review* **67**:802–819.

Mitchell C (1995). The right moment: Notes on four models of "ripeness" paradigms. *Kent Journal of International Relations* **9**:38–52.

O'Neill B (1986). International escalation and the dollar auction. *Journal of Conflict Resolution* **30**:33–50.

Patchen M (1988). *Resolving Disputes between Nations*. Chapel Hill, NC, USA: Duke University Press.

Pruitt DG (1997). Ripeness theory and the Oslo talks. *International Negotiation* **2**:91–104.

Ross J (1998). Escalation theory in labor–management negotiations. In *Advances in Qualitative Organization Research*, Vol. I, ed. Wagner J III. Greenwich, CT, USA: JAI Press.

Singer MS & Singer AE (1986). Is there always escalation of commitment? *Psychological Reports* **56**:816–818.

Staw BM & Ross J (1978). Commitment to a policy decision: A multi-theoretical perspective. *Administrative Science Quarterly* **23**:40–64.

Teger AI (1980). *Too Much Invested to Quit: The Psychology of the Escalation of Conflict*. New York, NY, USA: Pergamon Press.

Zartman IW (2000b). *Traditional Cures for Modern Conflicts*. Boulder, CO, USA: Lynne Rienner.

Zartman IW & Rubin JZ (2000). *Power and Negotiation*. Ann Arbor, MI, USA: University of Michigan Press.

Part II
Escalation Forms and Outcomes

Chapter 2

Deadlocks in Negotiation Dynamics

Guy Olivier Faure

One day, a clam opened its shell to sunbathe on a beach. Suddenly, a snipe stuck its beak in the clam. The latter closed its shell immediately, and trapped the snipe's beak. The clam refused to open its shell, and the snipe refused to remove its beak. Neither of them would make a move to overcome the deadlock. Finally, a fisherman came along and caught both of them.

"The Snipe and the Clam," A Chinese folktale

2.1 Introduction

Escalation and deadlocks share complex mutual causal relations. On the one hand, escalation may lead to a deadlock; on the other, a deadlock may trigger an escalation strategy. In the first case, a deadlock appears to be one of the few possible ways to escape an escalation process as both parties start to fear that the consequences of a bidding war will lead far beyond what was expected. The escalation may also have mobilized so many means of action that the parties feel resources have been exhausted, which thus greatly limits further escalation. Then may come a stage of equalization in threats, in pain inflicted or endured. In the second case, in the midst of a negotiation, a deadlock may trigger an escalation strategy from one party with the goal of moving out of the impasse and forcing the other party to restart the process. Thus, functionally deadlock can be a producer and a product of an escalation process.

Escalation may stop as a result of a swing in the process orientation. This turning point can be a lowering of the demands of both parties or a reduction of the resources they mobilize. Most often, however, the turning point signals that a new stage has been reached. This stage reflects a stagnant situation, of which redundant arguments are often the symptom. Each party sticks to its initially stated positions and refuses to budge. As the parties' positions are incompatible, a deadlock situation arises.

In the Clausewitzian way of looking at action, if escalation is the continuation of negotiation by other means, a deadlock is an incitement to those means, for it is most often the condition required to restart an exchange or readjustment process. The existence of tactical deadlocks strengthens this observation. Indeed, a tactical deadlock fictitiously provides the necessary condition to revive the process. The point is to make the other party believe or understand that one party is at the limit of the concessions that can be made, on the assumption that this is also the case for the other party. Thus, deadlock can be both reality and image.

There are also deadlocks that are not merely the product of an interrupted escalation, for example, a standstill in concession making on both sides. However, the extension of a deadlock over time – an inherent part of the definition of deadlock – already expresses time-frame escalation.

In international relations, deadlocks over grievances, conflicts, or conflicting assessments of a situation are numerous (Kelman 1979; Rothman 1992; Hopmann 1996; Berton *et al.* 1999; Faure 2003). The Mutual and Balanced Force Reduction (MBFR) talks in Vienna provide a good example of a negotiation that continued for many years without any result. These talks started in 1975 between the North Atlantic Treaty Organization (NATO) and the members of the Warsaw Pact and were not able to produce any agreement. One of the major issues that produced the deadlock was whether the verification question should be part of the global agreement or be subjected to a distinct negotiation.

Cease-fires that cannot be turned into peace treaties are typical examples of protracted deadlocks. The longest continuous deadlock that still resists all attempts to overcome it is probably that which began with the Korean truce meeting at Panmunjom. The first meeting was held in 1953 between a US general for the United Nations (UN) command and a North Korean general. No agreement has yet been reached, although hundreds of encounters have taken place since.

The work that follows aims to

- provide a definition of the concept of deadlock in its strategic and cultural aspects;

- identify the signals that show the imminence or the reality of a deadlock;
- identify the possible origins of a deadlock;
- survey the various incentives to break a deadlock; and
- categorize the strategies to overcome a deadlock.

The chapter will present illustrations drawn from international cases.

2.2 Concept of Deadlock

Webster's dictionary defines a deadlock as "a state of inaction or neutralization resulting from the opposition of equally powerful uncompromising persons or factions" (*Webster's Tenth Collegiate Dictionary* 1997). Stalemate and impasses are concepts also found in the current literature. There is a subtle but clear distinction between the concepts. A *deadlock* is an impasse in terms of position, a situation in which no concession or constructive action takes place. A *stalemate* is an impasse in terms of movement and offers no more possibilities for escalation. "Stalemate is the high-water mark for the conflictual ark" according to Rubin *et al.* (1994). For Pruitt (1981, p. 122), who emphasizes the concession-making aspect of negotiation, "A deadlock is a situation in which neither party seems capable of conceding," specified further by the author as "unwilling or unable" (p. 202).

How do actors end up in a situation of deadlock or stalemate? Here again, Pruitt offers an explanation: "this happens because demand levels move increasingly close to limits, producing heightened resistance to further concession making. In a deadlock, competitive actions also become decreasingly attractive because the other party seems quite firm" (Pruitt 1981, p. 133). The author also says that stalemate is a situation in which "all the threats, commitments and debating points that can be made have been made, and the opponent, while duly impressed, is unwilling to make further concessions" (Pruitt 1981, p. 210). Rubin *et al.* go further, suggesting that in deadlocks, "Party (and often the Other) comes to regard the conflict as intolerable, as something that should be ended as soon as possible" (Rubin *et al.* 1994, p. 151). In this view, deadlocks are turning points for negotiation, an opportunity to move into a de-escalation process, as indicated in ripeness theory, discussed by Karin Aggestam in Chapter 12 of this book.

In the scientific literature, the concept of deadlock is either embedded in a concession-making dynamic or viewed as a point of reversal in an escalation process. Though quite useful, the sense given to these concepts limits their analytical scope and instrumental reach. In fact, the concept has a much broader reach, for a deadlock more generally means a halt in the process, a protracted standstill of the dynamics of the negotiation system. The absence of concession does not necessarily mean that both parties are caught in a deadlock. There are a number of ways to keep a negotiation process moving, especially if the discussion still addresses the construction of an agreement formula. Ideas, suggestions, and offers can be exchanged, and thus fuel the development stage of the process with a global aim of exploring as many options as possible before entering a concession-making process.

A deadlock can also be viewed as the sign that a system has reached a state of equilibrium. It corresponds to a balanced situation in which no party can do without the other, or where each party could change only at a prohibitive cost. Zartman (1989, p. 268) argues that "Deadlock cannot be seen merely as a temporary stalemate, to be easily resolved in one's favor by a little effort or even by a big offensive or a gamble or foreign assistance. Rather, each party must recognize its opponent's strength and its own inability to overcome it." Thus, deadlock can also be defined in structural terms – in this case, in terms of power symmetry with one of its major consequences, namely, the inability of each party to relaunch the negotiation dynamics.

From a biological viewpoint, a deadlock can be defined as a negative adaptive reaction of a living organism confronted with a new situation. This is precisely what happens in a negotiation caught in stalemate logic. The evolution that could lead to an agreement – here, an adaptation of one negotiator's positions – does not operate. In this situation, the concession-making mechanism is only one of the many means that may keep the negotiation process going.

Seen through the lens of another semantics, that of the Chinese language, the most common sense of deadlock is represented by two associated characters, *jiang* and *ju*, which mean a locked situation, a neutral gear position, an impasse. *Jiang* is drawn with the symbol of man before two paddy fields separated by bars to show that it is impossible to go from one field to another. *Ju* stands for a situation, a state, a condition, or a fact of things (Faure and Chen 1999).

The breaking off of a negotiation is a fait accompli. A deadlock is an event one stage before a break-off. It can be framed as a situation of mutual threat. Each side issues a tacit message to its target, the other side, concerning the possible interruption of the process or, if it is already viewed as a stalemate, the restarting of the discussions. This type of communication falls into the category of compelling threats (Schelling 1960), in which each party strives to obtain concessions from the other party to restart the negotiation process.

Confronted by a threat, a party has four possible options: give in, tough it out, undermine the threat, or issue a counterthreat. A stalemate is typically a situation in which each of the parties has chosen the fourth option. This counterthreat may be sufficient to counterbalance the impact of the other's threat, but not powerful enough to force the other to submit.

The effectiveness of a threat depends mainly on its credibility. Resorting at the initial stage to a fait accompli at least ensures that the desired event has taken place. However, the term plays an essential part because, for each of the parties, the point is to estimate how long the other party will be able to stand the drawbacks linked to the deadlock, especially the costs entailed by the absence of agreement. The status of the message sender (Faley and Tedeschi 1971), its reputation based on similar acts in the past (Heilman 1974), and the real self-inflicted cost of the implementation of the threat (Mogy and Pruitt 1974) are factors that contribute to the credibility of the threat.

It seldom happens that a long and complex negotiation reaches completion without any period of deadlock. This is why a deadlock should not be viewed as a dramatic circumstance that directly challenges the negotiation as such, but more reasonably as one of the numerous events that stand out as landmarks in any negotiation process. Contrary to the pessimistic view, which sees it as an omen of a failed negotiation, a deadlock can be interpreted as the sign of a well-conducted process in which everyone has explored the possibilities to their limits, a sign of a positive-sum game or a Pareto-optimal process. Similarly, the absence of deadlock could be interpreted as an indication that the level of demand made by each party could be higher, that the security point of the other has not been properly probed, and that not all the possible options have been considered. An efficient negotiation is a process in which each side has made optimal use of the potential of the game, and this can seldom be achieved without deadlocks. The point, then, is to avoid becoming stuck in a stalemate and to move on as soon as an opportunity arises.

In conflict-resolution situations, according to Kreisberg and Thorson (1991), people typically do not sit down to negotiate until they have reached a point of stalemate at which each one no longer believes it possible to obtain what he or she wants through efforts to dominate or coerce. Ripeness theory (Zartman 1989, 2002; Touval and Zartman, 1985) even considers that negotiation can take place only when stalemates occur or when a decision is impossible by other means. Stalemate typically characterizes a situation that is ripe for negotiation and can be viewed as a signal to implement new strategies.

A deadlock situation presupposes structural equality between the parties to the negotiation. A deadlock often, although not always, occurs because of a symmetry in the power distribution or in the dependence relations. Otherwise, one side may be in more of a position to impose its own will. Drawing the consequences from this, Zartman (1991, p. 66) observes that the attempts of parties to overcome the perceived or impeding deadlock and escalate their way out of the stalemate are efforts to disprove the structural equality and to seek something other than a negotiated solution. It is when the deadlock is perceived, in terms of power distribution, to be completely symmetrical structurally, with no hope remaining of forcing one's own solution, that parties may renounce escalation and shift to another strategic option, such as negotiation.

A conflict can be a cause but also a consequence of a deadlock. However, the two concepts do not overlap, because deadlocks can crop up through simple divergence or differing visions of the problem to be solved. These types of deadlocks do not shape an antagonistic relationship and do not elicit a conflictual spiral. A deadlock is not a break-off situation, the indication of a negotiation failure, but rather the sign of a motionless process, so paralysis rather than death.

Deadlocks, especially if protracted, entail a great variety of consequences beyond simply that the negotiation process has stopped and that no more productive dynamics are going on around the negotiation table (assuming that the parties are still sitting there). Besides giving the impression that one's demands have gone as far as possible (and maybe even too far), since people usually state and repeat their views many times a deadlock contributes to anchoring their position deeply. It may turn the negotiation into a kind of trench warfare in which it becomes too risky and too costly for the protagonists to move out of the trenches.

Another possible consequence of a protracted deadlock is a shift from a classic conflict of interest to a conflict between people as they gradually become assimilated to the position they defend. Attribution may also play an active role. After some time, each actor no longer looks for solutions but for culprits, naturally putting the blame on the other party, possibly demonizing him or her in an escalation of images.

One of the main consequences of a protracted deadlock is the tacit message the situation conveys that there is no opportunity to restart the process. Thus, people are deterred from continuing to negotiate with the same counterparts unless there is an absolute need to do so and/or no alternative. The focus of the discussion may also be affected by a protracted deadlock. People strongly mobilize themselves to fight over the bone of contention and easily lose sight of the broader picture, unconsciously depriving themselves of the means of action to unlock the situation.

During a deadlock, parties may still escalate their efforts (means) in the hope of moving forward; not being able or willing to make a concession does not prevent them from taking other actions, such as issuing warnings or threats, even resorting to a fait accompli, until they reach a stalemate situation. Escalating from a deadlocked position to a stalemate may bring additional resources to the conflict, and so increase the price the other party has to pay or the risk it incurs, or it may change the way the other party is represented, for example through its demonization. When stalemate occurs, the escalation of efforts stops, for stalemate is a sign that no party can find any more acceptable initiatives to escalate further. The cessation of escalation can be justified in various ways, such as the parties thinking that proceeding further may elicit consequences too harmful for them, or simply seeing no more convenient means of action to resort to.

2.3   Deadlock Diagnosis

In negotiations, two major types of cultural practices can be distinguished, the direct and the indirect game. The two lead to very different methods of observation. In Western cultures, intentions and opinions are expressed rather openly. Thus, when someone is not really happy with what has been offered, his or her dissatisfaction can be easily decoded or perceived. A deadlocked situation is observed when none of the parties makes any more concessions or any move that could fuel the negotiation dynamics, be they acts or words. An example of a clear deadlock is the case of the partitioning of Cyprus into a Greek and a Turkish zone, which has already lasted for more than 25 years.

However, many situations do not have such visible characteristics, especially when they involve relations between individuals. In addition, the cultural dimension can make it more difficult for the actors to realize they are caught in a true deadlock. Applying criteria that signal the existence of a deadlock in a culture that emphasizes direct games will not lead to the diagnosis of a deadlock in a culture that emphasizes indirect games, such as in Asian cultures (Lang 1998, p. 39). If the situation is characterized by the absence of concessions, negotiation may still involve exchanges of information, offers, suggestions, and statements that continue to nourish the verbal dynamics. These exchanges may lead the observer to believe that the negotiation process is still moving, when, in the other actor's culture, it is in reality totally deadlocked.

Taking into account the diversity of the cultural contexts, numerous indications enable an attentive negotiator to realize that a negotiation is in a deadlocked situation:

- Meetings are empty at the substance level. The counterparts may go on exchanging nice words and large smiles in what looks like a serene context, but in the meantime no further real moves are made, such as concessions, information exchange, or the offering of suggestions.
- Answers are so complicated that they become totally incomprehensible, and all that they really convey is the embarrassment of their producer. The opacity of the explanations given by the negotiator expresses the care taken not to offend the other or make the other lose face, but at the same time it reflects the effort made not to show vulnerability and not to reveal the difficulties encountered.

- The same arguments and explanations are repeated endlessly. The quantity of energy spent compared with the actual result of the activity becomes quite excessive.
- One of the parties pretends to be unavailable for further meetings, invoking an acceptable reason and not using any unpleasant words or showing any sign of discontentment. This is a way to demonstrate social skills and to give proof of the creativity that is often missing in the development of the negotiation process.

These tenuous clues, while quite significant, are often ambiguous as to their meaning. For example, repeating the same arguments again and again does not always mean a deadlock is occurring, but may simply indicate that the counterpart is anxious to show concern about some highly prized issue. Answers to proposals that are delayed far beyond what one would reasonably expect do not necessarily mean a refusal to move, but may indicate that the other party is facing a lengthy decision-making process. This may be a result of the number of people involved in the decision, the complexity of the decision-making structure, the lack of available information, or other difficulties in making a decision. To save face, the opponent will not disclose the cause of this delay at the negotiation table.

The art of decoding consists of spotting significant signals, however weak or ambiguous, amplifying them, relating them to their initial context, and then drawing an inference. The Chinese have a saying: "The ginkgo tree has lost its first leaf, and the whole Empire knows that autumn is on its way." In Asian cultures, a slight modification in attitude, the way the relationship is handled, routines, protocol, or rituals can be used to indicate that more significant changes are going to take place (Faure 1998; Li 1999).

2.4   Origins of Deadlock

The essence of escalation is reciprocity. Initiatives taken by each party are legitimized because they abide by this principle. Deadlocks function in a similar way, for they also express a sort of behavioral equivalence, but in non-action. If we consider only escalation, the range of reasons behind a deadlock is very broad. The reasons can have a cognitive origin or be linked to perception, be of a personal or relational nature, be linked to the negotiation context, arise from the very structure of the negotiation, or arise from the process and the actors' behavior (*Table 2.1*).

Table 2.1. Causes of deadlock

Categories	Causes
Cognitive–perceptual	Differences in understanding of the rationale of the game and in perceptions; fear of uncertain consequences
Personal–relational	Lack of affinity; aggressive, arrogant, or condescending attitude; seemingly dishonest behavior; conflict of interest turned into a personal conflict; absence of trust
Contextual	Pressures from peer group, organization, administrative authorities
Structural	No more resources available; power relationships; strongly conflicting issues
Process–behavioral–strategic	Concessions not made in an appropriate way; process inconsistencies
	Insufficient information; deluded expectations, unkept promises, and unfair trade-offs
	Attempts to influence a third party, to gain side benefits, to move the negotiation to a higher level of authority
	Costs inflicted on the other party are higher

2.4.1 Cognitive and perceptual aspects

A cognitive or perceptual reason is implied when deadlock occurs because the parties understand the situation differently. Often, neither party realizes that the other has a totally different view about the global project or its final purpose, as no one openly states his or her objectives. For instance, during the Vietnam War, US President Lyndon Johnson (in 1965) used a carrot-and-stick strategy to try to end the conflict, issuing both a promise and a threat simultaneously. On the one hand, he offered the North Vietnamese US$1 billion in aid to rebuild the parts of their country destroyed during the war. On the other hand, he threatened to resume the bombing of vital places in North Vietnam if the North Vietnamese did not agree to the whole deal. Such a strategy was totally counterproductive, because the Vietnamese not only interpreted the financial offer as a cynical attempt by capitalists to buy them out, but also regarded the threat as just additional proof of the extreme hostility of the USA toward them and of the contempt the Americans always displayed for the Vietnamese.

In some cases, the picture may slowly become clearer, and one of the parties may discover that the other has incompatible objectives or does not act according to acceptable principles. As a defensive action, this party must at least freeze the whole process.

Sometimes, differences in cultural codes in communicating with adversaries may elicit very strong deadlocks. During the nuclear test ban negotiations between the USA and the Soviet Union (1958–1963), the word "control" became a source of misunderstanding that long made any agreement impossible. As underlined by Jönsson (1990, p. 130), the English word "control" has the connotation of "steering, command," whereas its semantic Russian equivalent *kontrol* means only "verification, supervision." As one of the major issues of these negotiations was the "arms control" aspect, such a misunderstanding became a stumbling block that prevented both parties from reaching any accord.

Differences in understanding the rationale of the game may also lead to a deadlock. If one party conceives of the negotiation as an integrative game and the other party sees it as a distributive game, the former may be quickly deterred from making any more cooperative moves.

A deadlock may arise because, in the eyes of one of the parties, continuing to negotiate implies making concessions. These concessions entail risks that can be perceived as being considerable because of the uncertainties they carry concerning several components of the negotiation process, such as the true intentions of the other party, how much it is willing to concede, and what the final consequences with respect to the possible outcome would be.

Another reason for being caught in a deadlock could be that the negotiation is perceived as a kind of tennis game. Once the ball is sent to the other party, it has to be returned with something more than in the previous exchange. If nothing additional is sent back – if there are no more concessions and no new offers – the first party tends to view the ball as still being "in the other's court" and so makes no further move. When both parties view the situation in these terms, we typically have a cognitive deadlock.

Another cause of deadlock is the misperception of the intent behind the actions of the counterpart (Bazerman and Carroll 1987; Rubin 1989; Jönsson 1991). Attribution theory provides a clear explanation of this phenomenon. Negotiators tend to assume that individuals' actions reflect their inner disposition, especially in cases of negative initiative, and rather underevaluate the impact of external factors beyond the other party's control. Furthermore, moves from the other side that look positive are attributed to attempts at manipulation. Thus, if both parties react in this way, the negotiation process may be reduced to a standstill as long as these cognitive aspects continue to play an important role in the bargaining interaction.

Finally, escalation of images may elicit a deadlock. This is particularly true if the other party is demonized, which prevents a negotiator from making any additional concessions so as not to be seen as compromising with the devil. The same type of escalation may induce the fear of being cheated, because of the reputation of the other party, and thus freeze the negotiation process. These cognitive aspects always play an important part in the bargaining interaction.

2.4.2 Personal and relational causes

A personal and/or relational origin is implied when a lack of affinity, or one party's aggressive, arrogant, condescending, or seemingly dishonest attitude, generates a deadlock. Since it is individual people who represent parties at the negotiation table, the conflict of interest that has to be dealt with may turn into a personal conflict. In such cases, any concession can be perceived as a sign of submission and will result in a loss of face, even if the aggressive party is careful enough to "point at the pumpkin to insult the calabash," a Chinese classic in indirect communication. Minimum consideration is given to the counterpart, especially if he or she enjoys a high status or has a non-negligible power position. Sometimes little is needed to drastically transform the relationship. Since everyone pays careful attention to every move or gesture made by the other side and gives it their own interpretation, any signal that is even the least bit dissonant can elicit dramatic reactions. The absence of the conditions needed to give rise to trust may also lead to a paralysis of the system by locking both parties into a defensive attitude. Information exchange is diminished, misunderstandings and suspicion grow, and bluffing becomes a major tactic. As a result, the dynamics of the whole system grind to a standstill. A sense of trust must prevail in the relations, and any commitment must be translated into acts that provide proof of goodwill, and even of honesty, to the other. Otherwise, the discussion will be carried out in vain.

Trust is a relational attribute that considerably helps parties to behave cooperatively. Conversely, a lack of trust leads to an escalation of conflict and deadlock, once the costs become too high to increase further. This was typical of the US–Soviet relations during the Cold War period. Each country faced a choice: agree to disarm or build more armaments. Basically, it was more advantageous for each party to disarm, but if one did while the other cheated, the cheater would gain a critical strategic advantage. Thus, although the best collective option was to disarm, the fear of being cheated made both parties highly reluctant to conclude any agreement. This absence of trust finally led to an impressive escalation in the arms race, which lasted for over 40 years, harmed both economies, and probably contributed to the destruction of the Soviet Union.

2.4.3 Contextual causes

The negotiation context that causes deadlock is a function of the external structure that bears upon the situation. These settings can be of a social, political, legal, or administrative nature. The negotiator may be under pressure from his or her peer group, department, organization, or administrative authorities to not concede any further. On the one hand, hiding behind a strong power carries a number of advantages in terms of leverage against the other side; on the other hand, it also entails some drawbacks, such as a dependence that may be difficult, even risky, to break off. There are moments in many negotiations when a party finds that the only available strategy involves resorting to some external factor, such as a regulation that one can try to interpret or play with. This runs the risk of locking that negotiator into the present position, thus causing a deadlock.

The East European situation that prevailed after World War II offered a context of political glaciation that broadly turned East–West relations into a permanent deadlock. Before 1989, no significant sign of ripeness occurred to indicate a new context more propitious to unlocking the impasse in relations.

2.4.4   Structural causes

Structural causes concern the parties involved in the negotiation and the internal resources available to solve the issues at stake. "Stalemate exists when the circumstances prevent either party to a dispute from creating a solution alone. Each party has necessary but insufficient ingredients of a solution" (Zartman and Berman 1982). Even when the counterpart wants to be open-handed, there are obvious limitations to this generosity. In deadlocks no further concession can be made for reasons of a quantitative or qualitative nature. Perhaps one party has reached its security point, or perhaps small concessions cannot succeed because they are not sufficient to modify the attitude of the other party. There are also situations in which nothing more can be given, because in doing so the whole balance of one's own system would be destroyed. Additionally, there are efforts that cannot obtain something in return, even if made in the most skillful way.

Another element of structure is the power relationships, perceived or real, that exist across the table and the stakes behind them. There is always the risk of being caught in a game between two powerful parties, which sensitizes everyone to the smallest differential. In an asymmetric power situation, the weaker party may find it advantageous to protect his or her interests by blocking progress and hence avoiding an agreement that reflects the existing power imbalance. If this were not the case, the end could be quite predictable.

2.4.5   Process, behavioral, and strategic causes

Process, behavioral, and strategic factors can freeze the negotiation process because concessions made in an inappropriate way can be the start of a deadlock or cause an existing deadlock to continue. As an illustration, a concession made too early or one of an unexpected size can raise the level of expectation of the other party and make reciprocity impossible. A late concession or one that is too small can break the momentum and have no – or even a negative – impact on the process. Introducing inconsistency during the course of the negotiation can interrupt the process because of a lack of sufficient reference points. An example is handling the financial aspects of an issue before the technical ones are dealt with. An insufficient amount of information exchange can also make it impossible to imagine solutions that would help to maintain the dynamics or devise constructive proposals.

A deadlock may also be the direct consequence of deluded expectations, unkept promises, or trade-offs considered fair by one party and rejected by the other. Sometimes the effort occurs too late and has no influence on the other's behavior. Such a deadlock ranks as a retaliatory procedure. Usually this has limited consequences, for it does not commit the parties to enter an escalation process. However, if one party decides to make the other party pay for its "bad deeds" and is happy with the idea that "at least, they will suffer more than we," a lose–lose game may be triggered. Indeed, our experience of this type of situation shows that a prudent approach is needed when the costs that may result from an escalation process are known.

Situations structurally framed as a Prisoner's Dilemma often entail deadlocks in a lose–lose logic, because it seems difficult for both parties not to anchor themselves in a defensive strategy, especially for one-off negotiations or negotiations not often repeated. If the counterpart responds, the player can take advantage of this and obtain a significant gain; but if the counterpart does not respond and remains tough and distrustful, the player also has to adopt a tough and distrustful strategy for protection. In both cases, the structure of the paradigm and its many expressions in real life induce a non-cooperative attitude that leads to conflictual situations and deadlocks.

Siegel and Fouraker (1960) suggest that the level of aspiration is a factor that determines the initial disposition and subsequent rate of concession. The negotiator who gains the best outcome is the one who opens with a high demand, has a small rate of concession, and is perceptive and unyielding. This maximalist bargaining strategy is weakened by the fact that its potential gain tends to be overshadowed by possible costs. As observed by Iklé (1964), the most serious of these costs is a deadlock. The other party may not make any move as long as he or she thinks that the opening demand is only a "bargaining position."

When both parties to a dispute consider that it is in their interest not to make any concession, conditions are set for a negotiation deadlock. This was the case with US Secretary of State James Baker and Iraqi Foreign Minister Tariq Aziz in the Geneva talks (1991) prior to the Gulf War. The US envoy threatened to take military action if Iraq did not withdraw its troops from Kuwait. Given the asymmetry between the military capabilities of both parties, it was not in the interest of the US secretary of state to give in. However, for the foreign minister of Iraq, capitulation would have been more harmful than a military defeat, because, in the latter case, the government and Saddam Hussein still had a chance of surviving politically, as there is no shame in being defeated by a much stronger enemy. Tariq Aziz just had to appear brave, and so the USA had to win without merit, a triumph without glory.

A deadlock may be the direct outcome of a tit-for-tat strategy if the negotiation dynamics become coercive. Reciprocity in refusing or in threatening leads to a balance in terms of fairness that sets up a paralysis in the negotiation system. Sometimes this locks the negotiation in a cycle of mutual hostility with an inherent risk of escalation.

Druckman (1978) states that the level of expectation produces an impasse fueled by a high level of mutual toughness, which in turn is readjusted according to the negotiation pattern. Whatever the cause of the deadlock, the negotiation itself may be considered as having entered a process of escalation that has led, at least, to a situation of positional deadlock, because none of the parties is able or willing to make any more concessions.

2.5   Incentives to Break a Deadlock

As pointed out by Rubin (1991), it is tempting to sit back, do nothing, and hope that the mere passage of time will turn events to your advantage. "Only time resolves conflicts, but time needs help" observes Zartman (1989, p. 273). Indeed, before taking any action to escape a deadlock, each of the parties must feel a need to do so. Each party has to find a good reason to move from the current situation. "The moment is propitious for negotiation when both sides perceive that they may be better off with an agreement than without one" (Zartman and Berman 1982). If the costs incurred by the deadlock are negligible and the related advantages of breaking the deadlock are not visible, there is no effective incentive to escape the deadlock. This is the case, for instance, in a business negotiation in which each of the parties negotiates at the same time with other counterparts. In this regard, time does not really put any pressure on the actor in terms of the costs incurred by not moving; transaction costs and opportunities lost or competitors taking advantage of the standstill are difficult to quantify. There may also be reasons to prolong the deadlock, especially if each of the parties considers that in the long run the position of the other will weaken. As the final agreement is believed to reflect the power balance that exists at the time of its making, the party that is becoming stronger will find it advantageous to conclude the negotiation at that time and not before.

The incentives to move from a deadlock are diverse and bear witness to an interest, at least a subjective one, to do so:

- The situation of a "mutually hurting stalemate" (Zartman 1989) provides one incentive. This occurs when the difference between the pain felt and the satisfaction gained from inflicting losses on the other party is no longer a sufficient driving force to protract the negotiation further. This is why, for instance, the independence of Algeria was finally negotiated between the Front de Libération Nationale (FLN) and the French government with the Accords d'Evian in 1962. One can hypothesize that there is a threshold beyond which a conflict reaches such an intense and painful level that it becomes obvious to everyone that a compromise has to be found. This threshold varies considerably according to the external conditions, stakes, and people involved. Cases such as World War I, with its four years of trench warfare and millions of dead, or the devastating war between Iraq and Iran (1980–1988) show how far people and governments can go before realizing that this threshold has been reached. Then, the mutually hurting stalemate performs a therapeutic function.

- The expectation of gain is reduced or a future fall is anticipated in the expected gains, as was the case in the negotiations between F.W. de Klerk and Nelson Mandela in South Africa.
- A new means appears by which to save face with a move that will not be viewed as a sign of weakness. This was the case with the UK–Argentinian negotiations over the Falklands. Another example is the signing of the Shanghai Communiqué between the USA and the People's Republic of China (PRC) on the normalization of their diplomatic relations (1979).
- A modification in the context of one or more of the components makes possible a new agreement formula. For instance, the Israeli–Palestinian negotiation process started after considerable changes in the Arab context. Another example is the Montreal Protocol on Substances That Deplete the Ozone Layer of 1987, which was signed after the discovery of major damage to the ozone layer.
- An influential third party intervenes and strongly encourages one of the parties to make a move. This was, for instance, the case with the Camp David negotiations between Egypt and Israel, with considerable leverage brought to bear by the USA acting as a mediator.
- A gain is anticipated – for instance, in terms of image with respect to a third party, such as international public opinion – if one takes an initiative that has been assessed positively. This is, for the time being, the case with the Israeli–Syrian negotiations over the Golan.
- A deadlocked situation that is going to lead to a major crisis, or to entail unbearable consequences, such as the action's moving from the negotiation table to the battlefield, may provide a commanding reason to restart the negotiation process. The shadow of the future, especially if the prospects are extremely dark, may become a strong incentive to avoid reaching a point of no return. The final agreement between the USA and the Soviet Union over the Soviet missiles in Cuba (1962), in which Soviet Premier Nikita Khrushchev agreed to

withdraw the missiles while US President John F. Kennedy agreed not to invade Cuba, provides a clear example of such a strong incentive to come to terms after the world had been brought to the verge of a global war.

2.6   Strategies to Overcome Deadlock

Human imagination has no limits when a solution to a problem has to be devised. From the viewpoint of the actor, these solutions are implemented by means of strategies. All of the strategies serve a common goal, the relaunching of the negotiation process, and their number is high because of the need to adapt action to the (very numerous) particulars of the situation or context.

Deadlocks are resolved by dealing with their causes. Therefore, the various possible solutions may also be classified within the causal categories used above. Strategies are actions devised and carried out by people within a cultural context. At the same time, they are induced by interests and cultural norms. They may vary according to the society within which the deadlock occurs.

Before taking any initiative to break a deadlock, if, as in many cases, the deadlock is grievous or linked to important stakes and dramatic consequences, the stress it has generated among the parties has to be dealt with. The stress may be overcome, reduced, removed, or lived with as painlessly as possible. Very few practitioners escape this reality.

2.6.1   Cognitive and perceptual strategies

For some problems there is no obvious solution. In such cases, it may be productive to reframe the problem in such a way that a solution can be devised. For instance, if the problem was structured according to the logic of a Chicken game, it may be better to turn it into a Prisoner's Dilemma. The Sino–US statement over the Taiwanese issue is an example of a successful reframing of a problem which had for decades been a bone of contention between the USA and China. Henry Kissinger and Chinese Premier Zhou Enlai agreed on the formula "All Chinese on either side of the Taiwan Strait maintain there is but one China."

As a general rule, stepping back from the narrow frame of action has virtues that many negotiators are sensitive to, because this positioning helps to distinguish what is essential from what is less important. The broadened viewpoint thus taken leads the negotiators to return to values of cooperation, which initially are the essence of an interaction. This "helicopter effect" enables the negotiator to incorporate more elements into his or her global perception, elements that pertain more or less directly to the negotiation situation, and thus provide a somewhat different picture of the situation. The source of the deadlock also may no longer be seen as a major divergence of interests, and the parties may realize that their quarrel is, to a certain extent, paltry. Considering the long-term consequences of cooperation is part of this global approach and often adds an integrative dimension to the problem that both sides face.

Distancing oneself from the details of a situation, which are possibly confusing in themselves if the number of elements involved in the deadlock is high, may be highly instrumental. It is also a part of oriental wisdom, as underlined by Ury (1991, p. 17): "In the ancient Japanese art of swordsmanship, students were instructed to look at an opponent as if he were a far-off mountain."

A change in the perception of the terms of the deal, their value, and their significance may help to restart a stalled process. For instance, in the Israeli–Arab negotiations, land for peace was seen by some of the stakeholders as a *marché de dupes*. Once the land is given it is really lost, whereas peace, which is just as necessary, is a much more uncertain achievement, the reality of which cannot be easily assessed and maintained over time. Again, a longer-term approach may help to revise these perceptions and reframe the nature of the global game.

One approach to breaking the vicious circle of mutually hostile images, with its spiral-type development, is to help each side to reevaluate their perceptions. The point is to show the inconsistency between the image of the other and the reality of that party's behavior. As suggested by Jönsson (1991), the party that wants to have its image modified should take initiatives that are clearly voluntary and costly. These initiatives should be repeated for some period of time, even if not initially reciprocated. This principle was applied by Soviet General Secretary Mikhail Gorbachev when, in 1986, during a deadlocked negotiation on conventional arms control in Europe, he announced his intention to unilaterally withdraw 240,000 Soviet soldiers and 10,000 tanks from Eastern Europe.

The cognitive changes may be facilitated by the intervention of a third party offering a new vision of the situation. This reframing activity is more likely to be accepted when promoted by an outsider to the conflict who is not part of the origin of the deadlock. Some empathy can be developed through specific techniques such as role reversal, when both parties agree to attend such exercises through training sessions. Instead of explaining its position and arguing for its own interests to prevail, each party is asked to present the position of the other party and to offer reasons to substantiate its demands. Inducing empathy does not challenge the interests of the concerned party, but simply helps that party to better understand the whole situation, including the interests and motivations of the other party; it does not require the party to share those interests.

2.6.2   Personal and relational strategies

A second set of strategies for breaking deadlocks deals with the personal and relational aspects of the negotiations. The purpose is to change an element of the
system, with the hope that the entire system will be modified. Negotiation is an
interaction between people, which means that their individual chemistries are at
work. It is difficult to foresee the result of this chemistry. If parties have no affinity or empathy, deadlocks may ensue. Changing one or several negotiators may
improve the relationship. When a negotiator is suspected of misconduct by the
counterpart, it is important that he or she leave the negotiation and that a new negotiator be chosen. The newcomer will not be tarnished by the misconduct of his
or her predecessor. After such a change, the overall chemistry may improve considerably. For instance, when Yitzhak Rabin was elected prime minister of Israel
in 1992, a dramatic change in the atmosphere of the Israeli–Palestinian relations
occurred. This contributed greatly to a resumption of constructive discussions over
the future of Gaza and the West Bank, which had hardly moved under the leadership of Rabin's predecessor, Yitzhak Shamir. Talking about oneself and revealing
some personal aspects of one's own life may also trigger some empathy from the
other side, and thus contribute to changing the nature of the relationship.

Emotions may considerably affect the negotiation atmosphere. Traditionally,
Asians are suspicious of emotions and tend to strongly restrict their expression.
For them, "the heart has passions like trees have worms." The only emotions that
have a constructive role are those that are still under control. Instead of continuing in a negotiation process that is constantly circular (progressing nowhere), it
is advisable to try a different approach, such as a social treatment of the deadlock
(Chen and Faure 1995). The point is to improve the atmosphere of the negotiation,
in the hope that this will improve negotiator flexibility, possibly by adding to the
mix some recreation, small gifts, dinners, banquets, or karaoke. Large gifts, of
course, can restart the negotiation process, but this is a matter not so much of social
improvement as of buying the other negotiator, a practice that, although morally
condemned, is still widespread. It is also possible to be more direct across the table
and lavishly praise one's counterpart, express consideration, and give "face" (Faure
et al. 2000).

Face is the "public self-image that every member of a society wants to claim
for himself/herself" (Brown and Levinson 1978). Face concerns are probably quite
universal, but people from oriental cultures have developed a special sensitivity to
them (Pye 1982; Fang 1999). Saving and giving face are questions of prestige,
reputation, and dignity that directly bear upon self-esteem. In China, shame has
traditionally been used as a means of social control. In a "group-oriented culture"
(Lockett 1988), this informal social credit is of crucial importance. This is also why

in business an efficient negotiator is someone with a "thick skin" or "thick face," who does not force his company to bear the costs of his concern for reputation and pride. Face is a fragile commodity, and its loss always implies some form of retaliation against those responsible. The worst situation is when someone has lost face in front of his or her subordinates. This can be considered an unforgivable offense, and the victim will certainly be merciless when taking revenge (Faure 1998, 1999).

Keeping the negotiation process moving implies being able to stand some level of risk, because there are always consequences that cannot be foreseen. A way to lower the level of risk is to build trust between the parties or to re-establish it when it has been challenged. This is a relational process whose reality has to be checked. As underlined by Zartman and Berman (1982), "Trust is enhanced by step-by-step agreements with 'accounting points' along the way."

Personal reasons or a particular concern for reputation may be behind the re-launching of a negotiation process. For instance, a negotiator who fears that a protracted deadlock could be seen as a personal failure, a manifestation of his or her inability to achieve an agreement, may invest more effort in restarting the negotiation process. Among the many personal reasons, career concerns and self-image can be considered strong incentives to overcome a deadlock.

Another type of relational approach, the informal go-between solution, involves an appeal to one's own social resources. One finds common acquaintances or friends who can intervene to improve one's credibility, to bear testimony to one's good intentions, to facilitate communication, or to ensure a better understanding of the other party. Such go-betweens must enjoy credibility and reputation to be accepted by both sides. The party who is suffering the most from the deadlock is, of course, the one who is more likely to look to someone else for help. This acting mediator may sometimes manage to obtain a concession from one side knowing that an unspoken rule compels reciprocity, which will restart the negotiation process.

2.6.3 Contextual strategies

The context of the deadlock offers opportunities to overcome it through negotiation. For instance, Zartman underlines that, in decolonization situations, the differences in terms of values carried by both parties "give a maximum flexibility and fungibility for negotiation" (Zartman 1991). In the negotiation process, the various cultures may combine the sets of values that they express and thus simultaneously increase the potential for flexibility and the number of functions that can be fulfilled.

A change in the overall balance of the external system may lead to the restarting of a negotiation that was previously at a standstill. Thus, for 15 years meetings were organized on a regular basis at the Chinese embassy in Warsaw between the US ambassador and the PRC chargé d'affaires. The first 134 encounters were totally useless. The 135th meeting, held in 1970, unlocked the situation, mainly because of the changes brought to the international arena by the Soviets (Kissinger 1979).

A whole set of strategies oriented toward the negotiation context can also play an important role in getting the process moving again. The first approach of this kind aims at contracting an alliance with external partners to increase one's leverage in the negotiation. Large numbers are important in some cultures because they reassure people psychologically and strengthen them physically.

When the causes of deadlocks are pressures from the peer group, their organization, or administrative authorities, these have to be considered as true parties to the negotiation and dealt with accordingly. To this end, one can draw from the panoply of strategies in the five different categories.

Another strategy that is meant to modify the context of the relationship and make it more cooperative consists of emphasizing all that has been accomplished together and shared in common, and all the difficulties that have been overcome together. An additional element that can prove effective in unlocking an impasse is to go over the joint projects to be carried out, provided that the conflict at the origin of the deadlock does not concern the content of the joint project, but only the means to achieve it.

When the range of possible options has been reviewed again and again, and when everyone has become convinced that nothing new can be expected from this procedure, another strategy is to introduce a superordinate value and thus transform the priorities of both parties. This new value may be mutual interest, friendship, long-lasting relations, long-term goals, government policy, the higher interest of the country, or the wish of the party. Such strongly persuasive, if not totally compelling, new constraints tend to modify the other negotiator's objectives and encourage that party to put the negotiation back on track. Generally, introducing a new value tends to modify the set of functional norms of the system or the logic of the game. To some extent, it is a new game that the parties are invited to join. The parties are not supposed to make costly or unilateral concessions, with all the reservations or refusals that entails, but simply to play differently.

Introducing a new norm of fairness, a new principle of justice, may also re-launch the negotiation process and enable both parties to base their actions on the "bicycle theory." This implies a dynamic of constant reciprocal moves to keep the whole process in motion, or to counterbalance the inequality in the power structure.

The Congress of Vienna offers a good example of what can be achieved with the introduction of a new value. At the end of the Napoleonic Wars in 1814, Europe was deeply destabilized and the allied powers of the time (England, Austria, Prussia, and Russia) decided to act in concert. They engaged in a negotiation to ensure a stable future for Europe by redefining some of its borders. The point was mainly to share among themselves part of the remains of Napoleon's empire. France, as expected, was not invited to the negotiation table. A kind of deadlock within a situation of clear power asymmetry then ensued. Charles Maurice de Talleyrand, the representative of the king of France, newly re-established on his throne, explained that France and the king he was representing were the first victims of Napoleon. At first, Talleyrand worked at reducing the structural asymmetry by setting up informal relations with some of the main actors in the game. In fact, if the victorious powers had agreed among themselves to punish France, they disagreed on everything else. At a second stage, Talleyrand managed to break the deadlock and to be accepted at the negotiation table by invoking a new value, devised for this very purpose, that did not give rise to any opposition, the *bien public*, or "public good" (Orieux 1973).

Sometimes, the superordinate value is introduced by third parties upset by the protracted deadlock, such as local authorities that believe the success of a business negotiation will have positive consequences for the town's economy. In every respect, an economic initiative is *a priori* well received because it brings advantages to the environment, and everyone within it will benefit from it. Thus, the pressure of the context becomes an essential variable in relaunching the negotiation process.

2.6.4   Structure-oriented strategies

The strategies in the fourth cluster apply to the structure of the negotiation. These aim at modifying the structure to restart the process. For instance, Zagare (1978) observed that in the Paris peace talks (1968–1973) the structural coincidence of the preferences of the players and their best strategies, as defined by game theory, locked the players into a stalemate that was not resolved until the structure was changed. The two major parties to the negotiation, the USA and North Vietnam, decided to resort to back-channel diplomacy. Thus, Henry Kissinger and Le Duc Tho were able to come to an agreement. "Track 2" diplomacy offers a significant advantage compared with official negotiations. The negotiators escape from the formalism, rigidity, and public character that prevent negotiators from taking risks or proposing initiatives that would be their own. Those who engage in the "Track 2" diplomacy do so on their own behalf and enjoy much more freedom of action and have much broader margins of maneuver, a better quality of communication, and better conditions for creativity. Thus, they are able to build up more effective solutions to take the negotiation out of the impasse into which the official discussions have dragged it. By introducing one's own superior, the structural aspect may also be changed. The effect of this is to raise the status of the negotiation and to increase the power position of the one who involves his or her superior in the game.

Another way to restart a deadlocked negotiation, especially when the deadlock is caused by a power imbalance, consists in building up a coalition to exert a high degree of control over a situation. Setting up a producer cartel, such as the

Organization of Petroleum Exporting Countries (OPEC) to control the supply of oil on the world market, is a typical example of an attempt to gain enough leverage to bring the counterpart back to the negotiation table with more constructive intentions.

Resorting to a mediator belongs to the same logic of working on the structural aspects, for it changes a bilateral system into a triangular system. The mediator, while avoiding direct confrontation, can facilitate communication, increase the motivation to reach an agreement, homogenize the parties' viewpoints, suggest initiatives, propose modifications in the issue structure, or transform the game. A friend is, in these circumstances, a convenient means to escape the impasse into which the negotiation process has moved. Intervention by a mediator is not cost free, especially if the mediator has a strong sense of his or her own interests, and what has been offered may have to be paid back sometime or other.

In fact, if we consider a paradigm such as the Prisoner's Dilemma, breaking a deadlock means moving from the southeast box to the northwest box. The former expresses a deadlock with a rather poor outcome but a clear absence of risk, while the latter provides a higher outcome paired with a real risk. A mediator may be especially instrumental in helping both sides to make this move either by persuading each one to trust the other a little more or by providing some kind of assurance that no move will be made at the expense of the other. As underlined by Pruitt (1981) and Touval and Zartman (1985), mediator intervention in a deadlock may greatly facilitate new concessions by providing a convenient cover, so that the concession maker does not run the risk of appearing weak or lose face and ruin his or her reputation. For instance, during his step-by-step diplomacy in the Middle East, Kissinger submitted to Egyptian President Anwar Sadat a map of the Sinai indicating a provisional border as if the map were his own creation when in fact it had been drawn by the Israeli government. Thus, the US mediator obtained an agreement from Sadat that would have been much more difficult to secure had the Egyptian leader known it had been designed by his own enemy. An expert on the issue at stake, because of his or her technical knowledge and credibility, can also be used as a mediator, or even as an arbitrator if both parties agree beforehand to conform to the expert's advice.

Resorting to an external party to put pressure on one's counterpart in a deadlock is another technique that has proved its effectiveness. The Palestinian authorities have systematically used such a method, hoping the US government will induce their Israeli counterparts to make an effort to escape the numerous impasses in which they have been caught. Similarly, in 1972 the USA tried to use their rapprochement with China to persuade the Chinese government to encourage the Vietnamese prime minister to take a more flexible stance in the negotiations with the USA.

It is also possible to operate directly on the structure by modifying the number of issues at stake, because adding or subtracting issues leads to changes in the game, the interests, and related assessments of the possible gains and losses. When Homans' theorem (1961) is properly applied, packaging and logrolling provide a potential for win–win formulas, attractive outcomes that will help to restart the negotiation process. The order in which issues are dealt with is also important, for it is essential to deal with sensitive issues at the right psychological moment.

Some deadlocks arise because the parties focus all their attention and energy on one issue considered to be crucial, such as the financial aspects in a business negotiation, and view its acceptance as a precondition to any further move in the negotiation process. In such cases, the point is to avoid this psychological or symbolic fixation and simultaneously propose a concession with compensation on another issue; for instance, in the case of the purchase of equipment, this could be spare parts, a shorter delivery time, or free installation. Adding issues to the negotiation changes the scope or the shape of the set of issues and thus enables everyone to look for "packages" that integrate trade-offs that will help reach a jointly satisfying balanced solution. With this new prospect in view, the negotiation process may restart.

This approach is also called issue aggregation. If each one of the issues were treated separately, each would lead to deadlock. As the costs and benefits are not symmetrical for both parties, the overall evaluation may be positive enough to make both sides restart discussions. Such a formula was tested in the US–Soviet negotiations (1972–1979) on the second Strategic Arms Limitation Talks (SALT II) Treaty. Originally, the Russians devised a classic concession–convergence approach to reduce the number of SS-18s on the Soviet side and the number of air-launched cruise missiles (ALCMs) on the US side. However, the USA did not want the ALCMs to be considered strategic missiles, because their range was rather short. They preferred to put them in the category of gravity bombs. A protracted deadlock resulted from this basic divergence. The two issues were not structurally linked, but they were ranked as high priorities for each country. Each party was more eager to strengthen its own military capabilities than to reduce those of the other. The two issues were finally linked, and an agreement was reached in which the Soviets could retain their SS-18s and the Americans were allowed to deploy a specified number of ALCMs (Hopmann 1996, pp. 83–84).

In some cases, the audience plays a role and contributes to the stalling of the negotiation process; a way to deal with this difficulty is to leave the public stage and operate behind the scenes. The successful conclusion to the Camp David negotiation between Anwar Sadat, representing Egypt, and Menachem Begin, representing Israel, owes much to this very specific device. Camp David was especially chosen to isolate both negotiators from their national audiences, which enabled them to be more flexible than they would have been had the whole process been held under the anxious and critical scrutiny of their media.

"Secrecy is the very soul of diplomacy" wrote de Callières (1716). To preserve secrecy and to avoid unwanted audiences, the parties to a stalled negotiation may look for an inaccessible site, such as a military base, a warship, or a remote village in the mountains. This is precisely why, for instance, the Korean cease-fire negotiations were moved from Kaesong to Panmunjom in 1951. Cambon, a French diplomat, even stated that "The day secrecy is abolished, negotiation of any kind will become impossible." Most of the talks between Henry Kissinger and Chinese Premier Zhou Enlai over the establishment of diplomatic relations between the USA and the PRC (1971) were held secretly in Beijing, in the house of the Chinese premier. Kissinger, who was in Pakistan, left unnoticed on board a Chinese airplane and returned the same way three days later. During that time, his staff spread a rumor that he was having digestive problems and had to take a rest in a quiet place, the personal residence of the Pakistani president (Kissinger 1979).

Another classic solution is to look for a precedent, a rule that is usually applied, or a traditional way of handling a particular type of difficulty that will legitimize the offer made by a party. Even precedents that are an exception to the normal rule have more than just the merit of existing: they can provide highly functional insights for future actions. The point is to look for a similar situation that has occurred elsewhere, see what was used to escape the stalemate, and suggest replication of this solution if the final result was satisfactory to both parties. In addition, as the solution has already been adopted by other people, it will not leave the impression that the parties are sailing into uncharted waters and therefore taking a large risk. It is because he found a precedent in history that Talleyrand, who played a prominent role in the Congress of Vienna, could marry with the blessing of the Catholic Church. This was quite a challenge, first, because he was a bishop and, as such, had to remain unmarried, and second, because his fiancée was a divorced woman who could not marry again according to the rules of the church. Nevertheless, Talleyrand managed to overcome these obstacles and move the negotiations out of the impasse.

2.6.5   Process-related strategies

A fifth and final group of strategies consists of intervention in the negotiation process. Two types of intervention can be devised according to their basic orientation: coordinative strategies that play on the positive repertoire and the win–win approach, and coercive strategies that operate with competitive tactics and are based on the zero-sum game concept of negotiation.

Coordinative strategies involve offers of exchanges of concessions or the sending of decipherable signals of goodwill. The point is to restart the process by providing some new reason for hope. This small contribution, which may be viewed as a trial balloon, may be able to trigger a new dynamic in terms of the "bicycle theory," which says that what is essential in a negotiation process is to keep the process in motion.

Introducing new information, unknown data, or the account of an unexpected event may induce, by the effect of surprise, a change of attitude that entails a revision of the other side's security point and more cooperative behavior, thus enabling the whole process to restart on a new basis.

Creating a focal point that is attractive enough to remove the process from its present fixation can be instrumental. This typically makes strategic use of a structural element that is accepted as being prominent. This element has to meet some kind of requirement – such as a social norm or a sense of fairness, justice, or what is considered reasonable and balanced – and thus be able to generate a consensus. A dynamic of convergence may then be re-established. Round numbers, the idea of equidistance, of uniqueness, of prominence, symbolic values, and natural boundaries such as rivers, mountains, or seas are examples of focal points. In conflict resolution, even geographic parallels have exhibited their longevity as focal points (Schelling 1960). A kind of intrinsic magnetism of a particular outcome, qualitatively differentiable from the continuum of possible alternatives, operates in providing a salient solution to an otherwise everlasting problem.

It is also possible to operate upstream of the process by providing a "decommitting formula" that eliminates a reason for being unwilling to concede. This formula can call on motives alien to the situation, such as the health of one of the negotiators, an external event, or a parallel action. It has to create a totally new situation that will subsequently be understood and assessed in a different way than before. This new situation elicits a redefinition of the problem and a different solution that may be easier to devise than was formerly the case. Even if the other side does not believe what has been said, he or she is likely to appreciate the effort that has been made to unfreeze the situation. This effort could elicit a similar gesture from the other side and contribute to a restarting of the process. For instance, in an extremely antagonistic business negotiation between a Dutch buyer and US sellers, a deadlock was clearly established and the atmosphere was very heavy. The only foreseeable future was ultimately a breaking off of the negotiation. But at the last moment, a Dutch negotiator got up and began playing a piano located at the other end of the room. Within a couple of minutes, attitudes were totally changed on both sides. After half an hour of music, the deadlock was overcome and an agreement was reached.

A technique often used is to take a recess in the hope that as time goes by tension will ease, people will cool down, and their attitudes will be modified. Another strategy that utilizes time is to temporarily set aside the thorny issue, moving it to a more favorable moment in the negotiation. This can also be done by postponing discussion of the thorny issue, if it is not essential to a framework agreement, leaving it to be managed at the stage of agreement implementation. This may work if different people are in charge of the implementation discussions, or if the context is so different that the initial problem no longer looms large.

In some cultures, parties caught in a deadlock resort to magic or religious rituals, or call on supernatural powers for help (Faure 2000). Divination and geomancy are popular with negotiators in some parts of the world, for they often provide explanations for failures and recipes for success. The geomancer, for instance, operates as an arbitrator surrogate and helps each party to make some moves without appearing submissive to the other's will. For instance, he reads his sun and moon compass, sounds the dragon's breath, and derives from his observations directions that leave no room for further discussion or personal decision.

To break away from the common principle of mutual yielding, which often produces two dissatisfied parties and does not necessarily lead to an agreement, joint explorations can be used as a technique to look at the issues at stake differently and to devise new solutions. Resorting to such an approach presupposes that a preliminary condition is met: the establishment of some level of trust between both parties. Then, techniques such as brainstorming, lateral thinking, or synectics may be utilized. These essentially aim to invent new options to be evaluated afterward by each party involved in the deadlock.

There are also a number of coercive strategies that incorporate a fair amount of cleverness, which is often of more value than is brute strength. It is common to create artificial confrontational issues that enable later dummy concessions to restart the negotiation with minimal cost; one such example is when in a business negotiation a party makes a concession on delivery time for the supplier when he or she actually has the product in stock.

Turning a negotiation into a war of attrition, harassing the other party to exhaustion, is another quite common practice, particularly in business negotiations, especially in Asian cultures. In a particular trade negotiation between Europe and China, the final discussion lasted for 49 hours with almost no halt, except to eat some food, but with absolutely no time for sleeping. The party that chooses such a strategy hopes the other party will simply collapse at the end.

Another way to force counterparts to resume negotiation is to deprive them of their means of action, including their logistics, to make it difficult for them to continue to withhold concessions. When the situation allows it, this stratagem combines with that of cutting adversaries off from their base of support, for instance by lengthening the geographic distance they must travel so as to deprive them of resources.

Resorting to threat is another competitive way to invite the other party to restart the negotiation process. Several options exist. The threat can be increasing the costs to the other party if the negotiation remains at a standstill. Ultimately, the threat can also go so far as to question the existence of the negotiation. However, this is a double-edged sword and can also lead to the opposite effect, with the counterpart becoming highly defensive or issuing a counterthreat to balance the initial threat. The risk that the negotiation will turn into an escalation process or an escalating conflict may become a reality.

Manipulating and destabilizing the other party is a classic technique that requires the use of two types of negotiators – the merciless one and the smiling one – coordinated in a two-stage process. The first drives the adversary to the wall, at the extreme limit of what he or she can stand. Then the conciliatory one comes to reap the benefits of the labor of his or her accomplice. This procedure is known in the West as the "good-cop/bad-cop" routine, and is depicted in China as the "red face" and the "white face," two stock characters of the Beijing opera.

2.7   Conclusion

Deadlock is a basic concept in negotiation analysis because of its frequency, its importance, and the vast array of variables that it mobilizes. To grasp such a phenomenon properly, the researcher must proceed through several stages: defining the concept, diagnosing its existence at the operational level, analyzing its causes, identifying why the parties to the deadlock might agree to make the particular effort required to break it, and finally establishing the strategies commonly used to overcome the deadlock.

A number of variables can be studied specifically to determine their influence on the procedures used to escape a deadlock, such as the hostility level between the parties. The degree of antagonism, a subjective factor, may play an essential role compared with the objective conflict of interest. The basic structure of the game – whether it is a zero-sum game or a variable-sum game – may also play an important part in the ability of the parties to overcome the stalemate.

It would be most useful when considering protracted deadlocks to see if a learning process exists, such as through the information exchanged and the behavioral signals sent. What are the consequences of the learning process? Does cognitive dissonance play a role in it?

Attribution theory may also have something to say, because once a deadlock has started, each party may find it necessary to build a negative image of the other to justify its own intransigent attitude.

Again, it would be intellectually interesting and practically quite instrumental to see if the approaches used to solve deadlocks operate along cultural lines. Each society produces its own techniques to handle conflicts (Faure 2000). Societies in China and Africa have developed specific methods at the village level that have withstood the test of time and demonstrated their effectiveness. Methods of solving deadlocks are strongly linked to the way people understand conflict and deadlocks, and the importance of overcoming or solving them. In addition, how to proceed implies resorting to values that, again, differ according to the culture. Thus, societies may offer quite distinct and effective panoplies of action developed through a whole range of techniques drawn from common wisdom.

References

Bazerman MH & Carroll JS (1987). Negotiation cognition. In *Research in Organizational Behavior*, eds. Cummings LL & Staw BM, pp. 247–288. Greenwich, CT, USA: JAI Press.

Berton P, Kimura H & Zartman IW (1999). *International Negotiation: Actors, Structure/ Process, End Values*. New York, NY, USA: St. Martin's Press.

Brown P & Levinson S (1978). Universals in language usage: Politeness phenomenon. In *Questions and Politeness: Strategies in Social Interaction*, ed. Goody E, pp. 256–289. Cambridge, UK: Cambridge University Press.

Callières F de (1963). *On the Manner of Negotiating with Princes*. Notre Dame, IN, USA: University of Notre Dame Press (originally published 1716).

Chen D & Faure GO (1995). When Chinese companies negotiate with their government. *Organization Studies* **16**:27–54.

Druckman D (1978). Boundary role conflict: Negotiation as dual responsiveness. In *The Negotiation Process*, ed. Zartman IW, pp. 87–110. Beverly Hills, CA, USA: Sage.

Faley T & Tedeschi JT (1971). Status and reaction to threats. *Journal of Personality and Social Psychology* **17**:192–199.

Fang T (1999). *Chinese Business Negotiating Style*. Thousand Oaks, CA, USA: Sage.

Faure GO (1998). Negotiation: The Chinese concept. *Negotiation Journal* **14**:137–148.

Faure GO (1999). The cultural dimension of negotiation: The Chinese case. *Group Decision and Negotiation* **8**:187–215.

Faure GO (2000). Traditional conflict management in Africa and China. In *Traditional Cures for Modern Conflicts: African Conflict Medicine*, ed. Zartman IW. Boulder, CO, USA: Lynne Rienner Publishers.

Faure GO (2003). *How People Negotiate*. Dordrecht, The Netherlands: Kluwer Academic Publishers.

Faure GO & Chen D (1999). Overcoming negotiation deadlocks in business: Lessons from the Chinese. *The SIETAR International Journal* **1**(Fall):73–94.

Faure GO, Mermet L, Touzard H & Dupont C (2000). *La négociation: Situations et problématiques*, second edition. Paris, France: Dunod.

Heilman ME (1974). Threats and promises: Reputational consequences and transfer of credibility. *Journal of Experimental Social Psychology* **10**: 310–324.

Homans G (1961). *Social Behavior.* San Diego, CA, USA: Harcourt Brace Jovanovich.

Hopmann PT (1996). *The Negotiation Process and the Resolution of International Conflicts.* Columbia, SC, USA: University of South Carolina Press.

Iklé FC (1964). *How Nations Negotiate.* New York, NY, USA: Harper and Row.

Jönsson C (1990). *Communication in International Bargaining.* London, UK: Pinter Publishers.

Jönsson C (1991). Cognitive theory. In *International Negotiation: Analysis, Approaches, Issues,* ed. Kremenyuk V, pp. 229–243. San Francisco, CA, USA: Jossey-Bass.

Kelman HC (1979). Reduction of international conflict: An interactional approach. In *The Social Psychology of Intergroup Relations,* eds. Austin WG & Worchel S. Monterrey, CA, USA: Brooks/Cole.

Kissinger H (1979). *White House Years.* Boston, MA, USA: Little Brown.

Kreisberg L & Thorson SJ (1991). *Timing the De-escalation of International Conflicts.* Syracuse, NY, USA: Syracuse University Press.

Lang N (1998). *Intercultural Management in China.* Wiesbaden, Germany: DUV.

Li X (1999). *Chinese–Dutch Business Negotiations.* Amsterdam, The Netherlands: Editions Rodopi BV.

Lockett M (1988). Culture and the problems of Chinese management. *Organization Studies* **9**:474–495.

Mogy RB & Pruitt DG (1974). Effects of a threatener's enforcement costs on threat credibility and compliance. *Journal of Personality and Social Psychology* **29**:173–180.

Orieux J (1973). *Talleyrand.* Paris, France: Flammarion.

Pruitt DG (1981). *Negotiation Behavior.* New York, NY, USA: Academic Press.

Pye L. (1982). *Chinese Commercial Negotiating Style.* New York, NY, USA: Oelgeschlager.

Rothman J (1992). *From Confrontation to Cooperation: Resolving Ethnic and Regional Conflicts.* Newbury Park, CA, USA: Sage.

Rubin JZ (1989). Some wise and mistaken assumptions about conflict and negotiation. *Journal of Social Issues* **45**:195.

Rubin JZ (1991). Psychological approach. In *International Negotiation: Analysis, Approaches, Issues,* ed. Kremenyuk V, pp. 216–228. San Francisco, CA, USA: Jossey-Bass.

Rubin J, Pruitt D & Kim SH (1994). *Social Conflict.* New York, NY, USA: McGraw-Hill.

Schelling TC (1960). *The Strategy of Conflict.* Cambridge, MA, USA: Harvard University Press.

Siegel S & Fouraker LE (1960). *Bargaining and Group Decision-Making: Experiments in Bilateral Monopoly.* New York, NY, USA: McGraw-Hill.

Touval S & Zartman IW (1985). *International Mediation in Theory and Practice.* Boulder, CO, USA: Westview Press.

Ury W (1991). *Getting Past No: Negotiating with Difficult People*. New York, NY, USA: Bantam Books.

Webster's Tenth Collegiate Dictionary (1977). Springfield, MA, USA: Merriam–Webster Inc. Publishers.

Zagare FC (1978). A game-theoretic analysis of the Vietnam negotiations: Preferences and strategies 1968–1973. In *The Negotiation Process*, ed. Zartman IW, pp. 115–130. Beverly Hills, CA, USA: Sage.

Zartman IW (1989). *Ripe for Resolution*, second edition. New York, NY, USA: Oxford University Press.

Zartman IW (1991). The structure of negotiation. In *International Negotiation: Analysis, Approaches, Issues*, ed. Kremenyuk V, pp. 65–77. San Francisco, CA, USA: Jossey-Bass.

Zartman IW (2002). Regional conflict resolution. In *International Negotiation: Analysis, Approaches, Issues*, second edition, ed. Kremenyuk V, pp. 348–361. San Francisco, CA, USA: Jossey-Bass.

Zartman IW & Berman M (1982). *The Practical Negotiator*. New Haven, CT, USA: Yale University Press.

Chapter 3

Deterrence, Escalation, and Negotiation

Patrick M. Morgan

3.1 Introduction

This chapter offers thoughts on the relationship between deterrence and escalation, on the one hand, and the broad topic of negotiation, on the other. The overall relationship is familiar – negotiations frequently take place in the shadow of deterrence, and negotiations also occur directly via deterrence efforts or other coercive steps. Escalation is one possible cause or result of deterrence efforts. It is also something deterrence is often used to prevent, frequently to make progress toward or in negotiations.

Before tackling this broad subject, however, several general comments must be made about deterrence, particularly those aspects relevant to the chapter topic. Deterrence is an effort to prevent someone from doing something unacceptable by threatening a harmful response if they do. Technically, the unacceptable action can be almost anything, and the painful response might involve all sorts of harm; but in security studies, the emphasis in the definition is normally on preventing someone from *attacking with force* by threatening a nasty *military* response. It is customary to distinguish deterrence by retaliation from deterrence by defense. Though both retaliation and defense can inflict harm after an attack, the use of threats of retaliation alone is considered the purer form. A party might use defenses primarily for protection and simply gain some deterrence as a bonus, but with a retaliatory capacity only, it is entirely dependent on deterrence to keep safe and is otherwise unprotected.

Deterrence is a psychological relationship because it is a particular way of *convincing* or *persuading* someone not to attack, using threats to adjust an opponent's perspectives and calculations. When an attack occurs, the harmful retaliation is not deterrence for that event, because the persuasion has already been attempted without the desired results. It can be, however, an effort to deter in the future by establishing a record or image that will enhance credibility for future deterrence threats.

Deterrence is, in an abstract sense, different from *compellence* (see Schaub 1998). Compellence is devoted not to preventing an attack, but to persuading someone to stop doing something they are already doing (to halt an attack already under way, or some other unwanted activity) or to undo something already done. On the eve of the Gulf War, the US–United Nations (UN) alliance made a last-ditch effort to prevent Iraq from invading Kuwait, a very late (and half-hearted) recourse to deterrence. They then mounted a strong threat to persuade Iraq to halt the invasion and, when that failed, to persuade Iraq to leave Kuwait. Those two threats were efforts at compellence.

While this is a fine distinction for theoretical purposes, it readily breaks down in practice and so cannot be taken too seriously. For instance, the Soviet government decided to send missiles to Cuba and initiated the necessary steps. The USA discovered this and warned that sending missiles to Cuba was a kind of attack on the USA and would be treated as such. Was this deterrence – since the decision had not yet been fully implemented – or compellence – because the USA demanded that the Soviet government stop what it was already doing and reverse a decision (with some implementation) already made? Quite often in conflicts the parties shift back and forth between compellence and deterrence. The USA ordered the Soviet Union to remove the missiles (compellence) and also not to fire any on pain of retaliation (deterrence).

There is also considerable emphasis in deterrence theory and the analysis of specific cases on the difference between the challenger and the defender. This distinction is also very useful for theoretical purposes, only to break down readily in actual deterrence situations. The problem is that being a challenger or a defender is allegedly important because the role adopted by a party in a deterrence situation affects the way it thinks or feels, and therefore its responses, as the situation develops. In fact, the reverse is often true – how each thinks or feels about the situation determines whether it responds as a challenger or defender. Students of negotiation know, better than deterrence analysts, that a good deal of what drives conflicts is the images of self and others that move the parties; often, both sides feel victimized, innocent, and justified, and thus both feel as if they are the defenders. Analysts therefore often disagree as to which role the actors played in specific cases (see Lebow and Stein 1989, 1990).

A distinction is also commonly drawn between *immediate* and *general* deterrence (Morgan 1983). In immediate deterrence, the defender faces an imminent attack or the imminent possibility of one – the other side is quite close to launching an attack – so deterrence is mounted in an effort to ward it off. Hence an immediate deterrence situation is a very serious crisis or confrontation, the source of the possible attack (the target of the deterrence threats) is known, and a good deal is understood about how the attack will be made.

In general deterrence, by contrast, the defender worries about a possible attack at an unknown time and place, perhaps even by an unknown assailant. The defender therefore issues a broad threat to the effect that it is armed and dangerous and will resolutely respond in a harmful way if attacked. General deterrence is obviously a far more common practice, even though a specific attacker and attack is uncertain or unknown and may even be almost entirely hypothetical. It is in general deterrence, for instance, that most of the steps are taken to establish commitments, develop capabilities to defend these directly or by threats of retaliation, and build the credibility to make the threats effective.

There is also the well-known differentiation between *direct* and *extended* deterrence. In the former, the defender seeks to prevent an attack on itself. In the latter, it seeks to prevent an attack on a third party. This is a fairly clear distinction, but not a rigid one, since an actor may say, actually or in effect, that an attack on a third party will be considered an attack on itself. To the extent it is known to take this position seriously, the deterrence involved becomes much less "extended."

Finally, while deterrence has been used as a broad and basic *strategy* to achieve security, which is how we came to study it so carefully during the Cold War, it is also often used as a *tactic*, which has some very different implications for the behavior involved. Using deterrence as a tactic, as a modest component within a larger strategy, is a very old practice in statecraft. For instance, our notion of how a balance-of-power system works involves deterrence, but deterrence is far from the only element involved in the actors' strategies to keep safe from attack. To have deterrence rise to the level of a broad and basic strategy requires that the threat relationship it involves be seen as the most important basis for keeping safe and just about the only one to be used. It is then the cornerstone, the everyday basis for security, and almost everything else becomes ancillary within deterrence as the master strategy. This was the fundamental basis on which the Cold War was conducted for years.

3.2   Deterrence, Escalation, and Negotiation during the Cold War

During the Cold War, deterrence emerged as the primary resource relied on by the superpowers and the two blocs to sustain their security. Within the overall rubric of containment, the USA's grand strategy of deterrence became its grand security strategy, and something similar emerged in the Soviet Union. This was not only deterrence to protect each country, but also extended deterrence to protect each country's friends and allies. While initially this was the pursuit of security via a *national* security strategy and posture, rising superpower interdependence led to an interplay between the national deterrence postures that resulted in a broad deterrence-based security structure and security management both for the international system as a whole and for particular regional systems.

In turn, deterrence was related to escalation in that escalation was the prime fear. In the very serious East–West political conflict, the constant fear was that it would escalate into open warfare, and that such warfare would then escalate into total disaster. The escalation of concern pertained not only to the intensity of the conflict, but also to its widening through additional participants, particularly ones with much greater resources, so that the scale of any fighting would be much larger. Deterrence was developed and employed primarily to prevent escalation. Deterrence theory came to focus on this objective, as did related investigations of crisis decision making, crisis management, coercive diplomacy, and arms control.

Deterrence theory was stimulated primarily by the emergence of mutual deterrence and the complicated problems it posed. Escalation was generally analyzed under the heading of the *stability problem* in mutual deterrence (see Brodie 1966). The goal was to keep mutual deterrence stable, to keep it from breaking down and having war result, particularly one that would destroy virtually everything. The risks of escalation were traced to various factors that could foster deterrence instability:

- Possibilities for misperception, particularly in a crisis
- Chances of accidental or otherwise unauthorized use of nuclear weapons
- Chances that minor combat between the superpowers would escalate through the dynamics of war or the emotional reactions it would stimulate
- The presence of flaws in deterrence postures that would give one or both sides incentives to launch an attack, especially in a crisis
- The possibility that the warning and reaction systems would be so primed to set off military responses that a minor glitch could have a cascading effect
- Fear that each side would attempt to erode the other's deterrence (developing first-strike capabilities or excessively good defensive capabilities)

There was elaborate analysis of how the stability problem might lead to escalation and the failure of deterrence, and studies of how this had occurred in historical cases. Kahn's escalation ladder tried to describe the steps that escalation could take (Kahn 1965). Schelling (1960, 1966) emphasized how an escalatory step during a war could lead to many further steps in this direction if there was no obvious reference point around which cooperation might develop informally to prevent it. Smoke (1977) investigated wartime escalation in selected cases to draw lessons on how to avoid it. Concern about escalation animated studies of crisis decision making, as analysts struggled to figure out how crises sometimes got out of hand and produced a war no party wanted (for instance, George 1991).

The doctrine and posture of flexible response was developed largely to help avoid escalation. The basic idea was to leave the burden of escalation on the other side by having the capacity to fight effectively at any level at which a conflict broke out, including even a nuclear war. In addition, with flexible response it was hoped that deterrence credibility would be strengthened, cutting down on the possibility that East–West political confrontations would escalate into war (Freedman 1981).

Finally, the theory and practice of arms control were dictated largely by the stability problem and concern about escalation. Negotiated agreements to avoid the development of first-strike capabilities emerged as a result, as did agreements to try to avoid crises, agreements to cooperate during crises to prevent escalation, efforts to expand transparency so as to reduce fears of surprise attack and allow more reaction time in a crisis, etc. (on arms control, see Morgan 1989).

Concern about escalation carried over into superpower relations with allies. Each made efforts to prevent nuclear proliferation within its bloc, and each tried to contain what it regarded as provocative actions by its clients. The objective was to minimize confrontations that would invite superpower involvement and thus escalate the stakes – and possibly the level and intensity – of the conflict. The superpowers used direct intervention to halt warfare between their clients, as in the Middle East, and sometimes tried to reduce or resolve conflicts among other states that looked like they might eventually stimulate greater power involvement if not dealt with. Fears about escalation led, in other words, to creation of a (somewhat ramshackle) security management system (Van Benthem van den Bergh 1992).

However, concern about deterrence stability and escalation was never fully as-suaged because of two factors. One was that the credibility problem could not be solved fully for the East–West conflict. Deterrence in that conflict, particularly extended deterrence, rested on threats a rational government would probably not be prepared to carry out if a true challenge arose. If credibility were lacking, deterrence could hardly be expected to be stable indefinitely. The solution adopted was to assert that nuclear deterrence was inherently credible because no government could guarantee to be fully rational under the extreme circumstances of a dire crisis or after a war had started (Jervis 1989). Deterrence was credible because escalation could not be precluded. Western governments embraced a mutually assured destruction (MAD) version of deterrence based on this explanation of its credibility. The Russians responded in kind by saying that they operated on the assumption that if a serious East–West war broke out, escalation to all-out war was inevitable, which implied they would initiate it rather than wait for it to happen. All of the things mentioned above about how deterrence might fail were cited to bolster this view. In effect, deterrence rested on the fallibility of human beings, on their potential inadequacies. But if the East–West conflict meant regular occasions when confrontations and crises could result, and escalation could not be precluded, how could deterrence be considered sufficiently stable over the long term?

Hence deterrence stability was also uncertain because it was never quite clear how the possibility of escalation was relevant. From one perspective, the risk of escalation was grave – deterrence might collapse. Whatever could be done to prevent escalation was vital. From another, the risk of escalation was what made deterrence work. The purist position of the latter view opposed flexible response plans and command systems, or missile defense systems, or other steps to slow escalation. West Europeans tolerated what were generally seen as inadequate arrangements to defend their territories because they believed that true security lay in leaving little to stand in the way of quick escalation to general nuclear war if an East–West conflict broke out (Schwartz 1983). Critics of this view, anticipating escalation some day, sought to go beyond deterring escalation to being ready to both use and survive it (see Gray 1984 on the "war-fighting approach").

As for the impact of all this on *negotiation*, we can start with the general point that, by leaning heavily on deterrence, the major actors in the Cold War did much to push negotiation into a subordinate, largely adjunct, role. First, deterrence received vast attention because negotiation was often considered futile. The early history of the Cold War seemed to demonstrate that the other side would not negotiate seriously, because the gap between the two sides was too great. Your enemy would therefore use negotiations mainly to undermine the cohesion of your side, and if possible to erode the credibility of your deterrence. Even if agreements resulted, the other side would cheat or end up abandoning them because the only agreements acceptable to you would be unacceptable in the long run to them.

Negotiation was not deemed a reliable tool to prevent escalation, which helps explain why so much effort went into making deterrence as good as possible for this purpose. It also followed that, in entering into negotiations, one had to guard against the negative consequences that could result, and deterrence was enlisted to help here as well. The second consideration, therefore, was the recurring fear that negotiations would be not only unproductive, but also damaging. This went beyond fear of being exploited by the crafty devils on the other side. It extended to the view that even being willing to negotiate might, in many cases, suggest weakness or fear, or that the onset of negotiations would lead to strong pressure against doing the things needed to keep deterrence sound, so as not to poison the atmosphere for the talks.

Not everything discouraged negotiations. What pushed in the other direction, eventually, was the insistence in arms-control thinking that negotiations could be a reliable route to enhanced deterrence stability. If both sides depended on deterrence stability and either could unilaterally disrupt it, then their overlapping interest in stability could lead them to agree on negotiated limits on their behavior (Schelling and Halperin 1985). However, of course, this reaffirmed the adjunct status of negotiations. They were not really suitable for dealing with the major issues of the Cold War, and instead were best used to shore up deterrence stability. While elements from the liberal side of the spectrum held out hope that arms-control negotiations would eventually generate a better political environment for broader talks on the underlying issues, the standard professional view considered this unlikely.

Third, there was the discussion by Schelling, Kahn, and others about manipulating the fear of escalation to engage in coercive diplomacy, using either direct threats of escalation or a willingness to risk it to shift the burden of making concessions to the other side. For Kahn, this required having a known superiority at each level on an escalation ladder – it would then be rational for you to escalate to win the negotiation, and rational for the other side to give in (Kahn 1960). For Schelling (1966), it was a matter of having a greater stomach for the terrible risks involved, admitting that a "competition in risk taking" had important irrational elements at times. In either view, negotiation went on, but it was akin to extortion.

In all these ways, nuclear deterrence and the fear (and possibility) of escalation were not particularly beneficial for negotiation as it is normally conceived. However, this was in a situation in which nearly everything seemed to rest on deterrence, the central security strategy on both sides. We need to look also at how deterrence, escalation, and negotiation can be interrelated when deterrence is a tactic and does not have broad system-management responsibilities.

3.3   Deterrence and Negotiations

In this section, the links between deterrence and negotiations are discussed in broad terms by envisioning deterrence as a dyadic relationship, the standard way in which deterrence is often conceived to generate and analyze hypothetical cases of it. The place to start is with the contention by Alexander George and Richard Smoke years ago that deterrence readily lends itself to being used as a substitute for negotiations (George and Smoke 1974). No serious effort is made to discuss issues with an opponent because you like the status quo and, with your effective deterrence in place, he or she cannot use force to make gains. To judge from the accounts, this was the Israeli–Egyptian relationship in the early 1970s, with a very powerful Israel unwilling to enter into serious negotiations (i.e., unwilling to consider the significant concessions, which would have to seem possible to the Arabs, to draw them to the table) and willing to wait for the Arabs to make them instead. This led Anwar Sadat to plot a war he knew he could not win. Thus, it is possible for deterrence to lead to negation or a substitute for negotiation, a point we return to later.

However, deterrence is often seen in exactly the opposite way, as a prerequisite to effective negotiations.[1] After all, deterrence is intended to preclude an opponent from choosing to try to resolve a conflict largely by an attack or threats of one. Deterrence narrows the opponent's options to accepting the status quo or seeking an adjustment and/or settlement by other means, such as negotiation. Indeed, in a harshly realist world, negotiations occur *only* when there are substantial penalties for governments who try to just bully their way through conflicts.

While deterrence, therefore, can be either a barrier to negotiations or a stimulus for them, most often it is an important underlying condition that shapes negotiations. To curtail the opponent's options is to undercut the opponent's negotiating leverage derived from threatening to attack, which places deterrence with other negotiation tactics that alter the parties' relative bargaining strengths. As such, deterrence can be an integral part of negotiations in a conflict that the parties take seriously enough to readily use force to have things their way. In fact, parties to such conflicts often develop, and use, capacities to do considerable harm, and the degree to which each can effectively bring deterrence to bear as a result is one factor that shapes the negotiations.

⁻Deterrence can be a great equalizer in bargaining. If each side can hurt the other seriously, at an "unacceptable" level, in retaliation or defense, then even though the relative level of harm each can actually do is quite uneven, the level is equal in psychological terms, which readily translates into political weight. To the extent that a rough equality of this sort between opponents may be needed to lure both to the negotiation table or to take steps needed to resolve the dispute, deterrence may contribute to both the resort to negotiation and its successful conclusion.

Thus, if the utility of deterrence is distributed unevenly in a conflict, the more deterrable party is at a significant disadvantage. This could lead it to accept an agreement it otherwise would reject, which makes negotiation successful at least for the time being. Alternatively, it might incite the superior party to forgo negotiations of a standard sort in favor of extortion. Or that party might feel free to up its objectives, harden its stance, and reduce its willingness to compromise on any

---

[1]For instance, the Republic of Korea (ROK) ambassador to the USA suggested in the late 1990s that the dialogue between the Democratic People's Republic of Korea (DPRK) and the ROK was based on deterrence (Boustany 2000).

point, thus making for greater difficulty in bringing negotiations to a successful conclusion. Finally, the deterrer could use its advantage to settle for being left free of fear of attack and negotiate earnestly to solidify the status quo, as the party most oriented to it. (It was the challenger that was eager to overturn the status quo and that therefore was most likely to resort to extortion if the deterrence balance was in its favor.)

Since deterrence can shape negotiations in these ways, alongside the main negotiation process there may be a parallel negotiation about the deterrence in the background. Since deterrence limits the range of violent actions each side feels able to take, and so somewhat affects their negotiating leverage, it is common for one or both parties to seek a dialogue, apart from the political issues, about curbing violent activity. This may be raised as something to be settled as a precondition to negotiations by one or both sides, and may also be seen by each as just an attempt to undercut its bargaining leverage. If the latter is the case, it usually leads to minimum demands for a significant compensation to make any such concession, a compensation either party may be unwilling to pay lest it increase its vulnerability to coercion, which could affect the rest of the negotiations. The USA and North Vietnam went round and round about whether serious talks could be conducted without a suspension of US bombing or of the attacks on the South Vietnamese government. A very similar side negotiation has occurred for years on the Northern Ireland conflict, and other examples could be cited. However, while the mutual deterrence capabilities (plus other abilities to hurt) are responsible for the problem, deterrence can contribute to resolving it once the actual or potential pain reaches levels deemed unacceptable or intolerable, so it is not a simple matter of cutting the capacities to hurt to initiate negotiations.

Deterrence can also be important to negotiation because, by narrowing the range of the opponent's options, it helps the opponent make more credible promises to abide by an agreement and to no longer resort to force. This can be quite significant. Various crisis studies point out that ending a confrontation takes promises by both sides to end their "bad" behavior and engage in "good" behavior, but each side is likely to have a serious credibility problem in this regard. In deep conflicts, one or both sides may fear being set up, lulled by agreement into greater vulnerability to attack thereafter. Deterrence can offset such fears, and so allow agreements that otherwise might not be possible. Many arms-control agreements have turned not just on the availability of adequate verification, but on the existence of an underlying general deterrence that would not be disturbed by steps required in the agreements.

Deterrence that guards against cheating and the like can be supplied by the parties themselves or by a third party, although the latter is relatively rare. This is unfortunate since it is probably far better that this be supplied by a third party in many instances. It is often too easy for the use of force by the two sides, for whatever reason, to deteriorate into a renewal of the conflict. For instance, retaliation for some violation of the agreement must appear proportional to the violation lest it stimulate escalation, or even a collapse of the agreement, but the party being punished is quite likely to find that the retaliation was disproportional and to reply accordingly. Taking steps to be able to retaliate for a future violation – buying new weapons, enhancing the training of one's forces, keeping forces on alert, etc. – can readily be taken as a lack of good faith and preparations to violate the agreement in the future.

Does it matter what kind of deterrence is involved when negotiations are sought or conducted? My suspicion is that it does. Immediate deterrence is not a terribly promising situation in which to promote and conduct negotiations. Such situations likely arise because negotiations have not gone well and appear unlikely to go well – a grave crisis is at hand. At this point the negotiation is done by threats, and deterrence largely displaces what we normally mean by negotiations in shaping the behavior of the parties. If deterrence works, then negotiations might again be resumed, maybe partly out of relief that the crisis was surmounted. This seems the best explanation for the sudden success of the atmospheric test ban treaty in the months after the Cuban missile crisis. This is not to say that negotiations are irrelevant or nonexistent in a grave crisis, because clearly there are cases in which this is not true, but in a really grave situation negotiation is apt to give way mostly to crude coercive efforts, with talks concerned with exiting the crisis rather than tackling the heart of the matter. Thus, deterrence is normally best used to get through such situations in the hopes of broader negotiations later.

General deterrence, however, is regularly a very important component of negotiations. As suggested earlier, it can also be an important stake in the negotiations, as was often the case during the Cold War. As noted above, in regard to East–West negotiations, even agreeing to take part was often criticized as likely to weaken one's deterrence credibility – allies would fear deals at their expense by the patron, who might lose his determination to continue the contest; concessions would generate an image of weakness or of being too fearful to fight; hopes would rise only to be dashed, with criticism landing on the government for not having tried harder. Secretary of State John Foster Dulles reiterated such views repeatedly in the Eisenhower administration. Hawks in the Reagan administration opposed serious negotiations during the first term, in part because they thought this was needed to avoid looking weak. From such a perspective, simply holding negotiations would reflect on the broad power and reputation of the two sides, whether or not any agreement was ever reached, a view repeatedly voiced in the Northern Ireland conflict, the Arab–Israeli conflict, and others. This reasoning was applied by some to negotiations of all sorts, not just those directly concerned with security issues.

US President John F. Kennedy came away from his summit with Soviet Premier Nikita Khrushchev in Vienna fearing that the overall image he had conveyed would damage American credibility, a view other observers shared. The USA repeatedly worried that European détente initiatives would weaken the overall credibility of the West, a favorite theme of Henry Kissinger when he was in office. It seems likely that the more intense a conflict, and the more concerned each party is that it will lead to the use of force, the more deterrence itself is seen as one of the things at stake in any negotiation and the greater the preoccupation with the presumed impact on deterrence credibility of almost any negotiating behavior.

General deterrence can also be related directly to negotiations in that deterrence capabilities are seen as a crucial component of overall strength, and thus as a key element of being able to "negotiate from strength," which may be touted as the only acceptable basis on which to treat with "those others." This was the other half of the motivation behind the early Reagan administration's decision not to pursue East–West negotiations: in its view, the Soviet Union had been inexorably gaining on the USA in military power and was about to attain, or had already reached, a position of superiority, and there was a determination to negotiate only when the Reagan military buildup had taken hold and this superiority had been canceled. Dulles often referred to the objective of negotiating from strength, and Kennedy saw such a favorable opportunity arising from the missile crisis, an opportunity he planned to exploit.

Overall, linking deterrence to negotiations by making it a major, if indirect, stake is a pernicious practice. Seeing credibility as being vital readily breeds an open-ended form of paranoia. Every aspect can come to be seen as a reflection on credibility, which erodes flexibility on many matters, inhibits making concessions, builds a preoccupation with saving face, etc. – attitudes that inhibit effective negotiations. The damage done can pertain to the possibility of negotiations directly on the conflict and on seemingly peripheral matters that are deemed relevant in this perspective. We know from careful studies that the American concerns on this score were almost certainly overblown – the Soviet government did not assess credibility in the ways this perspective suggests (Hopf 1994).

3.4 Deterrence and Escalation

As mentioned earlier, to talk about deterrence and escalation, we have to differentiate between deterrence as a tactic (a piece of a larger strategy) and deterrence as a fundamental strategy for security. In regard to the latter, we must first focus on the use of deterrence in this way in a dyadic conflict and then consider its use by a collection of states that seek to regulate an international system.

As noted above, deterrence is often used to try to prevent conflicts from escalating into outright fighting – to keep them at a prehomicidal stage and prevent them from becoming "hot." When credibly and successfully used in this fashion, deterrence can make a major contribution to inducing negotiations in serious conflicts by making attempts to settle the conflict by force look so unproductive that they are not or are no longer attempted. Here, deterrence is an escalation-control mechanism and, to the extent that the status quo is unacceptable to the parties and other barriers are eased, negotiations should then ensue.

It is widely accepted that one condition that often induces negotiations is a hurtful stalemate (Zartman 1996). It seems best to phrase this, within the context of this chapter, as the existence of mutual deterrence. The hurtful stalemate is then a condition in which the parties have repeatedly demonstrated a capacity to hurt each other and are now readily believed when they threaten to impose what amounts to unacceptable damage – a mutual deterrence situation that makes negotiations more plausible.

This suggests that in most serious conflicts, in which each side fears attack by the other, the participants benefit greatly from mutual deterrence in terms of the possibility of arriving at a negotiated settlement, or at least a negotiated relaxation of the worst features of the conflict. Of course, this may take a very long time, not least because of the way deterrence can serve as a substitute for negotiation. Put the two elements together and we have a good explanation as to why the Cold War lasted so long after mutual deterrence had been attained and why it then ended as a negotiated collapse, not in a violent fight.

By the same token, a serious conflict between a clear challenger and defender (if these roles are well established in the minds of the two parties) is pushed toward meaningful negotiation less by a hurtful stalemate than by the existence of *unilateral* deterrence possessed by the defender. The defender needs to be able to preclude the challenger from resorting to force or else negotiations are less likely. The same is possible, though much less so, in reverse. The defender may occasionally be willing to resort to force, and particularly to threats of force, to offset the challenger's many other advantages in any negotiation. (One thinks of the North Koreans, who for years have faced – in the USA – a very powerful state that dislikes the status quo; they have therefore been reluctant to enter into negotiations without issuing a panoply of threats and are suspected of sometimes staging incidents to bolster their reputation for being ready to use force.) In such a case, the challenger's deterrence may induce negotiations that otherwise could readily be precluded by conflict escalation.

Deterrence is regularly used to try to prevent escalation *after the fighting has already begun* – escalation not only of the political conflict (of the objectives or intensity of the political dispute), but also of the fighting. It can also be enlisted to help prevent a return to fighting after the conflict has died down. The deterrence involved can be provided by the parties themselves or by outsiders who seek to intervene to end the conflict or to contain it. Obviously, this injects deterrence into important aspects of negotiations. Escalation is a standard form of negotiation, an attempt to increase the opponent's incentives to enter into talks or to make more concessions by "making him an offer he can't refuse." Deterrence can be used to take a good deal of that leverage away.

Escalation is also a way of signaling; it can be used to convey frustration, determination, commitment, etc. Sometimes the opponent's deterrence actually aids the opposing side to convey just that message. Escalating a conflict in the face of serious threats of retaliation, particularly when retaliation has been delivered effectively by the deterrer before, is a transparent way to show the depth and intensity of the attacker's feelings and frustrations, as well as its resolve, its ability, and its willingness to suffer to achieve the kind of agreement it wants. This pattern in negotiations has been and continues to be all too evident in the Arab–Israeli dispute.

This raises the point that, unfortunately, while deterrence can block escalation, a deterrence capability sometimes has the effect of provoking it. The paradoxical result is that deterrence can end up *stimulating escalation* in various ways. One of the more obvious is that, in a relatively low-level conflict, introducing deterrence threats can be, in itself, an escalatory step. It conveys a fear of attack and lack of trust, which serves to signal that the conflict has entered a higher stage or become more serious. This may be resented by the other side and seen as a slur on its nature and character. It may also be seen as a fig leaf, a pretense of seeking self-protection to hide a new and higher willingness to use force to deal with the conflict.

As this implies, deterrence threats can stimulate escalation because they have a tendency to *provoke an emotional response*. This is not a well-understood feature of deterrence in the theoretical literature, in which analysis is often driven primarily by assumptions and/or conceptions of rationality. For instance, it has been said that it makes a difference whether a party threatens force out of an appetite for gain or out of frustration and fear, the latter being less dangerous because the opposite side can then accept the threat with more equanimity – a concession, for instance, might ease the frustration, whereas it would whet the aggressive appetite (Lebow and Stein 1990, 1994). However, plenty of evidence – and everyday experience – shows that nearly all threats produce a negative emotional reaction, a strong dislike of being threatened, and a tendency to feel irate. The reaction may be fear or irritation or outright hostility, or some combination of these, and is apt to be accompanied by anger. Deterrence threats can raise the emotional temperature in disputes, something rarely discussed in deterrence literature and often underestimated by practitioners because they focus on the fact that they have no aggressive intent.

One reason for the nasty reaction is that to be threatened, if only for purposes of deterrence, is to worry that, even though you had no intention of attacking, compliance will bring more threats in the future, or attempts to exploit your supposed weakness or readiness to back down. This misperception is possible because it is always difficult to tell why a deterrence threat was followed by no attack. Therefore, to introduce deterrence into a conflict is subtly (and sometimes unsubtly) to raise the stakes for both parties. The target state now faces the possibility that not attacking is evidence of weakness, which could make success in future conflicts, and their associated negotiations, harder to come by. It may feel strongly tempted to react in some harmful way just to show it cannot be "pushed around." Of course, the deterrer also acquires heightened concern about credibility once it issues the threats, which can lead to a readiness to react strongly to even a tentative or ambiguous challenge – clearly, not a good climate for avoiding escalation and taking negotiations seriously. In both cases some escalation of the dispute becomes more plausible. American insistence that there be no serious Soviet combat capability in Cuba after the missile crisis trapped the Carter administration into having to react strongly to the Soviet brigade in Cuba, even though it represented no significant increase in the Soviet military presence.

There is also either an open or almost subliminal message delivered with a deterrence threat. Threatening someone openly says something about how estranged from him or her you feel. Threats of force violate all the niceties of a normal relationship; they are not what would be resorted to in dealing with friends. The threat says, "I think so little of you that I can readily contemplate your hurting me and my hurting you."

This suggests that finding ways to deter cleverly so as to prevent escalation of a dispute, via threats that are not counterproductive, is very necessary, but apparently not easy. Not surprisingly, those who believe in minimizing stress to enhance negotiation often want to exclude threats completely. Given these considerations, deterrence threats should normally be kept implicit if possible (unless the conflict has reached a very dangerous stage) and be delivered in an indirect or symbolic fashion, rather than openly. For instance, threats can be left inherent in capabilities as opposed to being delivered deliberately. They can also be delivered privately, rather than being widely publicized. As a general rule, it is best to proceed by treating immediate deterrence (like blatant compellence) as a last resort, used only because all else seems to have failed. This offers the possibility of controlling escalation, but not the certainty of doing so.

Of course, efforts to leave threats implicit would violate some of the literature on deterrence. Classic treatments of deterrence theory often emphasize that threats should be stated openly to minimize misperception by rational actors. Cognitive-process students of deterrence have sometimes arrived at a similar conclusion because the actors are probably not rational; these analysts regard such threats as likely to be ignored, misperceived, or misinterpreted, even though they seem perfectly clear to the deterrer, and they urge that strenuous efforts be made to guard against this (Lebow 1981, 1989). Fears that arise out of both perspectives are certainly well founded, so this is a solution that is likely to be operative only in some cases. Evidence can probably be found to support either side – open deterrence threats are sometimes provocative, but they are also sometimes the only thing clear enough to finally get the message across – thus picking the right way to proceed will be consistently unclear.

We can also return once more to the point that deterrence threats have some potential effects *on the deterrer* that merit attention with regard to avoiding escalation and promoting negotiations. Deterrence may, if it appears to be working, lead the deterrer to harden his or her negotiation stance, escalate objectives, reduce flexibility, and take other steps that shrink the win set, which lowers the prospects of successful negotiations. This can also readily apply to the client in an extended deterrence arrangement – a client that is confident in the deterrence protection it enjoys may be more difficult to draw into serious negotiations.

We should recall once more the analysis by George and Smoke (1974) many years ago of some of the crises that arose in the first decades of the Cold War. They expressed the fear that the USA too often used deterrence to avoid serious negotiation with the other side. They predicted that a highly frustrated opponent would respond by creatively looking to skirt around American deterrence, for example by selective escalation through probes that could be reversed easily or by breaking a challenge into very small steps, none of which would appear sufficient to justify a retaliatory response.

The use of deterrence to prevent yet another kind of escalation can also be fraught with complications and difficulties. Deterrence can be used to try to prevent the widening of a conflict in terms of more parties becoming involved. The party that fears such an escalation must use threats to make outsiders think twice about joining the other side, and there is nothing complicated about this. However, with each new participant, actual or prospective, the credibility of these threats declines. In the meantime, the potential participants may have mounted deterrence threats to try to end or manage the conflict and might now feel it necessary to participate to sustain their credibility. They may also, in the classic view of balance-of-power theorists, fear the future impact of the deterrer's ambitions if it proceeds unchecked. The deterrence is likely to be challenged in a preliminary fashion, perhaps even in the ways George and Smoke (1974) suggested. The deterrer will have repeated decisions to make about just when these others have gone too far, in terms of shipping help to the enemy, stationing their military forces in the neighborhood, highlighting the danger to their citizens that the conflict is producing, which they must consider, and so on.

The best contemporary example might turn out to be the relationship among the USA, China, and Taiwan over the future of Taiwan. Here are two plausible scenarios:

1. China sends missiles against Taiwan, Taiwan defends itself, and the USA arranges protected flows of arms to Taiwan, gives Taiwan help from its reconnaissance capabilities, and has forces lurking that no military strategist could ignore in planning an invasion, but that never quite enter the fighting.
2. The USA does more, is more clearly involved, and China turns to limited attacks on American ships that deliver goods, drops missiles into the harbors when American ships are there, or tracks American surveillance planes by radar, etc.

In each case, the deterrer could find it difficult to convince allies and others that the other side has gone too far, that its patience is suitably exhausted, and that it is entitled to such escalation. And the whole conflict might gradually escalate from this sort of behavior.

It is possible to apply many of the preceding points in a case in which efforts at deterrence set off a deadly escalatory spiral. The US–North Vietnam relationship in the early 1960s was fraught with peril. Each side wanted very much to avoid at least one or two kinds of escalation. The USA wanted the guerrilla warfare toned down and sought to inhibit North Vietnamese involvement in it as the way to achieve this. Hanoi wanted to continue the war in the South, but avoid deep American military involvement – an escalation it could do without. Each felt it was the party being attacked, either the victim or on the victim's side. Each turned to deterrence to show that greater involvement by the other would provoke a very painful and costly response. The result was a recurring sequence. Each side's threats appeared to fail, as the other side did what it was not supposed to. This brought implementation of the promised punitive responses and (either then or after another provocation) the issuance of further threats that promised greater harm. If anything, the consistent result was a renewed determination on each side to persist, displayed both verbally and in their actions. Each feared that its credibility was on the line; for Americans, maintaining deterrence credibility globally was the primary rationale for the war. In the end, the war escalated in ferocity, geographic scope, and number of governments involved. This was negotiation via deterrence, via coercive diplomacy. The result was dreadful for all concerned.

The same sort of thing has happened repeatedly in the Middle East. It is a dangerous possibility whenever deterrence switches from a policy of mounting threats to forestall hypothetical attacks to the need to carry out previous deterrence threats, after being attacked, in the hope of deterring future attacks.

3.5   Deterrence and De-escalation

Deterrence can readily promote de-escalation of a conflict by discouraging one or both sides from continuing the conflict, for example by generating the hurtful stalemate that opens the door to serious negotiations. Deterrence can also facilitate de-escalation via a negotiated settlement by providing one or both parties with the confidence that they can control the risk in entering into an accommodation. While this can be a condition provided by the parties themselves, it can also be an important contribution by a third party when the opponents are modest in power and the third party can readily do serious harm if necessary. As noted earlier, it may be much better if the deterrence is supplied mainly by outsiders – there are too many possibilities for re-escalation otherwise. For instance, attempts to promote arms control during the Cold War ran into repeated difficulties because the parties engaged in arms buildups during the talks. The buildups were rationalized as providing "bargaining chips," but there was also the belief that stronger forces would hopefully deter cheating or exploitation. They were also necessary to mollify critics of the talks or agreements so as to build the necessary political consensus. Unfortunately, the buildups were readily challenged by skeptics on the other side as an absence of honest intent to negotiate seriously, with the talks being merely a cover for catching up or achieving military superiority. In effect, steps needed to make negotiations go forward weakened the de-escalation of either the general conflict or the arms race.

There is a general problem of military clashes that grow out of a desire by each side to show that it must be taken seriously under any proposed truce or peace agreement and that cheating will not be tolerated. These clashes are ideal for rekindling resentments and setting off cycles of retaliation. This is almost built into a deterrence relationship that rests on recurrent demonstrations that each side stands by its threats. There is a danger of a tit-for-tat strategy in reverse. The Axelrod (1984) version of tit-for-tat considers players who gradually achieve a high level of cooperation. However, in cases of deterrence demonstrations it is easy for each side to seek occasions to show its muscle as an important way, maybe the only way, to keep domestic critics of cooperation neutralized. The logic of politics can undermine the logic of cooperation under the shadow of deterrence.

An outside supplier of the necessary deterrence might be able to escape most of this. Its application of force cannot be interpreted so readily as escalatory or be seen as a first step toward abandoning the agreement. The problem is whether the outsider can be sufficiently determined to make the deterrence stick, and thus whether it can gain and sustain sufficient credibility.

3.6   Collective Actor Deterrence

Thinking about an externally supplied deterrence makes a nice transition to deterrence, escalation, and negotiation when the deterrer is a collective actor (CA). The term is used here to refer not to just any association, such as an ordinary alliance, but to one that is meant to be providing security management for an international system as a whole – at the global or regional level. It can be a CA that embraces virtually all the system members, such as the Organization of American States (OAS), or only some members, like the North Atlantic Treaty Organization (NATO) today, or a small proportion, like the UN Security Council. The point is that it is supposed to, claims to, represent the "public" interest, not just the interests of its members.

During the Cold War, deterrence-based security management grew out of the interactive national deterrence activities of the superpowers and their blocs. However, the most venerable conceptions of deterrence for systemic security have emphasized CAs – a great power concert (the UN Security Council) or a Wilsonian collective security system (the League of Nations). We have an interesting variant today in NATO and its associates, which act as a collective hegemon in managing European security because, unlike a true collective security association, it is not fully comprehensive in membership. In these security arrangements, deterrence is supposed to be a crucial fallback capability, not the mainstay it was in the Cold War. The CA seeks to provide or promote capabilities to either conduct or facilitate negotiations (negotiation, mediation, conciliation, etc.), which include capabilities to discourage dispute escalation and bring about de-escalation, particularly after fighting has taken place. If a forceful presence is needed as well, the preference is for peacekeeping to facilitate the upholding of agreements between the parties, at least to stop any fighting. The deterrence available through the members collectively is a damage-control resource if negotiations do not work and, as a result, also serves as pressure on the parties to a dispute to resolve or contain their differences.

This is not a carefully studied topic in deterrence analyses. The standard approach has been to assume a dyadic conflict and look at unilateral or mutual deterrence within it. We do not yet have sophisticated treatments of the role of deterrence in security management by CAs.

It seems clear that deterrence remains necessary under such arrangements. Woodrow Wilson thought the weight a League of Nations could bring to bear would handle most conflicts well before force was necessary, and that the deterrent effect of economic sanctions or even threats of sanctions would often do the trick. This eventually turned out to be false. The chief alternative to such deterrence-based security management is the Deutschian pluralistic security community (Deutsch *et al.* 1968), championed by strong supporters of the Organization for Security and Cooperation in Europe (OSCE) as the best basis for European security. However, it seems this is not enough either, and that a deterrence capability is needed, as illustrated by the initial post–Cold War efforts to design security management in Europe. Those arrangements began to break down almost as soon as they were in place as trouble broke out in the Balkans. In the end, the bulk of the participants turned to NATO for peace enforcement and peace imposition.

The initial objective in CA security management has always been to promote negotiation and strongly discourage escalation; if fighting has already broken out, the initial objective is to de-escalate to negotiations. Although it is conceivable that one might operate differently, I know of no instance in which a true CA did not consistently oppose escalation and the use of force. Hence CA deterrence is to provide a fertile ground for negotiation first by persuasion, then by insistence, and finally by the threat of forceful intervention.

However, CAs have difficult problems here. The organization will most likely be slow to build consensus behind the view that a conflict is sufficiently serious to deserve intensive consideration and action. A second problem is that the CA is an expression of a desire not to have to use force,[2] so force is almost certainly going to be its last resort. This is reinforced by the inevitable problem of building sufficient consensus among the relevant members to use force – they will normally not agree, at least for some time, that force must be used or even seriously threatened. This might be because there is no consensus on this *within* a number of the members, or because they disagree about the importance or particulars of the case at hand. It reflects a strong reluctance to risk their citizens' lives unless absolutely necessary. Also, there will always be members or others who dislike the precedents set, as China and Russia did with Kosovo. Since discussions about all this take place at least partly in public, the uneasiness within the group or some members about the use of force will be readily apparent.

Therefore, the CA is rarely ahead of the game in mounting a threat in time to prevent serious escalation of a conflict or to de-escalate the fighting (Rosecrance and Schott 1997). By the time it moves, the conflict is likely to be far along in damage done and loss of life – in fact, such losses may be what finally prompts the CA to act. Even when it starts to threaten, there will still be good reason to suspect its credibility: it will look reluctant, display a soft consensus of the members, appear to lack staying power if using force proves costly, etc. Since it is slow to react, it will often be raising threats when the parties have long since turned to fighting, so

---

[2]NATO is an odd case here since it was definitely created and maintained to use force. However, it has been acting as a CA, and in that mode it has acted much like the UN Security Council or other organizations – not wanting to use force except as a last resort.

it is engaged less in deterrence than in compellence. The more serious the fighting and the greater the combatants' military might, the more suspect the credibility of the CA's threats.

This brings us back to the problems of compellence, which is always described as being more difficult than deterrence because there is more psychological resistance to giving in on the part of the target. One reason, it now seems, is that the mind more readily resists losses than the equivalent costs associated with gains. Prospect theory outlines both the resistance to losses – not only in having to retreat from a position or advantage, but also in having to stop doing something (because it is what you want to do) – and the related tendency to treat recent gains as now part of the status quo, so that giving them up becomes a loss and thus unacceptable (Levy 1992, 1996).

In view of this there is a serious possibility that the initial CA effort to promote negotiations will fail and then deterrence and/or compellence will fail, and thus that the conflict will continue to escalate and some effort to implement the threats will have to be made. Negotiations with the parties, with deterrence as a backdrop, turns out to be ineffective and escalation is not precluded. We have certainly seen instances of this in Bosnia, Kosovo, and Sierra Leone. At this point, the steps needed to control escalation involve, at least briefly, additional escalation – another party is added to the fighting. It would naturally be much better to have CA deterrence work without force, not just in a confrontation, but in inducing negotiations earlier in the conflict.

This is unfortunate, because CA deterrence has intrinsically appealing features. Rarely can it be taken as a cover for aggressive intent, with the threats seen as just an excuse to move forces into an area for other purposes. This is a defect of deterrence by third-party states, as with the Russians, who tried to bring order to the Caucasus and Central Asia, or with the USA's use of its forces for the same purpose in the Caribbean. (While many Russians made this charge about NATO's actions in Kosovo, they rang a bit hollow given the number of states that voted for those actions or demonstrated their acceptance by being associates of NATO and/or participating in the occupation.)

With CA deterrence for system management, it is also normally clear that deterrence and/or compellence is a last resort, that the primary or preferred approach is negotiation, both with the parties to persuade them to stop escalating the conflict and then among the parties to ease or resolve the conflict. Another attractive feature is that the fighting is unlikely to be carried too far, to an extreme level of force. Given the nature of most CAs involved in such activities, the force is likely to be measured, with considerable concern about the casualties and destruction the targets might experience. The contrast with superpower deterrence of the Cold War era could not be greater.

This leads to another point: the CA is more likely to be able to order up deterrence threats, and implement them, without thereby provoking or promoting escalation of the conflict, and thus it evades a periodic drawback of deterrence as practiced by parties to a conflict. There is less need for the parties to guard their credibility, or to strive to uphold an image of not being vulnerable to being pushed around, when the CA is not a direct party to the conflict. Also, its tendency to hold the use of force to a minimum will be less provocative.

However, this only limits the escalatory potential, it does not cancel it. Sometimes one party will treat intervention as clearly uneven, tending to benefit its enemy, and will be inclined to escalate in response. Sometimes, as in the Kosovo case, the CA is indeed a party to the conflict, and escalation in response to its intervention is then quite possible. Commentaries about the Gulf War refer to the way the UN coalition deterred Iraq from escalation. This is correct concerning the use of weapons of mass destruction (WMD), but in response to the intervention, Iraq tried hard to provoke a region-wide war through its attacks on Israel and its propaganda, very much an escalatory effort.

In view of its attractions, can CA deterrence against conflict escalation be made more effective early on in a conflict so that negotiations look much more attractive to the parties? It is difficult to see how. In Europe, CA intervention expanded the military capabilities involved. Peacekeeping was initially the preferred response, with its lightly armed observers, but NATO took up peace enforcement in Bosnia and peace imposition in Kosovo with heavily armed forces primed to respond to trouble with considerable firepower to deter violations of the peace agreements and attacks on NATO forces. This escalated the deterrence involved and eased considerably the credibility problem once the forces were in place. It is a precedent likely to be followed elsewhere. The Australian-led forces in East Timor follow this pattern, and many will wish this had been true from the start for the UN forces sent to Sierra Leone, where a similar shift toward seriously armed intervention forces took place. While this does little to resolve the CA credibility problem early in a conflict, at least it makes a serious contribution when intervention occurs. But this will look less attractive the first time such heavily armed forces are drawn into a major war. Somalia was not quite such a case, since the forces were drawn into only limited fighting through mission creep. But imagine if forces are sent to fight if necessary, and the necessity arises and then lasts and lasts and lasts.

No clear solution has emerged on the credibility problem for earlier CA deterrence. Disagreements among relevant members about when to act and what to do will mean disagreement about when the organization's credibility is at stake and how much it matters, so a consensus that the organization had better act (or face extinction, a powerful motive for NATO in the Bosnia and Kosovo cases) will still mean too little is done too late. In most cases the commitment to take action will be forged only when the conflict escalates, the bodies pile up, the refugees stream out, and the atrocities mount.

Altering this in the future would probably require an adjustment to contemporary international systems. When deterrence serves as the central basis for the security of leading actors and the stability of the system, the cornerstone of system-security management, then conflict escalations are major challenges with potentially grave consequences. This creates a very "tight" system – what happens in one part is readily seen as threatening the rest. Conflicts readily reverberate. The end of the Cold War also ended a long era of this sort in the global system. Of the various regional systems today, and the global system, few seem as "tight" as that system was.

What might produce this condition again? A grave decline in security would do it – the return of the Cold War in some form or the rapid proliferation of nasty dyadic conflicts accompanied by huge WMD proliferation. It could also be produced by a spreading insistence that any conflict is everyone's responsibility, a large normative shift. Of the current international systems today, Europe's is the tightest, with a widespread belief that Europe is not safe unless everyone in it is safe. The Middle East looks "tight" only because of the strategic significance of its oil; internally, it is not as tight as Europe, and the end of the Cold War reduced its salience for the security of others. However, the war on terrorism has tended to tighten it up again, with the Israeli–Palestinian dispute seen as promoting terrorism and American-led responses seen as threatening much of the region. Elsewhere, the East Asian regional system is somewhat tight, but not like Europe, and other areas are not tight at all.

This leaves us vulnerable to a really serious test of CA deterrence and security management in the future. We have yet to see such a test. It will be a peace imposition effort where there is very serious and substantial resistance. Peacekeeping does not put CA deterrence credibility sufficiently at risk, nor does peace enforcement. Even peace imposition does not, when it can be done in a casualty-sanitized way, as in Kosovo. And the 1991 war against Iraq went too smoothly to constitute a true test.

3.7   Summary Thoughts on Practice

Since deterrence and its relationship to escalation can affect negotiations in so many ways, what lessons for the policy maker flow from the preceding analysis? We can focus on two types of conflicts, those in an early stage of development and those that have grown into a very substantial and durable level of hostility or even war.

In an emerging conflict, it is natural for some or all of the parties to turn to deterrence to try either to prevent escalation or to have one's own escalation not be matched by the other side. The goal for each party is to keep the other side from doing harmful things and negotiating by the use of force (especially if this is what the party itself is doing or wants to do!). Analysis and experience indicate that this is very difficult to do well and should be approached with great caution. There is the possibility that deterrence threats, and their implementation when they fail, will contribute to escalation of the conflict and poison the atmosphere for negotiations. Care must also be taken to prevent deterrence from becoming a substitute for negotiations, or for meaningful concessions in negotiations, which can be very attractive to fend off domestic critics. Finally, the opposite problem is to fail to mount a timely and vigorous deterrence to deflect the other side from using force instead of negotiations, which is what the USA did in reaction to Iraq's buildup along the Kuwaiti border and what some analysts fear will be the result of the USA's "strategic ambiguity" on Taiwan.

This suggests that it is best to minimize deterrence posturing in public, particularly posturing for domestic political purposes; governments should learn to resist what is often a terrible temptation. An effort should be made to practice deterrence *sotto voce*; probably, the stronger the threat, the more quietly it should be delivered. This can be difficult to combine with the achievement of sufficient credibility, but blatant deterrence can be difficult to combine with negotiation. Recognizing this trade-off is essential in statesmanship. The inclination is normally to go public and err on the side of looking staunch and putting one's threats across. Better is the realization that deterrence is vital, but is often not enough and quite capable of making things worse. Finally, it is wise to combine deterrence with carrots and other positive steps like reassurance, something borne out in both broad surveys and detailed case studies (Huth 1988; Stein 1991). Deterrence by itself is much less likely to induce serious negotiations in an emerging conflict, negotiations that could prevent its escalation. However, precise judgment is needed lest the carrots induce the other side to think it can hold out for a better deal or press on with threats for this purpose (Tetlock *et al.* 1991).

The advice shifts a bit for CAs. They should normally find it easier to avoid having their deterrence make the problem worse – their threats can seem less self-interested, and so giving in to them is less likely to generate fears of future exploitation. Their problem is to gain sufficient credibility, and going public with deterrence threats does seem to help here – it generates fears among the members that the CA will be damaged badly if such public commitments are not carried out.

Many conflicts are not settled or contained as they emerge – they worsen. How is deterrence related to ending the escalation and then developing serious negotiations in a full-blown conflict, especially one of long standing (such as an enduring rivalry)? Here, deterrence seems most likely to encourage negotiations when one or more of the following conditions arises:

- Parties rely on a mutual deterrence that seems stable and effective in keeping the conflict at a tolerable level, but there seems to be a good possibility that one or more of the parties, or an outside actor, will soon do something that could unravel the stability.
- Mutual deterrence upholds a stalemate that is very burdensome and painful – the conflict is not worsening, but is close to intolerable.
- Deterrence itself is very burdensome and painful, both to sustain and in terms of there being a good chance that it will collapse with nasty prospective costs.
- Deterrence seems adequate to protect against exploitation if the parties pursue a negotiated settlement or other cooperation to ease or end the conflict.

By way of illustration of all of the above points, we can cite the conflict on the Korean Peninsula and recent developments: all four of these conditions eventually came to apply to that conflict in the 1990s. To North Korea, deterrence appeared to be threatened by American high-tech weaponry; and to the USA and the Republic of Korea (ROK), it appeared to be threatened by North Korea's missiles and nuclear weapons program. The burdens of the conflict became much less tolerable for a declining North and less acceptable to the USA and ROK once the Cold War context for it had ended. The deterrence on both sides involved massive forces on high alert at great cost, as well as the continuing presence of US forces that, however useful, both Koreas had often found annoying. However, all three parties continued to emphasize that their deterrence was crucial to entering into the negotiations and agreements that eventually proliferated, but that had started over a decade previously and took years to blossom.

However, in 2001, the Bush administration moved to increase pressure on the North, partly because it suspected the North was cheating on nuclear weapons, by introducing the threats of a preemptive attack, abandoning additional steps (including negotiations planned by the prior administration), and showing disenchantment with South Korea's drive for additional negotiations and greater engagement with the North. The North had begun to open up more to the outside world and to introduce serious economic reforms, while simultaneously developing a new nuclear weapons effort – whether simply to cheat, or to enhance its own deterrence, or to maintain the necessary internal consensus behind the reforms and the opening to the world is not clear. The American reaction was to insist that the North renounce its nuclear weapons program as a prelude to negotiations (why negotiate with a cheat?), while the North used the program to demand negotiations. The American threat was of eventual military action, but it was carefully kept low key and implied; the North's deterrence threat was once again loud and blatant, not ideal for promoting serious talks. As I write, the conflict has been escalating steadily, and much that had previously been negotiated is in danger of unraveling, in spite of mutual deterrence – perhaps partially because of it – and despite the fact that the conflict remains very burdensome for all three parties. Efforts to develop negotiations may well succeed eventually, but the concern that they will not succeed is widespread.

It has often been asserted that the practice of deterrence is fundamentally anti-thetical to negotiations, a view rooted in sensitivity to the possibility of a security dilemma. Fortunately, the twentieth century ended with a flurry of examples of negotiation and conflict abatement in advance of or parallel with declines in military postures – deterrence did not prevent, and in some instances seems to have facilitated, these developments. Deterrence and negotiations are not inherently in-compatible, they are just uneasy partners in a relationship that requires constant, careful attention.

Finally, we have entered into an age of greater recourse to CAs to deal with se-rious conflicts among states and within them. However, CA deterrence is not likely to be very effective in preventing the escalation of conflicts from verbal abuse and minor confrontation to serious fighting – we will probably find that if a conflict ends short of this, the most significant reason will not be the application of deterrence from CAs. However, until it fails a serious test, CA deterrence is likely to be con-sistently effective in stopping severe fighting or reversing its results *among smaller states*. The prospect of confronting a determined CA is likely to be very daunting. Still, this does not offer good prospects for conflict resolution via negotiation in the most intractable and serious conflicts that have the most potential for large-scale violence, and in conflicts that involve the most powerful of nations. But our other resources do not consistently promise a better outcome, and thus we cannot be too surprised or caustic about the limitations of this one.

References

Axelrod RM (1984). *The Evolution of Cooperation*. New York, NY, USA: Basic Books.

Boustany N (2000). Changing North Korean attitudes, one step at a time. *Washington Post*, September 1.

Brodie B (1966). *Escalation and the Nuclear Option*. Princeton, NJ, USA: Princeton University Press.

Deutsch K, Burrell SA, Kann RA, Lee M Jr, Lichterman M, Lindgren RE, Loewenheim FL & Van Wagenen RW (1968). *Political Community and the North Atlantic Area*. Princeton, NJ, USA: Princeton University Press.

Freedman L (1981). *The Evolution of Nuclear Strategy*. New York, NY, USA: St. Martin's Press.

George A (ed.) 1991. *Avoiding War: Problems of Crisis Management*. Boulder, CO, USA: Westview Press.

George A & Smoke R (1974). *Deterrence in American Foreign Policy: Theory and Prac-tice*. New York, NY, USA: Columbia University Press.

Gray C (1984). *Nuclear Strategy and Strategic Planning*. Philadelphia, PA, USA: Foreign Policy Research Institute.

Hopf T (1994). *Peripheral Visions: Deterrence Theory and American Foreign Policy in the Third World, 1965–1990*. Ann Arbor, MI, USA: University of Michigan Press.

Huth P (1988). *Extended Deterrence and the Prevention of War*. New Haven, CT, USA: Yale University Press.

Jervis R (1989). *The Meaning of the Nuclear Revolution: Statecraft and the Prospect of Armageddon*. Ithaca, NY, USA: Cornell University Press.

Kahn H (1960). *On Thermonuclear War*. Princeton, NJ, USA: Princeton University Press.

Kahn H (1965). *On Escalation: Metaphors and Scenarios*. New York, NY, USA: Praeger.

Lebow RN (1981). *Between Peace and War: The Nature of International Crises*. Baltimore, MD, USA: Johns Hopkins University Press.

Lebow RN (1989). Deterrence: A political and psychological critique. In *Perspectives on Deterrence*, eds. Stern PC, Axelrod R, Jervis R & Radner R, pp. 25–51. New York, NY, USA: Oxford University Press.

Lebow RN & Stein JG (1989). Rational deterrence theory: I think, therefore I deter. *World Politics* **41**:208–224.

Lebow RN & Stein JG (1990). *When Does Deterrence Succeed and How Do We Know It?* Occasional Papers No. 8. Ottawa, Canada: Canadian Institute for International Peace and Security.

Lebow RN & Stein JG (1994). *We All Lost the Cold War*. Princeton, NJ, USA: Princeton University Press.

Levy J (1992). Prospect theory and international relations: Theoretical applications and analytical problems. *Political Psychology* **13**:283–310.

Levy J (1996). Loss aversion, framing, and bargaining: The implications of prospect theory for international conflict. *International Political Science Review* **17**:179–195.

Morgan PM (1983). *Deterrence: A Conceptual Analysis*. Beverly Hills, CA: Sage.

Morgan PM (1989). On strategic arms control and international security. In *Security and Arms Control*, Vol. 2, eds. Kolodziej EA & Morgan PM, pp. 299–318. New York, NY: Greenwood Press.

Rosecrance R & Schott P (1997). Concerts and regional intervention. In *Regional Orders: Building Security in a New World*, eds. Lake DA & Morgan PM, pp. 140–164. University Park, PA, USA: Penn State University Press.

Schaub G (1998). Compellence: Resuscitating the concept. In *Strategic Coercion: Concepts and Cases*, ed. Freedman L, pp. 37–60. Oxford, UK: Oxford University Press.

Schelling TC (1960). *The Strategy of Conflict*. Cambridge, MA, USA: Harvard University Press.

Schelling TC (1966). *Arms and Influence*. New Haven, CT, USA: Yale University Press.

Schelling TC & Halperin M (1985). *Strategy and Arms Control*, second edition. Washington, DC, USA: Pergamon–Brassey's.

Schwartz DN (1983). *NATO's Nuclear Dilemmas*. Washington, DC, USA: Brookings.

Smoke R (1977). *War: Controlling Escalation*. Cambridge, MA, USA: Harvard University Press.

Stein JG (1991). Deterrence and reassurance. In *Behavior, Society, and Nuclear War*, Vol. 2, eds. Tetlock PE, Jervis R, Stern P, Husbands JL & Tilly C, pp. 9–72. New York, NY, USA: Oxford University Press.

Tetlock PE, McGuire CB & Mitchell G (1991). Psychological perspectives on nuclear deterrence. *Annual Review of Psychology* **42**:239–276.

Van Benthem van den Bergh G (1992). *The Nuclear Revolution and the End of the Cold War*. Basingstoke, UK: Macmillan.

Zartman IW (1996). Bargaining and conflict resolution. In *Coping with Conflict after the Cold War*, eds. Kolodziej E & Kanet R, pp. 271–290. Baltimore, MD, USA: Johns Hopkins University Press.

Chapter 4

Quantitative Models for Armament Escalation and Negotiations

Rudolf Avenhaus, Juergen Beetz, and D. Marc Kilgour

4.1   Introduction

Any inquiry into escalation and negotiation in an international context must pay special attention to arms races and their inherent tendency to escalate. Since these phenomena deal with quantities – numbers of ballistic missiles, aircraft, tanks, troops, etc. – it is natural that their scientific treatment includes *quantitative* analysis. On the other hand, arms races and escalation depend fundamentally on international negotiations, and international relations in general, so that the *qualitative* methodological tools of political science are also appropriate. The published literature on international negotiation and escalation contains considerable quantitative work on arms races as such, but little quantitative work on negotiations about such races. Thus, it is not surprising that very little quantitative work addresses both subjects at the same time. It is the purpose of this chapter to develop some new ideas on this and to identify directions for future research.

Richardson (1939, 1960) was the first to describe arms races quantitatively and phenomenologically using a system of coupled linear differential equations. His work was brought to a wider audience by the well-known review article of Rapoport and Lewis (1957), which unleashed a veritable avalanche of arms-race research, including both formal theory and empirical analysis. The wealth of theoretical and empirical studies of arms races has been well documented in bibliographies (Cioffi-Revilla 1979) and literature reviews (Busch 1970; Intriligator 1976, 1982; Moll and Luebbert 1980; Avenhaus and Fichtner 1984).

Some empirical work, such as Richardson's own study of the naval race between Great Britain and Germany before World War I, impressively corroborated Richardson's theory, although other tests were less positive. Still, accepted or not, Richardson's theory cannot answer many important questions. For example, it cannot explain the causes of armament spirals because it focuses only on the mechanism by which they proceed; in other words, the two sides in an arms race are depicted as virtual automatons (Downs and Rocke 1990).

In the 1970s, *normative* Richardson-type analyses were performed on models in which national decision makers maximize their citizens' social welfare subject to a resource constraint and a dynamic stock-adjustment constraint. Brito (1972) presented an optimal control analysis in which each of two rival states optimally allocates resources between civilian consumption and arms expenditure. Simaan and Cruz (1973, 1975) extended this analysis to a differential game perspective in which competitive and interactive aspects of the rival's optimization problem are taken into account more fully. An overview of such mathematically demanding analyses is given by Sandler and Hartley (1995).

The opposite approach is to emphasize the conflictual character of arms races. For this purpose, game-theoretic models are natural, and many developed during the past 20 years do provide insight, at least in principle, into why states behave in ways that can seem paradoxical. Putting it very simplistically, one may say that the game-theoretic viewpoint posits that all pure arms-race models are more or less complicated variants of well-understood elementary models, of which the best known is the Prisoner's Dilemma.

Unfortunately, game models easily become complicated, both conceptually and technically. It is therefore not surprising that, to date, models have taken into account only a few important features of armament and negotiation. Parenthetically, we note that game theorists usually claim to address only bargaining models, which apparently reflects the view that "bargaining" is a fundamental interaction, whereas "negotiation" implies bargaining with additional structures that complicate the model. Assessing bargaining models, Morrow (1994, p. 237) concludes that "this field has a long way to go to capture what most of us think of as bargaining. Nevertheless it is one of the most promising areas in game theory, both in theory and application." We agree, and we believe that Morrow's statement is even more accurate if one tries to analyze bargaining in combination with other phenomena, such as arms races.

One very important consideration in the realistic modeling of decision problems in the areas under discussion is the amount of mutual information or lack of information that antagonistic states have about each other. Game-theoretic models deal with three kinds of uncertainty:

- Unforeseeable chance moves (which obviously cannot be ignored when dealing with real-world problems)
- Imperfectness of information (which means that, at some point, some decision maker makes a decision without complete knowledge of prior events in the game)
- Incompleteness of information (which describes a decision maker's uncertainty about the preferences of others)

Clearly, all of these sources of uncertainty are important for our area of interest.

In this chapter, several models of arms races, escalation, and negotiation are presented in increasing order of complexity. Each is discussed in some detail, with special emphasis on the conditions under which states in conflict tend to enter into an arms-race spiral or to avoid one by negotiation. In particular, we attempt to identify the states of information and other factors that have the greatest influence on behavioral predictions.

The first and simplest model is a one-step armament model, which turns out to be a variant of the well-known Prisoner's Dilemma paradigm. The second model, still very simple, includes a chance move if one player escalates. This model was developed by Ordeshook (1986, pp. 220ff). Neither of these models takes negotiation into account explicitly; they are presented here to demonstrate the formalism and serve as baselines against which to compare the more complex models that take negotiation into account.

Our third model, developed for this study, includes a form of negotiation; a variant of this model that relies on one-sided imperfect information is also included. The fourth model we discuss, developed by Morrow (1994, pp. 199ff), describes an asymmetric situation in which one player (the "challenger") lacks information about the willingness of its opponent (the "defender") to resist a challenge. Morrow's approach is compared briefly to the more complex models used by Zagare and Kilgour (2000) to describe interactions between two states, both of which are uncertain of the other's true preferences.

We do not really attempt to apply the results of our analyses to historical arms races, partly because we wish to emphasize the modeling itself, and partly because most other models published to date lack an empirical component. However, we offer a few remarks on applications because we feel that empirical corroboration is essential if models of this kind are to be established as methodological tools of

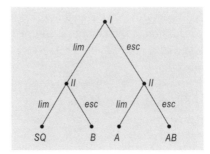

Figure 4.1. Extensive form of the simplest armament model. The states are I and II, and the outcomes are SQ (status quo), B (advantage for state II), A (advantage for state I), and AB (arms race). Roman numerals at decision nodes represent players, and letters at terminal nodes represent outcomes.

security analysis. In the final section we return to the questions raised initially: referring to a recent controversy, we discuss why quantitative analyses of arms races and negotiation are important, and conclude with some ideas on future research directions.

4.2   One-Decision Arms-Race Models

We start with the simplest model of armament escalation: Two antagonistic states I and II must decide whether to participate in an arms race; that is, whether to escalate (esc) by building up their forces or limit (lim) them at their current levels. If the two sides do not talk to each other, this conflict situation is modeled as a *two-person non-cooperative game*. For now, we suppose that both states have complete information and, in particular, that each knows its opponent's preferences over the possible outcomes. We begin by assuming that each state has *perfect information* (i.e., knows all previous decisions in the game) and that state I moves first. This model is best represented by the extensive form shown in *Figure 4.1*.

As an illustration of this model, consider the situation in 1949 when the Soviet Union (state I) had to decide whether to explode an atomic bomb and the USA (state II) had to decide whether to continue its nuclear program. Information was perfect in the sense that, after the Soviets escalated, the Americans learned that the Soviet nuclear weapon had been developed much faster than expected. "Truman and his advisers were shocked when a B-29 flying over the South Pacific on September 3, 1949 … detected a higher than normal radioactivity count. It indicated that, at some time in late August (the 29th, it was later determined), the Soviets had exploded an atomic device" (Powaski 1987, p. 53).

The US response was to counter-escalate. Surprised that it no longer had a monopoly on atomic weapons, and therefore a sure deterrent, the USA set out to produce a hydrogen bomb. According to Secretary of Defense Louis Johnson, the USA wanted "a military establishment sufficient to deter [an] aggressor and sufficient to kick the hell out of her if she doesn't stay deterred" (Johnson, quoted in Powaski 1987, p. 56).

Let $\succ_S$ represent the ordering relation for state S based on preference, so $X \succ_S Y$ means that outcome X is preferred to outcome Y by state S. In any common-sense model, state I must prefer its own advantage in armament to the uncertainty of an arms race, but it must also prefer an arms race to an armament advantage for state II. Moreover, state II should have the opposite preference. In symbols, we assume

$$A \succ_I AB \succ_I B \tag{4.1}$$

and

$$B \succ_{II} AB \succ_{II} A . \tag{4.2}$$

Use of Equation (4.2) in *Figure 4.1* shows that if state I escalates, then state II should escalate as well to achieve its most preferable outcome, AB. In other words, the outcome we identify with an arms race occurs. The important question, therefore, is whether state I will escalate. There are two possibilities:

1. If state II prefers to have an advantage over state I to the status quo, that is, if

$$B \succ_{II} SQ , \tag{4.3}$$

   then state II will escalate in any case. Equation (4.1) means that I will rationally decide to escalate to achieve outcome AB, which it prefers to outcome B. Thus, the two sides, each making decisions in its own interest, inevitably escalate and enter into an arms race.
2. If Equation (4.3) fails (ignoring the indifference case – as we shall do throughout – because it is impossible to estimate preferences precisely), then

$$SQ \succ_{II} B . \tag{4.4}$$

   It follows that state II will limit if state I does (because it prefers outcome SQ to outcome B), and escalate if I does (because it prefers outcome AB to outcome A).

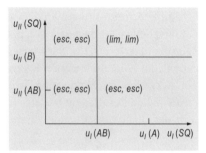

Figure 4.2. Equilibrium strategy pairs of the perfect-information model (*Figure 4.1*) depending on the states' relative preferences for the status quo.

Consequently, the two sides together either maintain the status quo or enter into an arms race, in accordance with I's preference between SQ and AB. Symbolically, the prediction is

$$\begin{matrix} (lim, lim) \\ (esc, esc) \end{matrix} \quad \text{if} \quad SQ \begin{matrix} \succ_I \\ \prec_I \end{matrix} AB . \tag{4.5}$$

Note that the outcomes we have identified are subgame-perfect equilibria, so-called because the strategies induced in any well-defined subgame constitute an equilibrium in that subgame (see, e.g., Osborne and Rubinstein 1994). In particular, subgame-perfect equilibria reflect the principle that all players make decisions in their own best interests and expect the same of their opponents.

For reasons clarified later, we introduce the players' (von Neumann–Morgenstern) utilities for the outcomes, u_I and u_{II}, also called their payoffs. It is understood that outcome X is preferred to outcome Y for a player if and only if that player's utility is greater at the more preferred outcome, formulated as

$$X \begin{matrix} \succ \\ \prec \end{matrix} Y \quad \text{iff} \quad u(X) \begin{matrix} > \\ < \end{matrix} u(Y) . \tag{4.6}$$

A player's von Neumann–Morgenstern utility represents not only its relative preferences between outcomes, but also the risk attitude that governs its preferences over probabilistic combinations of outcomes. This feature is utilized below.

Figure 4.2 shows in graphical form all subgame-perfect equilibrium strategy pairs in four possible cases, depending on the state's preferences for the status quo outcome, relative to the arms-race outcome and the state's own advantage. Note that the situations of the two states are not symmetric, because of the sequential nature of the game.

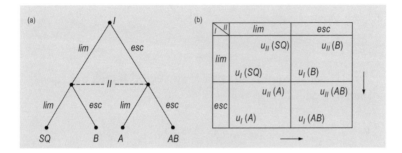

Figure 4.3. Extensive (a) and normal (b) forms of the simplest armament model with imperfect information. (a) The dashed line in the extensive form indicates state II's information set. (b) The arrows in the normal form indicate the directions of preference among the adjacent outcomes, according to Equations (4.1) and (4.2).

In summary, the two natural assumptions (4.2) and (4.3) imply two necessary and sufficient conditions for an arms race in the model of *Figure 4.1*. Either state II prefers outcome B to outcome SQ, or state II prefers outcome SQ to outcome B, but state I prefers outcome AB to outcome SQ. Note that in the first case, both states may prefer SQ to AB, which corresponds to a Prisoner's Dilemma; the two states rationally enter into an arms race, even though both would prefer the status quo.

Let us now consider an *imperfect-information* arms-race model in which state II does not know state I's decision at the time it (state II) has to make its own decision. This game is shown in extensive and normal forms in *Figure 4.3*.

Whereas the perfect-information model (*Figure 4.1*) could be analyzed just by exploring the consequences of the preferences in subgames, we now need a well-defined *solution concept* to identify decision choices that can reasonably be recommended to the players. Following Nash (1951), we define a *Nash equilibrium* to be a strategy (in this case, a decision) by each player with the property that a unilateral deviation of either player from its equilibrium strategy does not improve its outcome. (Note that some authors call an equilibrium pair of strategies a solution only if it is unique, or if it is distinguished among several equilibria for good reasons.)

The normal (or strategic) form of our game is also shown in *Figure 4.3*. Based on the preference directions shown in the figure, we see immediately that, because of the assumptions (4.1) and (4.2), the pair of strategies (esc, esc) does, indeed, fulfill Nash's equilibrium condition, and thus represents an equilibrium of the game.

If, furthermore, for state I

$$SQ \prec_I A ,\tag{4.7}$$

or for state II

$$SQ \prec_{II} B ,\tag{4.8}$$

then (lim, lim) is not an equilibrium pair of strategies. If both Equations (4.7) and (4.8) hold, and if in addition

$$SQ \succ_I AB ,\tag{4.9}$$

and

$$SQ \succ_{II} AB ,\tag{4.10}$$

then we again have a Prisoner's Dilemma situation, because (esc, esc) is the only equilibrium pair of strategies, even though (lim, lim) leads to a more preferred outcome for both states. To summarize, this Prisoner's Dilemma occurs if and only if the players' preferences are as follows:

$$A \succ_I SQ \succ_I AB \succ_I B\tag{4.11}$$

and

$$B \succ_{II} SQ \succ_{II} AB \succ_{II} A .\tag{4.12}$$

On the other hand, if both Equations (4.7) and (4.8) fail, then (lim, lim) is also an equilibrium strategy pair. There are then two Nash equilibria, a situation said to cause an equilibrium selection problem. However, in this case our basic assumptions (4.1) and (4.2) imply Equations (4.9) and (4.10). In other words, SQ, the outcome that results from the equilibrium strategy pair (lim, lim), is preferred by both players to AB, the outcome that results from the equilibrium strategy pair (esc, esc). The former is therefore a *payoff-dominant equilibrium*: both states are well advised to use the strategies that correspond to the preferred equilibrium, namely, to maintain the status quo, which is called the *solution* of the game. For completeness, note that this model has a third equilibrium in so-called mixed strategies (i.e., strategies that are chosen using a random device). It turns out, however, that the mixed equilibrium is also payoff-dominated by (lim, lim).

Figure 4.4 shows all pure Nash equilibrium strategy pairs in the nine possible cases defined by the states' relative preferences for the status quo, an arms race, and their own armament. However, in contrast to the previous case of perfect information, the situation is symmetric for both states.

Finally, note that this model can be generalized to n decision steps, such that after each step has been completed, each state knows its adversary's move on all the

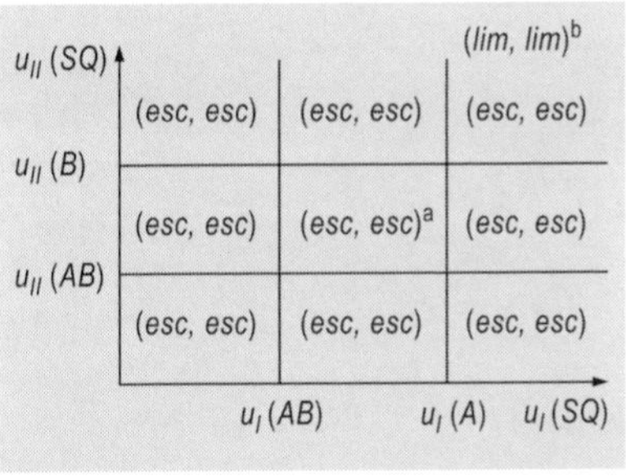

Figure 4.4. Pure equilibrium strategy pairs of the imperfect-information model (*Figure 4.3*) as functions of each states' relative preferences for the status quo. [a]Prisoner's Dilemma; [b](lim, lim) is the payoff-dominant equilibrium.

previous steps. For this purpose, both armament costs and gains must be measured in appropriate utility units, the estimation of which may turn out to be difficult in practice.

In summary, we have shown that, in the model with perfect information, there is one equilibrium pair of strategies, which can be either (lim, lim), if both players prefer the status quo to an arms race, or (esc, esc) otherwise. In the model with imperfect information, the states' choices are effectively simultaneous, and so the best strategy for a state cannot depend on knowledge of the opponent's choice. The strategy pair (esc, esc) is always an equilibrium; in special cases, there is another equilibrium, (lim, lim), which is payoff-dominant and therefore recommended to the players whenever it is an equilibrium. In both models, the relative preferences of both states together determine whether the status quo will be maintained or whether escalation is inevitable.

4.3 Models for Arms Races with a Chance Move

Ordeshook (1986), elaborating on Wagner's (1983) discussion, designed a simple arms-race model with *complete and imperfect information* that incorporated a *chance move*: If one state escalates and the other limits, then the latter may detect the situation, in which case it escalates in response. *Figure 4.5* shows the extensive form of this model. For consistency, we have modified Ordeshook's notation. Note that when detection probabilities are zero, this model is identical to the imperfect-information model of the previous section (*Figure 4.3*).

Ordeshook's model can be understood as being "between" the two models of Section 4.2. When detection probabilities are zero, this model is identical to the imperfect-information model (*Figure 4.3*). On the other hand, when detection is

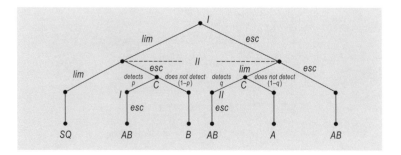

Figure 4.5. Extensive form of the Ordeshook (1986) model. The chance move is denoted C; p and q are I's and II's probabilities for detecting an escalation. Other symbols are as in the previous section.

certain, the game is a symmetric version of the perfect-information model (*Figure 4.1*) that incorporates automatic response: a player who learns that the opponent has escalated escalates immediately, consistent with (4.1) and (4.2).

To see how this model might illustrate real-world events, consider the interwar scenario involving Germany and Great Britain. In the 1920s, Germany escalated. We can suppose that the ability of Great Britain to detect escalation was uncertain and model it as a chance event. Initially, Britain did not detect escalation, but it did so when the game was replayed in the late 1930s and responded by counter-escalating.

To provide more details, Germany (state I) began an arms buildup shortly after World War I. Hans von Seekt, who assumed command of the Reichswehr in 1920, implemented a program under which violations of the Treaty of Versailles were coordinated centrally. The 100,000 troops allowed under the treaty were only the core of an army planned to have a strength of several million, supported by secret caches of weapons throughout the country (Glynn 1992, p. 63).

Initially, German rearmament went unnoticed by Britain (state II). As late as April 1934, Prime Minister Ramsay MacDonald explained that his government was not spending more money on arms because "the Government could not announce a new programme when the question [of disarmament] was still open" (MacDonald, quoted in Glynn 1992, p. 76). But later Germany's escalation was no longer in doubt, and Britain finally overcame its reluctance to build up arms. Referring to the decision to impose conscription on 27 April 1939 as a "belated awakening" on the part of the government, Winston Churchill assigned the main credit to the secretary of state for war who, he said, took a grave risk and "was never sure that each day in office would not be his last" (Churchill 1948, p. 317).

To analyze this game, we must consider explicitly the concept of mixed strategies and expected utilities, which we avoided earlier. If, for example, state I limits

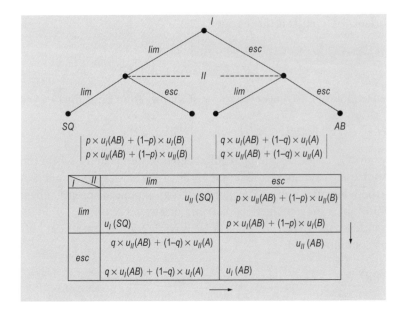

Figure 4.6. Reduced extensive form and corresponding normal form of the game of *Figure 4.5*. Outcomes when exactly one side escalates have been replaced by expected utilities.

and state II escalates, then with probability p I detects II's escalation and escalates in response, to obtain utility $u_I(AB)$. Otherwise, with probability $(1-p)$, I does not detect the escalation and therefore does not respond, obtaining utility $u_I(B)$. Thus, I's *expected utility* is

$$p \cdot u_I(AB) + (1-p) \cdot u_I(B) \,, \tag{4.13}$$

which is I's "weighted average" utility, in which the weight associated with an outcome is its probability of occurrence. A similar calculation can be carried out for state II. Using the expected utilities of I and II, the model of *Figure 4.5* can be reduced to the game shown in both extensive form and normal form in *Figure 4.6*.

For the sake of completeness, we repeat our common-sense assumptions (4.1) and (4.2), that is, we assume again that for the two states the following preferences hold:

$$A \succ_I AB \succ_I B \tag{4.14}$$

and

$$B \succ_{II} AB \succ_{II} A \,. \tag{4.15}$$

An important observation is that because

$$u_I(AB) \quad - \quad [p \cdot u_I(AB) + (1-p) \cdot u_I(B)]$$
$$= (1-p) \cdot [u_I(AB) - u_I(B)] \, , \qquad (4.16)$$

and because $(1-p) > 0$ whenever $p < 1$, it follows from Equation (4.14) that

$$p \cdot u_I(AB) + (1-p) \cdot u_I(B) < u_I(AB) \qquad (4.17)$$

whenever $p < 1$. A corresponding relationship holds for state II whenever $q < 1$. It follows that the strategy pair (esc, esc) is always a Nash equilibrium provided p and q are both less than unity. (The game of *Figure 4.5* has no proper subgames, so this equilibrium is subgame-perfect, but only in a trivial sense.)

The strategy pair (lim, lim) is a second Nash equilibrium if and only if the following conditions hold:

$$u_I(SQ) > q \cdot u_I(AB) + (1-q) \cdot u_I(A) \qquad (4.18)$$

and

$$u_{II}(SQ) > p \cdot u_{II}(AB) + (1-p) \cdot u_{II}(B) \, . \qquad (4.19)$$

These conditions are more conveniently expressed in the equivalent form

$$q > q_{cr} \qquad (4.20)$$

and

$$p > p_{cr} \, , \qquad (4.21)$$

where the *critical probabilities* q_{cr} and p_{cr} are defined by

$$q_{cr} = \frac{u_I(A) - u_I(SQ)}{u_I(A) - u_I(AB)} \qquad (4.22)$$

and

$$p_{cr} = \frac{u_{II}(B) - u_{II}(SQ)}{u_{II}(B) - u_{II}(AB)} \, . \qquad (4.23)$$

If it happens that both states prefer the status quo to a one-sided advantage, that is, if

$$A \prec_I SQ \qquad (4.24)$$

and

$$B \prec_{II} SQ \qquad (4.25)$$

hold, then Equations (4.18) and (4.19) are true, and (lim, lim) is an equilibrium for any values of p and q. Whenever it occurs, the equilibrium (lim, lim), which corresponds to the outcome SQ, is payoff-dominant.

On the other hand, if either state prefers escalation to the status quo, that is, if

$$A \succ_I AB \succ_I SQ \tag{4.26}$$

and

$$B \succ_{II} AB \succ_{II} SQ \tag{4.27}$$

hold, then the pair (lim, lim) cannot be a Nash equilibrium. Finally, if it happens that

$$A \succ_I SQ \succ_I AB \tag{4.28}$$

and

$$B \succ_{II} SQ \succ_{II} AB \tag{4.29}$$

hold, then (lim, lim) is an equilibrium pair of strategies if and only if $p > p_{cr}$ and $q > q_{cr}$. Whenever there are two pure Nash equilibria, there exists a third equilibrium in mixed strategies, just as for the incomplete-information game in the preceding sections. If $p < p_{cr}$ and $q < q_{cr}$, the model is again a variant of the Prisoner's Dilemma.

Figure 4.7 shows all pure equilibrium pairs in nine cases defined by the states' relative preferences for the status quo, an arms race, and their own advantage. (Note that only pure Nash equilibria are considered here.) In all nine cases, (esc, esc) is an equilibrium strategy pair. Whenever (lim, lim) is an equilibrium, it is payoff-dominant over (esc, esc).

If at least one state prefers escalation to the status quo (i.e., $AB \succ_I SQ$ or $AB \succ_{II} SQ$), then (esc, esc) is the only equilibrium, which implies that an arms race is the only possible outcome. If both states prefer the status quo to escalation (i.e., $SQ \succ_I AB$ and $SQ \succ_{II} AB$), then (lim, lim) is also an equilibrium strategy pair, subject to one possible condition on a state's probability of detecting its opponent's escalation. If state I prefers its own armament to the status quo (i.e., $A \succ_I SQ$), then for (lim, lim) to be an equilibrium, state II's probability of detecting I's escalation, q, must exceed a critical value, q_{cr}, and similarly for state I. If a state prefers the status quo to its own armament, there is no condition on its detection probability.

In summary, as seen best by comparing *Figures 4.4* and *4.7*, the Ordeshook (1986) chance-move model is very similar to the imperfect-information version of the previous section, as long as the detection probabilities are sufficiently small. The critical thresholds q_{cr} and p_{cr} fall as the utilities for one-sided advantage and

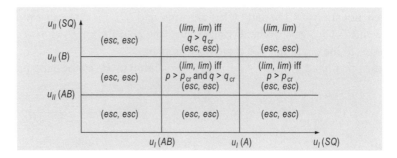

Figure 4.7. Equilibrium strategy pairs for nine cases defined by the states' relative preferences for the status quo. Whenever (lim, lim) is an equilibrium, it is payoff-dominant.

status quo approach each other, and as the utilities of one-sided advantage and escalation separate. Interestingly, each state's critical probability depends only on its opponent's utilities, a feature typical of non-cooperative game models. Our analysis of the Ordeshook model has thus added some nuances and some context to our conclusions about the simple one-decision models in Section 4.2. It also provides some new insight into the situation of Germany and Great Britain in the 1920s and 1930s, when detection of initial escalation was possible but not certain.

4.4   Arms-Race and Negotiation Models with Imperfect Information

We start with a *perfect-information* game model that explicitly includes different ways of negotiating. State I is involved in a protracted conflict, for example, a border dispute, with state II. State I must decide to start negotiations either by offering what it considers to be a reasonable starting position or by demanding a concession, backing its demands with the threat to increase its armament level. State II can respond with either a counteroffer or a similar challenge. In case one state threatens to escalate while the other attempts to negotiate, the latter can decide to make a concession, or not. The extensive-form representation of this model is given by *Figure 4.8*.

In broad outline, the negotiations surrounding the Cuban missile crisis illustrate the game of *Figure 4.8*. Under perfect information, the USA (now state I) made a demand of the Soviet Union (state II), which attempted to negotiate but ultimately conceded to US demands.

We now trace the negotiation scenario in more detail. The interaction be-gan with a demand by the USA, through its United Nations ambassador, Adlai

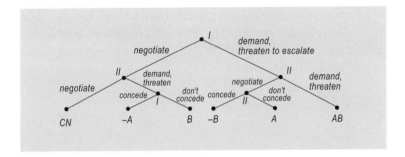

Figure 4.8. Extensive form of the perfect-information armament negotiation model. Outcomes are CN (status quo, i.e., continued negotiation), $-A$ (I concedes, II does not carry out its threat), B (II unilaterally increases its arms), $-B$ (II concedes, I does not carry out its threat), A (I unilaterally increases its arms), and AB (both sides increase their arms, i.e., escalation).

Stevenson. The USA declared its knowledge of Soviet activities in Cuba and demanded the removal of weapons. Stevenson declared: "We do have the evidence . . . clear and incontrovertible. And let me say something else. Those weapons must be taken out of Cuba" (Stevenson, quoted in Kennedy 1969, p. 75).

The Soviet Union responded by attempting to negotiate. Soviet Premier Nikita Khrushchev attempted to compromise in his letter to US President John F. Kennedy: "We will remove our missiles from Cuba, you will remove yours from Turkey . . . The Soviet Union will pledge not to invade or interfere with the internal affairs of Turkey; the US will make the same pledge regarding Cuba" (Khrushchev, quoted in Kennedy 1969, p. 94).

President Kennedy's letter of response stated:

> the key elements of your proposals – which seem generally acceptable as I understand them – are as follows:
> 1. You would agree to remove these weapons systems from Cuba under appropriate United Nations observation and supervision . . . ;
> 2. We, on our part, would agree – upon the establishment of adequate arrangements through the United Nations – to ensure the carrying out and continuation of these commitments, (a) to remove promptly the quarantine measures now in effect, and (b) to give assurance against an invasion of Cuba. (J.F. Kennedy, quoted in Kennedy 1969, p. 103)

Note that President Kennedy did not agree to remove US arms from Turkey. But Khrushchev conceded, responding to Kennedy's letter with a message indicating that the Soviet Union agreed to "dismantle and withdraw the missiles under adequate supervision and inspection" (Kennedy 1969, p. 110).

In the following, to reduce the large number of possible cases, we assume, for simplicity, that both states have the same preference orderings. Furthermore, as in the previous section, we assume that the states' relative preferences for outcomes A, B, and AB are as follows:

$$A \succ_I AB \succ_I B \tag{4.30}$$

and

$$B \succ_{II} AB \succ_{II} A . \tag{4.31}$$

To analyze this model, we observe first that if both states prefer the opponent's armament to their own concession, that is, if

$$B \succ_I -A \tag{4.32}$$

and

$$A \succ_{II} -B , \tag{4.33}$$

then a first-step backward induction leads to the game model of *Figure 4.1*. (The two games are the same in terms of outcomes, but not in terms of strategies. Whereas in the game of *Figure 4.1* both states decide immediately to limit or to increase their forces, in the game of *Figure 4.8* they either negotiate without intending to increase their arms – which corresponds to immediate limitation – or they threaten to escalate, but plan to implement the threat only if the opponent does not concede.)

In other words, independent of the preferences for the status quo, if concessions are less preferred than A, B, and AB for both parties, second-step negotiations do not make sense at all; if neither state is prepared to consider conceding, then negotiating is useless.

Now suppose that the preferences of Equations (4.32) and (4.33) are reversed, that is,

$$-A \succ_I B \tag{4.34}$$

and

$$-B \succ_{II} A . \tag{4.35}$$

Then the game of *Figure 4.8* can be reduced to the one shown in *Figure 4.9*. Depending on the preferences, all four remaining outcomes may occur as equilibria. In particular, the status quo is maintained if and only if

$$CN \succ_{II} -A , \tag{4.36}$$

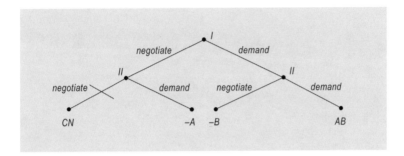

Figure 4.9. Reduced extensive form of the game given by *Figure 4.8* using assumptions (4.34) and (4.35).

$$CN \succ_I -B \,, \tag{4.37}$$

and

$$CN \succ_I AB \,. \tag{4.38}$$

Although admittedly not very plausible, this condition does not mean that the status quo must be preferred to all other outcomes. If Equations (4.31) and (4.36) hold, for example, then SQ is an equilibrium for any preference ordering of A that satisfies

$$A \succ_I CN \succ_I AB \succ_I B, \ -A \succ_I B \tag{4.39}$$

and

$$CN \succ_I -B \,. \tag{4.40}$$

Let us now consider the related *imperfect-information* model in *Figure 4.10*. This game assumes that I must make its choice before it knows whether II has decided to negotiate or demand. We see immediately that this game tree is structurally identical to that in *Figure 4.5*; the difference is that the two chance nodes in *Figure 4.5* are replaced by decision nodes in *Figure 4.10*. Thus, backward induction is applicable to the game of *Figure 4.10* for the subgames that begin at the two final decision nodes. Again, for simplicity we consider in the following only symmetric preferences.

We begin the analysis of the game of *Figure 4.10* by assuming preferences (4.32) and (4.33). Again, we are led back to the game of *Figure 4.3*, and thus in this version also second-step negotiations do not make sense.

Now we assume preferences (4.34) and (4.35). By backward induction at the final two decision nodes, we obtain the reduced game given in extensive and normal form in *Figure 4.11*.

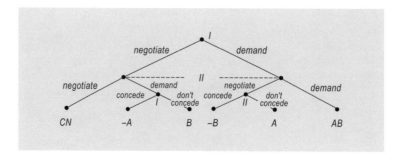

Figure 4.10. Extensive form of the imperfect-information armament negotiation model. Notation is the same as in *Figure 4.8*; the dashed line indicates the information set of state II.

Without discussing all possible cases we note, in particular, that maintenance of the status quo is equilibrium if

$$CN \succ_I -B \tag{4.41}$$

and

$$CN \succ_{II} -A \,, \tag{4.42}$$

which again is not very plausible. (Still, continued negotiations need not be the most preferred outcome to represent an equilibrium.)

For the reduced game of *Figure 4.11*, the escalation outcome (AB) is an equilibrium if

$$AB \succ_I -B \tag{4.43}$$

and

$$AB \succ_{II} -A \,. \tag{4.44}$$

When CN and AB coexist as equilibria, further assumptions are required to determine whether either equilibrium produces an outcome preferred by both states.

To summarize, if neither side is willing to concede, our simple models that include negotiation produce the same results as the simple models treated previously. In particular, maintenance of the status quo is the unique equilibrium only if it is the most preferred outcome for both states. The situation is different if concessions are rated higher than facing the other state's threat. Here, the status quo may be an equilibrium, even though it is not the most preferred outcome.

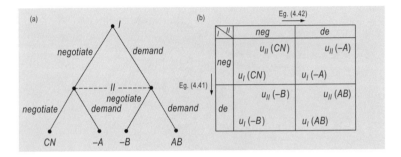

Figure 4.11. Reduced extensive (a) and normal (b) form of the model given by *Figure 4.10*, with assumptions (4.34) and (4.35).

4.5 Arms Race and Negotiation Models with Incomplete Information

One feature of negotiations often regarded as crucial is that parties do not necessarily know other parties' preferences. Formally, this situation can be modeled by so-called *games of incomplete information*. Morrow (1994) developed and analyzed such a model, which is described below. (The terminology has been changed to make it consistent with the rest of this work.) Morrow's game is shown in extensive form in *Figure 4.12*. A similar but more complex game model was advanced and analyzed by Kilgour and Zagare (1991) and Zagare and Kilgour (2000, Chapter 5).

State I begins by deciding whether to "challenge" state II by demanding a concession, or not. In the latter case, the game ends at the status quo outcome (SQ). State I must make its decision without complete knowledge of state II's preferences: it knows only that state II is resolute (r) with probability γ and irresolute (i) with probability $1 - \gamma$. (Formally, state II is informed as to its exact status, while state I retains only probabilistic knowledge.)

After a challenge, state II must choose either to resist or to concede. In the latter case, state II makes a concession and the game ends at outcome $-B$. However, if state II resists, then state I must decide whether to back down, which produces outcome $-A$, or to push, which leads to the escalation outcome (AB).

The relative preferences of state I and state II are assumed to be independent of state II's nature (or *type*) – irresolute or resolute – for three of the four possible outcomes: status quo (SQ), concession by state II ($-B$), and concession by state I ($-A$). However, the ranking of the escalation outcome (AB) depends on state II's

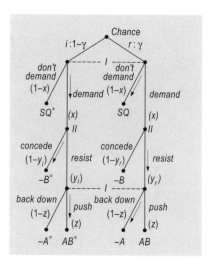

Figure 4.12. Extensive form of the incomplete-information game between state I and state II. Dashed lines indicate information sets; x, y, and z are mixed strategies. Explanations of all the symbols are given in the text.

nature. Denoting with an asterisk outcomes at which state II is irresolute, we assume (with Morrow 1994) the following preference ordering for state I:

$$\begin{matrix} -B \\ -B^* \end{matrix} \succ_I \begin{matrix} SQ \\ SQ^* \end{matrix} \succ_I AB^* \succ_I \begin{matrix} -A \\ -A^* \end{matrix} \succ_I AB . \tag{4.45}$$

And we assume the following preference ordering for state II:

$$\begin{matrix} -A \\ -A^* \end{matrix} \succ_{II} \begin{matrix} SQ \\ SQ^* \end{matrix} \succ_{II} AB \succ_{II} \begin{matrix} -B \\ -B^* \end{matrix} \succ_{II} AB^* . \tag{4.46}$$

Before analyzing the incomplete-information game, consider for a moment the two complete-information games that it subsumes: state I against a resolute state II, and state I against an irresolute state II. In terms of *Figure 4.12*, these games arise simply by cutting state I's information sets. Treating them as games of perfect (and complete) information enables them to be solved immediately by backward induction, as above. In the first (left-hand) game, the subgame perfect equilibrium is that state I challenges and state II concedes, to produce the outcome $-B^*$. In the second (right-hand) game, state I does not challenge, and the outcome is the status quo (SQ).

    A natural expectation is that the former strategies will be pursued if it is unlikely that state II is resolute, that is, if the probability γ is small, but there will be no challenge if γ is large. Thus, we expect there to be a threshold value of γ below which state I initiates and state II concedes, and above which state I does not challenge.

However, the game of incomplete information has another new aspect. It can be analyzed only using mixed (probabilistic) strategies, ultimately because of state I's uncertainty over the nature of its opponent. We assume that state I challenges with probability x, and thus does not challenge with probability $1 - x$. Should the opportunity arise, state I plans to push with probability z, and to back down with probability $1 - z$. If state I demands, state II plans to resist with probability y and concede with probability $1 - y$. But note that state II knows its own nature, and may behave differently depending on its type. For this reason, we assume that state II selects two mixed strategies, y_r and y_i, for use when it is resolute or irresolute, respectively.

To solve this game, we must introduce the players' utilities for all outcomes. With Morrow (1994), we assume that, except for the arms-race outcome (AB), all outcomes have equal utilities whether state II is resolute or irresolute. Thus we assume that state I's utilities satisfy

$$1 = \frac{u_I(-B)}{u_I(-B^*)} > \frac{u_I(SQ)}{u_I(SQ^*)} > u_I(AB^*)$$

$$> \frac{u_I(-A)}{u_I(-A^*)} = 0 > u_I(AB) \tag{4.47}$$

and that state II's utilities satisfy

$$1 = \frac{u_{II}(-A)}{u_{II}(-A^*)} > \frac{u_{II}(SQ)}{u_{II}(SQ^*)} > u_{II}(AB)$$

$$> \frac{u_{II}(-B)}{u_{II}(-B^*)} = 0 > u_{II}(AB^*) . \tag{4.48}$$

There are two requirements for a perfect Bayesian equilibrium (see, e.g., Osborne and Rubinstein 1994), the natural solution concept for games like the one of *Figure 4.12*. At a perfect Bayesian equilibrium, each player's choice must maximize its expected utility based on its current beliefs about the opponent. And, at a perfect Bayesian equilibrium, a player must adjust its beliefs about the opponent based on the opponent's choices that it has observed. In the game of *Figure 4.12*, state I has only one type, so state II always has complete information about state I. However, state I is uncertain as to state II's type – resolute or irresolute. At the beginning of the game, state I's probability that state II would be resolute was γ. But if the second information set is reached, state I has some new information about the nature of its opponent – it knows that state II has resisted. Since state II's probability of resisting may depend on whether it is resolute or irresolute, state I can and should revise its probability that state II is resolute, based on this new information.

To formalize this idea, let us define the probability β that state II is resolute given that it has resisted,

$$\beta = \Pr\{II\text{resolute}|II\text{resists}\} . \tag{4.49}$$

According to Bayes' theorem, we have

$$\beta = \frac{\Pr\{II\text{resolute}\} \cdot \Pr\{II\text{resists}|II\text{ resolute}\}}{\Pr\{II\text{resists}\}} . \tag{4.50}$$

Thus, with the help of the law of total probability, we find

$$\beta = \frac{\gamma \cdot y_r}{\gamma \cdot y_r + (1 - \gamma) \cdot y_i} , \tag{4.51}$$

provided the denominator on the right-hand side of Equation (4.51), that is, the probability that state II resists, does not vanish. However, if the denominator vanishes, there is no condition on the selection of β.

For the game of *Figure 4.12*, a *perfect Bayesian equilibrium* is a 5-tuple $(x^0, z^0, \beta^0; y_r^0, y_i^0)$ such that β satisfies Equation (4.51), provided the denominator identified above does not vanish, z^0 maximizes state I's expected utility at its second information set, given that it assigns probability β to state II being resolute, y_r^0 and y_i^0 maximize state II's expected utilities at its two decision nodes, and x^0 maximizes state I's expected utility at its first information set (where state A assigns probability γ to the defender being resolute). Note that maximization by state II takes place under complete information.

To illustrate the kind of computations that yield all perfect Bayesian equilibria, we see that, at its second information set, state I must maximize

$$z \cdot [(1 - \beta) \cdot (u_I (AB^*) - u_I (-A)) - \beta (u_I (-A) - u_I (AB))] . \tag{4.52}$$

To repeat, this means that state I makes its decision whether to push or back down based on its expected payoffs calculated using updated beliefs that account for state II resisting – otherwise the game would not have reached this information set. It is not difficult to show that I rationally decides to push ($z^0 = 1$) if $\beta < \beta_{cr}$ and to back down ($z^0 = 0$) if $\beta > \beta_{cr}$, where the critical probability β_{cr} is given by

$$\beta_{cr} = \frac{u_I (AB^*) - u_I (-A)}{u_I (AB^*) - u_I (AB)} . \tag{4.53}$$

Note that if $\beta = \beta_{cr}$, there is no restriction on the value of z^0 at a Bayesian equilibrium.

The utilities of the two types of state II are given by

$$
\begin{aligned}
F_{IIr} (x, z; y_r) &= (1 - x) \, u_{II} (SQ) + x (1 - y_r) \, u_{II} (-B) \\
&\quad + x y_r [(1 - z) \, u_{II} (-A) + z u_{II} (AB)] ,
\end{aligned}
\tag{4.54}
$$

$$F_{IIi}(x, z; y_i) = (1 - x) u_{II}(SQ) + x (1 - y_i) u_{II}(-B)$$
$$+ xy_i [(1 - z) u_{II}(-A) + zu_{II}(AB^*)] . \tag{4.55}$$

However, state II's maximization problem concerns only the parts of these expressions affected by II's choices. If $x > 0$, these are

$$y_r [(1 - z) u_{II}(-A) + zu_{II}(AB) - u_{II}(-B)] \tag{4.56}$$

for a resolute state II and

$$y_i [(1 - z) u_{II}(-A) + zu_{II}(AB^*) - u_{II}(-B)] \tag{4.57}$$

for an irresolute state II.

The choice of a resolute state II at a perfect Bayesian equilibrium is easy to determine. Expression (4.56) is equal to

$$y_r [(1-z)\{u_{II}(-A) - u_{II}(-B)\} + z\{u_{II}(AB) - u_{II}(-B)\}] \geq 0 , \tag{4.58}$$

with equality if and only if $y_r = 0$, because of Equation (4.46). It follows that at any perfect Bayesian equilibrium, $y_r^0 = 1$; in other words, a resolute state II always resists.

The situation is not so definite for an irresolute state II. Based on Equation (4.57), it can be shown that at any perfect Bayesian equilibrium, an irresolute state II should resist $(y_i^0 = 1)$ if $z < z_{cr}$, and should concede $(y_i^0 = 0)$ if $z > z_{cr}$, where

$$z_{cr} = \frac{u_{II}(-A) - u_{II}(-B)}{u_{II}(-A) - u_{II}(AB^*)} . \tag{4.59}$$

Any value of y_i^0 is consistent with a perfect Bayesian equilibrium if $z = z_{cr}$.

Finally, given the values of y_r, y_i, z, and β, state I's choice of $x^0 = x$ must maximize its expected utility in its first information set,

$$F_I(x, z; y_r, y_i) = (1 - x) u_I(SQ) + x\gamma\{(1 - y_r) u_I(-B)$$
$$+ y_r [zu_I(AB) + (1 - z) u_I(-A)]\}$$
$$+ x (1 - \gamma) \{(1 - y_i) u_I(-B)$$
$$+ y_i [zu_I(AB^*) + (1 - z) u_I(-A)]\} . \tag{4.60}$$

Relation (4.60) is simplified slightly by inclusion of the observation above that $y_r^0 = 1$ at any perfect Bayesian equilibrium. The determination of all perfect Bayesian equilibria requires the exhaustive verification of 27 cases, which reflects that, at least in principle, each of x, z, and y_i could equal zero, one, or some number in between. The details are not presented here. Instead, we simply describe the two main perfect Bayesian equilibria. First, define the critical value for γ by

$$\gamma_{cr} = \beta_{cr} \cdot \frac{u_I(-B) - u_I(SQ)}{u_I(-B) - u_I(-A)} . \tag{4.61}$$

[Note that Equation (4.46) shows that $\gamma_{cr} < \beta_{cr}$.] If $\gamma < \gamma_{cr}$, the only perfect Bayesian equilibrium is

$$x^0 = 1, \quad z^0 = z_{cr}, \quad y^0_r = 1, \quad y^0_i = \frac{\gamma}{1-\gamma} \cdot \frac{1-\beta_{cr}}{\beta_{cr}}, \quad \beta^0 = \beta_{cr}, \qquad (4.62)$$

with expected utilities

$$F^0_I = \frac{\gamma}{\beta_{cr}} \cdot u_I(-A) + \frac{\beta_{cr} - \gamma}{\beta_{cr}} \cdot u_I(-B) , \qquad (4.63)$$

$$
\begin{aligned}
F^0_{IIr} &= \frac{u_{II}(-A) - u_{II}(AB)}{u_{II}(-A) - u_{II}(AB^*)} \cdot u_{II}(-B) \\
&+ \frac{u_{II}(AB) - u_{II}(AB^*)}{u_{II}(-A) - u_{II}(AB^*)} \cdot u_{II}(-A) ,
\end{aligned}
\qquad (4.64)
$$

$$F^0_{IIi} = u_{II}(-B) . \qquad (4.65)$$

If $\gamma > \gamma_{cr}$, the only perfect Bayesian equilibrium is

$$x^0 = 0, \quad z^0 = 0, \quad y^0_r = 1, \quad y^0_i = 1, \quad \beta^0 > \beta_{cr}, \qquad (4.66)$$

with expected utilities

$$F^0_I = u_I(SQ), \quad F^0_{IIr} = u_{II}(SQ), \quad F^0_{IIi} = u_{II}(SQ) . \qquad (4.67)$$

Thus, our initial guess has been confirmed: there is a threshold value of the probability, γ_{cr}, that state I assigns to the event that state II is resolute, given by Equation (4.61). For $\gamma < \gamma_{cr}$, state I initiates a crisis, otherwise it does not. The value of γ_{cr} increases as state I's preference for the status quo decreases, and as the gap between its utilities for war against an irresolute or resolute state II widens. Interestingly enough, this critical value depends only on state I's utilities.

The solution has at least one interesting and unexpected aspect: for $\gamma < \gamma_{cr}$, there is a positive probability that an irresolute state II will resist. State I may then push, which results in the escalation outcome. Recall that escalation cannot occur when there is complete information since, as we saw, state I will challenge the irresolute state II and the latter will concede, whereas state I will not challenge a resolute state II. Thus, we conclude that *escalation can occur under incomplete information when it would not occur under complete information.*

A natural extension of this model would postulate that both states have incomplete information about each other's preferences. To solve such a two-sided incomplete-information game, we would have to deal with four player types, instead of the three in Morrow's model. As above, we would look first at four possible games of complete information between two players: a resolute or irresolute state I against a resolute or irresolute state II.

Kilgour and Zagare (1991; see also Zagare and Kilgour 2000, Chapter 5) have performed this analysis, which is more complex than that for the game described here. Instead of one threshold for each side, as one might expect, it turns out that there are two for state *II* and one for state *I*, and that as a consequence four different forms of perfect Bayesian equilibria can arise.

Another model developed by Morrow (1989a) allows both states to be resolute or irresolute and includes a third random draw (the first and second determine the types of both states), the outcome of which the players do not learn until war is on the point of breaking out. The outcome of this third event, which affects the probability of success in war, is revealed to one player only, who uses it to decide whether to accept the adversary's offered settlement. It turns out that this game has eight different forms of perfect Bayesian equilibria, according to the initial beliefs of both states. These solutions were used by Morrow (1989b) to develop a model of repeated crises, built by repeating this model of isolated crises.

4.6 Conclusions

A recent controversy in the journal *International Security* is a good introduction to our views on the general importance of game models. Assessing the impact of formal approaches to political science, Walt (1999) claimed, "The central aim of social science is to develop knowledge that is relevant to understanding important social problems. Among other things, this task requires theories that are precise, logical, consistent, original, and empirically valid. Formal techniques facilitate the construction of precise and deductively sound arguments, but recent efforts in security studies have generated comparatively few new hypotheses and have for the most part not been tested in a careful and systematic way."

Walt's views drew considerable reaction from Bueno de Mesquita and Morrow (1999), Martin (1999), Niou and Ordeshook (1999), Powell (1999), and Zagare (1999). Rather than join in, we simply quote from Powell's representative response, "The modeling enterprise is a way of trying to improve our understanding of empirical phenomena. Models serve in this enterprise as a tool for disciplining our thinking about the world. ... When mathematical models are well constructed, they offer us a relatively clear and precise language for communicating ideas and intuitions."

Of course, we would not have spent so much effort presenting and developing formal escalation models had we held Walt's view. Like many participants in the controversy, we believe that there are at least three different reasons that justify game-theoretic studies of, for example, negotiation processes. Game models enable the analyst to

- *describe* negotiation processes using a general theory to formulate strategies, information, payoffs, etc., and interpret the outcome – if there is one – in terms of general principles that govern human interaction;
- *gain insight* into negotiation processes, to show how apparently strange or irrational behavior can be understood in terms of a general theory; and
- *advise* those involved in a concrete negotiation process, and to assess outcomes of completed negotiations, in terms of the negotiator's preferences and strategic possibilities.

For the first two purposes, we view game theory as a *descriptive* theory; for the third, we consider it to be a *normative* theory.

As a descriptive theory, game-theoretic models and methods are tools in the search for truth, but in a different way from the natural sciences. According to Muthoo (1999, p. 341), "it cannot be over-emphasized that this theory . . . does not purport to generate falsifiable predictions . . . à la Popper – and indeed it cannot do so, since some of its key ingredients (such as the rationality of the players – which is implicitly embodied in the equilibrium concepts employed) are neither observable nor controllable. As such this theory cannot be tested by an appeal to experimental or field data." We note that this caution is a fundamental restriction on the growing area called experimental game theory or gaming (e.g., Selten 1998), of which the objective is not primarily to confirm or reject theories, but rather to uncover the utilities, and therefore the motivations, of specific individuals or groups.

As Raiffa (1991) pointed out, the purpose of quantitative models of negotiations is insight. We now summarize the insights gained in our study of quantitative models of armament escalation in the context of negotiation.

The generalized Prisoner's Dilemma structure proposed as a simple deterministic model for armament escalation explains the strategic tendency for mutual escalation, even though both sides prefer the status quo. Escalation avoidance is not even an equilibrium unless both sides are relatively content with the status quo and both act symmetrically – without knowledge of the opponent's behavior. And even in this case, mutual escalation remains an equilibrium and tends to occur when each side believes the other is likely to escalate. Thus, there appear to be strong strategic reasons why mutual escalation, though less preferred, is a common occurrence during a negotiation.

The range of occurrence of the no-escalation equilibrium is increased when each side has a probabilistic opportunity to learn the opponent's choice, but the stability of mutual escalation is unchanged. Thus, the tendency to escalate for strategic reasons is somewhat mitigated by the anticipation of future opportunities to react.

In a model of escalation as a negotiation tactic, the two sides choose simultaneously whether to continue negotiation or to escalate. When there is one-sided escalation, the non-escalator may concede or hold firm. This variant leads to outcomes similar to those of the earlier models if neither side is willing to concede. However, willingness to concede can produce a no-escalation equilibrium, which can sometimes be unique. Still, this model seems to corroborate earlier conclusions by suggesting a choice between concession and escalation.

Incomplete information models show that a crisis can sometimes occur when one or both sides is uncertain about the opponent's preferences – even though it would not occur under certainty. These models suggest that escalation can sometimes be an appropriate response to lack of knowledge about the opponent.

In summary, our study shows that quantitative models can provide quantitative assessments of the relevance of various parameters to escalation in negotiation, as well as qualitative insights into some apparently paradoxical negotiation behavior.

Our survey is, of course, incomplete; other applications of quantitative analysis to questions traditionally addressed only by qualitative methods include Wagner (1989) and several models in Zagare and Kilgour (2000). And much research remains to be done, not only in constructing and analyzing models, but also in carrying out case studies that combine careful qualitative analyses of historical arms-race negotiations with solid quantitative modeling.

Overall, we believe that quantitative modeling is crucial to the study of negotiation, and in particular to the study of escalation in negotiation. Raiffa (1991, p. 9) described the situation very well:

> Regrettably, a lot of profound theorizing by economists, mathematicians, philosophers, and game theorists on topics related to negotiation analysis has had little or no impact on practice. An important question for the PIN Project to answer will be why this is so. An important reason is clearly the lack of effective communication and dissemination of theoretical research results. Such communication could be improved if there were more intermediaries who are comfortable in both worlds and who could act as inventive go-betweens to facilitate the transfer of information that shows how theory can influence practice and how practice can influence the research agendas of theorists. The information must flow in both directions: many practitioners have developed valid, extremely useful, and often profound insights and analyses, which should help to guide the agendas of researchers in this field.

References

Avenhaus R & Fichtner J (1984). A review of Richardson models. In *Quantitative Assessment in Arms Control*, eds. Avenhaus R & Huber RK, pp. 143–178. New York, NY, USA: Plenum Press.

Brito D (1972). A dynamic model of an armament race. *International Economic Review* **13**:359–375.

Bueno de Mesquita B & Morrow JD (1999). Sorting through the wealth of nations. *International Security* **24**:56–73.

Busch PA (1970). Appendix: Mathematical models of arms races. In *What Price Vigilance?*, ed. Russett BM, pp. 193–233. New Haven, CT, USA: Yale University Press.

Churchill, WS (1948). *The Gathering Storm*. Boston, MA, USA: Houghton Mifflin.

Cioffi-Revilla CA (1979). *Mathematical Models in International Relations: A Bibliography*. Technical Paper No. 4. Los Angeles, CA, USA: Institute for Research in Social Science.

Downs GW & Rocke DM (1990). *Tacit Bargaining, Arms Race, and Arms Control*. Ann Arbor, MI, USA: University of Michigan Press.

Glynn P (1992). *Closing Pandora's Box: Arms Races, Arms Control, and the History of the Cold War*. New York, NY, USA: Basic Books.

Intriligator MD (1976). Formal models of arms races. *Journal of Peace Science* **2**:77–88.

Intriligator MD (1982). Research on conflict theory. *Journal of Conflict Resolution* **26**:307–328.

Kennedy RF (1969). *Thirteen Days: A Memoir of the Cuban Missile Crisis*. New York, NY, USA: Norton.

Kilgour DM & Zagare FC (1991). Credibility, uncertainty, and deterrence. *American Journal of Political Science* **35**:305–334.

Martin LL (1999). The contributions of rational choice: A defense of pluralism. *International Security* **24**:74–83.

Moll KD & Luebbert GM (1980). Arms race and military expenditure models. *Journal of Conflict Resolution* **24**:153–185.

Morrow JD (1989a). Capabilities, uncertainty and resolve: A limited information model of crisis bargaining. *American Journal of Political Science* **33**:941–972.

Morrow JD (1989b). Bargaining in repeated crisis: A limited information model. In *Models of Strategic Choice in Politics*, ed. Ordeshook P, pp. 207–228. Ann Arbor, MI, USA: University of Michigan Press.

Morrow JD (1994). *Game Theory for Political Scientists*. Princeton, NJ, USA: Princeton University Press.

Muthoo A (1999). *Bargaining Theory with Applications*. Cambridge, UK: Cambridge University Press.

Nash JF (1951). Non-cooperative games. *Annals of Mathematics* **54**:286–295.

Niou EMS & Ordeshook PC (1999). Return to the Luddites. *International Security* **24**:84–96.

Ordeshook PC (1986). *Game Theory and Political Theory*. New York, NY, USA: Cambridge University Press.

Osborne MJ & Rubinstein A (1994). *A Course in Game Theory*. Cambridge, MA, USA: The MIT Press.

Powaski RE (1987). *March to Armageddon: The USA and the Nuclear Arms Race, 1939 to the Present*. New York, NY, USA: Oxford University Press.

Powell R (1999). The modeling enterprise and security studies. *International Security* **24**:97–106.

Raiffa H (1991). Contributions of applied systems analysis to international negotiation. In *International Negotiation*, ed. Kremenyuk VA, pp. 5–21. San Francisco, CA, USA: Jossey-Bass.

Rapoport A & Lewis F (1957). Richardson's mathematical theory of war. *Journal of Conflict Resolution* **1**:249–304.

Richardson LF (1939). Generalized foreign politics. *British Journal of Psychology* **23**(Suppl.):1–91.

Richardson LF (1960). *Arms and Insecurity*. Pittsburgh, PA, USA: Boxwood Press.

Sandler T & Hartley K (1995). *The Economics of Defense*. Cambridge, UK: Cambridge University Press.

Selten R (1998). Game theory, experience, rationality. In *Game Theory, Experience, Rationality*, eds. Leinfellner W & Koehler E, pp. 9–34. Dordrecht, The Netherlands: Kluwer Academic Publishers, 1998.

Simaan M & Cruz JB (1973). A multistage game formulation of arms race and control and its relationship to Richardson's model. *Modeling and Simulation* **4**:149–153.

Simaan M & Cruz JB (1975). Formulation of Richardson's model of the arms race from a differential game viewpoint. *Review of Economic Studies* **42**:67–77.

Wagner RH (1983). The theory of games and the problem of international cooperation. *American Political Science Review* **79**:330–346.

Wagner RH (1989). Uncertainty, rational learning, and bargaining in the Cuban missile crisis. In *Models of Strategic Choice in Politics*, ed. Ordeshook P, pp. 177–205. Ann Arbor, MI, USA: University of Michigan Press.

Walt SM (1999). Rigor or rigor mortis. *International Security* **23**:5–48.

Zagare FC (1999). All mortis, no rigor. *International Security* **24**:107–114.

Zagare FC & Kilgour DM (2000). *Perfect Deterrence*. Cambridge, UK: Cambridge University Press.

Chapter 5

Entrapment in International Negotiations

Paul W. Meerts

5.1   Introduction

Entrapment is drowning in a swamp: the more we move, the more the swamp drags us down. It is playing roulette: the more we lose, the more we want to compensate our losses. We can be emotionally tied to a negative development. Rationally speaking we should stop, but we do not want to lose face or the resources already invested in the process, so instead we continue, running the risk of eventually losing much more than if we had cut our losses at an early stage. According to prospect theory (Kahneman and Tversky 1979), people are much more willing to take risks in order to prevent losses than to gain profits. Positive prospects generate risk avoidance; negative prospects induce risk taking if and only if one of the parties has already invested substantially and is in the process of risking the loss of those investments.

Escalation is a mark of conflict's dynamics, as is entrapment. Like escalation, entrapment is an increase in a conflict situation. However, in entrapment, the balance will be lost: one party is getting a stronger grip on the other party, which is losing its grip. In many cases it is the stronger party that sees its alternatives diminish, often through its own actions. This is due both to the reactions of the weaker party and to the specific landscape in which the entrapment situation develops. Escalation is betrayed by smoke, caused by the heat of an ever-intensifying fight. Entrapment is smoke and mirrors: reality lies behind smoke screens and cannot be judged in a balanced and objective way. One is not sure about the enemy, its strengths and weaknesses, or its actual position and intention. If escalation is a mutually coercive mechanism embedded in a conflict perspective, then entrapment is a mutually coercive mechanism embedded in a conflict with gradually diminishing perspectives for one of the parties involved – often the one that seemed to be in the most favorable position at the beginning of the process. Slowly but surely, the odds turn: the weaker becomes the stronger.

Entrapment is characterized by a specific context favorable for limiting the freedom of one contender and enhancing that of the other. The ladder image of escalation holds for entrapment, but the direction is reversed: one goes down the ladder, not up. The aim, however, is the same, namely, trying to reach a specific objective. Entrapment is downward escalation – not in the sense of de-escalation, but in the sense of moving toward an ever-intensifying conflict that limits our abilities. By investing more, we hope to regain our freedom to maneuver, recoup our investments, and win the game. Since we are stronger than the other party, this hope is well grounded. However, we overlook the funnel effect that limits our choices. The context, not the other party, is our real enemy. While escalation is an increase in new dimensions, entrapment is an increasing loss of alternatives. We are losing dimensions, becoming a one-dimensional man with only one choice: move on or withdraw. As long as the last option is not seen as realistic, the caravan will move on and the dynamics of entrapment will continue unabated.

Like escalation, entrapment means increasing efforts, expanding demands, adding unrelated issues, upping investments, drawing in other actors, demonizing the other party, enhancing risks, increasing expenditures, and making stronger commitments. But entrapment is more than escalation; it also comprises loss of choice, loss of freedom, loss of alternatives, and thus loss of power. In other words, step by step, one of the parties is losing out as the process develops, and this loss of strength becomes more and more apparent. As it becomes known to the outside world, another negative factor adds to the sorrow of the losing party, namely, the loss of face or honor. In other words, emotions enter the stage and add to the material losses. Whereas escalation is often quite businesslike and tends to remain a relatively objective development, entrapment turns subjective. While the emotional argument is normally completely overshadowed by logical reasoning at the beginning of the process of entrapment, it often becomes dominant by the end. A normative stand overtakes rational reasoning, at which point those who support reason are often seen as traitors.

As with escalation, in entrapment the stakes are raised, but the options become limited, at least for one of the parties. The process becomes unbalanced, and often the weaker party compensates for its lack of strength by using the context to its advantage. While in escalation the transitive element remains dominant in many cases, in entrapment the intransitive or "irrational" factor often dominates the scene. As in escalation, judgmental bias is one of the motors for entrapment. The factors that might de-escalate the process are the same for escalation and entrapment. The main difference is that the options for using them are less frequently available in the latter as a consequence of the one-dimensional character of entrapment processes. In this sense, entrapment can be regarded as a subcategory of escalation, stressing the importance of the context in which the process of international negotiation develops.

Entrapment in international negotiations is a form of escalation whereby parties involved in an interactive, nonviolent decision-making process with others with whom they have both common and conflicting interests find themselves unable to escape from the costs and investments they have already made. Brockner and Rubin (1985, p. 5) define entrapment as a decision-making process in which individuals strengthen their commitment to a previously chosen, though failing, course of action to justify or recover the prior investments. This chapter addresses entrapment in international negotiations and focuses on the behavior of states when they attempt to reconcile divergent interests in situations in which common ground is scarce and control difficult. As a form of escalation, entrapment can be a transitive (i.e., initiated) or intransitive (i.e., phenomenal) process, although these two types are dealt with together as they are not always easy to keep apart in practice and they share similar characteristics.

Entrapment in the context of international negotiations is one of the most fascinating and destructive of negotiation processes. A party that is "entrapped" (or that entraps itself) is in an unenviable position. For individuals who find themselves entrapped, the consequences can be serious in the sense that they lose out on a deal they had hoped to achieve. For organizations or countries, the effects can be disastrous. Whole international systems can become entrapped, and the consequences of such a situation often run out of control. An example of this is the situation in the world during the period of US–Soviet confrontation from 1950 to 1990. "The Cold War" is simply a shorthand way of describing the entrapment of the two superpowers at the time, caught in a "Balance of Terror" (Schelling 1963, p. 239). Nuclear power led the protagonists into the trap, and because of the global nature of the force involved, the whole world was caught in that trap as well. The same kinds of mechanism can also be seen in the nuclear and conventional arms races between countries such as India and Pakistan, albeit on a regional rather than a global scale.

The essence of entrapment is that, even though one or more of the parties may not like the agreement they seem to be moving toward, they find it extremely difficult to extricate themselves from the process. Entrapment occurs when the shape of the negotiation process is like a gorge that has a wide entrance that slowly but surely becomes narrower and narrower. One or more of the parties is left with increasingly less room for maneuver, so that at a certain point they can no longer turn back and are forced to work toward an agreement that they are finding less and less attractive. Even when they can still turn back, entrapped parties – like gamblers who are very much aware that they are losing but want to recover some of the losses they have already suffered – are often compelled to continue. When individuals or groups find themselves in this situation, an appropriate response is pity. However, when it happens to countries or the international system itself, then alarm bells should really start to ring. Leaders can guide a nation into entrapment situations, without its citizens being aware of it. "The apathy of the masses and their need for guidance has its counterpart in the leaders' natural greed for power" (Michels 1966, p. 205). Entrapment is both transitive and intransitive escalation, feeding each other.

Entrapment is thus a special form of escalation, in which the process itself has an enormous impact on the party's perception of the best alternative to a negotiated agreement, or BATNA (Fisher *et al.* 1991). The alternatives are at the same time increasingly better and increasingly worse. In this chapter, I first offer an analysis of the characteristics of entrapment (choice, uncertainty, investment, and repetition) and then consider the various levels at which it occurs (personal, interpersonal, national, and international). I then turn to examine the major factors involved (planning, information, communication, and control) and present and analyze a case study that is suitable for teaching negotiators about entrapment, and draw appropriate lessons from it. I had the opportunity to train diplomats from 60 countries all over the world and was therefore able to observe their behavior in exercises on strategy and tactics, skills and styles, risk and trust. In this chapter, I use the outcomes of these exercises to illustrate entrapment processes. In a final section, I summarize my main findings and briefly discuss entrapment as a strategic mode.

5.2   Characteristics

5.2.1   Choice

Entrapment is the result of choices made – not just one or two, but many of them; small, step-by-step decisions that result in a step-by-step loss of room for maneuver. In principle, a party that enters negotiations has complete freedom of choice. (In practice, this is not always true, of course, and in any event complete freedom of choice is probably an illusion.) Although there may be different degrees of freedom of choice at the start of entrapment processes, some freedom – or at least the *perception* of a certain degree of freedom – is a prerequisite for any negotiations. Brute force cannot be regarded as a type of international negotiation; rather, it should be seen as an alternative to negotiation. In negotiations, the parties decide on matters jointly, although power is rarely evenly balanced.

A dreadful example of entrapment was the treatment of the Jews by the Nazis during the Holocaust. They often tried to make Jews responsible for the deportation of other Jews. To persuade them to cooperate, the Nazis tried to hide their true intentions until the Jews had been sufficiently entrapped so that they could no longer escape from the process. The Nazis divided Jewish communities into several groups to whom they gave different guarantees of protection. Many of those with the highest degree of protection were willing to cooperate in the selection and transportation of their fellow Jews to save the other echelons. At the same time, these collaborators, who were often well intentioned, found themselves in an increasingly difficult position as a result of their collaboration. The deeper they became involved in the process, the more difficult it became for them to extricate themselves. They believed that negotiation with the Nazis over the fate of some of their kinsmen would save the lives of many others by buying time. However, as the German clergyman Martin Niemoeller once said, "First they came and took the communists, and I didn't protest because I wasn't a communist. Then they came and took the trade unionists, and I didn't protest because I wasn't a trade unionist. Then they came and took the Jews, and I didn't protest because I wasn't a Jew. Then they came and they took me . . . and there was nobody left to protest against that."

The behavior of these collaborators ensured that the process of the Holocaust could proceed smoothly, with a minimum of effort on the part of the Nazis and with a minimum loss of time. This meant that the Nazis did not need to use too many resources. Although they probably would have been able to force the Jews into the death camps without using entrapment techniques, doing so would have reduced their capacity to wage war on their military enemies. The Jews – and prisoners of war – were also forced to work for the Germans and thus support their captors against their potential protectors, the Allies. The Germans tended to use these tactics more in Western Europe (where the situation was more transparent and the population less anti-Jewish) than in Central and Eastern Europe, where mass killings were often committed. However, as we shall see, even there entrapment tactics were used, as in the city of Vilnius, for example (Szur 1997).

By choosing to embark on a process, you weaken your ability to exit that process. However, this particular loss of control may be more than compensated for because participation in the process could give you greater control over some matters within the process that would otherwise have been beyond your reach. This means there are two kinds of choice: those related to the process and those related to the situation. Entering into an alliance with others entails sharing control over the process and the structures that direct that process. Creating greater situational control within the main process and within the structures may be a better choice than trying to keep what in theory is absolute control, but may actually turn out to be control over nothing. What is decisive is the substance of control: for what purpose does a state desire control and freedom of choice? If the result is reduced control over a more substantial economy, a state may decide to cede absolute control in exchange for less control over a better situation. Leaders can decide to force their people into a situation by destroying their alternatives, and so deliberately limit choice. "He [the general] puts his troops in a position where they have no choice but to fight and stay alive" (Chung 1991, p. 12). However, it is important to consider to what extent this situation is actually an improvement. One cannot be certain that entrapment is not just around the corner – which brings up the question of uncertainty.

5.2.2   Uncertainty

Uncertainty is a hallmark of any negotiation. Negotiators have a natural tendency to keep their hands as free as possible, and thereby create uncertainty. In the simulation game "Crisis in Yugoslavia," participants "tried to prevent attacks by keeping their positions veiled as long as this seemed possible" (Meerts 1989, p. 346). Negotiators start off with a lack of knowledge, not only of the other party, but often of their own situation as well. Their instructions are often fuzzy, being the result of a bargaining process within the bureaucracy. Some diplomats are quite outspoken on this. "I never," wrote Lord Malmesbury, "received an instruction that was worth reading" (Nicholson 1998, p. 81). Negotiators need time before and during the actual negotiations to gather as much information as possible, not only about the subject matter, but also about the negotiators they have to deal with: their skills, style, character, and culture, as well as the political system and bureaucracy they represent, and so on. Culture has a decisive effect on the question of exploring for information. In some cultures, people shy away from a lengthy process of ambiguous reconnaissance, and negotiators want to tackle the business "straightaway." In other cultures, the exploration phase is considered essential for a proper evaluation of the negotiation situation.

But however much exploration occurs before the process starts and however much time is spent on exploration before the actual bargaining phase, one will not have all the information needed until the entire negotiation process has occurred. The negotiation process is not a neutral instrument. It has an impact on itself, because complete information can only be obtained in a step-by-step sequence; as information is released in small bits, this influences the direction of the process as a whole. In other words, obtaining all the information required takes time. But time can be dangerous. It can be manipulated – for example, by setting deadlines and thereby forcing the negotiators into taking decisions. Without deadlines, international negotiations have a tendency to go on forever. This is because certain countries want to make progress on certain problems, but they know that the other states will not accept certain proposals unless several months or years of negotiations have been invested in them, and so the former procrastinate. So much progress would not have been made in the European Union (EU), for example, without the deadline of the change of the Presidency every six months. It is, of course, possible to exclude uncertainty about one's intentions, as in the Chicken game (Garnett 1975). However, this might have disastrous consequences.

Conversely, deadlines can be moved or not set. If the situation changes in favor of one of the parties, that party may use time to change the balance of power, in which case time works in their favor. Without having to make any additional demands, one of the parties may maneuver itself into a stronger position and entrap the other side by using time as its weapon. Time, often overlooked by the other party, is one of the most effective tools in an entrapment strategy. It adds to uncertainty, which makes it one of the elements negotiators need to focus on if they want to avoid (or create) a trap. Negotiators need time to be sure about certain points in the negotiations. However, time may also create uncertainty: the context may change and the direction in which it is changing may be unpredictable.

Uncertainty about the nature of the relationship between the negotiators on the two sides can also be used as a tool in entrapment, because the relationship can be manipulated. By creating the impression that you and your opponent have an excellent relationship, it is possible to suggest the existence of a degree of trust that is not really there. Trust is therefore an element of uncertainty that should be added to the role of time management. Negotiators need to examine the negotiation situation closely to decide whether the other party can be trusted. If one of the parties benefits from breaking the relationship, additional measures need to be taken. A good relationship is no longer enough, and guarantees need to be asked for. Prisoner's Dilemma games are an excellent tool for training negotiators to deal with the matter of trust (Siebe 1991, pp. 181–185; Hayes 1991, pp. 365–366).

The more insecure the situation, the more trust is needed and the more difficult it is to build up trust. If emotions enter into the proceedings (and trust is, after all, closely related to emotion), negative influences may be expected. Positive emotions can reduce the uncertainty and can therefore lower the chances that a process of entrapment will arise. However, positive emotions can also lead to entrapment. If they are absent (i.e., if trust is low and the relationship is not good), negotiators take care not to be trapped. They may move slowly and seem indecisive, like Fabius the Procrastinator, who avoided joining battle with Hannibal. However, if positive emotions are present, entrapment may result for two reasons:

- first, because one side may trust the other without there being a good reason to do so;
- second, because if negotiators within the same team like one another, they may not be sufficiently critical of one another's behavior, which leads to "group think."

An example of the second case was the entrapment of the Dutch during the negotiations on the Maastricht Treaty. Negotiators within the Dutch Foreign Ministry's team failed to react to negative signals because they were convinced that their own strategy was right and no one within the group dared to criticize the others. Positive emotions may thus be dangerous (see Chapter 4 on the effects of uncertainty).

The Roman Senate was not happy with Fabius' procrastination and replaced him with two consuls who stormed forward and were – quite literally – trapped at Cannae. Hannibal did not really do anything. He just started off with a certain formation, and the Romans, through their own push and power, simply entrapped themselves. In this case, it was not so much uncertainty that led to entrapment as the false sense of security that arose because the Romans underestimated their enemy, or overestimated their own strength. More powerful countries often overestimate themselves, which can lead to their entrapment by the weaker party. Uncertainty may give rise to caution, while certainty may lead to recklessness and to entrapment. Uncertainty can function as a warning signal and is therefore a factor that can help cautious negotiators to avoid entrapment.

5.2.3   Investment

To avoid entrapment, it is therefore important to keep control of the investments: losing track of these may easily lead to entrapment. A party that is losing control of its investments may try to regain control with new investments that escalate the investment process. If these investments are also lost, entrapment becomes more difficult to avoid. Abandoning this situation may mean losing invested concessions, and since such a loss may be unacceptable on the home front, more investments may have to be made to try to recoup those that have been lost. Huge losses can be sustained during such a process of entrapment, but the gradual nature of the process means the magnitude of such losses may not become apparent until the mid-game phase, by which time too much has been invested to make turning back an option. On the other hand, further investments may lead to even greater losses and further entrapment. In this dilemma, a higher authority needs to step in to take responsibility for cutting losses. In other words, a General de Gaulle is needed to call a halt to the spiral of entrapment. He or she should be careful not to become part and parcel of the entrapment process. If this happens, the intervention of the "Deus ex machina" might create an even more dangerous situation.

Investment in the negotiations may take either a material or an emotional form. Negotiators are tied to the success or failure of the negotiations: their position, their status, their face is involved. Depending on their cultural backgrounds, this investment of the self can be serious to a greater or lesser degree. In many cases, emotional investment is a more serious matter than material investment. This is because material investment can be viewed with a certain distance, a certain objectivity. Losses are never pleasant, but they may be compensated by gains elsewhere. The more senior the officials are, and the greater the overview and power they possess, the more likely they are to be in a good position to compensate for the loss of A by the gain of B. If B is more important than A, this combination of losses and gains may even be part of a deliberate strategy of gambits. Decisions may be taken on a purely businesslike basis, even to the extent of ruthlessly sacrificing negotiations in one sector to give negotiations in another sector a chance of being successful.

However, such a chess game cannot be played easily if emotional investments are at stake. People are not flexible in matters such as face and status. "People responsible for a losing course of action will invest further than those not responsible for prior losses . . . people can become so committed to a position that they will pay more for a monetary reward than it is worth" (Staw and Hoang 1995, p. 474). It is not easy to "separate the people from the problem," and it is often not desirable to cut the links between the two (Fisher *et al.* 1991). Negotiators are human beings, and like most human beings they prefer to win, not lose. This is again very much a cultural matter. To prevent loss of face and faith, negotiators are often inclined to invest at a stage at which investment is no longer wise. This self-propelling nature of the immaterial side of investment may be of greater importance in explaining the dynamics of entrapment processes than the material side. The emotional side of investment is more difficult to handle than the material side. To keep control of the situation, the negotiators themselves need to be brought under control. The way to do this is to send in a higher-level person, if one is available and willing. High-ranking officials are often unwilling to step into an entrapment situation, as they will be blamed if things go wrong. And the higher they are in the hierarchy, the farther they may fall. High-ranking people are also in a position to shy away from involvement, as they are not easily commanded by others.

Much depends, therefore, on the position of the negotiator in the hierarchy of his or her organization. If the negotiator has a very senior, or even the most senior, position, entrapment is an imminent danger. Who is going to turn the minister around? Who dares to contradict the dictator if it means endangering one's life? The higher the rank of the negotiator directly involved in an entrapped situation, the greater the danger that entrapment will escalate. A Dutch minister who criticized Japanese policy relating to the World Trade Organization did not appear to know, for instance, that Japan had been a member of the organization from the very outset. Obviously, she was mistaking Japan for China. To make such a mistake during a visit to Japan is, of course, unforgivable. The civil servant who sat next to the minister, however, did not dare to correct such an enormous blunder. As a result, the minister repeated the mistake. The minister's civil servant did not dare to lose credibility (i.e., investments) by contradicting her, and left it to the situation to correct his superior. Even after the mistake was ultimately made clear to her, she tried to justify herself. One reason for this self-justification is the tendency to "associate persistence ... with strong leadership" (Staw and Ross 1987, p. 70). "[R]egardless of any need to justify, individuals may also learn that consistency in action is a more desirable leadership strategy than experimentation. Such an implicit theory of leadership would mean that many individuals would choose to remain committed to a dubious course of action simply because the opportunity to receive a positive evaluation by others would be greater in the case of consistency than with experimentation" (Staw and Ross 1980, p. 259).

5.2.4 Repetition

Entrapment is made up of a series of incidents. This makes it relatively invisible, and also relatively stable. One of the parties (or sometimes both) is devoured, bit by bit. The first move in entrapment is often made by the party that will ultimately be trapped, and the entrapment occurs through the assertiveness of that party. This is one of the most interesting characteristics of entrapment processes: victims are often trapped by their own actions. The party that uses the circumstances in which entrapment becomes possible often plays a somewhat passive role – with entrapment being rather like quicksand or a gin trap that is already there. Victims become increasingly ensnared as a result of their own actions and emotions in an intransitive escalation. Each move forward by the victim serves to make the trap more effective. Neither the trap nor the trapper needs to do much to add to this.

Entrapment may be seen as an escalator moving downward, not upward. In this sense, entrapment may be viewed as the counterpart of escalation. It shares the step-by-step nature of a development in which tension mounts with each successive step. Steadily, the crisis evolves until an almost inevitable finale. It is a balanced evolution that leads to revolutionary consequences. The differences between this and escalation are, however, the step-by-step growth of an imbalance in power and the step-by-step fixation of the situation. Entrapment could be defined as a stable process of escalation in which one (or more) of the parties systematically loses out as a result of his or her own actions. The growing imbalance of power is channeled into an environment that creates a kind of self-fulfilling prophecy, a kind of predestined situation. As in escalation, exit options begin to disappear, but normally only for one of the two parties; and step-by-step investments are increasingly made, but more by one party than the other. It is possible, however, for both parties to be entrapped, with the same mediation working on each.

Roger Fisher used a Prisoner's Dilemma game – the Alba–Batia game – to train people to understand entrapment. This has been used extensively to confront players with issues such as trust; insecurity; implementation; win–win, win–lose, and lose–lose situations; and emotional, rational, and irrational behavior. By replacing Alba and Batia with real names of countries and realistic situations (such as Iran and Azerbaijan negotiating an oil deal, or Mongolia and China negotiating a cashmere wool deal), cultural elements can be brought into play as well. Depending on how the game develops, it can illustrate either one-sided or mutual entrapment. As trust diminishes and emotions rise, an entrapment context is created, and one or both negotiation teams may fall victim to it. They will win much less than they could, and the third party will gain from this lack of cooperation. Again, we see the hallmark of entrapment: the third party, doing nothing, not being present, not being able to act or exert power, may win because of the counterproductive actions of the negotiating partners.

In this exercise, two negotiation teams decide on the price of oil or other product deliveries to a third country. In the first round, the delegations decide on a price without being able to negotiate on it. In a second, third, or fourth (etc.) round, parties may bargain about the price to be set for the round under consideration. The game master can introduce variation by calling for negotiation in only even-numbered rounds, inserting a mediator, adding additional negotiators to the actual talks, calling for an international conference of all parties, or doubling or tripling the stakes. In a normal game, the parties discuss their strategy and tactics, and formulate a mandate for one of the team members, who is sent to meet the envoy of the opposing side. The two envoys negotiate a price, but they need to "sell" their results to their own delegations. Each delegation then either decides to stick to the agreement or to renege on it. Only after they have taken their final decision at the end of each round do the teams hear the results.

This creates, of course, the typical insecurity of the Prisoner's Dilemma, or a price war. Teams are inclined to start in an avoidance manner by setting the lowest price on which they cannot be undercut. In a subsequent round, they try to negotiate trust and to raise the price for the absent third party. If both raise their prices, the third party suffers. If one of the two decides on a lower price than its counterpart in the negotiation, that party undercuts the market of the other side and therefore makes a good profit. The third party, by choosing the cheapest product, therefore provides that product's party with a relative gain, while the opponent who set too high a price makes a relative loss. The losing side normally retaliates by lowering its price at the next step and both often end up charging the lowest price possible.

They are in a mutually entrapped situation, which is beneficial for the consumer country. The producers can only escape from the trap by investing in their mutual relationship, that is, by risking a gambit – by conceding in the next round, and thereby compensating the side that made a relative loss in one of the earlier rounds. In most cases, the teams end up with a relative joint loss. In some cases they regain trust and end up well. In exceptional cases, by keeping their promises from beginning to end, they do not become trapped in the downward spiral of mistrust.

These oil-price exercises are a fine illustration of the impact of successive rounds on tendencies toward entrapment. The repetitive character of the rounds raises the tension, but the repetition is also a resource. It creates opportunities for doing better and restoring trust, as time is available. Depending on the skills and styles of the negotiators, their communication with each other and with their own party is decisive in overcoming the tendencies toward entrapment. The game therefore also demonstrates how effective negotiation can offer the option to restore trust and escape entrapment. Handling the emotional side is an essential factor here. More than the actual relative losses, emotions are the difficult factors in the game. People feel betrayed: they are angry and they want revenge. They end up in an entrapped lose–lose situation. They could escape, but they are often unwilling to take the risk. They prefer to punish the other side, and thereby punish themselves as well. They know that a good settlement would be good for both sides, but they no longer want the other side to benefit. They are prepared to lose, provided that the other side loses as well. Although they normally start out with full confidence in the other party, the structure of the game often leads them into entrapment.

5.3   Levels

5.3.1   Personal

Given that human beings react not only to their environment, but at least as much to their inner world, entrapment cannot be seen solely as a contextual development. To adapt Marx, to a large extent the basic structure determines the upper structures. The psyche of the negotiator is as important to understanding the mechanics of entrapment processes as the factors analyzed in the previous section on characteristics. The inner world of the negotiator can be viewed from many angles, but here we limit ourselves to the question of how to deal with the psychological dimension of one's own behavior and of the actions of the other side in the context of the entrapment process in international negotiations.

In psychoanalysis, we need to examine the negotiator's past to understand part of his or her reactions during the process of entrapment. As this process develops and stress builds up, personal characteristics start to play an increasingly important role. Matters and feelings that lurk in the shadows will appear as higher levels of stress force them out into the open. When these become explicit, they affect the entrapment process as an important semi-autonomous factor. Furthermore, negotiators themselves spend a lot of energy trying to understand the other party, and thereby forget about their own psychological processes. If the negotiators are part of the crisis they are bargaining about, there is a serious risk that they will be carried away by their own experiences and traumas. They become ensnared in their own and their opponents' psychological frames, and thus complicate and exacerbate the entrapment process as it proceeds.

As it is impossible to dig into the psyche of the other negotiator, it absolutely essential to at least investigate the background of one's opponent and the culture and the political history of his or her country, while at the same time being aware of one's own culture and experiences, and their impact on one's own behavior. It is difficult to judge the negotiation behavior of Armenians in negotiations with the Turks if one is unaware of the genocide that took place in the early twentieth century. How could we judge the Israelis' negotiation behavior in talks with Palestinians if we were to overlook the Shoah and the probability that old enmities and sufferings would affect negotiations with others who might also be seen as enemies? This shadow of the past, the projection of old images on fresh situations, is a quite common phenomenon in international relations, not only in the Balkans, the Caucasus, and the Middle East, but also in Western Europe between, say, the French and the Germans, the Irish and the British, and so on. Negotiators have to live with these "facts of life"; since they cannot be stamped out, the negotiators must teach themselves how to deal with them.

Observing the behavior of the opponent is the second tool negotiators use to better understand the motivation and psychological needs of those on the other side of the table. Nonverbal behavior, especially nonverbal leaks, unveil the real intentions of the negotiator. However, for a nonexpert it is extremely difficult to read them correctly (Goodfield 1999). Behavioral analysis as such is not sufficient and has to be supplemented by the background knowledge mentioned above. One may combine both by making good use of the corridors. In the informal talks that take place there, as in plenary sessions, both verbal and nonverbal signs should be registered. The informal talks may disclose more about the personality of the other negotiator, while in plenary sessions we are probably limited to observations of more superficial signals. To probe deeper in informal talks, it is often necessary to open oneself up to an extent that could be dangerous during the rest of the negotiations, as it might give the other side material that could be used for the purposes of blackmail. On the other hand, trust can only be established by opening oneself up, at least to a degree. This is one of the more difficult dilemmas in negotiation processes in general, and in entrapment in particular. Openness can work both ways. There are many dreadful examples of negotiators doing things to cover up mistakes that, when discovered by the other party, trigger serious entrapment processes.

All negotiators view reality through their own spectacles; these are necessary if one is to come to grips with reality, but they also shape and color the situation one observes. "The moment we want to say *who* somebody is, our vocabulary leads us astray in saying *what* somebody is . . . with the result that his specific uniqueness escapes us" (Arendt 1958, p. 181). The greater the gap between oneself and the other negotiator, the greater the risk of a serious distortion and the greater the risk of miscommunication. Being misled by one's own and the other negotiator's misperceptions creates an ideal breeding ground for entrapment. This leads to the conclusion that one must check the negotiators' understanding of their own mandate and the negotiation process as such. They will need to check their own perceptions as well, especially in processes prone to entrapment, since misperceptions are one of the main sources of entrapment and one of the most difficult to eliminate.

5.3.2 Interpersonal

The chemistry between negotiators is one of the factors that determines the success or failure of a negotiation. If the chemistry is not good, then entrapment processes are unlikely to occur as a result of the psychological dimension of the process. Negotiators who have negative feelings toward their opponents are very careful not to become trapped: negotiators are unlikely to be trapped if they feel they cannot trust the other party. The paradox of entrapment is that the negotiators need to build trust for the trap to work. And since entrapment is not just a question of creating a one-time trap situation, trust needs to be implemented in such a way that the other side only starts to mistrust the opponent when it is already too late to withdraw. However, since entrapment also very much depends on the situation and the way in which that situation arises, outright deception may not be necessary. Also, the action is mainly undertaken by the entrapped party, not the "entrapper." But it is vital that the entrapped side take the view that the only way to escape the trap is to move forward, not to withdraw. It is here that the entrapper needs to create certain carrots and sticks with which to entice or goad the party into the trap.

The relationship between the two parties is therefore an important factor. It might be argued that if the negotiators know each other well, entrapment is unlikely to occur. After all, ambiguity is an important element of entrapment. However, it could also be argued that negotiators who do not know each other well view the actions of the other side in a more distant and rational way. They may therefore notice the entrapment signals quite early in the process. Those who are emotionally close to the other party, by contrast, may overlook the signals of entrapment, since their feelings prevail over their reason. Indeed, many entrapment situations occur if there is emotional closeness between the parties. Emotional closeness blurs one's view, which has already been shaped by past experiences. It is extremely difficult to change one's focus from what one is accustomed to or expects and to see things differently.

Here we have another paradox in entrapment negotiation: to avoid being entrapped, one must try to understand the other party. It is therefore necessary to keep an eye on the psychological makeup both of the other party and of oneself. However, one should not become engrossed in this, as it distorts the clarity of one's vision, which can lead to entrapment. Emotional closeness should therefore be avoided, as it is one of the elements of entrapment processes. The closer people work together, the more likely they are to become emotionally attached and the more likely they are to become entrapped. For example, during the hostage crisis in Iran "President Carter ultimately lost faith in the reports of his 'man-on-the-spot' in Teheran, William Sullivan. But . . . Carter continued to rely on some of Sullivan's reports for some time . . . and . . . did not dispense with a resident ambassador but sent out a second one" (Berridge 1995, p. 42). Another example is provided by the Dutch Foreign Ministry during the Dutch Presidency of the EU. A group of diplomats who worked on a draft treaty for the Maastricht meeting knew each other well and had the same views about the content of the treaty they wanted. They turned a deaf ear to warnings from the Dutch Permanent Representation in Brussels that the Germans would not agree. This "group-think" led to entrapment. In general, diplomats are quite open to signals from the outside world. They have developed a sixth sense about potential traps in international relations. Civil servants, however, often are not very sensitive to the entrapments of international politics. As civil servants are becoming more important as international negotiators and are even taking over the hegemony of the diplomat within the EU (Meerts 1999), entrapment processes may become more frequent and more successful in the sphere of international relations. In general, negotiators should be open to one another, but in some cases it can be useful to avoid being influenced by the people on the other side of the table. The famous Dutch captain of industry Frits Philips "admonished his negotiators not to listen too well to their opponents because by listening they would run the risk of being convinced" (LePoole 1991, p. 34). At the same time, however, negotiators should be close enough to their opponents to detect certain signals that can be used to avoid entrapment.

5.3.3 National

Systemic factors are also at work. If a society is very individualistic, then entrapment in negotiation may be less likely, whereas if a society is more collectivist, then entrapment may occur more often. Hofstede (1980) defines individualism as a situation in which people look after themselves and their immediate family only. Collectivism is seen as a situation in which people belong to in-groups (families, clans, or organizations) who look after the group members in exchange for loyalty. In a collectivist political system, civil servants see their ministry as a network of alliances, whereas in an individualistic political system, the ministry may be seen as a machine. In an individualistic system, people may be less vulnerable to entrapment, as they are less dependent on relationships. Entrapment may therefore occur more frequently in Asian countries, which often score high on collectivism, than in European countries. However, to claim that entrapment is encountered less frequently in wealthier countries than in poorer countries would certainly be going too far.

Interpersonal communication depends partly on the systemic environment, and that environment differs depending on the society or the ministry in which one lives or works. But individuals exercise their own judgment as well, and they can go against the undercurrents in the system within which they operate. People's characters also influence their interpersonal relationships in an entrapment situation, their norms, their values, their experiences in life, and, of course, their living conditions. Hofstede (1980) also introduced the distinction between competitive and cooperative societies (although he used different terms). In competitive societies, the dominant values are achievement and success; in cooperative societies, the dominant values are caring for others and quality of life. To entrap another party is a competitive, or distributive, activity. We may therefore expect entrapment to happen more often in societies in which negotiators take a competitive stand. In line with this, we may expect entrapment to be more frequent in distributive (i.e., win–lose) negotiations than in integrative processes.

5.3.4   International

Entrapment processes occur frequently in negotiations between states and within international organizations such as the United Nations (UN), the Organization of African Unity, the EU, or the Association of Southeast Asian Nations. Entrapment processes in international politics often start with serious misjudgments of the intentions of countries that are perceived as enemies (De Rivera 1968, p. 71). The USA became entrapped in Vietnam, just as the Soviet Union became entrapped in Afghanistan. "[The USA was] caught in an intervention which [could] not be brought to a successful ending . . . [while being] reluctant to admit defeat" (Frankel 1969, p. 232). The consequences of entrapment at the international level are more serious than those at the national, personal, or interpersonal levels. But are they more likely to occur? Entrapment may be a greater danger at the international level because the consequences may easily spiral out of control. There is no international authority strong enough to exert the same degree of control that states can.

However, precisely because of this lack of control, which can be seen as a sign of less intimate relationships, entrapment may occur less often at the international level than at other levels. If it is true that entrapment is more likely if parties are closer to each other, the lower of the four levels (the personal and interpersonal levels) may show a higher frequency of entrapment than the higher levels (the national and international levels). Also, if it is the case that the higher the level, the more serious the consequences to be faced, parties may (or at least should) be more vigilant against it.

The consequences of entrapment in international negotiations can be very far-reaching. "Caught up in the investment that has already been made in some course of action, foreign policy decision makers may find themselves unable to bring to bear the kind of rational, dispassionate analysis that is necessary to make wise decisions in the throes of international crisis" (Rubin 1991, p. 224). Since entrapment may occur less frequently at the international level than at other levels, negotiators may be less prepared to deal with it. However, the effect is such that diplomats and other negotiators need to be trained to be aware of the phenomenon. If the parties decide not to be restrained, international cooperation and control will break down. An example may be found in the decision of the North Atlantic Treaty Organization (NATO) to attack Serbia to gain control of Kosovo. Since the UN Security Council was unwilling to agree to such a step, NATO either had to settle for doing nothing or decide to circumvent the UN. They decided to take unilateral action and as a consequence NATO became entrapped in the Kosovo situation. It was only through the use of excessive force that the organization managed to destroy the trap (and Serbia in the process).

In international negotiations, as in other negotiations, it is often the more powerful party that becomes entrapped through its own actions. Entrapment is a tool of the weaker party and a trap for the strong. Guerrilla warfare is based on the same principle. The weaker side tries to bog down the stronger party by avoiding direct confrontation, luring the stronger party into its web. Numerous examples of this kind of entrapment can be found in warfare, such as the weaker Flemish foot soldiers who lured the heavy French cavalry into the swamps during the Battle of the Golden Spurs, or the Mongol horsemen who avoided direct confrontation with the heavily armored European knights, but attacked them first with arrows until they were so weakened that the lightly armed Mongol horsemen could easily defeat them. Weaker parties look for the weak spots of their more powerful opponents and then exploit those weaknesses to entrap them. The problem of entrapment at the international level is not only the seriousness of the consequences, but also the difficulty of repairing the damage done. Once a party has been entrapped, no other mechanisms are available to make good the damage done. When more powerful countries entrap smaller ones, there is a risk that the smaller countries may not survive.

In multilateral international negotiations, an additional problem is that of coalition building. Seeking allies does help weaker parties to survive in entrapment situations, but it creates more entanglement at the same time, which makes it more difficult to free oneself from the spiderweb. "[I]f you are representing some group or constituency, it may be hard for you to explain sunk costs; once engaged in the negotiations, you may be forced to stay longer than you want" (Raiffa 1982, p. 89). At the same time, one's coalition might become more dependent on the other caucus: "if the no-agreement alternatives of one coalition improve, the zone of possible agreement . . . correspondingly shrinks" (Lax and Sebenius 1994, p. 182). Steering away from such a situation is more difficult if a whole group of countries is involved, with all their fears of losing face. Stepping out of the coalition might be seen as treason. Such defection is not easily accepted by the more powerful member(s) of the group, who will use the resources they have to stop the smaller country that tries to withdraw and thereby weaken the allied forces. "If an organization has the ability to exact a high price for exit, it thereby acquires a powerful defense against one of the member's most potent weapons: the threat of exit" (Hirschmann 1972, p. 96).

5.4 Factors

5.4.1 Planning

If there is one way a party can save itself from becoming entrapped, it is by carefully planning the negotiation in which entrapment may arise. Overall planning, including strategy, is probably the best tool for avoiding entrapment. Overall planning not only reveals potential traps, but also indicates potential linkages and opportunities for package deals. One of the characteristics of the entrapment process is overcommitment to certain issues, which creates blind spots. This problem can be alleviated by incorporating other issues: the broader the net, the less likely is entrapment. The greater the number of issues that are brought into play, the greater the number of escape routes that are available. What are the options in creating a strategy? Looking at the Thomas–Kilmann model of determinants of conflict behavior (Saner 1997, p. 111), we can distinguish five main strategies: competition, accommodation, avoidance, compromise, and collaboration. In general, parties that employ the first two strategies are more likely to become entrapped than parties that use the last two. Since parties may move from one strategy to another as the context changes, the Thomas–Kilmann model actually provides for 16 potential strategic paths.

Competition is an effective strategy for a situation in which the stakes are high and the competitive party has a power advantage over the opponent. At the same time, the interdependence of interests and the quality of the relationship may be relatively limited. A competitive strategy may lead to entrapment because the weaker party can use the assertiveness of the stronger party to entrap it in a situation in which the best option is to go on, moving deeper into swamps that are not yet apparent. In my training groups, negotiators often score quite low on competitive behavior, unless they have experienced warlike situations from which they have learned that competitive behavior leads to the resolution of conflicts in ways that, for them at least, are effective. Israelis and Croats, for example, score high on competition in the Thomas–Kilmann self-assessment exercise. Men tend to score higher on competition as a natural mode of conflict resolution than women, but there are exceptions. Women who have to fight for their posts as diplomats may score high on competition as an intuitive mode of conflict management. In an Omani group, the highest score on competition was achieved by the only woman diplomat.

Accommodation, the converse of competition, may also lead to entrapment. A party that continuously appeases the other side quickly finds itself trapped through salami tactics applied by the other side. That party will be eaten bit by bit, slice by slice. While each slice is digestible, the final result will be disastrous, as the opponent will have gained much more than originally foreseen. By focusing on short-term problems, the long-term effects remained out of sight.

In distributive international negotiation processes, the competitive side generally wins and the accommodating side generally loses. In this win–lose situation, compromise may provide a middle-of-the-road solution. In any event, strategies along the win–lose dimension run the risk of creating opportunities for entrapment. Accommodation, like competition, is one of the strategies that score low in self-assessment exercises. Negotiators dislike making concessions; they prefer other modes of conflict resolution. Women generally score higher on accommodation than do men. In some countries, accommodation hardly exists as a mode of negotiation: negotiators would rather fail to reach agreement than reach an agreement that benefits not only their own side, but also the other side. The win–lose axis is very much the emotional dimension in the model. Negative feelings toward the other party may lead to competitive (or avoidance) strategies, while positive feelings may lead to accommodative (and collaborative) approaches. EU negotiators score relatively high on accommodation.

Avoidance can be seen as the start of a collaborative strategy. The avoidance–compromise–collaboration axis could be described as the win–win dimension, provided the parties are moving from avoidance toward collaboration and not from avoidance to competition or accommodation. Avoidance can be seen as the most effective of the anti-entrapment strategies. However, since action is obviously needed to create a negotiated settlement, avoidance is also one of the more powerful anti-negotiation strategies. Avoidance is only effective for a while. (For example, in recent conflicts, as long as the Western allies had air superiority, both Iraqi leader Saddam Hussein and Serbian leader Slobodan Milosevic confronted them with an avoidance strategy, preferring to avoid confrontation with a stronger enemy than to be defeated in open battle.) In that sense, avoidance may be the most effective strategy for the entrapping party to adopt to lure its opponent into the trap by withdrawal. In the Thomas–Kilmann exercise used during workshops, men score quite high on avoidance as a preferred mode of dealing with problems. In addition, we see that people who have suffered in conflicts also often choose avoidance as their main intuitive strategy, as a way to wait for better times and not waste resources in the meantime. Palestinian intellectuals, for instance, score high on avoidance as a preferred mode of behavior in conflict situations.

Collaboration or cooperation is the hallmark of integrative bargaining, under the motto "We either sink or swim together." By integrating values, this approach leads to a negotiation result whereby each side wins more than it loses. Collaboration that is genuine may be a good strategy with which to counter entrapment. If collaboration is competition in disguise, however, then entrapment is just around the corner. As it is halfway between avoidance and collaboration, compromise may be an ill-balanced strategy. It is not as effective a tool against entrapment as avoidance or solid collaboration. It leaves open the danger that parties will fall back into competition or accommodation. In the oil-pricing exercise described above, compromise is a dangerous halfway house on the path from avoidance to collaboration. If one of the parties is lured into competitive behavior, a relapse into avoidance, and thus to lose–lose situations, is imminent. Normally, both men and women score high on compromise as their natural inclination to deal with conflicts. Consequently, by definition, they are not prone to entrapment; however, a change in circumstances may signal that entrapment is lurking. Women often score quite high on collaboration: it is often their second highest score (men's second highest score, by contrast, is avoidance).

5.4.2   Information

An important anti-entrapment tool is information. Keeping well-informed helps to avoid entrapment; being ill-informed increases one's risk of entrapment. As more information trickles in, the entrapped party notices that the trap is tightening, and that the swamps (if the party has spotted them at all) are actually much more extensive than originally thought. The pathways through the swamps may be narrower than expected, so that more information is needed. However, in the negotiation processes, complete information is not available. The parties need to enter the process to obtain more information, but in doing so they need to realize that entrapment is one of the factors they have to reckon with. In international negotiations, it is even more difficult to collect trustworthy information. It is therefore absolutely vital in negotiations with other states to be as well informed as possible. As intercultural and other factors add to the fog, reliable information is a prerequisite to avoiding entrapment. Besides having good security services, embassies can be very useful in helping negotiation teams prepare by providing them with in-depth and (hopefully) reliable data. However, it is equally important to use the available information in an appropriate manner.

Information, and especially misinformation, can also be used to create entrapment situations. As long as the Russian people remained ignorant of how the war in Chechnya was proceeding, the danger of President-elect Vladimir Putin's becoming entrapped was relatively slight. By contrast, the government of the USA was entrapped by news coverage of the Vietnam War, between North Vietnam and the Vietcong, on the one hand, and domestic public opinion, on the other. And in World War II, the Germans used misinformation to trap members of the Dutch resistance in what became known as the "England Spiel." Information about possible coalition partners in a negotiation, about alternatives, about the strengths and weaknesses of the other party, and about the road ahead is vital to create or avoid entrapment. The Germans entrapped their Jewish victims by giving them false information about the concentration camps. Pretense is an important element in entrapment, so being well informed is often an effective antidote. However, this antidote works only if the information is credible and if it is accepted by the negotiation party. If the negotiation party doubts the accuracy of the information, then entrapment will again be imminent. Why, for instance, did Joseph Stalin not heed the warnings he was given that the Germans were on the verge of attacking the Soviet Union?

5.4.3 Communication

This brings us to communication as a strategic device with which to create or avoid entrapment. Entrapment may occur through lack of communication, but in general communication is a neutral tool that can be used either to create or to avoid entrapment. The crucial factor, of course, concerns the reliability and quality of the communication. The entrapping party can communicate a willingness to negotiate an agreement favorable to both parties. By concealing matters that may lead to entrapment and by stressing issues and options that may look attractive to the other side, the entrapper can try to create a trap. From the point of view of honesty, this can be seen as untrustworthy behavior. In diplomacy, however, such communication is more often the rule than the exception. Diplomatic negotiators are inclined to tell the truth, but not the whole truth; by not mentioning certain matters, they construct a partial image of the real situation. They know this about each other and are therefore cautious in their communication. Diplomats communicate by sending the signals needed to allow the negotiations to progress while still keeping their options as open as possible. This forces diplomatic negotiators to know the "language" of diplomacy, to know the "codes," and to be able to decode them.

This caution shown by diplomats in communicating with others is often a major source of irritation to people from other professions in which communication is more direct. As a result, misunderstandings may occur in negotiations with non-diplomats. Military officers, in particular, are often outraged at the "fuzziness" of diplomatic communication. Civil servants, too, are less inclined or able to use diplomatic smoke screens. Diplomatic ambiguity may lead to entrapment, but diplomats know how to handle it, and their patient approach often produces dependable outcomes. A civil servant who is more forthcoming and seemingly more assertive, on the other hand, may form a prime target for entrapment. Viewed in this light, diplomats, with their special mode of communication, are well armed against entrapment, whereas other international negotiators may be more prone to walk right into the swamps, with disastrous consequences. Since non-diplomats increasingly play a major role in international discussions, especially within the EU (Meerts 1999), entrapment may occur more frequently in future negotiations.

By keeping communication lines open, by creating a good understanding and a positive atmosphere between the parties, and by using communication as a tool to improve transparency, it may be possible to keep entrapment at bay. After all, entrapment only flourishes when mists shroud what is going on. Transparency lifts the mists to reveal the swamps ahead and can thus save one of the parties from becoming entrapped. As diplomats are (or should be) communicators *par excellence*, they should be able to avoid entrapment or to use it as a defensive weapon against non-diplomatic international negotiators. Indeed, entrapment is often a tool they need, as diplomats have to rely on words to achieve their goals, unable as they are to use force. Certainly, diplomats can ask others to use weapons of force, but they themselves must rely on their verbal and nonverbal behavior. Communication is at the heart of their profession, and since they have fewer means at their disposal than do other professions, they need to resort to those strategies that are available to the weak, entrapment being one of them. This implies that diplomats are also entrappers *par excellence*. If this is true, and if diplomats are, indeed, likely to be less dominant in international negotiations in the future, then we may see a decline in the frequency with which entrapment occurs in that context.

5.4.4   Control

Entrapment is a process whereby one party gains control at the expense of the other. To create an entrapment situation, a party must therefore aim continuously to gain more control over the other side (i.e., to change the balance of power in its own favor). Of course, entrapment also creates its own shift of power, in a mixture of transitive and intransitive effects. Once the process has started, this shift of power becomes visible. While one side tightens its grip on the other (or watches it embroil itself into a situation in which its options diminish), the other side senses a loss of control. In entrapment, this shift in control from one side to the other is not a zero-sum game. The party that gains the upper hand certainly acquires greater control, but an essential part of entrapment is that this increase of power is not blatant. The entrapped party loses a great deal of control because of the situation it encounters. In other words, the context itself becomes a controlling device. However, this device is only partially in the hands of the entrapper: the entrapper can only control the situation up to a point and does not have full control. The situation itself plays a kind of autonomous role in the loss of control by the party being entrapped, which is only partly managed by the entrapper, who sometimes is not managing it at all. If this were not the case, it would be impossible to explain cases of double entrapment, in which both negotiating parties become trapped and no third party can be held responsible (see, for example, the oil-pricing dilemma described above).

To avoid entrapment, it is therefore necessary to keep control of the situation; and to keep control, it is necessary to have an overall strategy, to be well informed, and to create transparency through effective communication. But this is not enough. It is easier to exercise control if one is well organized. Internal organization is almost a prerequisite for external control. Thorough decision making, minimum goal setting, threat reduction, and accountability for decision processes and outcome (Simonson and Staw 1992, p. 421) are internal control mechanisms that dampen the risk of entrapment. To keep control, one needs to have alternative escape routes in place and use them if necessary. Control can be kept up to date by participating in good coalitions. However, such bandwagons also have negative effects on control and may enhance entrapment instead of stopping it, as discussed above concerning entrapment at the international level. If you are weak, ally yourself with those who are stronger. Surely, this is one of the central tenets of the EU – or NATO for that matter: have skilled negotiators to exercise control and to use it effectively. Having control over the situation is, indeed, a necessary prerequisite to avoiding entrapment, but power as such is not enough. Power itself can lead to entrapment if you try to control the outcome of the negotiations; power used to control the environment of the negotiations can lead to entrapment avoidance.

5.5   Case Study

Roy Lewicki (1993) wrote a very illustrative case study on entrapment, "Pacific Oil Company," which effectively conveys the idea to both skilled and unskilled negotiators. The case study provides us with four lessons for avoiding or escaping entrapment.

Lesson One: *To avoid entrapment, make sure that you have received a clear mandate from those who have the legitimate power to issue it, and make sure that internal information flows and communication are transparent and effective.*

Pacific Oil (in reality, Gulf Oil: these negotiations apparently actually took place) supplies Reliant with a chemical that Reliant uses to manufacture plastics. Some time ago, the parties agreed to a contract at a price favorable to Pacific. However, the contract has to be renewed in two years' time, and conditions are changing from a seller's market to a buyer's market. This change in the environment persuades the people at Pacific's Paris office to go for early renegotiations. Although Pacific's head office in New York seems to like the idea, they issue no explicit mandate to the Paris office to reopen negotiations. One reason for this is that Pacific's management structure is unclear. Reliant has a pyramidal organizational structure. In the confrontation to come, this difference in structures favors Reliant: a more transparent command structure always gives a party a clear advantage in conflict situations.

Lesson Two: *To avoid entrapment, make sure you have a realistic perception of the strength of the other party, develop an overall strategy, and set deadlines.*

Since Pacific had always been more powerful, the company's Paris negotiators entered the renewal negotiations full of self-confidence. They prepared the negotiations carefully and believed that the talks would be short and deal with only one issue, the question of price. In the past, Pacific had always been able to convince the other party to accept the price they preferred. As a result, they failed to consider the possibility that things might be different this time. In planning for only one issue, and being blind to the need to create an overall strategy covering all the elements that could come up during the negotiations, they overestimated themselves and underestimated their opponents. The whole process became fuzzy, opportunities for package deals went unnoticed, and unnecessary concessions were made. Furthermore, time could not be managed as no deadlines had been set. And as time worked in favor of Reliant, the delaying tactics of that company had disastrous consequences for Pacific.

Lesson Three: *To avoid entrapment, make sure that you check your assumptions about relationships and create good, clear workable relationships but avoid becoming too close, and avoid the possibility of emotional blackmail.*

Right from the start of the negotiations, Pacific were eaten up bit by bit as a result of Reliant's salami tactics. The Pacific people thought they had a good relationship with Reliant, but failed to realize the significance of the fact that the Reliant team did not contain people they knew from previous negotiations with the company. These new negotiators felt no loyalty toward the Pacific team on account of any earlier relationship, and no emotional attachment to Pacific that might hold them back in their entrapment strategy and tactics. On the contrary, their attitude toward Pacific was actually rather hostile. This situation often occurs when a weaker party feels it is being obliged to accommodate a stronger party. It is interesting to note that in such cases the dominant party does not share such negative emotions, having no reason to do so. As a result, it often fails to notice the hostile attitude of its opponents and the consequences this may have for the negotiations. When this hostile attitude eventually becomes apparent, it often comes as a surprise to the stronger and more successful party and leads to cognitive dissonance.

Another relationship issue that played a part in the Pacific–Reliant negotiations was the distorted communications between the head office of Pacific in New York and the branch office in Paris. New York had not really been following the negotiations and was surprised by the bad turn they took. By the time the bosses became aware of it, it was too late to do anything about the situation: things had gone too far. The head office may have had a good reason for not monitoring the negotiations closely: they had more important things to worry about and they wanted to keep their hands clean. However, this meant they shied away from taking responsibility. Paris, for its part, was happy enough not to have to deal with "unnecessary" intervention by people "who don't know the situation" in the field: a typical embassy–foreign ministry relationship. The problem was made worse because the Paris people were old colleagues and worked very well together. As a result of this excellent relationship, they did not criticize one another, which led to unrealistic "group-think."

Lesson Four: *To escape from entrapment, make sure that you are well represented in the power center of your organization and take care that those in power see your priority as their priority.*

Before the start of the negotiations, Pacific's Paris team had received reasonably optimistic information from the head office in New York about how the market was developing, despite the shift from shortage to abundance of the product they were selling to Reliant. They were also told about Pacific's plans to build its own factory for making plastics. This alternative to a deal with Reliant – Pacific supplying chemicals to its own future factory – gave the negotiation team a powerful counterweight to the shift in market conditions. However, without consulting the Paris team, the head office decided to drop the idea of building their own chemical factory and made this information public straightaway. This meant that, in a single stroke, they had deprived the Paris negotiation team of an important means of control. This sort of thing is not uncommon – the lack of consultation, the unthinking publication of information, and general ignorance at the head office of what is going on at the branches. In the overall balance of interests, one set of negotiations is often only part of a greater whole. Higher levels may decide to sacrifice those negotiations because there are more pressing priorities. They may not bother to inform or consult the team involved, who are seen as merely minor executive players. Unless those negotiations fit in with their line of thinking, they tend to be overlooked. Being unimportant, they can be discarded. Moreover, the higher levels may be afraid that consulting a minor player may be interpreted as weakness on their part as macho decision makers. However, as insignificant as these negotiations may have been to the managers in New York, they were nonetheless very important to the negotiators in Paris. The New York people were not emotionally attached to the negotiations with Reliant. Their interest was purely material. Of course, investments had been made and, of course, they would lose something, but they had to set priorities and the Reliant negotiations were not an overriding priority. The Paris people, however, had invested their credibility, their face, their energy, their self-image in these negotiations. For them, these negotiations were their only priority. Now this meant that they were unable to exit the negotiations. They had to bet more money to try to recover their losses. They were emotionally trapped and could not turn back. The head office was trapped in material terms, but had enough resources to pull out. In the end, the boss flew to Paris and used the "Take it or leave it" tactic on Reliant and Reliant signed the contract. Why? Because it was now so valuable to Reliant that by not signing the contract they had more to lose than to win. They no longer had any best alternative to a negotiated agreement. The power relationship had shifted again.

To summarize, the Pacific negotiators became entrapped because they had no overall and integrated planning, incomplete information, clogged internal and external communication, and no control, as they had no power over the negotiation process itself or over top-level decision making. They were therefore unable to select the most attractive options. The situation became more uncertain as the process unfolded. The investments mounted and, as long as the final stage could not be reached, the returns were virtually nil. The salami tactics of the other side resulted in delays and a lengthy series of concessions. These repeated concessions tended to hide the extent of the losses and make them more acceptable. The rule of thumb "Whenever you offer a concession, ask for one in return" had not been applied. Emotional factors made it difficult to withdraw, interpersonal relationships broke down or lost their function, and even national differences may have made matters worse through communication problems between the Americans, French, and Germans. Finally, the international dimension of the negotiations made matters even more difficult to control. The entrapment worked, in the sense that one of the parties gained more out of the negotiations than the other. The process could only be stopped by an actor who was not closely involved in the negotiations, who intervened when the potential agreement had become too valuable to the winning party to lose it.

5.6   Conclusions

Entrapment is a decision-making process whereby individuals escalate their commitment to a previously chosen, though failing, course of action to justify or recover previous investments. Entrapment is an intransitive process, a process that happens beyond the will of the entrapped, and as such is difficult to see in its early stages of development. Unfortunately, by the time it has begun to become apparent, it is often too late to escape from it. This is one of the dangers that countries most fear when they have to decide on peacekeeping or peace-enforcing matters. Gross violations of human rights, refugee flows, and media coverage can draw nations, individually or in groups, into entrapment processes (Von Hippel 2000, pp. 98–100). The "do something" effect can entrap whole organizations, such as NATO or the UN. To avoid entrapment, negotiators should have a clear understanding of their own aims and the aims of the other party. To escape from entrapment, a party must regain control over the dynamics that operated beyond its control. Through careful and overall planning, sufficient information, transparent communication, and control over the inner and outer environments, it is possible to contain the impetus toward entrapment. In other words, avoiding intransitive entrapment calls for careful and forceful negotiation tactics, with internal support and external control built up as much as possible, and information and communication keeping the actors up to date. Sometimes, these actors may need to be changed. "New senior executives are likely to provide a fresh perspective . . ." (Staw *et al.* 1997, p. 140). Exit options (Ross and Staw 1993, pp. 726–728) are vital to counter entrapment processes.

Entrapment can also be used in a transitive way, as a deliberate strategy on the part of one negotiating party over the other. Entrapment is a powerful option open to the less powerful countries of the world. Just as in judo, such countries can try to use the strength and assertiveness of the more powerful nations so that those nations become entrapped through their own actions. To use entrapment as a transitive strategy, a country should plan carefully to create as many smoke screens as possible, while laying bait down at the same time. It is not enough just to have a carrot to lure the opponents into a process in which a number of traps are carefully hidden along the way. One should also have a stick available to narrow down the other side's options. As the process unfolds, the opponents' choices need to be limited, insecurity generated, and concessions forced – and this will need to be done repeatedly. The other side needs to be driven forward in such a way that, psychologically, it sees the route ahead as the most effective way to satisfy its needs. Feelings of guilt may be very useful in forcing the other side not to leave the charted course. In the interpersonal sphere, the suggestion of a trusting relationship should be created. Care should be taken to arouse no suspicions. National characteristics should also be studied and used. For example, the impatience of the other side can be very powerful in luring them into an entrapment situation; also, honor and fear of losing face are very effective mechanisms. Information should be distorted; communication should look more open than it actually is. All this serves to strengthen control over the other party's crises. Although entrapment can, of course, be used by powerful countries, it is predominantly a strategy used by the smaller countries to compensate for their lack of power.

Yet entrapment within or outside negotiations does not always have to be negative. Entrapment can also have a positive side – and not only for the party that introduces it into the process. Lack of central control (or lack of push) at the international level can easily lead to procrastination, and indecisiveness can easily lead to disaster (although the opposite is also true). In situations that require action, but where countries are unwilling to act because the costs will be too high, entrapment could very well be the answer: it forces them to act. Natural disasters are a classic example. Investment in combating global warming may not be opportune for any individual country, but the collective community of states will be entrapped in the long run if it does not take appropriate measures in time. Here, we see countries using entrapment as a transitive strategy on themselves (i.e., as a self-transitive process).

Entrapment is both a danger to watch out for and an opportunity to be taken. As with almost everything in international relations, it has both a darker and a more positive side. Using entrapment on oneself is a very interesting phenomenon. People who are afraid of doing something may trigger a process that they know will lead to their own entrapment. They know that they need results in the long run, and they know that immediate decisions are psychologically unacceptable to them. A slice-by-slice salami process, however, would be something that they could deal with psychologically. They therefore deliberately force themselves into taking the necessary decisions by embarking on a process of entrapment. The same is true of countries. Populations are often unwilling to accept tough measures. Their governments are therefore unwilling to direct their delegations to go in the preferred direction. The delegation leader, however, seeing that a particular course of action is required, but unable to convince his or her superiors of this fact, may very well lead the delegation into entrapment on purpose to let "fate" decide. The salami character of entrapment in international negotiations is therefore something of a double-edged sword and can be wielded like that by the effective diplomatic negotiator. In that sense, even the EU itself can be used as a self-entrapment strategy: if a government has to do something that is unpopular with its people, it can simply point to "Brussels" as a way to let itself off the hook.

References

Arendt H (1958). *The Human Condition*. Chicago, IL, USA: The University of Chicago Press.

Berridge GR (1995). *Diplomacy*. London, UK: Prentice Hall.

Brockner J & Rubin JZ (1985). *Entrapment in Escalating Conflict: A Social Psychological Analysis*. New York, NY, USA: Springer Verlag.

Chung TC (1991). *Sun Zi, the Art of War*. Singapore: Asiapac Books & Educational Aids.

De Rivera J (1968). *The Psychological Dimension of Foreign Policy*. Columbus, OH, USA: Charles E. Merrill Publishing Company.

Fisher R, Ury W & Patton B (1991). *Getting to Yes: Negotiating without Giving In*. New York, NY, USA: Penguin Books.

Frankel J (1969). *International Politics*. London, UK: Allen Lane.

Garnett J (1975). Limited war. In *Contemporary Strategy*, Vol. I, eds. Baylis J, Booth K, Garnett J & Williams P, pp. 187–208. London, UK: Croom Helm.

Goodfield BA (1999). *Insight and Action: The Role of the Unconscious in Crisis from the Personal to International Levels*. London, UK: University of Westminster Press.

Hayes RE (1991). Negotiations with terrorists. In *International Negotiation*, ed. Kremenyuk VA, pp. 364–408. San Francisco, CA, USA; Oxford, UK: Jossey-Bass Publishers.

Hirschmann AO (1972). *Exit, Voice, and Loyalty*. Oxford, UK: Oxford University Press.

Hofstede G (1980). *Culture's Consequences: International Differences in Work-Related Values*. Beverly Hills, CA, USA: Sage.

Kahneman D & Tversky A (1979). Prospect theory: An analysis of decision under risk. *Econometrica* **47**:263–291.

Lax DA & Sebenius JK (1994). Thinking coalitionally. In *Negotiation Analysis*, ed. Young PH, pp. 153–193. Ann Arbor, MI, USA: The University of Michigan Press.

Leeson N (1996). *Rogue Trader: How I Brought Down Barings Bank and Shook the Financial World*. Boston, MA, USA: Little Brown.

LePoole S (1991). *Never Take No for an Answer*. London, UK: Kogan Page.

Lewicki R (1993). Pacific Oil Company. In *Negotiation: Readings, Exercises, and Cases*, eds. Lewicki R *et al.*, pp. 659–687. New York, NY, USA: The McGraw-Hill Companies.

Meerts P (1989). Diplomatic games. In *Simulation-Gaming*, eds. Klabbers HG, Scheper WJ, Takkenberg C & Crookall D, pp. 340–347. Oxford, UK: Pergamon Press.

Meerts P (1999). The changing nature of diplomatic negotiation. In *Innovation in Diplomatic Practice*, ed. Melissen J, pp. 79–93. London, UK: Macmillan Press.

Michels R (1966). *Political Parties*. Toronto, Canada: Collier-Macmillan Canada.

Nicholson H (1998). *The Evolution of the Diplomatic Method*. Leicester, UK: University of Leicester.

Raiffa H (1982). *The Art and Science of Negotiation*. Cambridge, MA, USA; London, UK: Harvard University Press.

Ross J & Staw BM (1993). Organisational escalation and exit: Lessons from the Shoreham nuclear power plant. *Academy of Management Journal*, **36**:701–732.

Rubin J (1991). Psychological approach. In *International Negotiation*, ed. Kremenyuk VA, pp. 216–228. San Francisco, CA, USA; Oxford, UK: Jossey-Bass Publishers.

Saner R (1997). *Verhandlungs-technik*. Bern and Stuttgart, Germany; Wien, Austria: Verlag Paul Haupt.

Schelling TC (1963). *The Strategy of Conflict*. New York, NY, USA: Oxford University Press.

Siebe W (1991). Game theory. In *International Negotiation*, ed. Kremenyuk VA, pp. 180–202. San Francisco, CA, USA; Oxford, UK: Jossey-Bass Publishers.

Simonson I & Staw BM (1992). Deescalation strategies: A comparison of techniques for reducing commitment to losing courses of action. *Journal of Applied Psychology* **77**:419–426.

Staw BM & Hoang H (1995). Sunk costs in the NBA: Why draft order affects playing time and survival in professional basketball. *Administrative Science Quarterly* **40**:474–494.

Staw BM & Ross J (1980). Commitment in an experimental society: A study of the attribution of leadership from administrative scenarios. *Journal of Applied Psychology* **65**:249–260.

Staw BM & Ross J (1987). Knowing when to pull the plug. *Harvard Business Review* **65**:68–74.

Staw BM, Barsade SG & Koput KW (1997). Escalation at the credit window: A longitudinal study of bank executives' recognition and write-off of problem loans. *Journal of Applied Psychology* **82**:130–142.

Szur G (1997). *De Joden van Wilno*. Amsterdam, The Netherlands: Uitgeverij Jan Mets.

Von Hippel K (2000). Democracy by force: A renewed commitment to nation building. *Washington Quarterly* **23**:95–112.

Chapter 6

The Role of Vengeance in Conflict Escalation

Sung Hee Kim

Something about revenge breeds its escalation. It is an all too familiar pattern. Someone harms us, and we retaliate, which in turn brings about yet another harmful response – and so on. This progression of retaliatory actions often incurs costs that are out of proportion to the harm that initiated the conflict in the first place. What causes this costly, often deadly, pattern of vengeful behavior? The main goal of this chapter is to examine the role of vengeance in escalating conflict. While acknowledging that many factors often contribute to conflict escalation (see Pruitt and Kim 2004), I argue that the desire for vengeance is a key driving force behind many escalating conflicts. I also try to show that an understanding of the nature of vengeance, especially as it operates at the collective level, reveals why it is such an important factor. Finally, I briefly suggest a few ways that the escalatory pattern of vengeance can be curbed.

6.1   The Nature of Vengeance

6.1.1   Potency of vengeance

> O child, child
> now I begin my mourning,
> the wild newly-learned melody
> from the sprit of revenge
>
> Euripides, *Hecuba*

In Euripides' great tragedy, Hecuba suffers unimaginable harm at the hands of the Greeks. They destroy her beloved Troy, kill her husband and most of her children, and reduce her, the queen of Troy, to a Greek slave. Remarkably, despite these torments, her heart remains relatively free from the desire for vengeance. Even when the Greeks use her remaining daughter for a human sacrifice, she appears simply to resign herself to her miserable fate. However, when she learns that her young son has been brutally murdered by her trusted friend, Polymestor, her heart is flooded with vengeful fury. It is her desire for vengeance that transforms her from a helpless victim ("helplessness of age!/ Too old, too weak, to stand," she laments early on) into a fearless, commanding avenger. Hecuba is energized and empowered by this desire and finds a way to undo the injury. She lures Polymestor and his two sons into her tent and satisfies her vengeful desire by murdering the sons and gouging out the eyes of their father.

Euripides' *Hecuba* illustrates the potency of the desire for vengeance. In fact, many scholars, from ancient (e.g., Aristotle) to modern times (e.g., Frijda 1993; French 2001), have argued that the desire for vengeance is one of the most power-ful human passions, perhaps *the most powerful* (e.g., Marongiu and Newman 1987). It is undoubtedly implicated in many forms of extreme behavior, including homi-cide (e.g., Elster 1999), suicide (e.g., Meng 2002), terrorism (e.g., Mylroie 2000), workplace violence (e.g., Aquino *et al.* 2001), and genocide (e.g., Scheff 1994). Certainly, there are times when the thirst for vengeance becomes so powerful that no other human desire or need seems to surpass it. People are sometimes willing to risk everything, including their own lives, to carry out their revenge against the harm-doer. In the language of research on game theory, vengeance alters people's preference structure. Hecuba knows her vengeance will bring about her own death; it will also strip away her humanity, as she will turn into a dog with blazing eyes. But her desire for vengeance overwhelms any other concerns: "What do I care how I die? I have my revenge."

The power of vengeful urges may explain why upward revenge – a weaker party's vengeful attack against a stronger party – often achieves its fulfillment. A prevailing pattern seen in many conflict episodes is that parties of low power are usually *less* likely to take revenge against a more powerful harm-doer (see, e.g., Lawler and Yoon 1993). However, occasionally parties of less power take revenge against a more powerful harm-doer, sometimes in dramatic fashion, despite their low-power status and despite the potential costs (Baumgartner 1984; Kim *et al.* 1998). Anthropological analyses of suicide show that a wife (the weaker party) commits suicide largely to take revenge on her abusive husband or his relatives (the stronger party).[1] Similarly, "Kamikaze revenge" is used frequently by a weaker

---

[1] For example, Jeffreys (1952) noted that many African suicides occur because the individuals believe their ghosts or spirits will torment their enemies, or because they know that their relatives will

party against a stronger party in intergroup conflict, as shown in many suicide bombings (see Jaber 1997). For a weak party, it may be often be the case that revenge is the only means available to turn against the stronger party (Frijda 1993).

The potency of vengeful urges can also be appreciated from the satisfaction it typically gives the avenger (e.g., Bain 1859; Heider 1958). In fact, the sweetness of revenge may help explain why its fulfillment can outweigh the utter misery and pain the avenger brings on him- or herself (Bain 1859). This is Geronimo's (1906, pp. 53–54) account of his joy when he and his Apache warriors were able to avenge their group's suffering at the hands of the Mexican force (cited in Daly and Wilson 1988):

> Still covered with the blood of my enemies, still holding my conquering weapon, still hot with the joy of the battle, victory, and vengeance, I was surrounded by the Apache braves and made war chief of all the Apaches. Then I gave orders for scalping the slain. I could not call back my loved ones, I could not bring back the dead Apaches, but I could rejoice in this revenge.

While fulfilled vengeance often brings such supreme joy, unfulfilled vengeance "leaves a person incomplete, as if he were maimed" (Burnett 1998, p. 2). It often has an unrelenting, corrosive effect on one's mind and creates quite unbearable psychological pain. In some cultures, it is believed that unfulfilled vengeance prevents a person's spirit from being purged; instead, the spirit must endure in a form of wretched purgatory. Indeed, this is the reason why the spirit of Hamlet's father urges Hamlet to avenge his father's death at the hands of his uncle; otherwise, his spirit cannot rest. It is the surviving kin who must take action so that the spirit can find eternal rest.

6.1.2 Main causes of vengeful desire

Many scholars point out that vengeful urges most obviously follow from the perception of a particular kind of harm, namely, *unjust* harm (e.g., Westermarck 1898; Mackie 1985; Vidmar 2000). The fact that the harm is perceived to be unjust seems to give vengeful urges staying power. However, another contributing factor to vengeful urges involves a particularly important human need – the need to maintain and enhance self-esteem (Westermarck 1912; Murphy and Hampton

---

inflict penalties upon their enemies. Jeffreys claims that such revenge through suicide has evolved as a way to restrain the stronger party from its excessive use of power against the weaker party.

1988; Baumeister 1997). As much theoretical and empirical work shows (e.g., Kunda 1987; Tesser 1988), we have a strong need to view ourselves in a positive light. We want to see ourselves as moral, good, kind, and competent human beings, and many behaviors can be traced back to this underlying need, the need for positive self-esteem (see Aronson 1992; also see Brown 1998 for further discussion on self-esteem). When we are harmed, this positive view of the self is compromised. The very fact that another person is willing to harm us suggests that this person holds us in low regard. Any injury to our self-esteem tends to produce strong reactions. When injury is caused by another person's harm, we may be most likely to feel a constellation of other-directed emotions, such as anger, hostility, and hatred. Urged on by these emotions, we often want to hurt the harm-doer in return.

Intentional, unjust harm carries the message that the harm-doer has less than full respect for us (see, e.g., Nietzsche 1887/1967; Westermarck 1912). As Murphy and Hampton (1988, p. 25) suggest,

> One reason we so deeply resent moral injuries [someone's unjust wrongs against us] done to us is not simply that they hurt us in some tangible or sensible way; it is because such injuries are also *messages –* symbolic communications. They are ways a wrongdoer has of saying to us, "I count but you do not," . . . or "I am here up high and you are there down below." Intentional wrongdoing *insults* us and attempts (sometimes successfully) to *degrade* us . . . It is moral injury, and we care about such injuries. [Italics in original.]

The fact that harm (especially intentional, unjust harm) translates into a blow to one's self-esteem (or moral injury) explains why, even after the inflicted physical injury has disappeared, we may still desire to take revenge against the harm-doer. Physical healing itself does little to undo the symbolic message of disrespect that the harm-doer conveyed to us. As social beings, we deeply care about other people's opinion of us. In fact, much of our self-esteem tends to derive from it (Cooley 1902; Meade 1934).[2] People's high opinion of us elevates our self-esteem, while their low opinion degrades it. Their low opinion of us, which is conveyed through their wrongdoing, tends to shake the foundations of our self-esteem.

---

[2]The urge for revenge becomes particularly intense when such harm is committed in public view. Public humiliation is likely to lower our self-esteem as well as our esteem both in the eyes of the harm-doer and in the eyes of the audience. Such "loss of face" can produce acute pain in us, and we become highly motivated to restore our face (see, e.g., Goffman 1959; also see Chapter 2 in this volume). Face-restoration behavior often takes the form of revenge, as many studies demonstrate (e.g., Brown 1968).

6.1.3 Functions of vengeance

Restoring damaged self-esteem

As mentioned above, vengeance is partly a response to injuries to our self-esteem. Thus, a main function of vengeance is the restoration of self-esteem degraded by unjust injuries (Brown 1968; Kim and Smith 1993; Baumeister 1997). As Westermarck (1912, p. 23) noted in his extensive analysis of vengeance, retaliation serves "to enhance the 'self-feeling' which has been lowered or degraded by the injury suffered." Heider (1958) is even more explicit about the self-esteem-restoring function of vengeance. He argues that revenge is a pointed attempt by the victim to change the harm-doer's low opinion of the victim, which gave rise to the act in the first place. By changing the harm-doer's belief about the victim through retaliation, the victim can enhance self-esteem that has been hurt or degraded by the injury. After all, what are the consequences of the victim's doing nothing? Such inaction will be viewed as a silent agreement that the victim is, indeed, inferior to the harm-doer or is deserving of harm (Berscheid *et al.* 1968).

Heider's (1958) claim that the victim takes revenge to restore self-esteem by changing the harm-doer's beliefs about the victim suggests that the victim is likely to reveal his or her *identity* to the harm-doer in carrying out revenge, rather than to conceal it. Aristotle's quote from *The Odyssey* by Homer makes this point: Odysseus makes sure that Polyphemus knows who blinded him "as if Odysseus would not have considered himself avenged, had Polyphemus remained ignorant who had blinded him and for what" (cited in Heider 1958, p. 265).

Deterring future harm

Vengeance and deterrence are seemingly unrelated concepts in that vengeance involves the restoration of *past wrongdoing*, while deterrence involves the prevention of *future potential wrongdoing*. Yet a vengeful act, in some cases, serves both functions. By avenging, or threatening to avenge, the victim may want to demonstrate to the harm-doer (as well as to other people) that he or she is equal or even superior to the harm-doer and that any harm is not inflicted upon him or her with impunity. In this regard, vengeance is both restorative and preventive.

Its restoration and deterrence functions mean that vengeance is backward-looking in that it aims to inflict harm in response to already inflicted harm, but at the same time it is also forward-looking in that it aims to deter or prevent further harm from the attacker (or from other potential attackers). The line between deterrence-motivated vengeance and restoration-motivated vengeance can often blur, particularly when the parties involved in a conflict have an ongoing relationship. One's retaliatory behavior is likely to be motivated both to restore lost self-esteem and to prevent further harm from the attacker.

Although it may be quite difficult precisely to differentiate deterrence-motivated vengeance from restoration-motivated vengeance, it may still be plausible to assume that these two types of revenge perhaps differ in terms of their *intensity*. If one retaliates against the harm-doer mainly to restore justice, one may try to return the *same* amount of harm to the harm-doer. For one thing, repaying the same amount of harm may be sufficient to restore lowered self-esteem, and for another, repaying harm in a tit-for-tat fashion is likely to suppress unwanted counter-revenge from the harm-doer (Kim and Smith 1993; Tripp *et al.* 2002). By contrast, if one retaliates against the harm-doer mainly to deter further harm, one may try to inflict more severe harm upon the harm-doer than the initial harm. Doing so perhaps enables the victim to clearly demonstrate that he or she is *far* superior to the harm-doer.

Indeed, history is filled with incidents showing that this deterrence-motivated vengeance often leads to a calculated, cruel genocide (Kelsen 1943; Scheff 1994; Horowitz 2001). Sometimes, the avenging party seeks "permanent deterrence" by literally exterminating the opposing side. The bloody feud between the Hatfields and McCoys provides a good example. On New Year's night of 1888, the Hatfields tried to end the ongoing feud by killing *all* of the remaining members of the McCoy family (Rice 1982). Similarly, ethnic cleansing committed in more recent conflicts, such as in Bosnia-Herzegovina, Kosovo, and Rwanda, supplies a vivid example of deterrence-motivated vengeance.

Fulfilling a duty

Taking revenge was long considered a moral imperative, a sacred duty (Jacoby 1983; Marongiu and Newman 1987; Daly and Wilson 1988), while forgiving the harm-doer was considered a sign of weakness or lack of honor (Westermarck 1912). This view of revenge is captured aptly by Aristotle in his *Rhetorica*: "It belongs to the courageous man never to be worsted; to take revenge on a foe rather than to be reconciled is just, and therefore honorable" (quoted in Westermarck 1912, p. 74). In Jibaro Indian culture, for example, a son whose father was murdered was compelled to take revenge against the harm-doer, even though he might not feel vengeful toward the harm-doer. By not fulfilling the duty of avenging his father's death, he would surely lose his honor and be ostracized by his people. Losing honor was considered worse than death (Karsten 1935).

Of course, in most modern cultures, taking revenge is no longer considered a sacred duty. In fact, revenge is now considered legally and morally wrong. However, taking revenge is still regarded as an honorable duty in some cultures (e.g., Albania) and in certain groups (e.g., the Mafia) and gangs.

6.1.4 Risks of vengeance

> If you seek vengeance, dig two graves.
>
> A Chinese saying

Revenge can take many forms. However, it appears that people have a natural inclination to retaliate against the harm-doer in a fashion similar to the way they were harmed (Westermarck 1912; Kelsen 1943; Gouldner 1960; Rawls 1971; Black-Michaud 1975). People tend to return harm with the *identical* amount and kind, especially in the initial stages of conflict, as many studies on aggression and conflict show (e.g., O'Leary and Dengerink 1973; Youngs 1986).

However, it is also clearly true that revenge often exceeds the initial harm, as many historical examples can attest. Hannibal's vengeance against the people of Himera is a case in point. It is said that in 409 BC, Hannibal finally avenged his grandfather, Hamilkar, who was murdered at Himera in Sicily. In response to this *one* death, he engineered the complete destruction of the city, the women and children were distributed as prizes among the soldiers, and over 3,000 male captives were dragged to the very place where Hamilkar had been slain and were slaughtered.

6.1.5 Sources of vengeful escalation

One source of vengeful escalation is that the parties involved have different views about the justification of the initial harm (Pruitt and Kim 2004). Both parties typically believe that they are "victims" of the other's unjust attack. The aggressor tends to justify his or her aggression as merely resulting from defending him- or herself from the other's aggression, even when it is clear not only to the victim, but also to a third party, that the aggressor is solely responsible for the harm-doing. Polymestor is no exception to this bias. He justifies his killing of Hecuba's son (Euripides 430–420 BC / 1958, p. 60):

> I killed him, and I admit it. My action, however, was dictated,
> as you [Agamemnon, the Greek commander who controls the area] shall see,
> by a policy of wise precaution. My primary motive was fear,
> fear that if this boy, your enemy, survived,
> he might someday found a second and resurgent Troy.

To Polymestor's mind, it is he who is the victim of Hecuba's unjust, vicious attack. As noted earlier, the sense of "being victimized" often provokes a powerful sense of injustice that motivates one to restore justice, typically through retaliation against the aggressor. Thus, Polymestor cries for justice and vows for revenge: "I'll claw her [Hecuba] to pieces with these bare hands!"

What happens when people realize that they are the perpetrators of wrong-doing rather than the victims? Are they likely to take appropriate steps to undo their wrongdoing – such as to apologize? Rarely: people tend to justify their action through a variety of means. Research on equity theory and just-world theory indicates that harm-doers, in an effort to convince themselves that their relationship with the victim is an equitable one, often blame the victim (Lerner 1975), minimize the victim's suffering (Baumeister *et al.* 1990), or deny their responsibility for the victim's suffering (Brock and Buss 1962, 1964). All these distortions and rational-izations are likely to prevent the harm-doer from admitting his or her responsibility, and thus give the victim a justification for counterattack.

Another source of the escalation of vengeful exchanges may be the victim's *subjective* assessments of the severity of harm – usually in the direction of over-estimation. There are many literary and historical examples of tragedies that re-sult from such asymmetric perceptions of injury (Black-Michaud 1975; Hallett and Hallett 1980; Jacoby 1983). Jacoby (1983, pp. 51–52) recounts the tale of Michael Kohlhaas, written in an 1806 novel by Heinrich von Kleist. Kohlhaas, a dairy farmer, is described as a model citizen whose nature is god-fearing, diligent, benevolent, and honest, yet one whose life is destroyed by "excessive" revenge. In his unbending quest to gain restoration for the abuse of his animals by a squire, Kohlhaas "eventually destroys his business and his marriage (his wife is killed by the enemies he has made); burns down the squire's house; murders innocent inhab-itants of the castle; and incites a revolt that lays waste to much of the surrounding countryside."

A third source of the escalation of vengeful exchanges is that individuals can easily frame a personal affront as an insult to their group. As an example, take the case of an incident that took place in Los Angeles in 1996 between the owner of a hat shop and a customer (described in Yamamoto 1999). The shop sells hats for women and, since the customer was a man, and since his presence appeared to make a female customer nervous, the shop owner asked the man to leave the store. But he refused to do so. Soon, a friend of the owner and the male customer began a verbal argument. Eventually, the customer left the store, vowing that he would come back. The customer felt insulted by the owner. This incident could have been handled as a case of personal affront, but what actually happened was that it was quickly framed as a case of group affront, as the shop owner was a Korean American, and the customer an African American. Even well before this particular incident occurred, racial tensions had existed between many Korean shopkeepers and their African–American customers. The customer contacted the Brotherhood Crusade, an African–American community organization that soon helped to orga-nize a protest in front of the store. The protesters demanded a public apology.

Despite the subsequent flurry of mediation efforts, this incident apparently left bitterness in both ethnic groups.

Once we frame our personal affront as the affront to *our group*, vengeance no longer operates at the personal level. It becomes collective vengeance (one group against another group), which can unleash its most deadly power. I examine some aspects of collective vengeance next.

6.2   Collective Vengeance

At the height of the genocide in Rwanda in 1994, over 800,000 people (Tutsis and moderate Hutus) were slaughtered in just 100 days – an average of about six people per minute. This appalling slaughter would have been impossible without the active or passive involvement of ordinary Hutu citizens (Gourevitch 1998). Apparently, many killings were done by Hutus who knew their victims – students killed by their own teachers, church-goers by their own ministers, and neighbors by their own neighbors. What drove ordinary Hutus to commit such horrible acts against their own countrymen? How were the Hutu power-holders able to mobilize Hutu citizens to slaughter their friends, neighbors, and students simply because they belonged to a different group?

Although many factors contribute to intergroup violence (see Kuper 1981; Staub 1989; Kaufman 2001), here, too, the desire for vengeance appears to be a driving force in many instances (Berke 1988; Scheff 1994). The history of relations between groups is often tainted with a series of wrongs and counter-wrongs, and so a group can easily dig up a past wrong inflicted by the other group. Indeed, it is reported that the Hutu hardliners skillfully inflamed vengeful feelings left in many Hutus' minds as a result of the wrongs committed by Tutsis in the past (e.g., 100,000 Hutu deaths, reportedly at the hands of Tutsis, in the 1970s). Similarly, the Serb government was successful in gaining its citizens' support for the ethnic cleansing of Kosovar Muslims by reopening the old wounds inflicted upon the Serbs by Turks. As these and other examples suggest, vengeance, often stirred purposefully by group leaders, appears to achieve its most full-blown expression at the group level (Scheff 1994; Volkan 2001).

6.2.1   The role of group identity

It is a universal human tendency to differentiate ourselves according to group membership (Tajfel 1982; Brewer and Miller 1996). As social beings, we tend to resort to a spontaneous categorization to simplify the social world: it is much more efficient and easy to base reactions to others on their group membership than on each person's individual characteristics (Hewstone *et al.* 2002). However, such categorization is beyond mere cognitive classification; it also carries emotional significance (Brewer and Miller 1996). We favor in-group members over out-group members, a phenomenon labeled *ethnocentrism* by Sumner (1906). He noted that

> [A] differentiation arises between ourselves, the we-group, or in-group, and everybody else, or the other-groups, out-groups. The insiders in a we-group are in a relation of peace, order, law, government, and industry, to each other. Their relation to all outsiders, or other-groups, is one of war and plunder . . . Ethnocentrism is the technical name for this view of things in which one's own group is the center of everything, and all others are scaled and rated with reference to it . . . Each group nourishes its own pride and vanity, boasts itself superior, exalts its own divinities, looks with contempt on outsiders. Each group thinks its own folkways the only right ones, and if it observes that other groups have other folkways, these excite its scorn. Opprobrious epithets are derived from these differences. "Pig-eater," "cow-eater," "uncircumcised," "jabberers" are epithets of contempt and abomination. (Sumner 1906, pp. 12–13)

Ethnocentrism expresses itself even when the basis for group identity is trivial. For example, Tajfel and his collaborators divided a group of British boys into two groups on the basis of whether they under- or overestimated the number of dots shown on a slide (Tajfel 1982). Needless to say, this group identity, under- or overestimators, should hardly carry any significance to the boys. Yet, when asked to allocate money to the participants, these boys showed in-group preference: they allocated more money to their "in-group" members. Ethnocentrism, as Sumner (1906) indicates, is more than just in-group favoritism; it also contains out-group discrimination.

Given that trivial group differences can trigger ethnocentrism, it is not surprising that real-life group differences (e.g., race, nationality, religion, etc.) can also produce ethnocentrism. It is interesting to note that the deep division between Hutus and Tutsis is a recent phenomenon. Although it is hard to imagine given recent bloody conflicts between these groups, for the past 500 years, "Hutus and Tutsis spoke the same language, followed the same religion, intermarried, lived intermingled without territorial distinctions on the same hills, sharing the same social and political culture in small chiefdoms" (Gourevitch 1998, pp. 47–48). But this harmonious relationship came to its end during the colonial period when ethnic lines were reinstituted and sharpened. In the early 1930s, the Belgian colonists classified the Rwandans into three groups: Hutus (85 percent), Tutsis (14 percent), and Twas (1 percent). Each Rwandan was given an "ethnic" identity card, "which made it virtually impossible for Hutus to become Tutsis. . . . Whatever Hutu and Tutsi identity may have stood for in the precolonial state no longer mattered: the Belgians had made 'ethnicity' the defining feature of Rwandan existence" (Gourevitch 1998, p. 57). Over 500 years of peaceful coexistence between these two groups was unable to withstand the ethnocentrism magnified by this augmented ethnic division (see Smith 1998 for a further analysis of the Belgians' division between these two groups).

What is the main cause of ethnocentrism? Research evidence suggests that ethnocentrism is rooted in the fact that our collective identity is an important ingredient in our overall sense of self (Tajfel 1982; Worchel 1999; McCauley 2001). Our feeling of self-worth derives from the status and achievements of the groups with which we identify, as well as from our own individual status and achievements. Thus, we elevate the relative position of our group in relation to out-groups to enhance our self-worth (Tajfel and Turner 1986). The close link between group-esteem and self-esteem means that any blows to our group-esteem may be perceived as blows to our self-esteem. Revenge against the out-group becomes a natural response.

6.2.2 Out-group homogeneity

After the suffering at the hands of Hecuba, Polymestor cries out (Euripides 430–420 BC / 1958, p. 62):

> On behalf of all those dead who learned their hatred of women long ago, for those who hate them now, for those unborn who shall live to hate them yet, I now declare my firm conviction: neither earth nor ocean produces a creature as savage and monstrous as woman. This is my experience. I know that this is true.

To Polymestor, all women, not just Hecuba, are evil. Thus, all women should be the target of his rage and vengeance. Similarly, we tend to view out-group members as all similar and interchangeable masses, a tendency known as "out-group homogeneity" (Hewstone *et al.* 2002). This tendency becomes especially heightened when we experience an injury at the hands of out-group members, which is in part why vengeance is not just limited to the original perpetrator, but also to anyone who shares the same group identity. In other words, collective vengeance typically takes the form of indiscriminate violence against the members of the target group.

6.2.3 Group validation

Personal vengeance frequently meets with strong social scorn and disapproval – at least in most modern cultures. Vengeance carries primitive, uncivilized, and barbaric connotations – something from which we should wean ourselves (Jacoby

1983; Solomon 1990; Govier 2002). Most societies have developed laws to curb private revenge.[3]

Collective vengeance, however, is relatively free from social condemnation; it frequently enjoys the approval and blessing of in-group members. Palestinian suicide bombers are granted martyr status, their photos are displayed in the streets, and their family members are bestowed with community respect, along with financial reward. Our own group's approval and encouragement provide us with a powerful *moral* justification to hurt the out-group. Taking revenge, even in an extreme form, can be considered heroic and virtuous if it is perceived as retaliation for sufferings at the hands of the out-group.

6.2.4   Longevity of collective vengeance

Collective vengeance can be long lasting. Even if current circumstances prevent vengeful actions, the desire for vengeance can bide its time. One reason for its longevity is that groups keep past wounds and humiliations alive through collective memories. Succeeding generations are handed down the songs, stories, and poems that detail, typically in an exaggerated fashion, the horrible wrongs suffered by their ancestors at the hands of out-group members.[4] Textbooks are often filled with a catalogue of injustices inflicted upon the in-group. As people's memories are typically self-serving, a very wide gulf can exist between what actually happened and what is remembered, in collective memory especially. We tend to remember only our own group's suffering, and not the suffering our group has inflicted upon the others. Collective memories of suffering perpetrated by the "evil" out-group enhance the likelihood that vengeful feelings will remain entrenched and powerful.

Another reason for the long shelf-life of collective vengeance has to do with modern technologies, in particular television and the Internet, which enable manipulative leaders or extremists to feed the general population a constant diet of biased

---

[3]The condemnation of private revenge within society has created a sense that justice has nothing to do with vengeful desire and, even further, that vengeance and justice are mutually exclusive (Jacoby 1983). There are many examples of how individuals can justify vengeful feelings by claiming that justice, rather than vengeance, motivates these feelings. Needless to say, seeking justice is a socially acceptable behavior, while seeking revenge is not. Jacoby (1983) describes a case of how vengeful feelings can be presented in the name of justice. A woman, a former officer of the Maidanek death camp who had married an American serviceman and lived a comfortable life, was brought to an American court. Most of the witnesses in the courtroom were Maidanek survivors. When the defendant's lawyer asked them whether they came to the court to seek revenge, all of them apparently replied in controlled, dispassionate tones that they only wanted justice. According to Jacoby (1983), they were obviously aware of the American cultural convention that makes it unacceptable to acknowledge any form of vengeance as a motivation.

[4]Past wounds at the hands of the out-group can provide a useful function for the group: they bond its group members and facilitate in-group cooperation. As Staub (1989) argues, a nation's identity "...is often defined by past hurt, pain, or injury" (p. 252).

portrayals of past and present wrongs. For over three years before the start of the 1991 war in the former Yugoslavia, Belgrade television stations, under the control of Serbian leader Slobodan Milosevic, broadcast programs that focused on the suffering inflicted on the Serbs by the Croats and Bosnian Muslims, complete with appeals to undo the suffering once and for all (Milosevi 1997). A similar process is seen in many Arab–Muslim countries, thanks to "an explosion of Arab satellite TV and Internet, which are taking the horrific [one-sided] images from the Intifada and beaming them directly to the new Arab-Muslim generation" (Friedman 2002, pp. 197–198). As a result, rage and vengeful urges become a constant theme in the minds of people who live in these countries.

Finally, collective vengeance persists because, when unfulfilled, it often leads to *hatred*, an especially intense, durable emotion characterized as "an enduring organization of aggressive impulses toward a person or toward a class of persons . . . a stubborn structure in the mental–emotional life of the individual" (Allport 1954, p. 363). At the group level, hatred is a blend of at least four elements (Horowitz 2001):

- an obsessive focus on the hated group;
- a belief that the hated group possesses evil traits that do not change – is inherently bad;
- a view that all members of the hated group are alike; and
- a sense of repulsion toward the hated group, which motivates the desire to destroy the hated group.

6.3 Appeasement of Collective Vengeance: A Step toward Reconciliation

As I have argued, the desire for vengeance is a key driving force behind many escalating conflicts, in particular many escalating intergroup conflicts. Vengeance provides the emotional charge to start the spiral of escalation. Theoretical analyses, as well as real-life examples, clearly suggest that vengeance demands its fulfillment – often at any cost. Compared with personal vengeance, collective vengeance carries the approval stamp of the in-group, which helps the vengeful desire surface in the form of deadly, unrestrained violence against the target out-group. As also mentioned above, unfulfilled vengeful desire can continue to brew in collective memories for a long time, waiting for the "right" moment to surface.

Given these features of collective vengeance, the realization that vengeance – and its accompanying hatred – poisons the relationship between the parties in conflict is hardly surprising. A salient case in point is the ruptured relationship between Palestinians and Israelis. Numbingly frequent killings, often motivated by vengeance, have damaged their relationship so deeply that any prospect of repairing it seems bleak.

When a relationship between two parties is so damaged, as it is with the Palestinians and the Israelis, any agreement to end the conflict is likely to fall apart. The parties remain entangled in a web of retaliatory actions as circumstances force them to continue interacting in the same confined space, a situation that characterizes many protracted ethnic conflicts (Kelman 1999; Pruitt and Kim 2004). It follows that gaining a durable peace between the antagonists requires that their relationship be repaired. Otherwise, vengeful desires are unlikely to diminish. How can this be done?

6.3.1 The goal of peace negotiation

It is only recently that *reconciliation*, the process of relationship repair and rebuilding, has attracted much attention from scholars (e.g., Kriesberg 2001; Shriver 2001) and practitioners (e.g., Lederach 1997). This growing focus is largely born out of the reality that traditional peace negotiation, typically brokered by third parties, is in general unresponsive to harsh intergroup conflicts (Azar 1990; Montville 1993; Kelman 1999; Fisher 2001). Consider a negotiated settlement that has halted the violent struggle between the Greek and Turkish communities in Cyprus: the deployment of United Nations (UN) troops. It appears that the continued presence of these troops since 1964 has been necessary to prevent renewed violence. In a sense, the 40-year presence of UN troops serves as a sign of the failure to promote reconciliation between the groups (Borris and Diehl 1998). Also consider the following finding: two-thirds of the negotiated peace agreements to end civil wars between 1945 and 1993 failed to yield a durable peace (Licklider 1995). (For a more comprehensive description of the track record of peace agreements in civil war, see Wallensteen 2002, pp. 134–139.)

Achieving a settlement to end a violent struggle can be itself considered a triumph, and one should not underestimate the benefits of such settlements (for one, it puts a halt to ongoing violence). But it is important to recognize that such settlements frequently fall short of a genuine repairing of the relationship between the antagonists. Rasmussen (2001) offers three reasons why traditional peace negotiations – which typically are designed to produce an agreement on the substantive issues (e.g., cease-fire, power-sharing provision, resource allocation) – have been largely ineffective in repairing the relationship between the parties. One reason lies in the typical goal of such negotiations: to gain an agreement designed to "produce macrolevel *changes in behavior*" (Rasmussen 2001, p. 112; italics added). These negotiations are not designed to bring about *attitudinal changes*, which are crucial for relationship repair both in the negotiators and among the members of each side.

A second reason is that such negotiations have largely failed to address the underlying causes that started and escalated the conflict. Many intergroup conflicts, on the surface, are over tangible issues such as land, property, and political structure, but at a deeper, more symbolic level, they are over basic human psychological needs such as recognition, dignity, justice, and identity (Kelman 1999). A third reason is that traditional negotiations have not mapped out specific ways for the antagonists to repair and rebuild their relationship.

In the light of these shortcomings of traditional peace negotiations, several theorists (e.g., Kelman 1999; Rasmussen 2001) argue that to deal with violent ethnic conflicts, the ultimate goal of peace negotiations should be to repair (or transform) the relationship between the parties. Such negotiations should be "designed not merely to produce a minimally acceptable political agreement, but to provide the basis for a stable, long-term peace and a cooperative, mutually enhancing relationship that contributes to the welfare and development of both societies" (Kelman 1999, p. 194). In other words, the key goal of peace negotiation should be to produce a blueprint for reconciliation.

6.3.2   Forgiveness, appeasement of vengeance, and reconciliation

Recent writings on reconciliation offer various suggestions on how to achieve it (see Deutsch 2000; Kriesberg 2001; Shriver 2001). What emerges as a common ingredient is forgiveness. Archbishop Desmond Tutu, an architect of the South African Truth and Reconciliation Commission – which is considered one of the boldest social and political experiments of the twentieth century – sums up the importance of forgiveness in reconciliation: "Forgiveness is not some nebulous thing. It is practical politics. Without forgiveness, there is no future" (cited in Wiesenthal 1997, p. 268).

Although forgiveness is defined in a number of ways (see Pruitt and Kim 2004 for its various definitions), one common theme is to let go of the desire for vengeance. Contrary to the trite advice to "forgive and forget," forgiveness does not mean forgetting or excusing the wrongdoing. Rather, it is a conscious decision, which often requires considerable effort, not to act upon the desire of vengeance (Pruitt and Kim 2004).

Forgiveness can be understood either as a *unilateral* or a *bilateral* process. Unilateral forgiveness takes an unconditional form, an unsolicited gift given to the offender. It does not require anything from the offending side, such as an apology, remorse, or plea for forgiveness. Three advantages of unilateral forgiveness are that

- it frees victims from the obsessive demand of vengeful desires and the resulting psychological pain;
- it can create a safe space for the perpetrators to acknowledge their wrongdoing and to express remorse; and

- like many other unilateral initiatives, it can break the cycle of mutual hurt (Pruitt and Kim 2004).

Unilateral forgiveness, however, has two possible problems in moving toward reconciliation (Govier 2002; Lamb 2002; Pruitt and Kim 2004). One problem is that unilateral forgiveness can invite further injury when it is perceived as a sign of weakness. Another problem is that, although it does promote victim healing, there is no sure guarantee that it also promotes healing in the *relationship* between the victim and the victimizer. A Tutsi woman may forgive her Hutu neighbor for his killing of her husband and children, even though he lives happily with his family in the same village without feeling guilty or expressing remorse over what he has done to her. But can her forgiveness sustain over time? Also, is it possible for her and her neighbor to resume their once friendly, food-sharing relationship? Given the reality of most intergroup conflicts in which the antagonists have to live together, often side by side, the practicality of unilateral forgiveness is probably limited.

Bilateral forgiveness is an interactive process that involves an exchange between the victim and the offender; that is, the victim forgives in exchange for genuine contrition by the offender (Jacoby 1983; Augsburger 1992; Montville 1993; Pruitt and Kim 2004). Unlike unilateral forgiveness, bilateral forgiveness requires a condition: genuine contrition on the part of the offender. When both parties are culpable – which is a common case in intergroup conflict – each side should offer authentic contrition. As Jacoby (1983, p. 347) points out, without such contrition by the offender, forgiveness has no "significance as a social bond, as a medium for restoring civilized relations between the injured and the injurer." When successful, bilateral forgiveness can free the victim and the offender from the painful, psychological bondage: the victim from vengeful desires, and the offender from shame and the burden of wrongdoing. With this mutual liberation in hand, both parties can work toward repairing and reconstructing their relationship.

Much empirical work supports that expressions of contrition promote forgiveness. Specifically, individuals are more likely to forgive offenders who admit their wrongdoing (see Exline and Baumeister 2000), express remorse (see McCullough *et al.* 1997), or make sincere apologies (see Ohbuchi *et al.* 1989). Forgiveness rarely occurs when offenders show little contrition or offer insincere apologies.

Forgiveness at the interpersonal level (e.g., between husband and wife) is difficult, slow, and often impossible to achieve (see, e.g., Finkel *et al.* 2002). And so, undoubtedly, it is even more intractable at the group level. Shriver (1995), a leading voice in the argument for collective forgiveness as a viable political concept, acknowledges the immense challenge in translating what we know about forgiveness at the individual level to forgiveness at the collective level. When political leaders pursue collective forgiveness, he argues, the translation has a chance. Some degree of forgiveness can be attained when the political leaders on each side exchange symbolic contrition with symbolic forgiveness; and symbolic exchange of this kind can bring about a collective turning away from stubborn vengeful feelings toward a rebuilding of the relationship.

6.4   Conclusion

This chapter explores the role of vengeance in escalating conflicts. While acknowledging that many other factors can contribute to the escalation of a conflict, I argue that the desire for vengeance plays a crucial role in many escalating conflicts – in intergroup conflicts in particular. Relying on theoretical analysis, literary work, and real-life examples, I discuss four key features of vengeance – its potency, its causes, its functions, and its long-lasting nature. Finally, I explore some ways that vengeful urges may be appeased.

It is my view that vengeance should receive increased empirical attention in conflict research, from the interpersonal to collective, international domains. As a research topic, it seems to enjoy much less focus than its everyday prevalence would seem to demand. Perhaps this is because the prevailing approach to the analysis of conflict seems to avoid looking squarely at the emotions that conflicts arouse in both parties (Adler *et al.* 1998). However, as recent work on the role of emotions in conflict (e.g., Horowitz 2001; Kressel 2002) is beginning to show, emotions play a critical role in conflict, and a full understanding of conflict requires an integration of emotion into other better-developed perspectives. The main theme of this chapter is that vengeful feelings are a main part of such an integration.

References

Adler RS, Rosen B & Silverstein EM (1998). Emotions in negotiation: How to manage fear and anger. *Negotiation Journal* **14**:161–179.

Allport GW (1954). *The Nature of Prejudice*. Boston, MA, USA: The Beacon Press.

Aquino K, Tripp TM & Bies RJ (2001). How employees respond to personal offense: The effects of blame attribution, victim status, and offender status on revenge and reconciliation in the workplace. *Journal of Applied Psychology* **86**: 52–59.

Aristotle. *Nichomachean Ethics* (translated by Ostwald M, 1962). Indianapolis, IN, USA: The Bobbs-Merrill Company, Inc.

Aronson E (1992). *The Social Animal*. New York, NY, USA: WH Freeman.

Augsburger DW (1992). *Conflict Mediation across Cultures: Pathways and Patterns*. Louisville, KY, USA: Westminster/John Knox Press.

Azar EE (1990). *The Management of Protracted Social Conflict: Theory and Cases*. Hampshire, UK: Gower.

Bain A (1859). *The Emotions and the Will*. London, UK: John W. Parker and Son.

Baumeister RF (1997). *Evil: Inside Human Violence and Cruelty.* New York, NY, USA: WH Freeman.

Baumeister RF, Stillwell A & Wotman SR (1990). Victim and perpetrator accounts of interpersonal conflict: Autobiographical narratives about anger. *Journal of Personality and Social Psychology* **59**:994–1005.

Baumgartner MP (1984). Social control from below. In *Toward a General Theory of Social Control, Vol. 1, Fundamentals*, ed. Black D, pp. 303–345. New York, NY, USA: Academic Press.

Berke JH (1988). *The Tyranny of Malice: Exploring the Dark Side of Character and Culture.* New York, NY, USA: Summit Books.

Berscheid E, Boye D & Walster E (1968). Retaliation as a means of restoring equity. *Journal of Personality and Social Psychology* **10**:370–376.

Black-Michaud J (1975). *Cohesive Force: Feud in the Mediterranean and the Middle East.* New York, NY, USA: St. Martin's Press.

Borris E & Diehl PE (1998). Forgiveness, reconciliation, and the contribution of international peacekeeping. In *The Psychology of Peacekeeping*, ed. Langholtz HJ, pp. 207–222. Westport, CT, USA: Praeger.

Brewer MB & Miller N (1996). *Intergroup Relations.* New York, NY, USA: Brooks/Cole.

Brock TC & Buss AH (1962). Dissonance, aggression, and evaluation of pain. *Journal of Abnormal and Social Psychology* **65**:197–202.

Brock TC & Buss AH (1964). Effects of justification for aggression in communication with the victim on postaggression dissonance. *Journal of Abnormal and Social Psychology* **68**:403–412.

Brown BR (1968). The effects of need to maintain face on interpersonal bargaining. *Journal of Experimental and Social Psychology* **4**:107–122.

Brown JD (1998). *The Self.* New York, NY, USA: McGraw-Hill.

Burnett AP (1998). *Revenge in Attic and Later Tragedy.* Berkeley, CA, USA: University of California Press.

Cooley CH (1902). *Human Nature and Social Order.* New York, NY, USA: Scribner's.

Daly M & Wilson M (1988). *Homicide.* New York, NY, USA: Aldine de Gruyter.

Deutsch M (2000). Justice and conflict. In *The Handbook of Conflict Resolution: Theory and Practice*, eds. Deutsch M & Coleman PT, pp. 41–64. San Francisco, CA, USA: Jossey-Bass.

Elster J (1999). *Alchemies of the Mind: Rationality and the Emotions.* Cambridge, UK: Cambridge University Press.

Euripides (430–420 BC). *Hecuba* (translated by Arrowsmith W, 1958). In *Euripides III*, eds. Grene D & Lattimore R, pp. 1-68. Chicago, IL, USA: The University of Chicago Press.

Exline JJ & Baumeister RF (2000). Expressing forgiveness and repentance: Benefits and barriers. In *Forgiveness: Theory, Research, and Practice*, eds. McCullough ME, Pargament KI & Thoresen CE, pp. 133–155. New York, NY, USA: Guilford Press.

Finkel EJ, Rusbult CE, Kumashiro M & Hannon PA (2002). Dealing with betrayal in close relationships: Does commitment promote forgiveness? *Journal of Personality and Social Psychology* **82**:956–974.

Fisher RJ (2001). Social–psychological processes in interactive conflict analysis and reconciliation. In *Reconciliation, Justice, and Coexistence: Theory and Practice*, ed. Abu-Nimer M, pp. 25–45. Lanham, MD, USA: Lexington Books.

French PA (2001). *The Virtues of Vengeance*. Lawrence, KS, USA: The University Press of Kansas.

Friedman TL (2002). *Longitudes and Attitudes: Exploring the World after September 11*. New York, NY, USA: Farrar, Straus and Giroux.

Frijda NH (1993). The lex talionis: On vengeance. In *Emotions: Essays on Emotion Theory*, eds. Van Goozen SHM, Van de Poll NE & Sergeant JA, pp. 263–289. Hilldale, NJ, USA: Lawrence Erlbaum.

Geronimo (1906). *Geronimo's Story of His Life*. New York, NY, USA: Duffield.

Goffman E (1959). *The Presentation of Self in Everyday Life*. New York, NY, USA: Doubleday Anchor.

Gouldner AW (1960). The norm of reciprocity: A preliminary statement. *American Sociological Review* **25**:161–178.

Gourevitch P (1998). *We Wish to Inform You that Tomorrow We Will Be Killed with Our Families: Stories from Rwanda*. New York, NY, USA: Farrar, Straus and Giroux.

Govier T (2002). *Forgiveness and Revenge*. London, UK: Routledge.

Hallett CA & Hallett ES (1980). *The Revenger's Madness: A Study of Revenge Tragedy Motifs*. Lincoln, NE, USA: University of Nebraska Press.

Heider F (1958). *The Psychology of Interpersonal Relations*. New York, NY, USA: Wiley.

Hewstone M, Rubin M & Willis H (2002). Intergroup bias. *Annual Review of Psychology* **53**:575-604.

Horowitz DL (2001). *The Deadly Ethnic Riot*. Berkeley, CA, USA: University of California Press.

Jaber H (1997). *Hezbollah: Born with a Vengeance*. New York, NY, USA: Columbia University Press.

Jacoby S (1983). *Wild Justice: The Evolution of Revenge*. New York, NY, USA: Harper and Row.

Jeffreys MDW (1952). Samsonic suicide or suicide of revenge among Africans. *African Studies* **11**:118–122.

Karsten R (1935). *The Head-Hunters of Western Amazonus*. Helsingfors, Finland: Societas Scientiarum Fennica.

Kaufman SJ (2001). *Modern Hatred: The Symbolic Politics of Ethnic War*. London, UK: Cornell University Press.

Kelman HC (1999). Transforming the relationship between former enemies: A social–psychological analysis. In *After the Peace: Resistance and Reconciliation*, ed. Rothstein RL, pp. 193-205. Boulder, CO, USA: Lynne Rienner.

Kelsen HJ (1943). *Society and Nature: A Sociological Inquiry*. Chicago, IL, USA: The University of Chicago Press.

Kim SH & Smith RH (1993). Revenge and conflict escalation. *Negotiation Journal* **9**:37–43.

Kim SH, Smith RH & Brigham NL (1998). Effects of power imbalance and the presence of third parties on reactions to harm: Upward and downward revenge. *Personality and Social Psychological Bulletin* **24**:353–361.

Kressel NJ (2002). *Mass Hate: The Global Rise of Genocide and Terror*. Cambridge, MA, USA: Westview Press.

Kriesberg L (2001). Changing forms of coexistence. In *Reconciliation, Justice, and Coexistence: Theory and Practice*, ed. Abu-Nimer M, pp. 47–64. Lanham, MD, USA: Lexington Books.

Kunda Z (1987). Motivated inference: Self-serving generation and evaluation of causal theories. *Journal of Personality and Social Psychology* **53**:636–647.

Kuper L (1981). *Genocide*. New Haven, CT, USA: Yale University Press.

Lamb S (2002). Introduction: Reasons to be cautious about the use of forgiveness in psychotherapy. In *Before Forgiving: Cautionary Views of Forgiveness in Psychotherapy*, ed. Lamb S & Murphy JG, pp. 3–14. New York, NY, USA: Oxford University Press.

Lawler EJ & Yoon J (1993). Power and the emergence of commitment behavior in negotiated exchange. *American Sociological Review* **58**:465–481.

Lederach JP (1997). *Building Peace: Sustainable Reconciliation in Divided Societies*. Washington, DC, USA: US Institute of Peace Press.

Lerner MJ (1975). The justice motive in social behavior: An introduction. *Journal of Social Issues* **31**: 1–20.

Licklider R (1995). The consequences of negotiated settlements in civil wars, 1945–1993. *American Political Science Review* **89**:681–690.

Mackie JL (1985). Morality and retributive emotions. In *Persons and Values: Selected Papers*, eds. Mackie J & Mackie P, pp. 206–219. Oxford, UK: Clarendon Press.

Marongiu P & Newman G (1987). *Vengeance: The Fight against Injustice*. Totowa, NJ, USA: Rowman and Littlefield.

McCauley C (2001). The psychology of group identification and the power of ethnic nationalism. In *Ethnopolitical Warfare: Causes, Consequences, and Possible Solutions*, eds. Chirot D & Seligman MEP, pp. 343–362. Washington, DC, USA: American Psychological Association.

McCullough ME, Worthington EL Jr & Rachal KC (1997). Interpersonal forgiving in close relationships. *Journal of Personality and Social Psychology* **73**:321–336.

Mead GH (1934). *Mind, Self & Society*. Chicago, IL, USA: University of Chicago Press.

Meng L (2002). Rebellion and revenge: The meaning of suicide of women in rural China. *International Journal of Social Welfare* **11**: 300–309.

Milosevi M. (1997). The media war: 1987–1997. In *Burn this House: The Making and Unmaking of Yugoslavia*, eds. Udoviki J & Ridgeway J, pp. 108–129. Durham, NC, USA: Duke University Press.

Montville JV (1993). The healing function in political conflict resolution. In *Conflict Resolution Theory and Practice: Integration and Application*, eds. Sandole DJD & van der Merwe H, pp. 112–127. New York, NY, USA: Manchester University Press.

Murphy JG & Hampton J. (1988). *Forgiveness and Mercy*. Cambridge, UK: Cambridge University Press.

Mylroie L (2000). *Study of Revenge: Saddam Hussein's Unfinished War against America*. Washington, DC, USA: AEI Press.

Nietzsche F (1887). *On the Genealogy of Morals* (translated by Kaufmann W, 1967). New York, NY, USA: Vintage Books.

Ohbuchi K, Kameda M & Agarie N (1989). Apology as aggression control: Its role in mediating appraisal of and response to harm. *Journal of Personality and Social Psychology* **56**:219–227.

O'Leary MR & Dengerink HA (1973). Aggression as a function of the intensity and pattern of attack. *Journal of Research in Personality* **7**:61–70.

Pruitt DG & Kim SH (2004). *Social Conflict: Escalation, Stalemate, and Settlement*, third edition. New York, NY, USA: McGraw-Hill.

Rasmussen JL (2001). Negotiating a revolution: Toward integrating relationship building and reconciliation into official peace negotiations. In *Reconciliation, Justice, and Coexistence: Theory and Practice*, ed. Abu-Nimer M, pp. 101–127. Lanham, MD, USA: Lexington Books.

Rawls J (1971). *A Theory of Justice*. Cambridge, MA, USA: The Belknap Press.

Rice O (1982). *The Hatfields and McCoys*. Lexington, KY, USA: University of Kentucky Press.

Scheff TJ (1994). *Bloody Revenge: Emotions, Nationalism, and War*. Boulder, CO, USA: Westview Press.

Shriver DW (1995). *An Ethic for Enemies: Forgiveness in Politics*. New York, NY, USA: Oxford University Press.

Shriver DW (2001). Where and when in political life is justice served by forgiveness? In *Burying the Past: Making Peace and Doing Justice after Civil Conflict*, ed. Biggar N, pp. 23–39. Washington, DC, USA: Georgetown University Press.

Smith DN (1998). The psychocultural roots of genocide: Legitimacy and crisis in Rwanda. *American Psychologist* **53**:743–753.

Solomon RC (1990). *A Passion for Justice: Emotions and the Origins of the Social Contract*. Reading, MA, USA: Addison-Wesley Publishing Company.

Staub E (1989). *The Root of Evil: The Origins of Genocide and Other-Group Violence*. New York, NY, USA: Cambridge University Press.

Sumner WG (1906). *Folkways: A Study of the Sociological Importance of Usages, Manners, Customs, Mores, and Morals*. Boston, MA, USA: Ginn and Company.

Tajfel H (1982). *Social Identity and Intergroup Relations.* Cambridge, UK: Cambridge University Press.

Tajfel H & Turner JC (1986). The social identity theory of intergroup behavior. In *Psychology of Intergroup Behavior*, eds. Worchel S & Austin W, pp. 7–24. Chicago, IL, USA: Nelson-Hall.

Tesser A (1988). Toward a self-evaluation maintenance model of social behavior. In *Advances in Experimental Social Psychology*, Vol. 21, ed. Berkowitz L, pp. 181–227. New York, NY, USA: Academic Press.

Tripp TM, Bies RJ & Aquino K (2002). Poetic justice or petty jealousy? The aesthetics of revenge. *Organizational Behavior and Human Decision Processes* **89**:966–984.

Vidmar N (2000). Retribution and revenge. In *Handbook of Justice Research in Law*, eds. Sanders J & Hamilton VL, pp. 31–63. New York, NY, USA: Kluwer Academic/Plenum Publishers.

Volkan VD (2001). Transgenerational transmissions and chosen traumas: An aspect of large-group identity. *Group Analysis* **34**:79-97.

Wallensteen P (2002). *Understanding Conflict Resolution: War, Peace and the Global System.* Thousand Oaks, CA, USA: Sage.

Westermarck E (1898). The essence of revenge. *Mind* **7**:289–310.

Westermarck E (1912). *The Origin and Development of Moral Ideas*, Vol. 1. London, UK: Macmillan.

Wiesenthal S (1997). *The Sunflower: On the Possibilities and Limits of Forgiveness.* New York, NY, USA: Schocken Books.

Worchel S (1999). *Written in Blood: Ethnic Identity and the Struggle for Human Harmony.* New York, NY, USA: Worth Publishers.

Yamamoto EK (1999). *Interracial Justice: Conflict and Reconciliation in Post-Civil Rights America.* New York, NY, USA: University Press.

Youngs GA (1986). Patterns of threat and punishment reciprocity in a conflict setting. *Journal of Personality and Social Psychology* **51**:541–546.

Part III
Negotiating out of Escalation

Chapter 7

Structures of Escalation and Negotiation

I. William Zartman

Escalation is an augmented effort to prevail. It can be either unilateral or bilateral, but in either case it is a responsive action. Unilaterally, a party escalates on its own, in response to its previous action or to that action's insufficiency. Bilaterally, the more common understanding of the term, each party responds to the other's increasing effort to prevail. Thus conceived, escalation is an expression of power, a rational approach to conflict, as parties take increasing actions to change the other party's behavior.[1] Escalation is the pursuit of conflict designed to end conflict, but the designed end can be either on the escalator's own terms, as in victory, or on jointly decided terms, as in negotiation. Escalation ends when the parties can or will escalate no more; that is, when one or both run out of resources, when one prevails, or when both come to an agreement that removes the incompatibility of positions.

Escalation and negotiation are opposite actions, one to increase conflict and the other to decrease it. Not only do they head in different directions, but they also demand different attitudes and convictions: one to beat the enemies and the

---

[1]This is not to ignore all the problems of misperception and miscalculation that the previous chapters of this book have identified, nor the effects of intransitive escalation, which carry the parties away in vicious circles. However, it does emphasize the essential role of escalation in the pursuit of conflict, and it highlights the basic rationality of increasing effort in order to win; see the discussion of rationality in escalation in Waltz (1954, pp. 191–192) and Young (1991, pp. 102–104, 115–116).

other to come to terms with them, sometimes referred to as a winning versus a composing mentality. They thus seem to be mutually incompatible. On closer look, this absolute incompatibility does seem to be conditional, since some escalations appear to be designed to bring the other party to negotiation while others appear designed to prevail. But this differentiation does not entirely erase the difference in attitudes and convictions required for the two actions. The need then remains to find out the relation between escalation and negotiation. The present interest is to place conflict resolution within the context of conflict dynamics.

7.1   The Many Faces of Escalation

When a party takes an escalatory action in transitive escalation, it does so to achieve a purpose, notably to produce an outcome to the conflict either by prevailing over the other side or by bringing it to settlement (Schelling 1960, 1966; Kahn 1965; Young 1968; Cross 1969; Snyder 1972; Pillar 1983; Morgan 1990, 1994). In so doing, it seeks to exercise power over the other party. Power is an action by one party intended to produce a change in another party's behavior (Tawney 1931; Simon 1953; Habeeb 1988; Zartman 1997; Zartman and Rubin 2000). It can be exercised by either a direct or a contingent action; that is, by an action done ("I have closed the Panama Canal; that will change your mind about our trade agreement") or an action to be done ("If you persist in your behavior, I will close the Panama Canal; that will change your mind"). As such, it can be reckoned as an added value, a cost–benefit increment that can be combined negatively, as a deprivation, or positively, as a gratification, with the current value of a given or demanded position to change a party's evaluation of a particular course. For example, the cost imposed by closing the Panama Canal, added to the value of a previous course of action, diminishes that value and makes the posited course of action worth less, thus motivating the party to reconsider its action compared with alternatives previously valued less. (An example of a gratification would be an action, done or contingent, to decrease Canal transit fees.) The value of the second party's position on the trade agreement is now lowered by the cost of the Canal's closing or raised by the benefit of decreased Canal fees.

Such added values can be the result of a volitional action by a party, positively as a promise or negatively as a threat, as indicated in the example. Or they can be the result of an involuntary effect, negatively as a warning or positively as a prediction. The warning might be, "If you maintain your position on the trade agreement, our mutual trade will dry up and your farmers will suffer." The prediction might be, "If you accept my position on the trade agreement, our trade will blossom and your farmers will grow rich." These two aspects of power – voluntary and involuntary – correspond to transitive and intransitive escalation, respectively. Threats and promises, and faits accomplis, are the ingredients of transitive escalation (decisions that are taken to increase or decrease the conflict), whereas warnings and predictions are references to intransitive escalation, both negative and positive (the inherent intensification and relaxation spiral of conflict). The latter show that even intransitive escalation can be used by conflicting and bargaining parties to try to alter each other's behavior. Escalation commonly refers to rising deprivations – threats and warnings – that parties impose on each other. The question then remains, "How can this escalation be used to bring itself and the conflict to an end?"

Preliminarily, this discussion is not a reconsideration of the ripeness issue and the mutually hurting stalemate, which is the subject of a separate consideration in Chapter 12 by Karin Aggestam. Escalation may, indeed, be related to ripeness, but it is not the whole subject, and the two topics are not identical. The focus here is on the dynamics of escalation, or the pursuit of conflict, to determine where conflict can and does contribute to its own resolution. Although the subject of the present inquiry is the relation between conflict (escalation) and negotiation, its purpose is not to establish whether escalation is a precondition, necessary even if not sufficient, to negotiation, as in the case of a mutually hurting stalemate (Zartman 2000), but, to the contrary, whether negotiation is the possible sequel to escalation; that is, not whether stalemate must take place before negotiation, but whether negotiation can take place after escalation.

Probably the most important characteristic of escalation for its use in negotiation is its distinction from mere intensification. Conceptually the difference is clear, even if reality does its usual trick of treating conceptual distinctions sloppily. Intensification refers to a gradual increase without a change in nature, whereas escalation – as its etymology indicates – refers to a step-like increase in the nature of conflict, a change in saliency (Schelling 1960; Smoke 1977). Against "more and more," escalation is "something else." These new measures form risers for the steps of escalation, rather than constituting the famous "slippery slope" (reinforcing the distinction between intensification and escalation, since the image of the slope runs down and that of the stairs runs up). Thus, the escalation considered here is a noticeable (even if not unambiguously so) and conscious or at least identifiable action, and as such a use of power.[2] In sum, escalation is a monumental staircase, with the stairways heading in all directions, but with clear treads (the horizontal "steps") and risers (the vertical "lifters"). Or rather, it is an assemblage of two-sided (or more) stepladders, on which each party tries to mount higher than the other in a strenuous climb. It should be emphasized that this competitive climb is perfectly

---

[2]This is not to imply that all escalation is a purposeful exercise of power. It may well be designed simply to hurt the other party, with no further relation to intended outcomes. Since, as the introductory chapter discusses, escalation can refer to many dimensions, there are aspects that escape the focus of this inquiry. On the other hand, such "purposeless" escalation may well also have the same effects in producing negotiations, even if it was only intended to produce pain.

rational, at least to a point (Patchen 1988, pp. 241–260). Something worth wanting is worth escalating for. Much folk wisdom testifies to this fact, such as "If at first you don't succeed, try, try again"; "In for a penny, in for a pound"; and "Put your money where your mouth is." However, at the same time, somewhere there is a limit at which the cost of escalation outweighs the benefits of prevailing. This is the emphasis of business discussions of escalation, which refer to an unproductive unilateral extension or entrapment, as discussed in Chapter 5 by Paul Meerts. Unfortunately, this limit is not a line, but a zone. Unfortunately, too, it depends on the action of the other. If one more increment wins the prize, it may be worth it, but if it only invites a counter-increment from the other party, it is not (unless, of course, the *next* increment ...). Finally, if the parties could see ahead how many increments each was willing to invest, they could calculate at the bottom of the ladder their relative strengths and interests, and decide whether to win, lose, or bargain (except, of course, it would then be rational for each party to bluff about strengths and interests ...).[3] So how and where does the process of escalation relate to the process of negotiation?

7.2   Escalation and Negotiation

The relation is in the treads and risers. Escalation is a succession of risers, and between the risers is a tread, which is the status quo after one escalation and before the next one. The risers continue until one party outrises the other, or until they match each other and can go no further; in either case, each must decide whether to hold out wherever they are (on the tread), escalate again, or negotiate their way out of the conflict. Two of these situations constitute dynamic conflict: escalation (risers) and outcome (treads). The analytical questions of interest here are, Where in the tread-and-riser process is the third outcome, negotiation, proposed, and when does it occur? It needs to be emphasized that the questions here concern the inauguration of negotiations, not their successful conclusion, since the latter depends on other factors, notably the ability of the parties to create an enticing opportunity in the course of their negotiations.

Hypothetically, there are many possible answers. The decision to negotiate can come from the escalator itself, in relation to its own escalation, at one of four points: *during* one's own riser (1a), right *after* one's own escalation (1b), once the effect of one's escalation has passed (1c), or just before, under *threat* of, one's

---

[3]Snyder and Diesing's (1977, p. 181) contention that "the escalation ladder as a series of preexisting escalation options usually does not exist for bargainers and is not used in crisis decision-making" seems both descriptively and prescriptively wrong. In many situations, including some of those considered as cases in this chapter, future escalations were considered; in any case, in general, if they were not they should have been. Situations concerned in the entrapment literature arise because the escalation ladder was not surveyed fully before the first (or third) step.

Table 7.1. Summary of 10 cases

Case	(1) Escalator	(2) Target	(3) Relation	Time from escalation to negotiation
Cuba 1962	After, threat	After	Call	4 days
Kashmir 1965	After	After	Raise	3 weeks
Vietnam 1972	After, threat	After	Stalemate	4 months, 3 weeks
Gulf 1974	After	Threat	Shortfall	6 months
Angola 1983	During/after	After	Stalemate	10 days
Angola 1987	After, threat	After	Shortfall	3 months
Gulf 1987	After	After, threat	Call	2–4 weeks
El Salvador 1989	After	After	Shortfall	4 months
Karabagh 1994	After	After	Raise/shortfall	3 months
Bosnia 1995	After	After, threat	Stalemate	1 month

planned escalation (1d) (see *Table 7.1*). In other words, is negotiation initiated during escalation, under the memory of a recent escalation, when that memory has faded and new prospects are not yet looming, or under the threat or warning of a new escalation? The first, second, and fourth actions are exercises of power undertaken to produce negotiations, whereas the third appears to be independent of the exercise of power.

The decision can also come from the target party, at one of three points: just *after* the other's riser (2a), which corresponds to the first two moments of the escalator, since the first moment needs a little time to sink in; in the middle of the tread with no relation to risers (2b); or just before the other's *threatened* riser (2c). All three of these points refer to the other party's escalation. In terms of power, the target party is responding with an offer to negotiate to the efforts of the escalator to prevail or to open negotiations in the first and third cases, whereas the second does not appear to have any relation to the other party's exercise of power.

In both series, "after" refers to a short period following the latest escalation, not just subsequent to it at any point in time, which would be meaningless. "Long after" is the second option in both cases, after the effect of the escalation has passed. The short period is necessarily a bit soft and difficult to define within specific limits. It is not clear whether it should be calculated from the beginning of the escalation or from some point during its course, and whether it should be calculated to the first mention of negotiations by one side, their opening by both sides, or some intermediate point. The period itself may vary for many reasons, including the length of the preceding conflict. The difficulty of precise calculation, however, should not invalidate an important measure and the concept behind it. Once the case examples of this effect (assuming that it exists) have been collected, it may be possible inductively to assign a time limit.

Finally, negotiation can take place in relation to the two escalation processes by combining the first two effects; that is, when one party's escalation has outrisen the other (escalation to *raise*; 3a), when it has met the other (escalation to *call*; 3b), or when it has returned to the other's position unilaterally (*shortfall*; 3c) or bilaterally (*stalemate*; 3d) (Zartman and Aurik 1991; see *Table 7.1*). In other words, the result of the first process – raise – is to produce an imbalance that forces the target to negotiate while leaving the initiator in a strong position; whereas the latter three – call, raise and shortfall, and stalemate – all contain the result of a deadlock or stalemate in which neither side sees the desirability or possibility of further escalation, as a result of one side's policy success (3b) or failure (3c) or both sides' inability. In any of these instances, however, the threat of further escalation by one party, especially if it sees that escalation as possible, but not desirable, can be instrumental in reinforcing the effects of the stalemate. These instances require further exploration into the intent of the exercise of power: in the case of escalation to call, the intent to produce negotiations is clear; whereas in the case of shortfall, the intent to produce victory is clear and it has failed; and the case of escalation to raise can be either outcome.

7.3   Instances of Escalation

Ten studies have been undertaken to throw some light on the relation between escalation and negotiation. The cases were chosen as major instances of conflict escalation; 10 others could have been used, and scholars are invited to test the preliminary conclusions presented here using other instances. The cases come from around the world and involve various levels of state power. The dynamics they show are similar, whether the case took place during the Cold War or after. A detailed history or careful analysis in each case would be longer than the space available here, so the dynamics are briefly summarized below and the type of relation identified. The escalator is marked (E) and the target (T) for identification purposes only; designations do not preclude prior escalations or counter-escalations by the target. References are given for fuller case analyses. This type of concise summary does not permit causal inferences beyond a sequential correlation; in all cases, however, fuller accounts show the causal link inferred here.

7.3.1   The Cuban missile crisis

In 1962, the Cuban missile crisis came to a quick end after one escalation, followed by some minor relaxation, and before a threat of a second major escalation (Kennedy 1969; Snyder and Diesing 1977). The USA (E) established a naval quarantine around Cuba on 22 October 1962, after it had discovered Soviet missile construction a week earlier; it reduced the perimeter from 800 to 500 kilometers two days later when Soviet ships turned around, but boarded a (non-Soviet) ship the next day as construction continued. Faced with urgent threats and warnings of air strikes (transitive) and nuclear war (intransitive), the Soviets (T) proposed an agreeable compromise on 26 October 1962, four days after the previous major escalation and two days after escalation in its procedural expression (1b and 1d above).

7.3.2 The Kutch and Kashmir crisis

In 1965, the Kutch and Kashmir crisis followed a series of ratcheted escalations until both sides were exhausted, but the initial attacker more so, and a peace agreement was mediated. Before the completion of an Indian military modernization program and after the death of Indian Prime Minister Jawaharlal Nehru, Pakistan opened a series of skirmishes in the Rann of Kutch, forcing the territorial dispute to an ad hoc international tribunal, and then began guerrilla attacks on Indian Kashmir in August. The Indians escalated with an attack with conventional forces and seized territory on the Pakistani side of the *de facto* border, whereupon Pakistan responded with a drive into southern Kashmir. India (E) then escalated again in early September with an attack across the *de jure* frontier well south of Kashmir and took and held territory near Lahore. With India in the more favorable position, having proved that Kashmir could not be taken from it by force, and Pakistan (T) out of spare parts, both parties agreed to a cease-fire demanded by the United Nations (UN) on 22 September 1965 and to a Soviet-mediated truce on 10 January 1966. The time between the last in a series of transitive escalations into a full war across the recognized international – that is, not Kashmiri – frontier and the cease-fire was three weeks (1b, 2a, and 3a above; Thornton 1985).

7.3.3 The US–Vietnam War

In the early 1970s, a series of escalations to call after inconclusive rounds of escalations to raise brought a negotiated settlement to the Vietnam War. The war in the 1960s was an escalating stalemate, as symbolized by the Pyrrhic repulsion of the North Vietnamese Tet offensive at the end of January 1968; the USA continued heavy air raids through the following nine months, while combat continued inconclusively on the ground. The Paris peace talks began at the end of the following January, but a month after their opening a major North Vietnamese offensive took heavy American casualties. An American peace proposal was offered in October 1970. The Paris and back-channel negotiations were punctuated by US (E) escalations into Cambodia in April–June 1970 and into Laos in February 1971, and by the North Vietnamese (T) conventional army's spring offensive of March 1972 and the US and South Vietnamese counteroffensive to retake Binh Dinh province in July 1972.

The US bombing and mining of Hanoi and Haiphong began in early May 1972, a move heavy with risks for further, intransitive escalation if Soviet ships were to hit a mine or if Soviet–US summit communications were to hit a snag. Instead, the escalating cost line for non-agreement crossed the declining benefit line for further US concessions, and the Vietcong Politburo decided to table significant proposals in early September and October 1972, which produced progress and then deadlock in mid-December. After a negative deadline constituted by the Christmas bombing of North Vietnam, the parties resumed negotiations on 9 January 1973, and an agreement was made within weeks thereafter. After the initial North Vietnamese effort in the early and mid-1960s in continuation of the previous war in Indochina, the war was a repeated set of US escalations matched by North Vietnamese responses. The time between the escalation and the opening of serious negotiations in mid-1972 was about four months, and that between the last escalation and the reopening of the final negotiations was three weeks (1b, 2a, and 3d above; Milstein 1974; Szulc 1974; Zartman 1987).

7.3.4   Iraq–Iran border conflicts

In 1974, the third round of the border crisis between Iran and Iraq took a specific turn with the involvement of Iranian support for the Iraqi Kurds, and the limited escalation of the previous rounds of 1959 and 1969 took a much more serious form, which led to stalemate and the negotiation of a mediated agreement in Algiers in March 1975 (Ghareeb 1981; Lieb 1985). After 1972, the central undemarcated portion of the Iran–Iraq boundary became the scene of increasing incidents, compounded by Iranian support of the restive Kurds on the other side of the border. A UN Special Representative mediated a cease-fire and border demarcation agreement between the two neighbors in March 1974.

However, Iraqi Vice President Saddam Hussein decided that the usual past sequence of a limited spring–summer offensive, winter stalemate induced by Iranian Kurds, and Iraqi late-winter negotiations was undesirable for his regime, and so he staked his career on a full-scale military offensive. Every Iraqi advance against its Kurds brought increased Iranian involvement on their behalf across the border, which violated the cease-fire. By September 1974, the Iraqi spring–summer offensive had captured almost every Kurdish town, which provoked a large flow of Kurdish refugees across the border, and most of the Iranian supply routes were closed. Iran (E) then produced an important escalation by introducing sophisticated weaponry (radar-guided anti-aircraft missiles and anti-tank batteries) that slowed the Iraqi offensive as the winter snows arrived. However, the Iraqis (T) maintained their pressure on the Kurds throughout the winter and prepared for a final decisive escalation when the spring thaws appeared. At the beginning of March 1975, both parties came to Algiers for the first Organization of Petroleum Exporting Countries (OPEC) summit, during which they came to an agreement on their common border and on the Kurdish question. The Iranian escalation had fallen short of its intended decisive impact, and faced with an impending counter-escalation by Iraq, Iran agreed to negotiate (1b, 2c, and 3c above).

7.3.5   The Namibian crisis

In late 1983, in the conflict between South Africa and Angola centered on Namibia, a South African military escalation was countered by an Angolan diplomatic escalation, which led to a brokered truce (Zartman 1989; Crocker 1992). After the South African invasion of Angola failed to bring the National Union for the Total Independence of Angola (UNITA) to power in 1975–1976, the South African Defense Force withdrew to fight the rebellion of the South West African People's Organization (SWAPO) in Namibia and to launch raids across the border against SWAPO and Angolan army camps. Increasingly deep and frequent raids in May 1978, March and October 1979, June 1981, and June 1982 reached the level and the length of the previous decade's invasion, without reducing SWAPO's attacks on Namibia. UNITA's advances also increased during the period, as its troops moved into northern Angola at the beginning of 1983 and to within 100 miles of Luanda in September; but its lines were stretched and it could not hold its advances.

At the beginning of December, UNITA and the South African Defense Force (E) launched their twelfth annual campaign into a more intense escalation than previous efforts. Operation Askari's deep penetration into northern Angola led only to increased Angolan (T) dependency on augmented Cuban forces and, in January 1984, to a large arms deal with the Soviet Union. The day Operation Askari began, US Assistant Secretary of State Chester Crocker met South African Foreign Minister R.F. Botha to urge some unilateral confidence-building gesture; 10 days later, South Africa proposed a cease-fire for the end of January, just before the rains. At the same time as Operation Askari was going on, amid much diplomatic activity, South Africa responded to US pressure by proposing a cease-fire and withdrew much of its military force a week before the cease-fire date, upon receiving assurances that Angola would not fill the gap, and negotiated a disengagement from southern Angola in Lusaka in mid-February 1984 (1a and 3c above).

In 1987, in the same Namibian conflict, a military escalation and counterescalation left the parties locked in a stalemate with the threat or danger of a massive escalation ahead, which led to a mediated conflict resolution (Zartman 1989; Crocker 1992). With the beginning of the dry season in July, both the Angolans with the Cubans (E) and South Africa with UNITA (T) launched major offensives in southern Angola, with heavy losses. The Angolan attack was halted and UNITA returned to the offensive against the Angolan base of Cuito Carnevale at the end of the year. After a massive US$1 billion Soviet arms buildup in May, the Cuban–Angolan side met in Moscow in early November 1987 and decided to out-escalate South Africa by doubling the number of Cuban troops, to a total higher than the 50,000 South African troops in the theater of operations. The new Cuban troops immediately moved south, across the tacitly agreed southern border for their operations, engaged South Africans wherever they met them, caused significant white casualties among South African troops, and announced a new doctrine of hot pursuit that could carry them across the border for the first time into South African territory. By March 1988, the battle for Cuito Carnevale was bogged down in the rains.

At the same time, both Cuba and the Soviet Union let it be known that they were tired of the Angolan adventure and were ready to negotiate an agreement, essentially on the "linkage formula" of paired Cuban withdrawals from Angola in exchange for South African withdrawal (i.e., independence) in Namibia. Diplomatic contacts had been going on under US persistence for a while, always to run up against the usual obduracy of both sides. However, in mid-January 1988, as Cuba announced new troop levels after the Moscow agreement, Angolan President José Eduardo dos Santos proposed a meeting with the USA, with Cubans present, that, at the end of the month, broached new details of major importance. The USA urged a precise timetable, which Angola produced in a first draft in mid-March, as the battle for Cuito Carnevale ended in a draw, which led to full exploratory talks among Angolan, Cuban, South African, and American delegations in May 1988. The November 1987 decision to escalate troop commitments by Cuba, Angola, and the Soviet Union, while South Africa and Angola, with their UNITA and Cuban allies, respectively, were checking each other's offensives to an escalated draw around Cuito Carnevale, effectively brought Angola to offer three months later, and South Africa to accept in another two months, negotiations that led to the paired withdrawal agreements signed in Brazzaville in December (1b, 2a, 3b, and 3c above; and Zartman 1989).

7.3.6   The first Gulf War between Iran and Iraq

In 1987, in the first Gulf War between Iran and Iraq, after eight years of inconclusive escalation and counter-escalation, Iranian attempts to win through escalation fell short with massive costs, and Iraqi counter-escalation to call, backed by the threat of a much more horrendous escalation, brought an end to the fighting. In that year, the last Iranian human-wave offensive, Karbala Five, in the battle for Basra was repulsed by Iraq with 50,000 and 20,000 killed, respectively, and Iraq began to gain the upper hand, regain its territory, and press the Iranians beyond their ability to respond. UN Security Council Resolution 598 of 20 July 1987 demanded a cease-fire, which Iraq accepted on condition of Iran's acceptance, safe in the belief that it would not be forthcoming; the rejection left Iran isolated diplomatically and hence short of military material, with its economic means and its cannon-fodder youth in ever-decreasing supply.

In a desperate response, Iran (E) re-escalated in February 1988 by reviving its missile "war of the cities" with raids on Baghdad, only to find that over the next six weeks every one of its surface-to-surface missiles was met by nearly three Iraqi missiles. Iraq (T) returned to the offensive in April with a succession of invasions into Iran, withdrawing to its border each time it took some territory. At the same time, reports again arose about the Iraqi use of chemical weapons, as had been verified in previous years, and confirmed by Iraq in July 1988. Added to the missile raids on urban civilian complexes, the use of poison gas raised the threat of a horrible escalation without its ever having to be mentioned explicitly. When Saddam Hussein called for negotiations and an "honorable peace" on 17 July, Iran accepted Resolution 598 the next day. When nothing happened, Iraq resumed its pattern of invasion and withdrawal, driving up to 40 kilometers into Iranian territory. The cease-fire was finalized on 8 August 1988, to go into effect on 20 August, and negotiations began in Geneva a week later. Iraq's escalation to call was accompanied by the threat of a huge escalation, followed in two weeks by an agreement to negotiate (1b, 2a, 2c, and 3b above; Preece 1988).

7.3.7   The El Salvador civil war

At the end of 1989, a decade of civil war in El Salvador burst into a major offensive by the Farabundo Marti National Liberation Front (FMLN) in which the FMLN failed to hold conquered areas in the capital, but could not be dislodged from its rural bases; four months later, UN mediation took hold, which led to eight agreements between April 1990 and January 1992 and ended the civil war. Initially in this civil war, the rebels had the military advantage and their victory, as in Nicaragua, was seen to be only a matter of time. However, after 1983 rebel leaders saw that even victory would be costly and, in the following year, the increased strength of the government and paramilitary forces, with US support, and the election of a moderate right-wing civilian president, José Napoleon Duarte, led to the opening of talks later in the year. The peace talks stalled, and government military fortunes continued to improve over the following three years.

The FMLN was able to mobilize public pressure in favor of peace talks, which counterbalanced the government's military power, but rebel proposals for negotiations were repeatedly rejected until late 1987 (Roett and Smyth 1988). Several months of contacts under an agreement mediated by Costa Rican President Oscar Arias Sánchez also collapsed at the end of the year. Seeking to overcome the failing popularity of his predecessor over the rising death and destruction of the civil war, the newly elected president, Alfredo Cristiani, proposed dialogue in his inaugural speech in June 1989. However, in November the rebels (E) launched their maximum effort of the war, penetrating into San Salvador and other cities. The offensive was repulsed and failed to spark a popular uprising in the cities, leading only to an increase in popular support for an end to violence. It also showed the government (T) that it could not overcome the rebellion. A month after the initiation of the offensive, UN Special Representative Alvaro de Soto made contacts with FMLN leaders and with President Cristiani, opening UN mediation. Intensive shuttle diplomacy finally brought the parties together in March 1990 and produced the first of the eight agreements at the beginning of April (1b, 2a, and 3c above; Byrne 1996; de Soto 1999).

7.3.8   The Karabagh problem

In 1993, after three years of steady conflict over the Armenian enclave of Karabagh within Azerbaijan, an escalation and repulsed counter-escalation led to a ceasefire (Mooradian and Druckman 1999). After a period of Azeri dominance in the hostilities over its Armenian enclave, following the independence of Armenia and Azerbaijan in 1991, the Karabagh legislature declared its own independence in January 1992 and Armenian irregulars (E) broke the Azeri blockade of the area and established a connection with Armenia through the Lachin Corridor. As fighting continued, cease-fires were signed in May, August, and September. However, new Karabagh offensives in February, March, and April 1993 widened the Corridor, and in June, August, and October escalated operations beyond the Corridor to larger Azeri towns to the south, taking a fifth of the country's territory. Armed forces from Armenia and Mountainous Karabagh then defeated a December Azeri (T) counterattack by February 1994, but were overextended; neither side was able to move the battle lines. After Kazakh, Iranian, and international – Conference for Security and Cooperation in Europe (CSCE) – attempts at mediation failed or were blocked, Russia began mediation in November 1993, bringing the parties together three months after the stalemate had set in to negotiate a cease-fire in May 1994, which managed the conflict without resolving any of its basic issues (1b, 2a, 3a, and 3d above).

7.3.9   The Bosnian crisis

In 1995, after three years of Serbian ethnic cleansing and military conquest of much of Bosnia, an escalation by Croatian and Bosnian forces, combined in a federation (E) since the previous March, followed by an escalated North Atlantic Treaty Organization (NATO) intervention, brought all parties to a settlement. In the first half of the year, Bosnian Serb (T) tactics continued to lead to new seizures of territory; the neutralization of the UN Protection Force (UNPROFOR), the UN peacekeepers; and the avoidance of NATO retaliation by tactical concessions. In July, these tactics culminated in the capture of Bosnian safe areas at Srebrenica and Zepa in the east and the massacre of their male populations. However, in the west the Croatian forces successfully regained the offensive to retake Western Slavonia in May and Krajina in August, and so destroyed the Serb objective of a single contiguous Serb Republic in Bosnia.

Two events at the end of August 1995 brought the conflict to a fragile stalemate. Serb mortar bombing of the Sarajevo market produced instant and continuous NATO bombing of Serb positions within two days, expanded 10 days later to include the use of cruise missiles and "smart bombs." At the beginning of September, the Croatian and Bosnian forces joined to continue their drive from Serb-held territories in Croatia into Bosnia itself, and regained significant parts of the lost territory and brought their holdings close to the diplomatic target of 49 percent of the Bosnian territory. By the end of the month, the drive was poised to enter the traditionally Serbian territories of Bosnia and take the Serb town of Banja Luka. Restrained by the US mediating team as Serbian President Slobodan Milosevic called for a cease-fire at the end of the month, the Bosnians delayed the cease-fire agreed on 5 October 1995 for an additional six days and took the Bosnian town of Sanski Most. As a result, the Serbs agreed to meet the Croats and Bosnians to begin negotiations at Dayton on 1 November (1b, 3a, and 3b above; Holbrooke 1997).

7.4 Initial Findings

The 10 cases are presented in a rather rough initial form (summarized in *Table 7.1*), but nonetheless they indicate some rather clear results that invite substantial refinement. First, the correlations indicate that decisions to negotiate follow a party's escalation of the conflict; deeper analysis into the course of the conflict, only alluded to here, confirms that these correlations do, indeed, have a causal effect. Parties escalate their conflict behavior and then, unable to win outright by that behavior, decide to explore coming to terms. Opposing parties feel the effects of the escalation and decide that the appropriate response is not a (further) counter-escalation, but a matching exploration of negotiation. The beginnings of a major change in attitudes and commitment occur after the escalation and give way to negotiation. It must be emphasized – because the discussions on ripeness have already indicated a huge propensity to misunderstanding – that what is caused is only the decision to explore negotiations, not the successful conclusion of a negotiated agreement, which depends in turn on many other things that the literature on negotiation itself explores. Escalation is – or at least can be – pre-negotiation behavior.

Second, the cases indicate that escalation (as distinguished on occasion from renewed conflict at a non-escalatory level) usually does not take place while negotiations are going on. However, there are exceptions, which only reinforces the idea that escalation can be intended to produce negotiations, not victory, and so the two are not incompatible.

Third, not all escalations produce a decision to negotiate (or else there would never be more than one escalation). The cases show three interrelated types of escalation: escalations to call, failed escalations to raise (or shortfalls), and escalations that stalemate (whatever they were intended to do). The typology is partially overlapping: both calls and shortfalls stalemate, so that types one and two are sub-types of three, although they may not constitute the entirety of type three. Calls are intentional stalemates, shortfalls are failed raises that do not change the previous stalemate out of which they sought to break.

As in many other pieces of life, the distinction between escalations to call and to raise is not always as clear in reality as it is at the conceptual level. It often takes a while for the distinction to become clear to the receiving side, so escalations to call often have to be repeated many times, as the Cuban missile crisis, the first Gulf War, and perhaps other cases show, which increases the risk of their being misunderstood. The problem with the distinction is compounded because it may be used tactically, as when an escalation to raise is presented as only an escalation to call and therefore justifies a response. In the midst of the second intifada, and the debate over reopening Israeli–Palestinian negotiations over the extent of the withdrawal of the Israeli occupation, the Hezbollah killing of an Israeli soldier was labeled by the USA as a "provocation" and was responded to by an Israeli deep raid on a Syrian radar station in Lebanon, "meant as a warning to Syria and not as an invitation to further conflict in the region." At the same time, Israel called Palestinian mortars firing across the Gaza border into Israel "really an escalation by Yasir Arafat himself." Edward Djeredjian commented, "I don't think that either Syria or Israel perceives any interest in a military escalation that can bring wider fighting. But the risks of miscalculation and escalation are always there, and that is the danger" (*New York Times*, 17 April 2001, pp. A1, A6). The next day the Israeli Defense Force occupied a portion of Gaza in retaliation, vowing to stay "days, weeks and months," but then withdrew under intense international criticism (*New York Times*, 18 April 2001, p. A1). The nature and message of the escalations were unclear.

However, some successful escalations to raise also produce negotiations, just as presumably some of the other types and results of escalations do not produce negotiations. This exercise focuses on the finding that escalation and negotiation are not incompatible and that the first can lead to the second, with some indication of subcategories of the first (escalation). It has not established (or sought to establish) the other side of the picture, namely, which escalations lead to negotiation and which do not. The constant or unknown factor is human will and free choice: some decision makers seize the opportunity (which they themselves may have created) and some do not. However, beyond free choice there are patterns that have only begun to be discovered here.

Fourth, one element of these patterns is time, with the cases showing a rather large range. Negotiations opened between four days (Cuba 1962) and six months (Gulf 1974) after the escalation. In the longer-range cases, the decision to negotiate was still clearly a result of the latest escalation, in most cases accompanied by the danger of worse to come, either transitively as a threat or intransitively as a warning. Threat was much less frequently necessary in the shorter-range cases. Length of time is determined by the amount of time it takes for the effect to sink in; escalations – like threats, as Patrick Morgan points out in Chapter 3 – need time to be perceived by the other side and to show their limits to the using side. The length of time, however, is also affected by the nature of the intervening conflict; in some of the longer periods, the war continued in the winter or wet-season period of lower activity while the parties hunkered down and considered their options. In the very short periods of time, a threatened deadline or a mediator's pressure focused the parties' attention. The only clear evidence of the cases is that it is impossible to specify (and hence to predict) the lapse of time before the effect is felt.

Fifth, the cases suggest that there is more to the decision to negotiate than simply stalemate. The preceding effort – that is, the escalation itself – is important too. The conflict is worth a try, a test, an investment. The escalation is a down payment on commitment, a measure of importance, like any intensification (Patchen 1988). However, by its stepped nature it is also an attempt to jolt the adversary into rethinking its own investment and commitment, raising the ante to provoke either withdrawal or negotiation by the other side. How many escalations it takes to accomplish this goal is still open to research – and may never be determined conclusively.

Sixth, by the same token, escalation is also a self-provocation for the escalator – one last try, after which the cost–benefits need to be reevaluated (at the same time as the adversary is doing the same thing). Escalation is therefore a catalyst to thinking about negotiation. And it is a catalyst to thinking about negotiation rather than withdrawal (by both sides) because it represents a major increment of sunk costs, both material and psychological, that prohibits out-and-out withdrawal and favors recuperating at least some benefits through negotiation. The cases, in their many varied ways, all support this complex calculation.

Seventh, even when it works, escalation is often not enough. Two additional measures are often necessary. One is the future shadow of more escalation, the reluctant threat. What clinched the target party's acceptance of the view that the time of counter-escalations was over was the danger of something worse on the horizon, something that the escalator was willing and able, but not eager, to do. Reluctance is a useful ingredient, inherent in many escalations, since escalation involves cost and the escalator is just as content to achieve the same results at a lower cost. But it also removes – or at least reduces – the element of challenge in the threat and confirms the presence of a way out of the conflict. Threat or precipice and way out or requital are also elements in classic ripeness.

The other additional measure is mediation. As is often the case in conflict resolution, even the presence of all the elements of pre-negotiation, including ripeness, are not enough to persuade the parties to overcome their fixation on the pursuit of conflict and instead seek settlement and reconciliation. They need help.

Eighth, the operational implication, therefore, is that adversaries and mediators should push for negotiations once an escalation has been attempted by the other side, as found in Chapters 8 and 9 of this book. Such a démarche is obviously best timed for when the escalation fails, or arrives at either a call or a shortfall. Even if it succeeds, by the reasoning of the previous point, it may be what the escalator needs, for its own domestic or psychological reasons, to enable it to now undertake negotiations. Unless the escalation actually won the war, in which case negotiation is moot, the escalation is likely to have restored the escalator's ability to negotiate – winning the battle perhaps, but still leaving the war tied. Escalations provide opportunities for negotiators to seize.

This is a very preliminary study, designed to document the importance of the topic and indicate research directions. A number of clear implications stand out for further research. First, studies of negotiation need to take into account the course of conflict, which few now do. The newness of the study of negotiation, the attempt to explain outcomes out of the negotiation process, and the focus on understanding and improving the practice of negotiation itself mean most accounts at best devote almost exclusive attention to "who said what to whom with what effect," and little to the ongoing conflict on the ground. The processes of conflict and conflict management, and their study, still tend to remain separate. Much of what happens in negotiation can be explained through an interactive process that still invites better understanding and conceptualization. However, some or much of that process reflects the course of the conflict itself. Except in the cases of the Cuban missile crisis and the Vietnam War, in which confrontation was the main element, there is little on escalation and its relation to the initiation and conduct of negotiation.

Second, studies on escalation and negotiation need to develop a higher degree of resolution, along many dimensions. A more finely tuned notion of correlation needs to be developed, with an appropriate explanation of lag times. Notions of "after," "between," and "before" are not sharply delimited. Correlation needs to be complemented by historical research on causality (see Mooradian and Druckman 1999 for a good example). More differentiation needs to be made in regard to the size of escalation and a non-tautological test of tolerance for pain (Carlson 1995). In dealing with size, proper attention must be paid to the problem of comparing different types of escalation. "The word escalation and all its synonyms are about to drop out of the lexicon as a result of overuse," it was noted with respect to the second intifada. "Over the last two weeks, the situation has been escalating, getting worse, intensifying and deteriorating almost daily [with no negotiation in prospect]" (Shalev 2001). As already indicated, if it has been established that escalation is (or can be) pre-negotiation behavior, research now needs to distinguish those escalations that lead to negotiations from those that do not, and why, and to consider how many escalations are needed to produce a negotiation.

Third, different types of controls are necessary to improve the robustness of findings. Studies of decisions to negotiate that correlate causally with escalations need to be tested by studies of decisions to negotiate that do not relate to escalations, and of escalations that do not produce decisions to negotiate. Only by comparing what did not work with what worked can one understand the latter. This study (at this stage) has shown that escalations, and especially escalations that intentionally or unintentionally produce stalemates, produce a decision to negotiate. The next round of research should help to answer whether both calls and falls can lead to negotiations, so that conflict and management can be brought together in a single phase.

References

Byrne H (1996). *El Salvador's Civil War: A Study in Revolution*. Boulder, CO, USA: Lynne Rienner.

Carlson L (1995). A theory of escalation and international conflict. *Journal of Conflict Resolution* **39**:511–534.

Crocker CA (1992). *High Noon in Southern Africa*. New York, NY, USA: Norton.

Cross J (1969). *The Economics of Bargaining*. New York, NY, USA: Basic Books.

De Soto A (1999). Ending violent conflict in El Salvador. In *Herding Cats*, eds. Crocker C, Hampson F & Aall P. Washington, DC, USA: US Institute of Peace.

Ghareeb E (1981). *The Kurdish Question in Iraq*. Syracuse, NY, USA: Syracuse University Press.

Habeeb MW (1988). *Power and Tactics in International Negotiations*. Baltimore, MD, USA: The Johns Hopkins University Press.

Holbrooke R (1997). *To End a War*. New York, NY, USA: Random House.

Kahn H (1965). *On Escalation*. New York, NY, USA: Praeger.

Kennedy RF (1969). *Thirteen Days: A Memoir of the Cuban Missile Crisis*. New York, NY, USA: Norton.

Lieb D (1985). Iran and Iraq at Algiers, 1975. In *International Mediation in Theory and Practice*, eds. Touval S & Zartman IW. Boulder CO, USA: Westview.

Milstein JS (1974). *Dynamics of the Vietnam War*. Columbus, OH, USA: Ohio State University Press.

Mooradian M & Druckman D (1999). Hurting stalemate or mediation? *Journal of Peace Research* **36**:706–772.

Morgan TC (1990). Power, resolve and bargaining in international crises. *International Interactions* **XV**(2):279–302.

Morgan TC (1994). *Untying the Knot of War*. Ann Arbor, MI, USA: Michigan University Press.

Patchen M (1988). *Resolving Disputes between Nations*. Chapel Hill, NC, USA: Duke University Press.

Pillar P (1983). *Negotiating Peace*. Princeton, NJ, USA: Princeton University Press.

Preece R (1988). *Iran–Iraq War*, Issue Brief 88060. Washington, DC, USA: Congressional Research Service.

Roett R & Smyth F (1988). *Dialogue and Armed Conflict: Negotiating the Civil War in El Salvador*. SAIS Foreign Policy Institute Case Study 12. Lanham, MD, USA: University Press of America.

Schelling T (1960). *The Strategy of Conflict*. Cambridge, MA, USA: Harvard University Press.

Schelling T (1966). *Arms and Influence*. New Haven, CT, USA: Yale University Press.

Shalev C (2001). Escalation in Israel. *Maariv*, 3 April, quoted in Sontag D (2001), In absence of talk, Israeli–Palestinian violence speaks, *New York Times*, 4 April.

Simon H (1953). Notes on the observation and measurement of power. *Journal of Politics* **15**:500–516.

Smoke R (1977). *War: Controlling Escalation*. Cambridge, MA, USA: Harvard University Press.

Snyder G (1972). Crisis bargaining. In *International Crises*, ed. Hermann C. New York, NY, USA: Free Press.

Snyder G & Diesing P (1977). *Conflict among Nations*. Princeton, NJ, USA: Princeton University Press.

Szulc T (1974). How Kissinger did it. *Foreign Policy* **15**:21–69.

Tawney RH (1931). *Equality*. London, UK: Unwin Press.

Thornton TP (1985). Tashkent. In *International Mediation in Theory and Practice*, eds. Touval S & Zartman IW. Boulder, CO, USA: Westview.

Waltz K (1954). *Man, the State and War*. New York, NY, USA: Columbia University Press.

Young HP (1991). *Negotiation Analysis*. Ann Arbor, MI, USA: University of Michigan Press.

Young O (1968). *The Politics of Force*. Princeton, NJ, USA: Princeton University Press.

Zartman IW (1987). Reality, image and detail. In *The 50% Solution*, ed. Zartman IW. New Haven, CT, USA: Yale University Press.

Zartman IW (1989). *Ripe for Resolution*. New York, NY, USA: Oxford University Press.

Zartman IW (1997). The structuralist dilemma in negotiation. In *Research on Negotiation in Organizations*, ed. Lewicki R. Greenwich, CT, USA: JAI Press.

Zartman IW (2000). The hurting stalemate and beyond. In *International Conflict Resolution after the Cold War*, eds. Stern P. & Druckman D. Washington, DC, USA: National Academy Press.

Zartman IW & Aurik J (1991). Power strategies in de-escalation. In *Timing the De-escalation of International Conflicts*, eds. Kriesberg L & Thorson S. Syracuse, NY, USA: Syracuse University Press.

Zartman IW & Rubin JZ, eds. (2000). *Power and Negotiation*. Ann Arbor, MI, USA: University of Michigan Press.

Further reading

Bonoma T (1975). *Conflict: Escalation and Deescalation*. Beverley Hills, CA, USA: Sage.

Brams S & Kilgour DM (1988). *Games and National Security*. New York, NY, USA: Basil Blackwell.

George A (1991). *Avoiding War*. Boulder, CO, USA: Westview.

Hopmann PT (2000). National disintegration disputes. In *Preventive Negotiations: Avoiding Conflict Escalation*, ed. Zartman IW. Lanham, MD, USA: Rowman & Littlefield.

Pruitt DG (1981). *Negotiation Behavior*. New York, NY, USA: Academic Press.

Ross J (1998). Escalation theory in labor-management negotiations. In *Advances in Qualitative Organization Research*. Greenwich, CT, USA: JAI Press.

Rubin JZ, Pruitt DG & Kim SH (1994). *Social Conflict*. New York, NY, USA: McGraw-Hill.

Smoker P (1964). Fear in the arms race. *Journal of Peace Research* 1:55–63.

Staw BM (1997). The escalation of commitment. In *Organizational Decision-Making*, ed. Shapiro Z. New York, NY, USA: Cambridge University Press.

Chapter 8

Conflict Escalation and Negotiation: A Turning-Points Analysis

Daniel Druckman

International negotiation is a dynamic process. Outcomes develop from patterned exchanges between negotiating parties and their constituencies. Of particular interest to analysts is the challenge of depicting these patterns. Some prefer sequential stage models (Douglas 1957; Zartman 1975; Gulliver 1979; Pruitt 1981; Druckman 1983), although they differ on just how the stages should be characterized. Others propose cyclical models in which monitoring and learning are central (Coddington 1968; Snyder and Diesing 1977; Cross 1983). For both, however, the guiding question is how to explain the relationship between processes and outcomes. Central to this explanation is the idea of turning points or events that move the process on a trajectory toward or away from agreement. One purpose of this chapter is to increase the usefulness of turning points as an empirical concept. It is a first attempt to perform a large-sample comparative analysis of negotiation processes.[1] Another purpose is to assess the role of turning points in the escalation of conflicts. The

---

[1] For a small-sample analysis of negotiating responsiveness, see Druckman and Harris (1990). For comparative analyses of negotiating objectives, attributes, events, and conditions, see Chesek (1997), Druckman (1997b), and Druckman *et al.* (1999). For large-sample analyses of international mediation, see Bercovitch and Langley (1993) and Bercovitch and Wells (1993).

negotiation process is analyzed in the context of the larger conflict between the parties.

8.1   Turning Points in Negotiation

There seems to be agreement on a broad conceptual definition of turning points. There is less agreement on how the concept should be operationalized for the analysis of negotiation processes. The concept is usually considered in conjunction with stages and defined as "events or processes that mark passage from one stage to the next, signaling progress from earlier to later phases" (Druckman 1997a, p. 92). It has been used to depict progress in such diverse negotiations as the military base rights talks between Spain and the USA (Druckman 1986), the North American Free Trade Agreement negotiations (Tomlin 1989), the Intermediate Nuclear Forces talks (Druckman *et al.* 1991), and 11 cases of multilateral environmental negotiations that took place between 1972 and 1992 (Chesek 1997). Turning points are indicated in these studies by such key events as resolving an impasse, signing a framework agreement, developing formulas and then bargaining over the details, and absorbing events outside the talks by either changing evaluations of the terms on the table or resolving the decision dilemma in the endgame. Each of these events is viewed as instrumental to moving the negotiation from one stage to the next. They can be procedural events, as when the format changes (e.g., from a plenary to a working committee structure), when the venue is changed from a public to a private location, or when deadlines are imposed. They can be substantive, as when new concepts are introduced that lead to a framework agreement or when different ways of packaging proposals are invented. Finally, they can be external to the talks, as when a leadership succession occurs in the country of one or more of the parties, when public opinion about the issues changes, or when a third party is sought to provide assistance. Many of these events were used as indicators of turning points in the four studies mentioned before.

While agreeing on the conceptual definition of turning points stated above, these investigators present considerable variety in the kinds of events chosen to indicate them. None of them has offered a typology that distinguishes among the various events – as, for example, procedural, substantive, or external events, or other turning points. None has clarified whether these types of events are precipitants of departures in the process (such as a new conceptualization of the issues) or are the departures (move from a stage of debating the issues to bargaining exchanges) themselves. This study seeks more precision in definition and analysis. It does so by distinguishing among three elements of turning points: precipitants, process departures, and consequences. By making these distinctions, we move the conception of turning points from identifiable events – as moments in time – to an analysis in three parts. Rather than identifying a turning point, we perform a turning-point analysis.

This concept of turning points is in some ways similar to, but in other ways different from, the concept of ripeness. Both concepts refer to changes in the course of a conflict or relationship. Both are thought to occur, often but not always, as a result of a crisis or impasse, also referred to as a hurting stalemate (Zartman 2000). And both are known better in retrospect, through analysis, than in prospect, during an ongoing process. Unlike ripeness, however, turning points are

- part of a negotiation (or pre-negotiation) process rather than only a condition for negotiation (or pre-negotiation);
- indicated by changes that occur during the process rather than by the conditions that lead to the change;
- less dependent on perceiving or seizing the opportunity when it presents itself; and
- indicative of downturns or escalations as well as upturns or de-escalations in the process.

In our three-part framework (Precipitants → Departures in process → Consequences), ripeness refers to the precipitants (or antecedent conditions), while turning points are indicated both by departures in the process itself and by the consequences of those departures.

Turning points are understood in relation to a chronology of events through the course of a negotiation. The chronology contains most of the information needed to analyze turning points. First, a departure must be observed and "coded." It is identified in comparative or time-series terms, in relation to earlier trends, and may be more or less abrupt. Second, precipitants must be identified, often but not always, within the process. These can be procedural or substantive decisions that occur in a proximate relation to the observed departure. They can also be external events responded to by the negotiating parties. They are identified through "backward tracing" from the departure. Third, the consequences of the departure are recorded in terms of movement toward or away from agreement. Progress toward agreement, indicated also by stage transitions, is regarded as being de-escalatory if it follows an impasse. Movement away from agreement, which may consist of an impasse or crisis, is "coded" as an escalation of the conflict. By distinguishing between immediate (proximal) and longer-term (distal) consequences, it is possible to project the path through future turning points that lead toward or away from agreement.

When viewed in terms of the complete chronology of a negotiation, a turning-points analysis can be construed as a form of process tracing. Following George and Bennett (2004), process tracing is an attempt to identify the causal chain that

proceeds from precipitating (independent variables) to consequent events or outcomes. The emphasis placed on causation renders process tracing more than a
historical description of a sequence of events. It attempts to infer causation within
cases and, as such, is similar to time-series analysis. It differs from the experimental logic of inferring cause from similar between-case (group) comparisons,
referred to as the method of controlled comparison (Faure 1994). The path being
traced proceeds from precipitating events to process departures to immediate and
then later consequences that lead to an outcome. This within-case analysis can,
however, be extended to comparisons between cases. By categorizing diverse cases
in terms of issue area (or other relevant distinguishing characteristics), paths from
different cases can be compared.

8.2   Negotiation and Conflict

The negotiation process is embedded within the context of a larger conflict between
the parties. The process reflects and influences the conflict. In their research on the
Partial Nuclear Test Ban talks (1962–1963), Hopmann and Walcott (1977) showed
reciprocal effects between the negotiation process and the level of tension in the international system and in the relationship between the parties: the process reflected
the tension and the tension was influenced by the outcome of the negotiations. An
implication of this finding is that escalatory (or de-escalatory) moves made outside
the negotiation produce escalatory (or de-escalatory) moves inside the talks and that
these moves further influence the trajectory of the conflict. However, international
negotiators have also been shown to take advantage of an increasingly positive relationship between their nations by extracting concessions that are not reciprocated
(Druckman and Slater 1979).

   Tensions and escalatory interactions within and outside negotiation can be understood in relation to various aspects of ongoing conflicts that include structures,
historical relationships between adversaries, and sources of conflict. By structures,
we refer to power symmetries or asymmetries between the parties. Whether defined
in terms of resources, threat potential, or alternatives to a negotiated agreement,
power differences (or similarities) have been shown to influence bargaining strategies (Haskel 1974; Hopmann 1978) and outcomes (Beriker and Druckman 1996).
With regard to relationships, we distinguish between cooperative, conflictual, and
transforming systems (Druckman 1980). Operating within a shared framework of
values, cooperating parties focus primarily on coordinating their interests for mutual benefits. Jockeying for advantage, conflicting parties focus on strategies that
influence the balance of power between them. And, concentrating on differences
in values, transforming parties seek to develop frameworks that lead to convergence. These relationships give rise to particular sources of conflict that are likely

to influence the negotiation process. In cooperative relationships, parties encounter conflicts of understanding. Competitive parties attempt to resolve their differences in interests, while parties in transforming relationships must confront their differences in values. These distinctions among sources of conflict provide a dimension of the larger conflict that is included in the comparative analysis to follow.

When conflicts occur because of misunderstandings, the parties may differ on the terms of reference or assign different meaning to procedures, concepts, or frameworks. The source of misunderstanding is cognitive, and this type of conflict has been found to be difficult to resolve through bargaining despite cooperative relationships between the parties (Brehmer and Hammond 1977). Conflicts of interest occur when parties have different preferences for an outcome that usually consists of material resources, such as territorial claims. This source of conflict is typically resolved through a bargained compromise (Axelrod 1970). When values are the source of a conflict, the parties often reject bargaining or attempt to separate the values from interests that are subject to bargaining. These conflicts are often difficult to negotiate and may lead to escalation as parties attach their identities to the values in dispute (Aubert 1963). Each of the cases in our sample was coded for the primary source of conflict, as based on misunderstanding, interests, or values. An attempt is made to assess the influence of source, as a dimension of the larger conflict, on the various parts of the turning-points framework, including escalation.

8.3   Comparative Analysis

The framework for analyzing turning points is generic in the sense of capturing processes that occur in a wide variety of cases. It is intended for comparative analysis. One advantage is that such a framework illuminates patterns that transcend specific cases. Another is that the impact of variations in each of the parts of the framework can be evaluated. Both contribute to theory development. Of course, generality is achieved at the cost of a less detailed or less penetrating analysis of individual cases. By moving from the case-specific language, used by authors of case studies, to a general conceptual language, used by theorists, we are able to discern similarities and dissimilarities between the cases. By doing both individual-case and comparative analyses, we can strike a balance between the kinds of historical analyses that emphasize uniqueness and those that seek general patterns. Since the individual-case analyses are the "data set" for the comparative work, we retain an archive of case-by-case chronological analyses. (See Stern and Druckman 2000 for a discussion of comparative case methodologies.)

The data set consists of 34 cases drawn mostly from the February 1999 compendium of Pew Case Studies in International Affairs (30 of the 34 cases; see the

listing of cases in Appendix 8.1).[2] They were selected according to the following
three criteria:

- a regional distribution that is roughly comparable with the universe of Pew
  cases, but somewhat over-represented by Asian and European countries [Africa
  (2), Asia (8), North America (2), Latin America (5), Europe (10), Middle East
  (2), global (2)];
- representative issue areas or types of negotiation [security (13), political (11),
  trade–economic (10)] and sources of the larger conflicts [interests (15), understanding (8), values (11)]; and
- sufficiently detailed descriptions of a negotiation process.

The diversity of cases facilitates comparisons by providing variation along a number of dimensions: which types of precipitants occur in which types of negotiation
with what consequences for short- and long-term processes? The diversity also allows for a robust evaluation of the turning-points framework: what kind of model
(or framework) best depicts the dynamics of international negotiation?

The Pew cases were prepared in a common format. Ranging in length from
10 to 15 printed pages, each case consists of four major sections: background information, description of the negotiation, analysis of the process and outcome, and
teaching notes, which include questions for discussion. All the cases were peer
reviewed before publication. These cases were chosen for this study for several
reasons. One is that they are coherently and uniformly organized. Another is that
many of them use primary sources, such as interviews with the participants, as the
bases for description and analysis. A third is that the series is the largest pool of
case studies in international negotiations and shows considerable diversity in topic
and geographic region. And a fourth reason is that they are more descriptive than
analytic, although not the kind of raw material presented by the two de-classified
cases in our data set from the Library of Congress archive of historical negotiations,
US Department of State, Foreign Relations of the United States.

This analysis contributes to the state of the art (science). The four previous studies of turning points concentrated on one type of negotiation, either trade (Tomlin
1989), security (Druckman 1986; Druckman *et al.* 1991), or environmental negotiations (Chesek 1997). This study expands the sampling in each of these categories.
Only Chesek's study was comparative. She analyzed 11 cases of multilateral environmental talks. This study extends the range and diversity of types of negotiations
included in the comparative analysis. Further, by developing analytical categories

---

[2]This set of cases was also used for analyses reported in a paper presented at the annual meeting
of the International Society of Political Psychology, 1–4 July 2000, in Seattle, Washington, and in
Druckman (2001). Some of the findings reported in these papers are presented in this chapter.

for each aspect of turning points – precipitants, departures, and consequences – we reduce the vagueness in definition often attributed to the concept (e.g., see Tomlin 1989). As noted above, in this analysis, turning points are defined as a sequence from precipitants to process departures to consequences.

Each case is described in terms of the five typologies:

- Sources of conflict
- Type of negotiation
- Precipitants
- Process departures
- Consequences

8.3.1 Sources of conflict

Each of the 34 cases was categorized by the source of the larger conflict between the negotiating parties. The threefold distinction of interests, understanding, and values was used to depict each conflict in terms of its primary source. Using the definitions mentioned above, two judges, working independently, coded each case. The separate codings were compared and discrepancies were resolved through discussion: only 5 of the 34 cases were coded differently, with a difference of opinion as to whether certain security negotiations were conflicts of values or interests. Examples, shown in Appendix 8.2, include the trade talks between Switzerland and the Allied Forces as a conflict of *understanding*, the security negotiation over the Beagle channel as a conflict of *interests*, and the political case of regime-change negotiations between the USA and Nicaragua as a conflict over *values*.

8.3.2 Type of negotiation

Based largely on the Pew case studies' subject index, the cases were categorized by issue area as security, political, or trade–economic. Security negotiations included cases on defense, strategic policy making, arms control, and war termination. Political negotiations included international (bilateral or multilateral) relationships; conflict management and resolution; global resources, energy, and the environment; and international law and organizations. Trade or economic negotiations included issues that concerned economic development, money and finance, trade and investment, and science and technology development.

8.3.3 Precipitants

To distinguish between factors inside and outside the negotiations, precipitants were categorized as being procedural (inside), substantive (inside), or external (outside). Procedural factors are defined as decisions made to change the structure or format of the talks including their formality, venue, and exposure to the media. Substantive factors consist primarily of new ideas or concepts introduced by one or more of the negotiating parties and include the way proposals are packaged for discussion. External factors are events that occur outside the negotiations, such as policy or leadership changes within one or more of the countries represented (proximal events), third-party interventions by non-negotiating parties, or events that occur elsewhere with possible global implications (distal events). The external precipitants often refer to the wider policy and relational contexts within which the negotiation process is embedded.

8.3.4   Process departures

The distinction made here is between more or less abrupt changes in the ongoing negotiating process. Abrupt changes are sudden departures from a pattern of give-and-take and include interim or final agreements or deadlocks as well as unexpected transitions from one stage to another, notably from proposal exchanges to a willingness to settle that marks an endgame process. Less abrupt changes include new proposals that alter the discussions somewhat or adjust the terms of trade, higher-level discussions, or third parties, as well as somewhat predictable stage transitions.

8.3.5   Consequences

Some departures lead to positive consequences, others to negative results. Positive consequences refer primarily to progress toward, or to the achievement of, agreements. Negative consequences refer to movement away from agreements toward impasses. The former are depicted as de-escalatory consequences ("upturns" in a trend); the latter as escalations in the process ("downturns" in a trend). As part of a three-part turning-points analysis, consequences follow immediately from the departures (t). To extend the consequences further in time, we also analyze the events that follow in the next turning-point sequence $(t + 1)$. By doing so, we can evaluate the extent to which escalation precedes (or follows) de-escalation.

8.3.6   Turning-points analyses

These definitions guided the decisions made to categorize the turning points in each case as shown in Appendix 8.2. (Three cases in each of the three issue areas are shown; a case with only one turning point, a case with three turning points, and a case with five or more turning points.) These case-specific decisions were made first by student analysts trained to code the case material in terms of the categories. Each analyst coded two randomly assigned cases. They based their decisions on chronologies constructed for each case based on the information provided by the authors of the Pew case studies. Each turning-point decision was then reviewed by the author in terms of the impact (escalatory, de-escalatory) of the departure on the unfolding process. The review either confirmed the initial decisions or revised them in favor of fewer turning points. This judgment was then presented to the student coders for discussion that led to a consensus decision, in the manner of Delphi paneling techniques. (See Frei and Ruloff 1989 for a discussion of the procedures.)

The analyses were designed to uncover relationships among the parts of the framework. These relationships contribute to the development of paths from the type of negotiation to consequences of the departures. One issue, however, is the unit of analysis. There are more turning points than there are cases. To the extent that the turning points that occur within a case are not independent – later turning points are influenced by earlier ones – they cannot be counted as separate instances. Thus, the case, not the turning point, is the unit of analysis. Each analysis is based on an N of 34 cases. This is done by calculating percentages on a case-by-case basis: for example, the number of external (procedural, substantive) precipitants divided by the total number of precipitants in a given case, or the number of abrupt departures (escalatory consequences) relative to all departures (consequences) in that case. For some analyses, the frequencies (number of external precipitants), rather than percentages, were used to facilitate statistical analysis.

The analyses consisted of assessing relationships among the various parts of the turning-points framework: sources of conflict (interests, understanding, values), type of negotiation (trade, political, security), precipitant (substantive, procedural, external), process departure (abrupt, non-abrupt), and consequence (escalatory, de-escalatory). Relationships are represented by cross-tabulations between pairs, or in some cases triads, of variables. For example, the cross-tabulation of type of negotiation by precipitant consists of the average percentage of the total in each precipitant category by case (how many substantive, procedural, and external precipitants for trade, political, and security cases, respectively). Other cross-tabulations included source of conflict by type, source by consequence, precipitants by departure, precipitants by consequence, departure by consequence, and type of negotiation by precipitant and departure (a three-way analysis). In addition, the sequence of consequences from one turning point (at time t) to another (at time $t + 1$) was analyzed. The question of interest is whether a previous escalation is followed by another escalation or by a de-escalation. These analyses provided the basis for the process tracing. Paths from the type of negotiation to consequences and/or outcomes at $t + 1$ were developed for each of the three types of negotiation cases.

Table 8.1. Type of negotiation by source of conflict

Type of negotiation	Source of conflict			
	Interests	Values	Understanding	Total
Trade	4	0	6	10
Political	4	7	0	11
Security	7	4	2	13
Total	15	11	8	34

8.4 Results

In this section, the results of each cross-tabulation are reported.

8.4.1 Source of conflict by type of negotiation

As shown in *Table 8.1*, the sources of conflict are distributed across the three types of negotiation. Six of the eight conflicts of understanding occur in trade cases. The conflicts of interest are distributed more evenly across the three types of negotiation: four are trade cases, four are political negotiations, and seven are security negotiations. Seven of the value conflicts occur in political talks and four occur in security negotiations. None of the political negotiations attempted to resolve conflicts of understanding, and none of the trade talks addressed conflicts over values. Although there is a prevalent source of conflict for each type of negotiation (understanding for the trade cases, values for the political talks, and interests for the security talks), more than one source of the larger conflicts between the parties is represented (see the rows in *Table 8.1*).

8.4.2 Type of negotiation by precipitant

As shown in *Table 8.2*, most of the precipitants in the security negotiation cases were external (78 percent). The fewest external precipitants occurred in political negotiations (19 percent). About half (44 percent) of the precipitants for political talks and somewhat more than a third (39 percent) for trade talks were substantive. Fewer procedural precipitants occurred in these negotiations (30 and 37 percent in trade and political cases, respectively). Trade and political negotiations were characterized primarily by precipitants that occurred inside the talks (69 and 81 percent, respectively), while security talks were characterized by outside precipitants (78 percent). The statistical relationship between type of negotiation and precipitant is significant, as shown in *Table 8.3* ($\chi^2 = 15.36$, two degrees of freedom, $p < 0.001$; Cramer coefficient, C, is 0.67).

Table 8.2. Type of negotiation by precipitant

	Type of negotiation		
Precipitant	Trade	Political	Security
Substantive	0.39	0.44	0.05
Procedural	0.30	0.37	0.17
External	0.31	0.19	0.78

Table 8.3. Type of negotiation by precipitant (based on 34 cases)

	Type of negotiation		
Precipitant	Trade	Political	Security
Inside	7	9	1
Outside	3	2	12

8.4.3 Type of negotiation by precipitant by departure

As shown in *Table 8.4*, the external precipitants that occurred in security negotiations led to the most abrupt departures in the process. Of the precipitants in the security cases, 50 percent were external followed by abrupt departures. None of the other precipitants within the other types of cases approached this number: the closest were the 27 percent of substantive precipitants in the trade cases being followed by abrupt departures and the 26 percent of substantive precipitants in the political cases being followed by non-abrupt departures. Further, the largest discrepancy between abrupt and non-abrupt departures occurred for the external precipitants in two of the three types of cases (0.26 for security and 0.09 for political cases). For trade talks, the difference between abrupt and non-abrupt departures is largest for substantive precipitants (0.18 for substantive versus 0.14 for external and 0.04 for procedural).

8.4.4 Source of conflict by precipitant and departure

The main distinction between types of precipitants is between the conflicts based on understanding and those based on either interests or values. Of these conflicts, 78 percent were driven by "inside" precipitants, of which 45 percent were substantive and 33 percent were procedural. The remaining 22 percent were driven by external precipitants. The interest and value conflicts were more evenly divided between the inside and outside precipitants: 49 percent of the interest and value conflicts were driven by external precipitants; the remaining interest conflicts were primarily driven by procedural precipitants (41 percent), and the remaining value conflicts were characterized primarily by substantive precipitants (33 percent). With regard

Table 8.4. Precipitant by departure

Departure	Precipitant		
	Substantive	Procedural	External
Trade negotiations			
Abrupt	0.27	0.16	0.25
Non-abrupt	0.09	0.12	0.11
Political negotiations			
Abrupt	0.18	0.18	0.14
Non-abrupt	0.26	0.19	0.05
Security negotiations			
Abrupt	0.03	0.11	0.50
Non-abrupt	0.00	0.13	0.24

Table 8.5. Precipitant by consequence

Consequence	Precipitant		
	Substantive	Procedural	External
De-escalatory	0.19	0.25	0.31
Escalatory	0.08	0.03	0.14

to process departures, more than three-quarters of the eight conflicts of understanding had abrupt departures after precipitants, while about half of the interest and value conflicts had abrupt departures after precipitants. The inside precipitants (usually substantive) led to abrupt departures for the cases in which the source of the larger conflict was in understanding.

8.4.5   Precipitant and departure by consequence

Although 75 percent of the consequences showed progress toward agreement (75 percent were de-escalatory), more than half the escalations occurred in response to external precipitants (see *Table 8.5*). Also, two-thirds of these escalations followed abrupt departures (16 of 24 were abrupt, 8 of 34 were non-abrupt), as shown in *Table 8.6*. Although there were also more de-escalations after abrupt departures, the ratio of abrupt to non-abrupt departures is larger for the escalations (2:1 [abrupt:non-abrupt] for escalations versus 4:3 for de-escalations).

Further insight into the relationship between external precipitants and escalations is provided by another analysis. External precipitants can be divided into those that involve the negotiation parties (e.g., policy changes or a leadership succession) and those that involve parties or events that are not part of the negotiation (e.g., decisions made by international organizations or agreements reached in other

Table 8.6. Departure by consequence

Consequence	Departure	
	Abrupt	Non-abrupt
De-escalatory	0.44	0.31
Escalatory	0.16	0.08

negotiation venues). Of interest is the question of whether the escalations occur primarily after changes closer to or more distant from the process. Of the escalations, 28 percent occurred after an external precipitant that involved one or more of the parties; about 40 percent occurred when the precipitant was further removed from the process. A ratio of about 3:1 (de-escalations:escalations) for negotiation parties compares to a ratio of 3:2 for parties or events further removed. Thus, escalations are somewhat more likely to occur in response to more distant events.

8.4.6   Source of conflict by consequence

More of the value conflicts resulted in escalatory consequences than did the conflicts of interest or understanding. A ratio of de-escalatory to escalatory consequences was calculated for each case. The average ratio for value conflicts was 66 percent compared with 80 percent for both the interest and understanding conflicts. (This is interpreted as meaning that roughly one in three conflicts over values escalated, whereas only one in five of the other sources of conflict resulted in escalations as a consequence of the negotiation process.) Although only 25 percent of the consequences were escalatory, most of these occurred in conflicts over values in security and political talks.

8.4.7   Sequence of consequences

The sequence from a consequence at time t to the next consequence at $t + 1$ is shown in *Figure 8.1* for all the cases with more than one turning point. The focus of this analysis is on the question of whether an escalatory consequence is followed (in the next turning point) by another escalation or by a de-escalation. This question is relevant to earlier findings that show a relationship between crises and positive turning points (Druckman 1986). The results are clear. Of the 25 sequences in which an escalation occurred in the 17 relevant cases, 20 show that a de-escalation follows a previous escalation in the negotiation process. This is a ratio of four positive consequences (de-escalations) to one negative consequence (escalation) of a previous escalation. It provides strong support for the earlier finding obtained from an analysis of the Spain–US base rights talks (Druckman 1986).

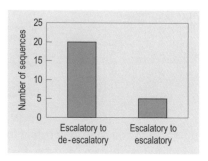

Figure 8.1. Consequences of a previous escalation ($t \rightarrow t + 1$).

8.5   Tracing Paths to Outcomes

Paths are traced for each case within types of negotiation cases in *Figures 8.2* (security cases), *8.3* (political cases), and *8.4* (trade cases). For each of the 13 security cases shown in *Figure 8.2*, the primary precipitant (which occurs in more than 50 percent of the turning points), primary type of departure (more than 50 percent abrupt or non-abrupt), immediate consequence, and later consequence (if more than one turning point occurred) are shown. In all cases except one (case 5), precipitants were external (ranging from 0.60 to 1.0) and departures were abrupt (ranging from 0.50 to 1.0). Although most consequences of the abrupt (or non-abrupt) departures are de-escalatory, when an escalation occurs (at least 0.50 in four of the cases) at t (immediate) it is followed in three of the four "escalation" cases by a de-escalation at time $t + 1$ (case 3 is the only exception). A typical path for the 13 security cases is as follows:

> Security negotiation: External precipitant $\rightarrow$ Abrupt departure in process $\rightarrow$ De-escalation at time $t \rightarrow$ De-escalation at time $t + 1$.

The 11 political cases are shown in *Figure 8.3*. In contrast to the security cases, only two of the precipitants were external. Nine were inside precipitants, of which three were substantive, two procedural, and four a combination of these types of precipitants. Only four of the departures were non-abrupt, and most of the consequences at t and at $t + 1$ were de-escalatory. These patterns suggest the following typical path for political negotiations:

> Political negotiation: Substantive and/or procedural precipitant $\rightarrow$ Abrupt departure $\rightarrow$ De-escalation at time $t \rightarrow$ De-escalation at time $t + 1$.

Case 1:	External precipitant (1.0) → Abrupt departure (0.75) → De-escalatory consequence (0.75) → De-escalatory consequence $(t + 1)$
Case 2:	External precipitant (1.0) → Abrupt departure (1.0) → De-escalatory consequence (1.0)
Case 3:	External precipitant (1.0) → Abrupt departure (0.67) → Escalatory consequence (1.0) → Escalatory consequence $(t + 1)$
Case 4:	External precipitant (0.80) → Abrupt departure (0.60) → Escalatory consequence (0.60) → De-escalatory consequence $(t + 1)$
Case 5:	Procedural precipitant (1.0) → Non-abrupt departure (1.0) → De-escalatory consequence (1.0)
Case 6:	External precipitant (0.80) → Abrupt departure (0.60) → De-escalatory consequence (1.0)
Case 7:	External precipitant (0.75) → Abrupt departure (0.75) → De-escalatory consequence (1.0)
Case 8:	External precipitant (1.0) → Abrupt departure (0.67) → De-escalatory consequence (0.67) → De-escalatory consequence $(t + 1)$ (also follows the escalation)
Case 9:	External precipitant (1.0) → Abrupt departure (0.50) → De-escalatory consequence (1.0)
Case 10:	External precipitant (1.0) → Abrupt departure (0.50) → Escalatory consequence (0.50) → De-escalatory consequence $(t + 1)$
Case 11:	External precipitant (1.0) → Abrupt departure (0.67) → De-escalatory consequence (0.67) → De-escalatory consequence $(t + 1)$ (also follows the escalation)
Case 12:	External precipitant (0.60) → Abrupt departure (0.60) → De-escalatory consequence (0.60) → De-escalatory consequence $(t + 1)$ (also follows the escalation)
Case 13:	External precipitant (1.0) → Abrupt departure (0.50) → Escalatory consequence (0.50) → De-escalatory consequence $(t + 1)$

Figure 8.2. Paths for security cases (see Appendix 8.1 for names of cases).

The 10 trade cases are shown in *Figure 8.4*. Interestingly, each of the types of precipitants occurs with roughly equal frequency. Four are external, four are procedural, and six are substantive. Each precipitant also occurs with two other precipitants, namely, external–procedural (1), external–substantive (1), and substantive–procedural (2).

This near-equal division of the substantive, procedural, and external precipitants is shown also by the percentages in *Table 8.2* (39, 30, and 31 percent, respectively). Only 3 of the 10 departures were non-abrupt, and the same number

Case 14:	Substantive–procedural precipitant (0.50)* →Abrupt departure (0.50) → De-escalatory consequence (1.0)
Case 15:	Substantive precipitant (0.75) →Non-abrupt departure (0.75) →De-escalatory consequence (1.0)
Case 16:	Substantive–procedural precipitant (0.50) → Non-abrupt departure (1,0) → De-escalatory consequence (1.0)
Case 17:	Substantive–procedural precipitant (0.50) → Non-abrupt departure (0.75) → De-escalatory consequence (0.75) → De-escalatory consequence $(t + 1)$
Case 18:	Substantive precipitant (1.0) → Abrupt departure (1.0) → Escalatory consequence (1.0)
Case 19:	Substantive–procedural precipitant (0.50) → Abrupt departure (0.75) → De-escalatory consequence (0.75) → De-escalatory consequence $(t + 1)$
Case 20:	External precipitant (0.80) → Abrupt departure (0.80) → De-escalatory consequence (0.60) → De-escalatory consequence $(t + 1)$
Case 21:	Substantive precipitant (0.67) → Abrupt departure (0.67) → De-escalatory consequence (0.67) → De-escalatory consequence $(t + 1)$
Case 22:	Procedural precipitant (1.0) → Abrupt departure (0.67) → De-escalatory consequence (1.0)
Case 23:	External precipitant (0.75) → Abrupt departure (0.50) →De-escalatory consequence (1.0)
Case 24:	Procedural precipitant (0.67) → Non-abrupt departure (0.67) → De-escalatory consequence (0.75) → De-escalatory consequence $(t + 1)$

*Refers to two precipitants of equal frequency.

Figure 8.3. Paths for political cases (see Appendix 8.1 for names of cases).

had escalatory consequences. In each case of escalation, however, a de-escalation followed, consistent with the security paths traced above. Thus, although about two-thirds of the precipitants are likely to be inside the negotiations, it is difficult to identify a primary precipitant. A typical path, then, takes the following form:

Trade negotiation: → Inside precipitant → Abrupt departure →
De-escalation at time t → De-escalation at time $t + 1$.

In summary, the paths make evident a difference between the security cases, on the one hand, and the political and trade cases, on the other. In practically all the security cases, external precipitants led to abrupt departures in the process which, more often than not, had short- and longer-term de-escalatory consequences. Inside precipitants were predominant in the political and trade cases leading mostly (but not always) to abrupt departures with consequences that were primarily positive (de-escalatory).

Case 25:   Substantive precipitant (1.0) → Abrupt departure (1.0) → De-escalatory consequence (1.0)

Case 26:   External–procedural precipitant (0.50)* → Non-abrupt departure (0.75) → De-escalatory consequence (0.75) → De-escalatory consequence ($t + 1$)

Case 27:   Procedural precipitant (0.67) → Abrupt departure (0.67) → De-escalatory consequence (1.0)

Case 28:   External–substantive precipitant (0.50) → Abrupt departure (1.0) → Escalatory consequence (0.50) → De-escalatory consequence ($t + 1$)

Case 29:   Substantive precipitant (0.60) → Abrupt departure (0.60) → De-escalatory consequence (1.0)

Case 30:   Substantive–procedural precipitant (0.50) → Abrupt departure (1.0) → Escalatory consequence (0.50) → De-escalatory consequence ($t + 1$)

Case 31:   Substantive–procedural precipitant (0.40) → Non-abrupt departure (0.80) → Escalatory consequence (0.60) → De-escalatory consequence ($t + 1$)

Case 32:   External precipitant (0.60) → Non-abrupt departure (0.60) → De-escalatory consequence (1.0)

Case 33:   Substantive precipitant (0.67) → Abrupt departure (0.67) → De-escalatory consequence (1.0)

Case 34:   External precipitant (1.0) → Abrupt departure (1.0) → De-escalatory consequence (1.0)

*Refers to two precipitants of equal frequency.

Figure 8.4. Paths for trade cases (see Appendix 8.1 for names of cases).

The role of sources of conflict

By superimposing sources of conflict on the turning-points framework, we can construct paths that develop from the sources themselves. A typical path for conflicts based on understanding takes the following form:

Conflicts of understanding → Trade negotiations → Substantive precipitants → Abrupt departures → De-escalatory consequences at time *t*.

This path is virtually the same as that shown above for trade negotiations, which indicates that this source of conflict does not alter the path set in motion by trade talks. In contrast, however, the other sources of conflict do alter the paths shown above. A typical path for conflicts of interest takes the following form:

Conflicts of interest → Trade or security negotiations → External or procedural precipitants → Non-abrupt departures → De-escalatory consequences at time *t*.

While combining elements of both trade and security talks, these sources of conflict also depart from those paths by having more non-abrupt departures than either of these types of negotiations. A typical path for value conflicts is

Conflicts over values → Political or security talks → External precipitants →
Abrupt departures → Escalatory consequences at time *t*.

These conflicts occur mostly in the political cases (see *Table 8.1*). However, they retain two key features of security negotiations, external precipitants and escalatory
consequences. The political negotiations that are driven by external precipitants
and lead to escalation are primarily conflicts over values. Also, the security negotiations that lead to escalations are primarily those in which the source of conflict is
differences in values rather than interests or understanding.

8.6   Discussion

Escalation is analyzed in this study in terms of both patterns in the negotiation
process and the influences of the larger conflict on those patterns. Most of the consequences of the process departures in the cases (75 percent) were de-escalatory
in the sense of showing progress toward reaching agreement. This finding is consistent with the idea that turning points in negotiation are benchmarks of progress.
This was evident in each of the earlier case studies of turning points. For example, decisions by Soviet General Secretary Mikhail Gorbachev and US President
Ronald Reagan concerning the intermediate-range nuclear forces (INF) galvanized
the process toward agreement, high-level interim activities in the base rights talks
led to a framework agreement, and the various substantive and political decisions
in the North American Free Trade Agreement pre-negotiation discussions led to
formal negotiations. To the extent that the cases analyzed in this study are representative of a larger universe of cases, we can conclude that precipitants, whether
internal or external to the process, serve to move a negotiation toward agreement.
To the extent that parties create these precipitants, they have control over the velocity of the process that leads toward or away from agreement. Yet to be explored is
the relationship between types of agreements and types of turning points.

Of more interest, however, are the later consequences of the escalatory or negative consequences that occurred in 25 percent of the turning points. Similar to
Druckman's (1986) earlier finding, a crisis or setback was confronted by the negotiating parties – although not necessarily by the negotiators themselves – and
reversed in the subsequent rounds. Most of the reversals were produced by such
external interventions as third-party actions in the security cases: seven of the nine
cases in which third parties played a role dealt with security cases. In contrast,
few external interventions were sought to reverse an escalation in the political and
trade cases: 8 of 10 were engineered from inside the talks, as either substantive
or procedural decisions. By separating precipitants from consequences and tracing

the path between them, we can distinguish between various actions taken in different types of negotiations (as precipitants) to reverse the course (as consequences of departures).

Less attention was paid in these analyses to the role of the parties in bringing about turning points. Our distinction between external and internal precipitants is relevant. In the political and trade cases, process departures were precipitated by either substantive or procedural activities, which are largely controlled by the parties. It can be argued that these are attempts made by the parties to control the process and so avoid the intrusion of outside influences. Format changes (procedures) and new ideas (substantive) are intended to move the process toward agreement when this is the goal of the negotiation. However, they can also be used to subvert a negotiation process to avoid an undesirable agreement or to prolong the process in the interest of obtaining side effects (Iklé 1964). Attempts made to prolong a process for its own sake were more characteristic of security negotiations than either political or trade cases. The uncertainties associated with the consequences of any new agreement in this area make the parties reluctant to bring about departures in the process that either escalate or de-escalate the process. Thus, the process is more vulnerable to outside influences, as documented in this analysis. Further analyses should illuminate the ways in which parties attempt to control the process by precipitating certain types of departures.

The security cases showed slow progress toward outcomes that often took the form of small incremental adjustments. A risk-averse or reactive approach taken by governments when dealing with their own security is reflected in a reluctance to alter the status quo or to take bold initiatives (the exception to this pattern, of course, is Gorbachev's nuclear and troop reduction initiatives during the latter part of the 1980s). For this reason, it is less likely that departures in the process will result from moves made by the parties themselves, as either substantive or procedural decisions. Progress often depends on outside intervention or on dramatic events within one or another of the negotiating parties, as these cases demonstrate. The frequency with which third parties intervened in these negotiations (7 of the 12 cases in which outside precipitants occurred) also supports the observation that these issues provoke widespread interest and encourage involvement.

The source of the larger conflict between the negotiating parties was shown also to influence the paths taken in the talks. Eight of the cases were depicted as conflicts of understanding. Since most of these conflicts were addressed in trade negotiations, it is not surprising that the paths are the same as those shown for the trade cases. Most of these cases resulted in de-escalatory consequences. The paths for the interest and value conflicts were more complex. These conflicts were divided among the types of cases: interest conflicts occurred in all three types (and were divided between inside and outside precipitants), while value conflicts were divided between the political and security cases. Although escalations occurred for all sources of conflicts and types of negotiations, they were somewhat more frequent for the value conflicts and security talks: 30 percent of the escalations occurred for value conflicts, compared with 25 percent and 20 percent for interest and understanding conflicts, respectively; similarly, 30 percent of the escalations occurred in security talks, compared with 22 percent and 20 percent for the political and trade cases, respectively. Further, more typical paths led to escalations in the security cases than in the political or trade negotiations.

These findings suggest that escalations occur somewhat more often in security talks, for which the source of conflict is primarily values or interests. They occur less often in conflicts of understanding, which are the primary source of conflict in trade talks. Another interesting finding is the relationship between process departures and consequences. Abrupt departures precede escalations for value conflicts, but they precede de-escalations for conflicts of understanding. For the former conflicts, the abruptness of the departure is a movement away from agreement. For the latter, it is a move toward coordination and agreement. These influences suggest that sources of the larger conflict and types of negotiations influence paths toward escalation or de-escalation of the process and, thus, for these cases, the larger conflict between the parties as well. Unraveling the separate and joint effects of sources and types is a task for further research.

More generally, these analyses reveal research opportunities and expose some limitations. With regard to opportunities, the study provides a framework for the analysis of change in negotiation. By separating the three parts of turning points, the framework disentangles driving factors (precipitants) from process and consequences. By defining each of these parts, it guides coding decisions and provides reproducible procedures. Going beyond the single case, the framework facilitates comparative research. A next step would be to perform controlled comparisons on a smaller, more homogeneous set of cases. To expand the sampling frame, the framework could be used to analyze other types of cases, including negotiations that occur within countries and those that are nongovernmental or unofficial. The framework could also be used to examine a sample of failed negotiations. These cases could be compared with the sample of primarily successful negotiations used in this analysis. It would be interesting to compare the paths that lead to de-escalation: for example, how often does de-escalation occur at $t+1$ (or beyond) in the failed versus the successful cases?

With regard to limitations, the analysis illuminates the well-known trade-off between large and small N studies. In our search for generality, we have forfeited a degree of depth for breadth. Focusing attention on comparison, the analysis is less revealing of the case-specific circumstances that would enrich the interpretation of the turning points. Although more of this detail is found in the earlier case studies of turning points, we do have an archive of the 34 case chronologies as well as the original Pew case studies (1999). Another trade-off for comparative research is between relatively homogeneous and heterogeneous samples. The former have the advantage of enabling an investigator to distinguish more precisely between similarities and differences among the cases. By limiting the sample to one type of negotiation, for example, the typical (or generic) causal paths can be inferred with more confidence, which enhances the internal validity of the findings (e.g., McDonald and Bendahmane 1990). The latter has the advantage of robustness. Findings obtained from heterogeneous samples of cases may generalize widely, but not precisely, which enhances the external validity of the findings (e.g., Bendahmane and McDonald 1986). We chose the latter strategy, in part because of the availability of descriptive material about the negotiation process. In stratifying our sample of available material by source of conflict, issue area, and region, we were able to represent a range of types of negotiations and conflicts. Less clear, however, is the universe(s) from which the cases were drawn. For this reason, the relevance of the findings for other cases is uncertain.

Another possible limitation of the analysis concerns the way that coding decisions were made. The typological distinctions made for each part of the analysis were limited to two or three categories. In several cases, we discovered overlapping categories. For some cases, it was difficult to distinguish between the interests at stake and the parties' values. A number of precipitants were combinations of substantive and either procedural or external causes. Several cases were complex mixtures of political and security concerns, and the four environmental cases were regarded as being primarily political. Although less ambiguous, the either/or distinctions for departures and consequences obfuscate the extent to which these are events that vary in degree. By capturing these variables in terms of gradations – as amount of escalation – a coder could provide more information with which to assess the sorts of relationships analyzed in this chapter. These findings can be regarded as hypotheses for further evaluation with other samples and coding schemes.

This turning-points analysis was embedded within the larger context of conflict between the parties. In this analysis, context was defined in terms of three sources of conflict. It could also be regarded in terms of other sources, as well as structures and experience, within the negotiation process or issues. With regard to other sources, it would be interesting to ask whether the negotiation process discussed in this chapter also applies to the sorts of identity issues that have arisen during the past decade. With regard to structures, we might ask whether the process is different for the more institutionalized negotiations than for those conducted outside organizational contexts. And with regard to experience, we would want to ascertain whether changes have occurred in the professionalization or efficiency of the process. Such changes may have implications for control over the velocity of the process and, thus, the way that precipitating events are introduced.

Escalation in negotiation turns on events, referred to here as precipitants, that may occur within or outside the negotiating process. They were shown in this analysis to have consequences for paths toward or away from agreements. Different kinds of paths were diagnosed for each of several sources of conflict and types of negotiation cases in our sample. Capturing change in the negotiation process, the paths (referred to as a turning-points analysis) highlight the dynamic aspects of international negotiation.

Acknowledgment

Thanks go to Mieko Fujioka for her many contributions to the analyses. Thanks also to Tatsushi Arai for his contributions to the coding and analysis of sources of conflict.

Appendix 8.1. Cases Categorized by Type of Negotiation

Case	Source*
Security negotiation cases	
1. Angolan Civil War	Pew #460
2. Beagle Channel, 1977–1979	Pew #401
3. French withdrawal from NATO	Pew #301
4. Troop withdrawals from Lebanon	Pew #310
5. US–Portugal airfields use	Foreign relations of the US
6. Intermediate nuclear forces	Druckman *et al.* (1991)
7. Base rights, USA and Spain	Druckman (1986)
8. Korea, 1951–1953	Pew #359
9. Making peace with Germany	Pew #435
10. NATO on INF, 1977–1979	Pew #305
11. SALT I	Pew #303
12. Ending the Vietnam War	Pew #337
13. Withdrawing Russian forces from the Baltic states, 1990–1994	Pew #371
Political negotiation cases	
14. Negotiating neutrality, Austria and the European Union	Pew #233
15. Camp David accords	Pew #445
16. Austrian state treaty	Pew #432
17. Mining the deep seabed	Pew #423
18. US–Nicaragua regime change	Pew #327
19. Montreal Protocol, 1987	Pew #447
20. Falklands/Malvinas dispute	Pew# 406
21. Future of Hong Kong	Pew #411
22. Minerals regime for Antarctica	Pew #134
23. Panama Canal	Pew #407
24. Normalizing US–Chinese relations	Pew #426
Trade negotiation cases	
25. Switzerland and Allied Forces	Foreign Relations of the US
26. Philippine debt, 1983–1986	Pew #133
27. US–Japan air service	Pew #104
28. Nigeria–IMF, 1983–1985	Pew #205
29. North American Free Trade	Pew #143
30. Renegotiating international debt	Pew #208
31. Japan's construction markets	Pew #145
32. Algerian gas	Pew #103
33. US–EC accession, Spain and Portugal	Pew #147
34. US–Canada soft lumber	Pew #141

*The Pew cases can be found in the 1999 *ISD Compendium of Case Study Abstracts and Indexes.*

Appendix 8.2. Examples of Turning Points in Selected Security, Trade, and Political Cases

Security Cases

Beagle Channel negotiations, 1977–1979 (Pew case #401)

Source of conflict	Interests
External precipitant	Crisis in long-stalemated talks leads both sides to prepare for war
Process	Papal mediation takes the form of shuttle diplomacy by Cardinal Samore; a vague agreement, referred to as "The Act of Montevideo," is crafted
Consequence	Both sides agree to continue the papal mediation process (+)

SALT I (Pew case #303)

Source of conflict	Values
External precipitant	Soviet Union nuclear arsenal approaches parity
Process	US domestic pressure for bilateral agreement to suspend further nuclear weapons development
Consequence	Bilateral talks begin (+)
External precipitant	China acquires nuclear weapons, US–China relations improve
Process	Soviets propose some concessions on weapons limitations
Consequence	USA rejects Soviet proposal, threatens to break off both front- and back-channel talks (−)
External–procedural precipitant	Summit meeting occurs, back-channel talks pursued simultaneously
Process	Soviets drop their demands on linking offensive and defensive weapons (SALT I agreement deals with offensive weapons limitations; corresponding anti-ballistic missile [ABM] agreement deals with defensive weapons)
Consequence	Drafting of treaty documents begins and leads to a treaty signed in 1972 (+)

Withdrawal of Russian forces from the Baltic states, 1990–1994 (Pew case #371)

Source of conflict	Interests
External precipitant	US, Sweden, and other European countries put pressure on Russian President Boris Yeltsin to withdraw troops
Process	Yeltsin and the Lithuanian president discuss the conditions
Consequence	An agreement is reached (+)
External precipitant	Moscow conservatives win seats in the Duma
Process	Talks break down with Latvia
Consequence	External intervention needed to revive talks
External precipitant	USA supports the Russian troop withdrawal
Process	Deals made with USA willing to provide financial support
Consequence	Agreement for a timed withdrawal signed (+)
External precipitant	Conservatives in Russia challenge Yeltsin, conservatives in Estonia demand a resolution
Process	Russian delegate states that withdrawal will occur on the Russian timetable
Consequence	Negotiations break down (−)
External precipitant	US President Bill Clinton intervenes
Process	Pressure put on Yeltsin to meet with the Estonian president
Consequence	Talks break down as Yeltsin recants his earlier statements (−)
External precipitant	Pressure placed on Moscow from several European countries and USA
Process	Yeltsin and the Estonian president meet in Moscow to discuss conditions for withdrawal
Consequence	A withdrawal agreement is reached (+)

(+) indicates a de-escalatory consequence of the departure in the negotiation process.
(−) indicates an escalatory consequence.

Trade Cases
Switzerland and Allied Forces (from Foreign Relations of the US)

Source of conflict	Understanding
Substantive precipitant	New understanding of Swiss interests (by UK) on 6 May 1942; in time the USA endorses this new understanding, namely, Swiss unemployment
Process	Discussion becomes focused on ways to deal with the problem of Swiss unemployment in the manufacturing sector and actions are taken by the Swiss to solve the problem
Consequence	Path to agreement, which was reached in December 1942 (+)

US–EC accession negotiations on Spain and Portugal (Pew case #147)

Source of conflict	Interests
Procedural precipitant	Ministerial meeting
Process	Set in motion a negotiation process
Consequence	Path to agreement (+)
Substantive precipitant	Pressure tactics by USA to obtain Spanish concessions
Process	New elements incorporated in the form of concessions to USA
Consequence	Interim agreement reached for USA to continue to export its grain at previous levels (+)
Substantive precipitant	USA signals that it could accept a package deal
Process	Agreement negotiated between USA and EC
Consequence	Relations between USA and EC improve (+)

Opening Japan's construction market to American firms, 1985–1988 (Pew case #145)

Source of conflict	Understanding
Procedural precipitant	Japan opens discussions on allowing foreign firms to participate in its construction market
Process	Discussions proceed, including a seminar co-sponsored by the USA and Japan
Consequence	Little progress made in getting Japan to open its markets (−)
External precipitant	US President Ronald Reagan meets with Japanese Prime Minister Yasuhiro Nakasone
Process	Some progress in negotiations, but no commitment from Japan on removing trade barriers
Consequence	Slow progress continues without an agreement in sight (−)
Procedural precipitant	Agreement on bidding procedures
Process	Stage shift from details of bidding procedures to discussion of projects to which such procedures would apply
Consequence	New conflicts surface from discussions between Japan and USA (−)
Substantive precipitant	Japan offers a new proposal
Process	USA responds with a recognition that the proposal meets only minimal requirements
Consequence	Negotiations move to a more detailed discussion of projects for US participation (+)
Substantive precipitant	Consideration of what constitutes a public work, since these are the kinds of projects in which USA can participate
Process	Hammering out the agreement to clarify the role of US participation
Consequence	Agreement reached in March 1988 (+)

(+) indicates a de-escalatory consequence of the departure in the negotiation process.
(−) indicates an escalatory consequence.

Political Cases

US–Nicaragua regime-change negotiations (Pew case #327)

Source of conflict	Values
Substantive precipitant	USA is convinced that Somoza will not compromise and will remain intransigent
Process	USA withdraws from the talks
Consequence	Negotiation ends (–)

Negotiations to normalize US–Chinese relations (Pew case #426)

Source of conflict	Values
Procedural precipitant	US President Richard Nixon's visit to China
Process	Discussion of normalization between the two countries
Consequence	Signing of the Shanghai Communiqué, leading to a transformed relationship (+)
Procedural precipitant	US President Jimmy Carter commits USA to a normalization plan
Process	Negotiations under way to implement plan
Consequence	Talks result in a stalemate as new issues arise (–)
Substantive precipitant	China embarks on a large economic modernization program
Process	Negotiations speeded up as secret talks are initiated with USA by Chinese Vice Premier Deng Xiaopeng
Consequence	A normalization agreement is reached in 1979 between USA and the People's Republic of China, including terms about US relationship with Taiwan (+)

Political–Environmental Case

Montreal Protocol, 1987 (Pew case #447)

Source of conflict	Values
Substantive precipitant	Scientific research on relationship between chlorofluorocarbons (CFCs) and ozone depletion
Process	Pre-negotiation debate on negotiability of the issue
Consequence	Path toward multilateral negotiations (+)
External precipitant	Scientific discovery of an ozone hole
Process	Transition to higher-level negotiations
Consequence	Path toward a major agreement on banning CFCs (+)
Procedural precipitant	Informal workshop convened
Process	Progress toward a solution
Consequence	Path to agreement (+)
Substantive precipitant	UK leads EC to oppose US plan
Process	Negotiation stalemated because of divisions
Consequence	No progress made until succession (–)
Procedural precipitant	Belgium succeeds UK as president of EC (negotiating as a bloc)
Process	Belgium leads EC to back US plan
Consequence	Agreement is reached to ban the production of certain types of CFCs (+)

(+) indicates a de-escalatory consequence of the departure in the negotiation process.
(–) indicates an escalatory consequence.

References

Aubert V (1963). Competition and dissensus: Two types of conflict and of conflict resolution. *Journal of Conflict Resolution* **7**:26–42.

Axelrod R (1970). *Conflict of Interest: A Theory of Divergent Goals with Applications to Politics*. Chicago, IL, USA: Markham.

Bendahmane DB & McDonald JW (1986). *Perspectives on Negotiation: Four Case Studies and Interpretations*. Washington, DC, USA: Foreign Service Institute.

Bercovitch J & Langley J (1993). The nature of the dispute and the effectiveness of international mediation. *Journal of Conflict Resolution* **37**:670–691.

Bercovitch J & Wells R (1993). Evaluating mediation strategies: A theoretical and empirical analysis. *Peace and Change* **18**:3–25.

Beriker N & Druckman D (1996). Simulating the Lausanne Peace Negotiations, 1922–1923: Power asymmetries in bargaining. *Simulation & Gaming* **27**:162–183.

Brehmer B & Hammond KR (1977). Cognitive factors in interpersonal conflict. In *Negotiations: Social-Psychological Perspectives*, ed. Druckman D, pp. 79–93. Beverly Hills, CA, USA: Sage.

Chesek P (1997). A comparative analysis of multilateral environmental negotiations. *Group Decision and Negotiation* **6**:437–461.

Coddington A (1968). *Theories of the Bargaining Process*. Chicago, IL, USA: Aldine.

Cross J (1983). *A Theory of Adaptive Economic Behavior*. Cambridge, UK: Cambridge University Press.

Douglas A (1957). The peaceful settlement of industrial and intergroup disputes. *Journal of Conflict Resolution* **1**:69–81.

Druckman D (1980). Social-psychological factors in regional politics. In *Comparative Regional Systems*, ed. Feld WJ & Boyd G, pp. 18–55. New York, NY, USA: Pergamon Press.

Druckman D (1983). Social psychology and international negotiations: Processes and influences. In *Advances in Applied Social Psychology*, Vol. 2, eds. Kidd RF & Saks MJ, pp. 51–81. Hillsdale, NJ, USA: Erlbaum.

Druckman D (1986). Stages, turning points, and crises: Negotiating military base rights, Spain and the United States. *Journal of Conflict Resolution* **30**:327–360.

Druckman D (1997a). Negotiating in the international context. In *Peacemaking in International Conflict*, eds. Zartman IW & Rasmussen L, pp. 81–123. Washington, DC, USA: United States Institute of Peace Press.

Druckman D (1997b). Dimensions of international negotiations: Structures, processes, and outcomes. *Group Decision and Negotiation* **6**:395–420.

Druckman D (2001). Turning points in international negotiation: A comparative analysis. *Journal of Conflict Resolution* **45**:519–544.

Druckman D & Harris R (1990). Alternative models of responsiveness in international negotiation. *Journal of Conflict Resolution* **34**:235–251.

Druckman D & Slater R (1979). *External Events and Arms-Control Negotiating Behavior*, Report P-14. Bethesda, MD, USA: Mathtech Inc. Analytical Support Center.

Druckman D, Husbands JL & Johnston K (1991). Turning points in the INF negotiations. *Negotiation Journal* **7**:55–67.

Druckman D, Martin J, Allen Nan S & Yagcioglu D (1999). Dimensions of international negotiation: A test of Iklé's typology. *Group Decision and Negotiation* **8**:89–108.

Faure AM (1994). Some methodological problems in comparative politics. *Journal of Theoretical Politics* **6**:307–322.

Frei D & Ruloff D (1989). *Handbook of Foreign Policy Analysis*. Boston, MA, USA: Martinus Nijhoff.

George AL & Bennett A (2004). *Case Studies and Theory Development in the Social Sciences*, Cambridge, MA, USA: MIT Press.

Gulliver PH (1979). *Disputes and Negotiations: A Cross-Cultural Perspective*. New York, NY, USA: Academic Press.

Haskel BG (1974). Disparities, strategies, and opportunity costs: The example of Scandinavian economic market negotiations. *International Studies Quarterly* **18**:3–30.

Hopmann PT (1978). Asymmetrical bargaining in the conference on security and cooperation in Europe. *International Organization* **32**:141–177.

Hopmann PT & Walcott C (1977). The impact of external stresses and tensions on negotiation. In *Negotiations: Social-Psychological Perspectives*, ed. Druckman D, pp. 301–323. Beverly Hills, CA, USA: Sage.

Iklé FC (1964). *How Nations Negotiate*. New York, NY, USA: Harper & Row.

McDonald JW & Bendahmane DB (1990). *US Bases Overseas*. Boulder, CO, USA: Westview.

Pew Case Studies in International Affairs (1999). *The ISD Compendium of Case Study Abstracts and Indexes*. Washington, DC, USA: The Institute for the Study of Diplomacy, Edmund A. Walsh School of Foreign Service, Georgetown University.

Pruitt DG (1981). *Negotiation Behavior*. New York, NY, USA: Academic Press.

Snyder GH & Diesing P (1977). *Conflict among Nations*. Princeton, NJ, USA: Princeton University Press.

Stern PC & Druckman D (2000). Evaluating interventions in history: The case of international conflict resolution. *International Studies Review* **2**:33–63.

Tomlin BW (1989). The stages of pre-negotiation: The decision to negotiate North American Free Trade. In *Getting to the Table*, ed. Stein JG, pp. 18–43. Baltimore, MD, USA: Johns Hopkins University Press.

Zartman IW (1975). Negotiations: Theory and reality. *Journal of International Affairs* **9**:69–77.

Zartman IW (2000). Ripeness: The hurting stalemate and beyond. In *International Conflict Resolution after the Cold War*, eds. Stern PC & Druckman D, pp. 225–250. Washington, DC, USA: National Academy Press.

Chapter 9

Escalation, Negotiation, and Crisis Type

Lisa J. Carlson

9.1   Introduction

In 1988, Vietnam and China engaged in a brief, but violent, military clash over conflicting claims of ownership regarding an archipelago known as the Spratly Islands
located in the South China Sea (Amer 1994; Furtado 1999). The crisis lasted several days and at least three Vietnamese were killed, dozens were missing, and no
meaningful resolution to the crisis was achieved (Brecher and Wilkenfeld 1997).
The crisis between Vietnam and China is a classic illustration of the "violence
begets violence" dynamic. One argument suggests that once violence is employed
in a crisis, states find it exceedingly difficult to switch to more de-escalatory or accommodative strategies to manage the crisis, especially to negotiation (Huth 1988;
Brecher 1993; Leng 1993a, 1994; Dixon 1994, 1996; Rubin *et al.* 1994; Miall
1996).

   The 1987 crisis between Uganda and Kenya offers a similar illustration of an
initially violent escalation phase. In response to Kenya's decision to impose tighter
border controls on traffic coming from Uganda into Kenya, Ugandan armed forces
crossed the border into Kenya. Border skirmishes ensued for days and led to the
deaths of several civilian and military personnel; it appeared, for a time at least, that
the two countries might go to war (*Time*, 11 January 1988). In this crisis, however,
the presidents of Uganda and Kenya met two weeks later in the town of Malaba to

negotiate a peaceful resolution to their conflict. Both sides agreed to withdraw their security forces and reopen their borders (Ofcansky 1996).

The Uganda–Kenya case suggests that it is possible for states to "wind down" their conflict even under the difficult conditions of an interstate crisis. De-escalation as a strategy, however, is not synonymous with negotiation as a conflict-management strategy. Clearly, a state can de-escalate a conflict (act to lower hostility levels or costs) without offering to negotiate differences (see Chapter 1, p. 6, in this volume). Since we know that some crises are managed using negotiations, the issue becomes to identify the conditions that make negotiation a more attractive option for actors in crises, even if the conflict began with a violent act.

Gaining an understanding of the conflict-management choices that states make in crisis situations is important in that "not nearly enough effort has been devoted to understanding the vast number of disputes in which militarized behavior occurs without escalation to war" (Jones *et al.* 1996, p. 164). Some very important research has focused on the role that regime type plays in affecting the decision to negotiate settlements (Brecher 1993; Dixon and Senese 2002; Huth and Allee 2002). However, other variables need to be identified to build a more comprehensive picture of the patterns that characterize crisis management (Bercovitch and Jackson 2001).

Recently, scholars associated with the International Crisis Behavior (ICB) Project (Hewitt and Wilkenfeld 1999) alerted researchers to the distinction between what they deem "one-sided" and "two-sided" crises (both crises mentioned at the outset of this chapter are "two-sided"). The authors found that crisis type (one- or two-sided) was a significant factor in explaining both the level of violence in crises and whether or not states adopted violent or accommodative crisis-management techniques. This variable was significant even when controlling for other factors, including geographic proximity, power, and regime type (Hewitt and Wilkenfeld 1999, p. 315).

The purpose of this research is to expand upon the Hewitt and Wilkenfeld (1999) findings by developing a theoretical argument that makes stronger claims regarding the non-coercive nature of one-sided crises. This argument is captured by developing a modest, non-formalized extension of the classic model of crisis decision making (see Morrow 1994). The extension involves giving an actor confronted with a challenge by another state the option of "offering negotiations," in addition to the standard acts of not responding or responding (at lower or higher levels of escalation). Rudolf Avenhaus, Juergen Beetz, and D. Marc Kilgour also analyze the Morrow model in Chapter 4 of this volume; however, instead of modifying the foregoing model, as is done here, they develop a separate model to capture certain kinds of negotiation tactics.

The argument leads to the expectation that states in one-sided crises are less likely than their two-sided counterparts to adopt violence or even indirect accommodative tactics in favor of bilateral negotiations. The hypotheses derived from this argument are tested empirically using the International Crisis Behavior (ICB) System data set[1] on 412 crises during the period from 1918 to 1994 (Brecher and Wilkenfeld 1997).

9.2 Discussion

In one view, a crisis is defined by three necessary conditions. An actor perceives that one or more of its basic values is threatened, it perceives a finite time in which to redress the situation, and it perceives that the probability of military hostilities or war has increased (Brecher and Wilkenfeld 1997, p. 3). If a state takes an action to challenge the status quo on some issue or if a demand is made and resisted, actors must make a series of decisions regarding how they will manage the crisis at any particular point in time. States can employ unilateral actions that may be non-coercive or coercive in nature. Non-coercive actions include withdrawing from the crisis, breaking off diplomatic relations, issuing a threat, imposing economic sanctions, or displaying military force. Unilateral coercive actions involve using force or violence (e.g., bombing the adversary's territory). The former are often considered low-escalation or more accommodative crisis acts compared with the latter, which entail high-escalation acts. I. William Zartman and Guy Olivier Faure point out that escalation can take place along several dimensions (see Chapter 1, pp. 7–8). The emphasis of the research here is on the escalation of means and costs where costs may accrue to both sides. Non-coercive techniques also include bilateral and multilateral efforts, which include negotiations, mediation, and, in some cases, adjudication.

Research has tended to emphasize either the nature or context of the crisis and its actors or the bargaining behavior of the players once the crisis is under way to explain the choice among conflict strategies (Snyder and Diesing 1977; Leng 1993b, 1994; Hewitt and Wilkenfeld 1999; Bercovitch and Jackson 2001). Empirical studies have been remarkably consistent in finding that negotiation or a negotiated settlement is more likely to occur if both actors are democratic or share a similar culture or set of values (Brecher 1993; Maoz and Russett 1993; Dixon and Senese 2002; Huth and Allee 2002; Kinsella and Russett 2002). In addition, some studies suggest that cultural variables, especially those pertaining to the ethnic or religious similarities or dissimilarities of the disputants, can lead toward or away from violent crisis escalation (Huntington 1993; Henderson 1997). The chances for negotiation also improve if the issues in the dispute are tangible or divisible and there are few of them (Kleibor 1996; Bercovitch and Jackson 2001). The duration of a dispute has also been linked to the actors' propensity to negotiate. Negotiation

---

[1] ICB data obtained from http://www.icbnet.org.

is more likely when a dispute is either very short or very long (Jones *et al.* 1996; Dixon and Senese 2002). In the former case, the actors' positions do not have time to become entrenched; in the latter, "a hurting stalemate" may be in effect (Zartman 1989).

The findings regarding the explanatory power of other independent variables, such as conflict intensity (as measured by fatalities) and the relative power of the actors have received either mixed or in some cases contradictory support. Some studies have found that states are more likely to negotiate if they are equal in power (Zartman 1989; Bueno de Mesquita *et al.* 1997; Bercovitch and Jackson 2001), while others have found that relative power has no effect on the probability of a ne-gotiated settlement (Dixon and Senese 2002). Similarly, both low and high fatality levels have been associated with negotiation or negotiated settlements (Jones *et al.* 1996; Bercovitch and Jackson 2001).

Regime type (non-democracy), heterogeneity (dissimilarity), relative power (equality), and contiguity (Bremer 1982) have also been found useful in explaining why states use violent escalation in a crisis (Brecher 1993, 1996). Not surprisingly, those attributes that lead to violent conflict escalation also lead states away from negotiation.

Researchers associated with the ICB Project recently identified another key variable that helps to explain a state's decision to employ one conflict-management strategy over another (Hewitt and Wilkenfeld 1999). The variable refers to the "type of crisis" and can assume one of two values: one-sided or two-sided. One-sided crises are defined as cases in which the perceptions of one actor (the crisis actor) satisfy the three conditions of a crisis mentioned earlier. The actor that acted and generated a crisis for another state (the crisis adversary) does not believe it is in crisis. The "initiator" may perceive a threat to its values and perhaps a finite time in which to respond to the threat; however, it appears that the missing belief is that the probability of hostilities or war has increased. In a two-sided crisis, the perceptions of both (or several actors if it is a multiparty dispute) satisfy all three conditions and this belief is *shared* between or among the actors (Hewitt and Wilkenfeld 1999, p. 311).

Hewitt and Wilkenfeld (1999) did not focus on identifying the theoretical con-ditions that lead to the two kinds of crises. However, they did discuss some inter-esting implications for crisis behavior when only one side believes that the proba-bility of war is unchanged. The authors expected that the level of threats to basic values, stress, and crisis violence would be lower in one-sided crises compared with two-sided disputes. The results of their empirical tests confirmed that actors in one-sided crises experience a significantly lower level of stress and violence in crises; that is, in such crises states are much more likely to rely on accommodative crisis-management techniques (Hewitt and Wilkenfeld 1999).

As noted earlier, states make general decisions as to whether they will employ coercive or non-coercive tactics in a crisis situation. If violence is rejected, states also have choices to make as to which of the elements in the set of accommodative or non-coercive tactics they will use. Thus, one way to deepen our understanding of different crisis dynamics is to disaggregate the concept of accommodative tools and to specify the conditions under which different techniques will be used. In what follows, I argue that the preferred conflict-management technique in one-sided crises is negotiation.

9.3   Theoretical Framework

The classic crisis model is given by Morrow (1994). There are three players: nature, a challenger, and a defender. Nature moves first and determines the defender's type: resolute or irresolute. The challenger moves second and has to decide whether or not to challenge the status quo. If no challenge is issued (there is no crisis), the status quo prevails. If the challenger acts, the defender has to decide whether to respond to the challenge (escalate) or not. A non-response ends the game with a win for the challenger and a loss for the defender. If the defender responds to the challenge, the challenger can press on or back down. Pressing on produces war and backing down results in a loss for the challenger and a win for the defender:

Challenger wins (defender loses) → Status quo →
Challenger loses (defender wins) → War.

A resolute defender has the following preference order:

Defender wins (challenger loses) → Status quo → War →
Defender loses (challenger wins).

An irresolute defender reverses the preference ordering of the final two outcomes:

Defender wins (challenger loses) → Status quo →
Defender loses (challenger wins) → War.

If the challenger has complete information regarding the defender's type, then the challenger initiates a crisis against irresolute defenders (challenger wins) and does not challenge the status quo when the opponent is resolute (status quo prevails). The reason is that a resolute defender will respond to a challenge and so leave the challenger with either war or loss as the outcome of the contest. Since the status quo is preferred to both of these outcomes, the challenger does not initiate a crisis.

To analyze the dynamics in one-sided crises, I propose a simple non-formalized variation on the foregoing model. If there is a challenge to the status quo, the defender retains the options of not responding or responding (at lower or higher levels of escalation). However, now the defender is endowed with a third act: proposing negotiations. If the defender proposes negotiations, the challenger can either accept or reject the offer. If negotiations are accepted, the game ends with some mutually agreed solution. That solution admits several different possibilities. The actors can agree to disagree (stalemate) or both sides can make concessions (compromise) or one actor can make all the concessions (defeat for one and victory for the other). A negotiated settlement may be designed to manage or end the current crisis or crafted to resolve the underlying conflict itself (see Chapter 1, p. 11). If the challenger rejects negotiations, the defender can back down (defender loses, challenger wins) or the defender can escalate. Escalation produces a violent military contest that may include war.

As noted by Hewitt and Wilkenfeld (1999), one of the unique features of one-sided crises is the absence of *shared* perceptions that the actors are both in a crisis. In other words, a challenger takes some action that generates a foreign policy crisis for the defender, but the challenger believes that the probability of war is unchanged. The authors speculate that this belief is based on the expectation that violence will not evolve from its actions. This means that the challenger knows its own unwillingness to engage in hostilities and/or believes the defender is irresolute and acts on the basis of that belief. Here, the challenger wants to alter the status quo on some issue and expects that the defender will not resist the attempt.

Another reason why a triggering entity may not expect violence to evolve from its actions is that it simply does not expect its actions to generate a serious crisis for another state. In other words, the triggering actor may not have intended to create a crisis, but did so more as a by-product of its action. The defender only knows that an adversary took an action and that as a result it now is in a crisis. However, the defender cannot be certain that the challenger knows this; nor can it be certain as to which state of the world the challenger is in (i.e., crisis or not).

The 1957 dispute between Tunisia and France illustrates the foregoing points. The status quo issue at stake for Tunisia was the fact that, in exchange for its independence, Tunisia granted France the right to maintain military bases in their country. France's primary concern in 1957 was not Tunisia; it was to crush the independence movement in neighboring Algeria. In May 1957, French and Tunisian soldiers clashed, leading to the deaths of seven Tunisians (Brecher and Wilkenfeld 1997). The clash was not the result of a deliberate French attempt to alter the status quo (French military presence in Tunisia). Nevertheless, from Tunisia's point of view, the threat to Tunisia was profound, the value of the status quo had declined sharply, and, most importantly, France needed to be made aware of those facts (Ling 1967; Messenger 1982).

Upon observing some act, a crisis actor can capitulate, escalate, or offer to negotiate. To capitulate immediately is to accept the hypothesis that the defender is resolute. For example, in July 1986 Mozambique publicly accused Malawi of providing safe haven to the Mozambique National Resistance (MNR), an insurgent group that had been trying for several years to overthrow Mozambique's government. Tense relations between the two neighbors prompted Mozambique both to close its border with Malawi and to issue a threat to deploy missiles along the frontier unless Malawi stopped harboring the MNR (Huffman 1992). Malawi initially denied the accusation, but eventually capitulated by issuing an expulsion order for all MNR insurgents operating out of Malawi. This act ended Malawi's foreign policy crisis and prevented one for Mozambique (Brecher and Wilkenfeld 1997).

If an actor forgoes immediate capitulation, a state can respond to the provocation by choosing to escalate (at lower or higher levels) or by offering to negotiate. A call to negotiate is a decision to suspend judgment over whether to capitulate or escalate until new information can be obtained about the opponent given its response (accept or reject the offer). If the costs associated with deferring judgment do not exceed the benefits of acquiring more information and reducing the risk of accepting a false hypothesis, offers to negotiate will be preferred initially to escalation, even if the triggering act was violent.

An actor is more likely to propose negotiations when it believes both that there is a good chance the offer will be accepted and that it can achieve everything it wants at the negotiation table. Assume that one-sided cases occur when a triggering entity either inadvertently creates a crisis (which produces a decline in the status quo for the target), or intentionally does so, even though it is not really prepared to fight, in the hopes that its action will lead to an improvement of the status quo. Put differently, one-sided crises may be situations in which one or both sides are irresolute. And since irresolute challengers are in general more likely to accept an offer to negotiate than resolute ones, offers to negotiate are even more attractive to actors in one-sided crises, given that there is a high probability that they will be accepted. In some ways, one-sided crises resemble what Leng and Gochman (1982) referred to as "dialogue" or perhaps "prudence" disputes. Not only are these dispute types the least likely to end in war, but they also lend themselves to negotiation.

The foregoing conditions that lead to negotiations also occur in two-sided crises; however, they occur less often in such crises, given the different mixes of player types that characterize these disputes. In other words, sometimes the contest is between two highly resolved actors (e.g., China and Vietnam) or some other combination of actors.

International crises (two-sided) have been characterized as competitions in risk taking or as contests in demonstrating resolve (Schelling 1966; Snyder and Diesing 1977; Jervis 1979; Maoz 1983). As Powell (1988) notes, this does not necessarily mean that the state with "the greater resolve" wins or that an irresolute challenger never escalates. This characterization does strongly imply, however, that the actors in crisis know what the disputed issue is and consequently act in such a way as to induce the other side to give in on that issue.

For a variety of reasons, offers to negotiate are not likely to be the first act selected in international crises. The basic reason is that when issues are known and threats to values are serious enough, an offer to negotiate may be interpreted as a sign of weakness (Molinari 2000). If so, the adversary may be induced to escalate, believing that the opponent will capitulate rather than risk further conflict. This logic even applies to democratic dyads, which seem to require a few rounds of meaningful escalation before they can achieve a negotiated settlement (Dixon and Senese 2002). Thus, offers to negotiate are more likely to occur once each side realizes that escalation will not induce the desired result. But first the actors have to tango. In this view, an actor switches acts, from escalation to negotiation, when she revises her initial estimates regarding the opponent or the conflict more generally. Put differently, one way that escalation is interrupted or stops and a settlement proceeds is via learning (see Chapter 1).

In one view, any action that a crisis actor (the defender) implements in response to the provocation, short of doing nothing or giving in, generates a perception of threat for the triggering actor (Brecher and Wilkenfeld 1997). If the latter responds, a full-blown international crisis ensues. However, this is precisely the situation that most actors in one-sided crises want to avoid (for actors in two-sided crises, generating a crisis may be the only way to establish one's seriousness concerning the issues at stake).

Assume that the defender is irresolute. Here, the defender takes a real risk of receiving its worst outcome if it opts to escalate (match the threat or use force), as its first act when the challenger is in fact resolute. Note that this is always the case irrespective of whether the crisis is one or two sided. What exacerbates the situation in one-sided cases is that escalation still carries an additional danger in that the act of escalation itself produces a crisis for a challenger who would not otherwise be in crisis mode. Now the defender is in an unnecessary fight. If, for whatever reason, the challenger is not in a crisis, and the defender is not interested in creating one because it can obtain what it wants without one, offers to negotiate will be the preferred method of conflict management. At worst, offers to negotiate may be rejected; however, it is hard to imagine that an offer to negotiate would elicit a perception of threat.

The argument suggests that negotiation, as a conflict-management technique, should be much more prevalent in one-sided crises than in two-sided ones. First, actors have a basic need to communicate threats and demands in one-sided crises to determine what state of the world they find themselves in. Actors in two-sided crises may be more certain as to what is at stake and take actions to signal their commitment to resolve the issue in their favor. Once escalation has occurred, an actor may attempt to wind down the conflict through an offer to negotiate. However, the offer may be interpreted as a sign of weakness (escalation was an attempt to bluff one's resolve) and may motivate the recipient of the offer to escalate again. In contrast, given the types of players that operate in one-sided crises, negotiation serves both as an information-gathering device and as a method of settlement.

The foregoing argument leads to two hypotheses:

(H1) Actors in one- (two-) sided crises are less (more) likely to use violence to manage their conflict, even if the triggering act was violent (they are more [less] likely to de-escalate).

(H2) Actors in one-sided crises are more likely to use negotiation to resolve their conflicts than are actors in two-sided crises.

In the sections that follow, these hypotheses are operationalized, followed by empirical tests and data analysis. The final section contains concluding remarks.

9.4   Research Design

The hypotheses are tested using the ICB Project system-level data set (Brecher and Wilkenfeld 1997). This data set contains a total of 412 crises from the period 1918–1994. A total of 336 cases were analyzed; 76 crises were excluded because they occurred during an ongoing war.

To test the first hypothesis, the concepts of escalation and de-escalation were defined and operationalized. A crisis either escalates or de-escalates compared with the action or event that triggered the crisis. The data set contains a variable called the "breakpoint" (trigger), which includes nine different triggering acts. The nine different values of this variable include verbal, political, and economic acts; external changes; other nonviolent acts; internal verbal or physical challenges to regime or elite; a nonviolent military act; indirect violent acts; and violent acts. These acts were grouped according to whether they were violent or not. The first seven acts are considered nonviolent (accommodative) and were coded as 0; the final two acts listed are violent and were coded as 1. The frequencies of each event reveal that 38 percent of all crises are triggered by a violent act, while the remaining 62 percent start off nonviolently.

The variable "Crisis Management Technique" (CMT) was used to measure the concept of response or how the actors coped once the crisis was under way. As the name implies, CMT pertains to the primary technique used overall by the actors to manage a crisis. This variable includes negotiation, adjudication or arbitration, mediation, multiple techniques that do not include violence, non-military pressure, nonviolent military acts, multiple techniques that include violence, and violence (exclusively). This variable was also dichotomized into nonviolent or accommodative CMTs (coded as 0) and violent CMTs (coded as 1). The combination of the trigger and CMT produces three different outcomes:

- Nonviolent or violent reciprocation (0, 0 or 1, 1)
- Escalation in which violent CMTs follow a nonviolent act (0, 1)
- De-escalation in which nonviolent CMTs follow a violent act (1, 0)

The final variable, called casetype, pertains to whether a crisis was identified as two-sided or one-sided according to ICB coding rules. A two-sided crisis is coded as 0 ($N = 216$); a one-sided crisis is coded as 1 ($N = 109$). There were also 11 cases in which a non-state actor triggered a crisis. The results of the empirical tests begin with a discussion of states' behavior without taking into account casetype. This analysis serves as a baseline against which we can later assess the additional explanatory power provided by the casetype variable.

9.5   Results

Consistent with previous studies, the test results confirm that there is a significant association between actors' behavior in crises.

When the initial act in a crisis is nonviolent, 63 percent of crises are managed nonviolently, whereas 71 percent of crises that begin violently remain violent (see *Table 9.1*). Escalation and de-escalation are less common, and occur 37 percent and 29 percent of the time, respectively. Once casetype is included in the analysis, the findings show that the propensity of a crisis to escalate and/or de-escalate is not independent of whether a crisis was one or two sided.

Of the 136 crises characterized by violent triggers, 90 occurred in two-sided crises and 38 occurred in one-sided contests (the remaining 8 cases involved a non-state triggering actor). The data show that if the triggering act or event involved violence, actors in two-sided crises de-escalated (pursued accommodative CMTs) in only 17 percent (*Table 9.2*) of the cases (15 of 90). The rarity of de-escalation in two-sided crises contrasts sharply with the likely outcome in one-sided events. De-escalation occurs in 23 of 38 cases, or 61 percent of the time. The propensity of crises to escalate is also revealing. If the triggering act was nonviolent, a violent

Table 9.1. Crisis trigger and management

	Trigger	
Crisis management technique	Nonviolent	Violent
Nonviolent	63%	29%
Violent	37%	71%
N	200	136

Based on a 2 x 2 contingency table; $X^2 = 39.536$; $p < 0.01$ two-tailed test.

Table 9.2. Crisis dynamic, management, and dispute type

	Crisis	
	One-sided	Two-sided
Crisis dynamic		
De-escalation	61%	17%
Escalation	18%	47%
Management technique		
Negotiation	53%	20%
N	109	216

Based on a 2 x 2 contingency table; two-sided crises, $X^2 = 29.713$ with two degrees of freedom, $p < 0.01$ two-tailed test; one-sided crises, $X^2 = 10.817$ with two degrees of freedom, $p < 0.01$ two-tailed test.

CMT was employed in 47 percent (59/126) and 18 percent (13/71) of two- and one-sided crises, respectively. The association between casetype and crisis escalation and de-escalation may help to explain one of the outstanding issues in the literature on why states deviate from violent matching behavior in crises (see Brecher and Wilkenfeld 1997).

The second hypothesis stated that, of the non-coercive, accommodative techniques available to states, actors in one-sided crises are more likely to employ negotiation as their primary strategy to manage their conflict. To test the hypothesis, accommodative techniques were disaggregated into cases that involved negotiation without any other actions being taken ($N = 60$) and the remaining accommodative techniques ($N = 106$). The findings led to a rejection of the null hypothesis that casetype and a specific accommodative CMT are independent.

The bottom part of *Table 9.2* shows that in two-sided crises, 16 of the 82 cases (20 percent) involved the exclusive use of negotiations to settle a dispute. However, actors in one-sided crises employed negotiations in a majority of cases, 43 of 81 (53 percent). It is also noteworthy that a full 40 percent (17/43) of the negotiations that took place in one-sided crises occurred even though the initial triggering act involved violence. Actors involved in two-sided crises only managed to negotiate 19 percent of the time when the crisis began with a violent act.

The findings contained here both reinforce and, more importantly, extend previous findings on the nonviolent nature of one-sided crises. Not only are actors in one-sided crises more likely to use accommodative CMTs, but they are more likely to de-escalate by opening up the lines of communication with offers to negotiate differences. The implication, of course, is that without taking crisis type into account, we may be overstating the likelihood that actors in two-sided crises will be able to manage their differences at the negotiation table. Unfortunately, this means that the crisis between Uganda and Kenya may, indeed, be exceptional. When actors in two-sided crises do negotiate, it is much more likely that other actions, including threats and displays of force, will be used in conjunction with negotiation offers. Actors in one-sided crises often find these additional actions unnecessary to cope with conflict.

9.6 Conclusion

The notion that different types of disputes lead to different outcomes is not novel. Over two decades ago, Leng and Gochman (1982) drew our attention to the war-proneness of different dispute types. However, the scholarly community is just beginning to recognize how important it is to identify the conditions under which states choose one type of conflict-management strategy short of war and at what point in a conflict these tactics are used. A number of important contextual factors explain when a state is more likely to employ accommodative or violent crisis-management techniques. However, the type of crisis actors find themselves in (or think they are in) is fundamental in shaping choices (Leng and Gochman 1982; Hewitt and Wilkenfeld 1999).

I proposed a modest, non-formalized extension of the classic crisis model to advance stronger claims regarding the non-coercive nature of one-sided contests. The findings from the empirical tests supported the hypotheses that, compared with two-sided events, one-sided crises are more de-escalatory and the form that that de-escalation takes involves negotiation. In contrast, issues in two-sided crises are mainly resolved through tacit bargaining techniques (Schelling 1966; Pruitt 1981).

The de-escalatory nature of one-sided crises may help to solve one of the puzzles in the literature that tries to account for deviations from violent matching behavior (Brecher 1993; Brecher and Wilkenfeld 1997). While we have solid models that account for escalation, powerful explanatory models of de-escalation are more elusive. The findings here suggest that de-escalation is in large part driven by crisis type.

This study provides a preliminary set of results that require expansion and refinement. Future research on the subject should investigate the role that relative power might play in generating a crisis for one actor, but not another. I suspect that in most cases it is a stronger actor whose action triggers a crisis for a weaker one. If so, this may partially explain why a crisis adversary proposes negotiation. However, power alone does not explain why offers to negotiate are more likely to be accepted.

More attention should also be devoted to understanding the content of a negotiated agreement when the parties agree to settle their issues peacefully. Negotiation often conjures up images of both sides making concessions that lead to a compromise agreement. However, negotiations often produce victory for one side and defeat for the other or the negotiations end in stalemate. One implication of the argument advanced here is that, since actors in two-sided crises usually negotiate only after escalation, their negotiated agreements are much more likely to involve compromises than those in one-sided cases, in which neither actor goes to the edge.

The results of this study are encouraging; however, I agree with Hewitt and Wilkenfeld (1999) that deeper attention needs to be given to the development of different crisis types. In the end, we have made great strides toward understanding the factors that drive decisions to escalate conflict. Leaders choose to escalate on the basis of psychological factors, their attitudes toward risk, and pressures stemming from domestic political conditions (Ellsberg 2002), among others. However, less emphasis has been placed on identifying the conditions under which a leader opts not to escalate or use force (DeRouen and Sprecher 2004). We have also seen advances in our understanding of the timing and effectiveness of negotiation, and mediation in particular. However, the development of a rigorous theory that "artfully" combines the processes of escalation and negotiation has been more elusive. Different contexts may call for different constructs. The factors that produce negotiation given escalation in episodic crises between states may be different from those that operate in protracted conflicts between and within states. To find out, it is imperative that we continue to build theories and models that disentangle the complex processes that produce escalation and negotiation.

References

Amer R (1994). Sino-Vietnamese normalization in the light of the crisis of the late 1970s. *Pacific Affairs* **67**:357–384.

Bercovitch J & Jackson R (2001). Research report: Negotiation or mediation? An exploration of factors affecting the choice of conflict management in international conflict. *Negotiation Journal* **17**:59–77.

Brecher M (1993). *Crises in World Politics: Theory and Reality*. Oxford, UK: Pergamon Press.

Brecher M (1996). Crisis escalation: Model and findings. *International Political Science Review* **17**:215–230.

Brecher M & Wilkenfeld J (1997). *A Study of Crisis*. Ann Arbor, MI, USA: University of Michigan Press.

Bremer S (1982). The contagiousness of coercion: The spread of serious international disputes, 1900–1976. *International Interactions* **9**:29–55.

Bueno de Mesquita B, Morrow JD & Zorick ER (1997). Capabilities, perception, and escalation. *American Political Science Review* **91**:15–27.

DeRouen K & Sprecher C (2004). Initial crisis reaction and poliheuristic theory. *Journal of Conflict Resolution* **48**:56–68.

Dixon WJ (1994). Democracy and peaceful settlement of international conflict. *Journal of Conflict Resolution* **88**:14–32.

Dixon WJ (1996). Third-party techniques for preventing conflict escalation and promoting peaceful settlement. *International Organization* **50**:653–681.

Dixon WJ & Senese PD (2002). Democracy, disputes, and negotiated settlements. *Journal of Conflict Resolution* **46**:547–571.

Ellsberg D (2002). *Secrets.* New York, NY, USA: Viking.

Furtado X (1999). International law and the dispute over the Spratly Islands: Whither UNCLOS? *Contemporary Southeast Asia* **21**:386–404.

Henderson EA (1997). Culture of contiguity: Ethnic conflict, the similarity of states, and the onset of war, 1820–1989. *Journal of Conflict Resolution* **41**:649–668.

Hewitt JJ & Wilkenfeld J (1999). One-sided crises in the international system. *Journal of Peace Research* **36**:309–323.

Huffman RT (1992). Repatriation of refugees from Malawi to Mozambique. *Africa Today* **39**:114–123.

Huntington S (1993). The clash of civilizations. *Foreign Affairs* **72**:22–49.

Huth PK (1988). Extended deterrence and the outbreak of war. *American Political Science Review* **82**:423–443.

Huth PK & Allee TL (2002). Domestic political accountability and the escalation and settlement of international disputes. *Journal of Conflict Resolution* **46**:754–790.

Jervis R (1979). Why nuclear superiority doesn't matter. *Political Science Quarterly* **94**:617–633.

Jones DM, Bremer SA, & Singer JD (1996). Militarized interstate disputes, 1816–1992: Rationale, coding rules, and empirical patterns. *Conflict Management and Peace Science* **15**:163–213.

Kinsella D & Russett B (2002). Conflict emergence and escalation in interactive international dyads. *Journal of Politics* **64**:1045–1068.

Kleibor M (1996). Understanding success and failure of international mediation. *Journal of Conflict Resolution* **40**:360–389.

Leng RJ (1993a). Reciprocating influence strategies in interstate crisis bargaining. *Journal of Conflict Resolution* **37**:3–41.

Leng RJ (1993b). *Interstate Crisis Behavior, 1816–1980: Realism vs. Reciprocity.* Cambridge, UK: Cambridge University Press.

Leng RJ (1994). Interstate crisis escalation and war. In *The Dynamics of Aggression: Biological and Social Processes in Dyads and Groups,* eds. Potegal M & Knutson JF, pp. 307–332. Hillsdale, NJ, USA: Lawrence Erlbaum Associates, Publishers.

Leng RJ & Gochman CS (1982). Dangerous disputes: A study of conflict behavior and war. *American Journal of Political Science* **26**:664–687.

Ling DL (1967). *Tunisia: From Protectorate to Republic.* Bloomington, IN, USA: Indiana University Press.

Maoz Z (1983). Resolve, capabilities, and the outcomes of interstate disputes. *Journal of Conflict Resolution* **27**:195–229.

Maoz Z & Russett B (1993). Normative and structural causes of democratic peace: 1946–1986. *American Political Science Review* **87**:624–638.

Messenger C (1982). *The Tunisian Campaign.* London, UK: Allan Press.

Miall H (1996). *The Peacemakers: Peaceful Settlement of Disputes since 1945.* New York, NY, USA: St. Martin's Press.

Molinari MC (2000). Military capabilities and escalation: A correction to Bueno de Mesquita, Morrow, and Zorick. *American Political Science Review* **94**:425–427.

Morrow JD (1994). *Game Theory for Political Scientists.* Princeton, NJ, USA: Princeton University Press.

Ofcansky TP (1996). *Uganda: Tarnished Pearl of Africa.* Boulder, CO, USA: Westview Press.

Powell R (1988). Nuclear brinkmanship with two-sided incomplete information. *American Political Science Review* **82**:155–178.

Pruitt DG (1981). *Negotiation Behavior.* New York, NY, USA: Academic Press.

Rubin JZ, Pruitt D & Kim S (1994). *Social Conflict: Escalation, Stalemate and Settlement,* second edition. New York, NY, USA: McGraw-Hill.

Schelling TC (1966). *Arms and Influence.* New Haven, NJ, USA: Yale University Press.

Snyder GH & Diesing P (1977). *Conflict among Nations: Bargaining, Decision Making and System Structure in International Crises.* Princeton, NJ, USA: Princeton University Press.

Time (1988). Back from the brink. January 11, **131**(2):53.

Zartman IW (1989). *Ripe for Resolution.* New York, NY, USA: Oxford University Press.

Chapter 10

Escalation in Negotiation: Analysis of Some Simple Game Models

D. Marc Kilgour

10.1 Introduction

The many negotiation tactics called "escalation" have at least one feature in common: they are all risky. One famous metaphor for escalation, recounted by O'Neill (1991; see also PBS 1983) makes this point graphically:

> In July 1964, US Undersecretary of State George Ball tried to dissuade Lyndon Johnson from sending ground forces to Vietnam *en masse.* Johnson intended to pressure the North Vietnamese to end the war on his terms, but Ball feared that escalation would become an autonomous force, impelling both sides to higher and higher levels of violence. "Once on a tiger's back," his memo argued, "we cannot be sure of picking a place to dismount."

The struggle in Vietnam can be interpreted as an implicit negotiation in which the status quo was simply the continuation of the conflict at its current level. From this perspective, Johnson's escalation strategy was to render the status quo less preferable for the opponent – ideally, to make it unendurable – and thereby pave the way for a resolution that Johnson preferred. This tactic, which can be called *settlement pressure escalation*, is implemented by reducing the opponent's comfort level – withholding services, impounding assets, supporting its domestic opposition, etc. Settlement pressure escalation is sometimes seen as a good if costly bet, which the initiator "wins" if the target gives in first. However, as more recent events in the former Yugoslavia clearly demonstrate, this bet is risky – success is far from certain, and the initiator's costs can easily exceed those of the target. Arms races constitute mutual settlement pressure escalation, as each side tries to motivate its opponent to drop out of the race rather than face the crushing burden of increasing arms costs (see Chapter 4 in this volume).

A related tactic is *conflict escalation*, in which a participant attempts to manipulate its adversary by changing the stakes. For ongoing international disputes, conflict escalation reflects the choice by one side to cross some identifiable (perhaps symbolic) boundary, such as by putting forces on alert, deploying them, using forces rather than threatening to use them, increasing the geographic scale of a conflict, or using more terrible weapons. Zagare and Kilgour (1998, 2000) argue that the possibility of escalation changes the initiator's strategic calculation and conclude that when conflict escalation is an option, decision makers are unlikely to forgo it.

Escalation is a risky bargaining tactic because both costs and consequences are unpredictable. Unleashing forces that resist later restraints means that even a victory for the escalating side can be pyrrhic; and losing after escalating can, of course, be disastrous. In 1964, US President Lyndon Johnson believed that a significantly increased US ground presence would make the status quo in Vietnam less preferable for Ho Chi Minh, North Vietnam's leader, and thereby increase the pressure on Ho to concede. Johnson escalated, but Ho did not give in. It is likely that the consequences were worse than anything George Ball imagined when he chose the "tiger's back" metaphor.

Escalation is a tactic sometimes used in international bargaining, often rhetorically, but sometimes concretely. For example, the Democratic People's Republic of Korea (North Korea) has tested missiles or re-commissioned reactors while bargaining, explicitly or implicitly, with the USA and Japan. The specific tactic we model might be called *demand escalation*. Perhaps the simplest version of escalation for formal modeling purposes, demand escalation presupposes an ongoing single-issue distributive bargaining problem that begins with conflicting fixed demands and a mutually unsatisfactory status quo. In our formal analysis of demand escalation, we ask whether escalation can help to achieve a preferred bargaining outcome and whether the outcome after escalation is likely to be better for the escalating side. Our method is to compare the consequences of demand escalation in some simple bargaining models.

Our approach bears similarities to other formal analyses of escalation in the literature. O'Neill (1991) investigated the consequences of escalation defined as deliberately changing the values of conflict outcomes. He compared two cases: symmetric escalation, in which each side's values change equally and simultaneously, and asymmetric escalation, in which values change in a leapfrog pattern reminiscent of open, ascending-bid (or "English") auctions.

Escalation is the focus of a well-known illustration and teaching device, the both-pay open ascending-bid auction (Shubik 1971), sometimes called the escalation game. This contest is designed to induce bidders to "throw good money after bad" by bidding far more than the object at auction is worth. About such auctions, Raiffa (1982, pp. 85–90) advises, "Avoid them – they're treacherous!" In classroom illustrations, the object (typically, a US$10 bill) has an unambiguous value, which ensures that the escalation game has only one issue – money. It is not unheard of for two bidders to bid (and therefore to pay) 10 times the object's value. The escalation game is assuredly not a distributive negotiation, because of the very real possibility of both sides losing.

Of course, terms like "escalation" have many other meanings in the literature. For instance, Fisher *et al.* (1991, p. 139) call "escalating demands" the tactic of demanding more on one issue while making a concession on another. This investigation does not address the integrative, multi-issue bargaining context relevant to that definition.

In the bargaining models analyzed here, the two bargainers choose to escalate their demands, to hold them fixed, or to concede. This is single-issue bargaining that is approximately distributive, insofar as settlements more preferred by one side are less preferred by the other. Of course, remaining at the status quo is an outcome that is relatively low in both sides' preferences. Compared with the both-pay auction, these models are more loosely structured (either bargainer can act, or not, at any time), but more constrained in outcome (only a few outcomes are possible, and they are fixed in advance and not subject to change).

This version of bargaining is admittedly coarse; it requires bargainers to select black or white and excludes the shades of gray typical of distributive bargaining. It specifically prohibits compromises created, for example, by structuring outcomes differently. The motivation for this stark picture of bargaining is the need to assess the consequences of increasing a demand without clouding the issue by allowing latitude for accommodation. And while the bargainers' possible actions are constrained, their timing or sequence is not.

Thus, although it cannot capture many essential aspects of negotiation, this simple model focuses directly on the tactic of demand escalation – increasing one's demands at the bargaining table – and thereby permits analytic conclusions about its consequences to be drawn. Of course, this is a preliminary study, and its insights are only tentative. Still, this simple approach suggests whether and when a negotiator benefits from the tactic of demand escalation.

10.2   The Negotiation Models

Four related negotiation models are used in this investigation. In all models, the two negotiating parties, A and B, are assumed to have made specific demands prior to the analysis. One compromise outcome is available. Each party prefers that its own demand be met and prefers not to accept the other's demand, but prefers any settlement to none at all. Antecedents for these interrelated models are found in Zagare (1987), Kilgour and Zagare (1991), Zagare and Kilgour (1993, 1998), and Kilgour (2004).

The base-case model is designed so that the parties achieve the compromise state, perhaps after some initial moves. The three additional models include moves that a party can use to complicate the bargaining process by escalating, that is, proposing an outcome more favorable to itself and less favorable to the opponent than the original demand. The object is to assess both how escalation affects the likelihood that the parties reach the natural compromise and when escalation benefits – or harms – a bargainer.

The special structure of the bargaining models makes them amenable to the methodology (related to game theory) employed to analyze them. Each party always has a *position*, which corresponds to its current bargaining stance with respect to its own and its opponent's demands. Together, the positions of the two parties determine the *state* of the model. If A's current position is x and B's is y, then the current state is xy. A party is free to change its own position at any time; the state of the model changes whenever one of the parties changes its position.

In all four models, the positions available to each party include concede (C), which is interpreted as "agree to the opponent's demand," and demand (D), which is "continue to press the original demand." In some of the models, a party can escalate by utilizing a third option, escalate (E), which represents the position of pressing a demand more extreme than the original – better for oneself and worse for the opponent. The objective of this investigation is to compare the likely outcomes of these four models to determine when a negotiator who escalates does better.

The *no-escalation negotiation model* is the base case. It is referred to here as Model a and is shown in *Figure 10.1*. Note that there are four states (CC, CD, DC, and DD) and that the possible changes of state are shown by the arrows in *Figure 10.1*. Each arrow is labeled with the name of the bargainer, A or B, who controls the change of state. Note that A can move only horizontally, and B can move only vertically.

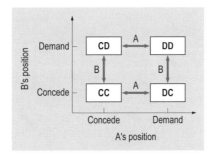

Figure 10.1. The no-escalation negotiation model (Model a).

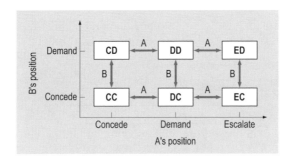

Figure 10.2. The A escalates negotiation model (Model b).

The model that includes escalation by party A alone is called the *A escalates negotiation model*. It is referred to here as Model b and is shown in *Figure 10.2*. Note that A now has three positions (C, D, and E), which combine with B's two positions (C and D) to produce six states. The states of Model b include the four states of Model a, plus EC and ED. Again, available changes of state are indicated in *Figure 10.2* by arrows, each labeled with the name of the party that controls it.

The third negotiation model included here is similar to the second, except that it is B and not A that escalates. It is called the *B escalates negotiation model* and is referred to as Model c. (It is not shown in a separate figure as it is the mirror image of Model b.) Model c has the four states of Model a, plus CE and DE, which represent the two additional states available after B escalates.

The model that encompasses escalation by both parties is called the *A and B escalate negotiation model*, referred to here as Model d and shown in *Figure 10.3*. Note that both A and B now have three positions (C, D, and E), which combine to produce nine possible states. The states of Model d include the four states of Model a, the two states added in Model b (reflecting A's escalated position), the two states added in Model c (reflecting B's escalated position), and one more state, EE, which

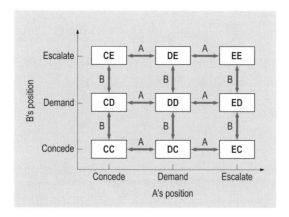

Figure 10.3. The A and B escalate negotiation model (Model d).

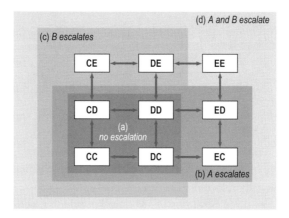

Figure 10.4. Interrelationship of Models a, b, c, and d.

represents both parties pressing their escalated demands. As in the other figures, feasible state transitions are indicated by arrows, each labeled with the name of the party that controls the transition.

The purpose of analyzing these four models is to assess the consequences of escalation by one or both parties. For this reason, the models have been constructed to overlap; in other words, states like CC and DD are common to all four models. The interrelationship of the four models is shown in *Figure 10.4*.

The objective here is to study the choices of decision makers. Because the methodology is game-theoretic, the negotiating parties' preferences over states play an important role. For example, a reasonable intuition is that a bargainer might be better off to demand more when the opponent has a strong preference against continuing disagreement, but that escalation might fail, and even backfire, if the opponent is highly competitive. Thus, it may be possible to predict behavior based on rankings only. With this observation in mind, we select (see below) an analysis methodology that depends only on ordinal preference information and does not require cardinal information, such as the usual von Neumann–Morgenstern utilities for outcomes. All that is needed are the parties' preference rankings of the states, which reflect the relative values for remaining at the states over the long term.

Many preference orderings can be encoded into these negotiation models. For convenience, all states that include at least one C position are called *settlement states*, and all others are called *conflict states*. Any state that does not include at least one E position is called a *base state*, and all the other states are called *escalatory states*. For this analysis, all preference orderings for a given party are required to satisfy the following assumptions:

(P1) Favorable settlement balance: among settlement states, those with a greater demand by a party are more preferred by that party, and those with a greater demand by the opponent are less preferred.

(P2) Embedded simple negotiation model: considering only the four base states, each party prefers any settlement to continued disagreement.

(P3) Pacific opponent: whatever a party's position, it most prefers that its opponent concedes and least prefers that its opponent escalates.

(P4) Escalation advantage: among the conflict states including one-sided escalation, a party prefers its own escalation to its opponent's.

(P5) Settlement preference: a party prefers compromise (CC) to any conflict state.

We write $S_1 \succ_X S_2$ to denote that negotiator X (strictly) prefers state S_1 to state S_2. The assumptions above then imply the following preferences for party A:

$(\text{P1})_A$ $EC \succ_A DC \succ_A CC \succ_A CD \succ_A CE,$

$(\text{P2})_A$ $\min_A\{DC, CC, CD\} \succ_A DD,$

$(\text{P3})_A$ $CC \succ_A CD \succ_A CE; DC \succ_A DD \succ_A DE; EC \succ_A ED \succ_A EE,$

$(\text{P4})_A$ $ED \succ_A DE,$

$(\text{P5})_A$ $CC \succ_A \max_A\{DD, ED, DE, EE\},$

where $\min_A\{DC, CC, CD\}$ refers to A's least preferred state among DC, CC, and CD, and $\max_A\{DD, ED, DE, EE\}$ refers to A's most preferred state among DD, ED, DE, and EE. The list of B's preference relationships, analogous to A's list above, can be obtained by reversing the two letters that define the state and changing "$\succ_A$" to "$\succ_B$." Assumptions (P1) to (P5) are independent in the sense that none is a consequence of the others.

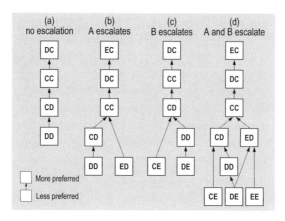

Figure 10.5. Partial ordering over all nine states for Models a, b, c, and d.

Together, (P1) to (P5) define a partial ordering of the nine possible states for each party. *Figure 10.5* shows their consequences for party A's preferences in all four models. The partial ordering over all nine states is shown in *Figure 10.5d*, which applies to Model d. In Model a, only four states are available, and they are linearly ordered by the assumptions, as shown in *Figure 10.5a. Figures 10.5b* and *10.5c* indicate that Models b and c lie between these extremes. (The partial orderings for party B, obtained by the transformation described above, are analogous.)

Of course, many linear (i.e., total or strict) orderings may be consistent with a given partial ordering. Three linear orderings are consistent with the partial ordering of Model b, three with the partial ordering of Model c, and 40 with the partial ordering of Model d. Of course, each one of these 40 orderings could be taken as defining a "type" for party A in Model d; this type would induce a type for A in Models b and c. However, it is too much to ask what the consequences are of all 40 x 40 = 1,600 combinations of types of the two parties.

The analysis used below works best with linear orderings, so this proliferation of possibilities is addressed more usefully by imposing more restrictions on a party's preferences over states. Two that are convenient, consistent with (P1) to (P5), easy to interpret, and distinct from each other define what are called the "beat the opponent" (BTO) type and the "minimize conflict" (MinCon) type.

- A BTO type has minimization of the opponent's demand as its first priority and maximization of its own demand as its second priority, with one exception: in accordance with (P2), the BTO type prefers the settlement state, CD, to the conflict state, DD.

- A MinCon type has minimization of the level of conflict as its first priority and maximization of concession differential as its second priority. The level of conflict is defined as the lowest demand selected by either party (C) if at least one side chooses C; D if at least one side chooses D and neither chooses C; and E otherwise. A party's concession differential is higher the more it demands (E greater than D greater than C) and lower the more the opponent demands.

Combining with (P1) to (P5) produces the following preference orderings in the four models:

(1) BTO type of party A:

   Model a: $DC \succ_A CC \succ_A CD \succ_A DD$
   Model b: $EC \succ_A DC \succ_A CC \succ_A ED \succ_A CD \succ_A DD$
   Model c: $DC \succ_A CC \succ_A CD \succ_A DD \succ_A DE \succ_A CE$
   Model d: $EC \succ_A DC \succ_A CC \succ_A ED \succ_A CD \succ_A DD \succ_A EE \succ_A DE \succ_A CE$

(2) MinCon type of party A:

   Model a: $DC \succ_A CC \succ_A CD \succ_A DD$
   Model b: $EC \succ_A DC \succ_A CC \succ_A CD \succ_A ED \succ_A DD$
   Model c: $DC \succ_A CC \succ_A CD \succ_A CE \succ_A DD \succ_A DE$
   Model d: $EC \succ_A DC \succ_A CC \succ_A CD \succ_A CE \succ_A ED \succ_A DD \succ_A DE \succ_A EE$

Preference orderings for the BTO and MinCon types of party B can be obtained by the usual transformation, plus interchange of Models b and c, as follows:

(1) BTO type of party B:

   Model a: $CD \succ_B CC \succ_B DC \succ_B DD$
   Model b: $CD \succ_B CC \succ_B DC \succ_B DD \succ_B ED \succ_B EC$
   Model c: $CE \succ_B CD \succ_B CC \succ_B DE \succ_B DC \succ_B DD$
   Model d: $CE \succ_B CD \succ_B CC \succ_B DE \succ_B DC \succ_B DD \succ_B EE \succ_B ED \succ_B EC$

(2) MinCon type of party B:

   Model a: $CD \succ_B CC \succ_B DC \succ_B DD$
   Model b: $CD \succ_B CC \succ_B DC \succ_B EC \succ_B DD \succ_B ED$
   Model c: $CE \succ_B CD \succ_B CC \succ_B DC \succ_B DE \succ_B DD$
   Model d: $CE \succ_B CD \succ_B CC \succ_B DC \succ_B EC \succ_B DE \succ_B DD \succ_B ED \succ_B EE$

Below, the analysis focuses on how these two types fare in the four negotiation models. Allowing each party to be of either type means that each model must be analyzed in 2 x 2 = 4 cases. Here we assume that the parties' types are common knowledge.

10.3   Analysis Methodology

GMCR II is a computer-based system for the analysis of strategic conflict (Peng 1999; Fang *et al.* 2003a, 2003b). Its theory and methodology are based on the graph model for conflict resolution (Fang *et al.* 1993). GMCR II provides for easy model input and revision, flexible analysis procedures, and efficient communication of analysis results. It was selected for this exploratory analysis because it facilitates the analysis and comparison of interrelated models under a range of preference assumptions.

Conflict models such as Models a to d can be input into GMCR II. The primary model components are the decision makers (DMs) and their options. Model a was input into GMCR II using one option (a course of action that can be selected or not), namely, concede. The interpretation is that a party either exercises the option, which represents position C, or does not exercise it, which represents position D. The same inputs are used for the parties who cannot escalate in other Models (B in Model b and A in Model c). A party that can escalate (A in Model b, B in Model c, and both A and B in Model d) is entered as a DM with two options, concede and escalate. The model is then restricted so that such a DM cannot exercise both its options simultaneously; this procedure is the simplest way in GMCR II to represent the parties' movements among positions C, D, and E.

As noted above, the graph model and GMCR II conceive of the conflict as evolving through changes of state controlled by DMs. No restrictions on the changes of state were included in this study, leaving for future work the consequences of restrictions on state transitions. (One interesting possibility is one-way escalation: it would be easy to input a model in which a party that has escalated cannot subsequently de-escalate.)

The graph model uses only ordinal preference information, and GMCR II models and analyzes a conflict using only the DMs' preference rankings of the states. The easiest of the several methods of preference entry is direct entry, which involves simply dragging and dropping states until the desired ordering is achieved. For the small models under consideration here, direct entry of preferences is the recommended method. Using it, the preference rankings for both BTO and MinCon bargainers were entered for all four of the negotiation models.

To analyze a conflict model, GMCR II applies a range of stability definitions (or solution concepts). The graph model analysis rests on the solutions of certain simple extensive games called *departure games*. Different stability definitions correspond to different procedures for constructing departure games, which always involve a focal DM and an initial state. The DM may move from the initial state in accordance with any transition it controls, or it may stay at that state. Most stability definitions allow follow-up moves by other DMs, always with the option of staying at the current state. Departure games are solved by determining the shortest-path subgame perfect equilibrium. If this equilibrium calls for the DM to stay at the status quo state, that state is called *stable* for the DM under the particular stability definition. A state that is stable for all DMs under a stability definition is an *equilibrium*.

Different stability definitions are attempts to capture different decision styles, levels of information, attitudes to strategic risk, etc. (Fang *et al.* 1993). Below, stability results for three representative stability definitions, Nash, sequential, and non-myopic, are reported.

The *horizon* of a departure game is the maximum number of moves and corresponds roughly to the level of foresight. For example, a game with horizon $h = 1$ ends after the focal DM has decided either to stay at the initial state or to move away from that state. Other departure games can be constructed by iteration; for example, in a simple departure game with horizon $h = 2$, each move by the focal DM is followed by a simple departure game with horizon $h = 1$ in which the new focal DM is the original opponent and the new initial state is the one attained after the first move. A simple departure game with $h = 3$ has simple departure games with $h = 2$ as subgames, etc. Other stability definitions, which represent more conservative, less strategic decision styles, can be defined using departure games with subgames that are not simple.

A state that is stable for a decision maker according to the simple horizon h departure game is said to be $L(h)$-stable. $L(1)$-stability is also called *Nash* stability, a terminology that reflects the observation that an $L(1)$-equilibrium, an outcome that is $L(1)$-stable for all DMs, would correspond to a Nash equilibrium if the graph model were (incorrectly) interpreted as a strategic-form or simultaneous game. It has been observed that some states may not be stable at every horizon, but are stable at any horizon that exceeds some minimum; such states are *non-myopically* stable. (They are appreciated by DMs with "sufficient" foresight.) This definition was originally proposed by Kilgour (1984); it is similar in spirit to but different in detail from Brams' (1994) definition for 2 x 2 games and is also related to Willson's (1998) proposal.

Besides Nash and non-myopic stability, *sequential* stability is reported below. Sequential stability is defined by departure games with horizon $h = 2$, in which

- the second mover (the "sanctioner") may consider only moves in its immediate interest (all sanctions must be credible), and
- the focal DM (the first mover) is deterred from any move for which there is a credible sanction (even if the credible sanction would not be the sanctioner's best response).

Table 10.1. Properties of selected GMCR II stability definitions

Name	Description	Decision-maker characteristics
Nash	Initial move, no response permitted	Very low horizon of foresight
Sequential	Initial move and response, no counterresponse permitted	Low horizon of foresight, conservative, considers only credible threats
Non-myopic	Unlimited sequence of responses and counterresponses	Unlimited foresight, willing to accept strategic risk

Sequential stability effectively captures a conservative, but shorter-foresight decision style.

Summary descriptions of the three GMCR II stability definitions selected for this study are given in *Table 10.1*. For further details and extensive references, see Fang *et al.* (1993).

10.4   Analysis

The four negotiation models described in *Figure 10.4* were input into GMCR II using parties A and B as the two DMs. Preferences of BTO and MinCon parties were modeled and analyzed separately. For brevity, the analyses below are subdivided into three cases, as follows:

(1) Both parties are of the BTO type.
(2) Both parties are of the MinCon type.
(3) One party is of the BTO type and one is of the MinCon type (for definiteness, A is assumed to be MinCon, while B is BTO).

For each of the two symmetric cases, (1) and (2), the following three models are analyzed:

(a) No escalation negotiation model
(b) A escalates negotiation model
(d) A and B escalate negotiation model

Comparisons lead to conclusions as to whether escalation by one party and counter-escalation by the other are beneficial choices when both parties are of the same type, BTO or MinCon.

For the asymmetric case (3), the following four models are analyzed:

(a) No escalation negotiation model
(b) A escalates negotiation model

(c) B escalates negotiation model
(d) A and B escalate negotiation model

From these four analyses, we can assess whether either party benefits from escalating and whether the other then benefits by counter-escalating, when one party is of the BTO type and the other is of the MinCon type. For example, comparing cases (3b) and (3a) shows whether a MinCon party benefits by escalating against a BTO party, and comparing (3d) and (3b) shows whether the BTO party would then be motivated to counter-escalate.

The GMCR II analyses for cases (1), (2), and (3) are shown in *Tables 10.2, 10.3, and 10.4*, respectively. In each of these tables, columns refer to states and rows refer to the escalation-behavior models described above; a state that does not appear in a model is indicated with "–". Within each row, stability results are reported under the three stability definitions described above. Stability is coded as follows: "x" indicates unstable for both parties; "A" indicates stable for A, but not for B; "B" indicates stable for B, but not for A; and "AB" indicates stable for both parties.

Model a (no escalation) is, in fact, identical in all three cases, because the BTO type and the MinCon type have the same preference rankings of the states CC, CD, DC, and DD. In fact, all preference orderings consistent with both (P1) and (P2) produce the same ordering of these four states. In other words, the first three lines of each table are identical.

Table 10.2 summarizes the stability results when both bargainers are of the BTO type. First, consider case (1a), the no escalation model. The preference pattern in this model is identical to the simultaneous game of Chicken, so it is not surprising that the Nash-equilibrium states (i.e., Nash-stable for both parties) are CD and DC. These states are also sequentially stable for both parties and are the only states with this stability. Recall that Nash stability has a horizon of one move (i.e., parties look ahead exactly one move in deciding whether to move or stay), and that sequential stability has a horizon of two moves. Taking the long view, state DC is non-myopically stable for A only (it is A's most preferred state), CD is non-myopically stable for B only (again, it is B's most preferred state), and CC, the compromise state, is non-myopically stable for both parties. (The details are not shown here, but in fact CC is stable for both parties provided their horizons are both at least three moves; see *Table 10.5* for a comparison.) In summary, the GMCR II analysis of the no-escalation model suggests that if the parties are short-sighted, then one must win and the other must lose, but if both have some foresight, then compromise and mutual concessions ensue. (Since CC is the only non-myopic equilibrium, it is to be expected that far-sighted parties will move from state to state until eventually they reach CC, from which neither would be motivated to move; see Kilgour 1984 for more details about non-myopic stability.)

Table 10.2. Stability results when both parties are of the BTO type

Negotiation model	Stability definition	States								
		CC	CD	CE	DC	DD	DE	EC	ED	EE
(1a) No escalation	Nash	x	AB	–	AB	x	–	–	–	–
	Sequential	x	AB	–	AB	x	–	–	–	–
	Non-myopic	AB	B	–	A	x	–	–	–	–
(1b) A escalates	Nash	x	B	–	AB	B	–	A	AB	–
	Sequential	B	B	–	AB	B	–	A	AB	–
	Non-myopic	B	B	–	AB	x	–	A	B	–
(1d) A and B escalate	Nash	x	x	B	x	x	B	A	A	AB
	Sequential	AB	AB	B	AB	AB	B	A	A	AB
	Non-myopic	AB	B	B	A	x	x	A	x	x

As case (1b) of *Table 10.2* shows, a party gains by escalating when both sides are of the BTO type. After a bargainer (A) has introduced an escalated demand, the states stable for A are those in which A holds to position E (i.e., presses its escalated demand) and, when foresight is greater, state DC, in which B concedes to A's original demand. On the other hand, a bargainer (B) that cannot match its counterpart's escalation is in a weaker position. Its stable states occur where A concedes despite escalation, and at ED, where both sides are as far from compromise as possible. The state DC is also stable for B and is the only non-myopic equilibrium. It is also an equilibrium according to the sequential stability criterion. The only other equilibrium is the Nash and sequential equilibrium at ED. Note that the compromise outcome, CC, is non-myopically stable for B, but unstable for A at any horizon of foresight.

Thus, when both sides prefer to better the opponent and one side has escalated, a reasonable expectation is that the maximum-demand state ED might arise if foresight is short; but if foresight is greater than minimal, the interaction may settle at DC, where B concedes to A's original demand. In summary, if BTO-type bargainers are not myopic, one-sided escalation seems to benefit the side that escalates and does not upset the overall stability of the system.

A comparison of cases (1b) and (1d) of *Table 10.2* shows that when both bargainers are of the BTO type and have sufficient foresight, counter-escalation is a good response to escalation. More specifically, if both sides have escalated, the Nash-stable outcomes for a party are exactly those in which the party's position is E; all states are sequentially stable except where the opponent's position is E and the original party's is not; and the non-myopically stable states for a party are those at which the opponent's position is C. It follows that the unique Nash equilibrium is EE, that both EE and CC are sequential equilibria (as are CD, DC, and DD), and that the unique non-myopic equilibrium is the compromise state, CC.

Table 10.3. Stability results when both parties are of the MinCon type

Negotiation model	Stability definition	States								
		CC	CD	CE	DC	DD	DE	EC	ED	EE
(2a) No escalation	Nash	x	AB	–	AB	x	–	–	–	–
	Sequential	x	AB	–	AB	x	–	–	–	–
	Non-myopic	AB	B	–	A	x	–	–	–	–
(2b) A escalates	Nash	x	AB	–	B	x	–	AB	x	–
	Sequential	x	AB	–	B	x	–	AB	x	–
	Non-myopic	B	B	–	B	x	–	A	x	–
(2d) A and B escalate	Nash	x	A	AB	B	x	x	AB	x	x
	Sequential	x	A	AB	B	x	x	AB	x	x
	Non-myopic	x	x	B	x	x	x	A	x	x

This propitious result, that after escalation and counter-escalation the strategic situation is stable and essentially unchanged from the no-escalation case, must be tempered by the observation that the required minimum horizon of foresight for the unique non-myopic equilibrium at CC is seven moves (see *Table 10.5*). Still, the most important conclusion from *Table 10.2* is that, provided both parties are of the BTO type, escalation does not really change the situation; the only long-term stable point is compromise.

Everything changes, however, when both sides are of the MinCon type (i.e., each bargainer's first priority is that the level of conflict be minimized). The three cases shown in *Table 10.3* refer to this situation. The analysis for case (2a), the no escalation model, is identical to what has been described above, and is not repeated here. For cases (2b) and (2d), however, the situation is strikingly different.

Case (2b) of *Table 10.3* shows that escalation by one side, when both parties are of the MinCon type, is risky and destabilizing. After A has introduced an escalated demand, the low-foresight equilibria are the two states in which one party concedes to the other's greatest demand – CD and EC. In addition, conceding to A's original demand is stable for B, though not for A. When foresight is high, no state is stable for both sides: B finds CC, CD, and DC non-myopically stable, but A's only non-myopically stable state is EC, where B concedes to A's escalated demand. Thus, when foresight is low (or decision making is conservative, as under the sequential definition), the predicted outcome is an extreme state – victory for one side or the other. When foresight is high, the only prediction is instability.

After A has escalated, the CC compromise state is non-myopically stable for B, but B's foresight must be at least three moves to achieve it. However, CC is not stable for any A whose foresight exceeds three moves, so CC is not non-myopically stable for A and is not a non-myopic equilibrium. To summarize case (2b), in which both sides are of the MinCon type and A has escalated, the most likely outcome is a

Table 10.4. Stability results when A is of the MinCon type and B is of the BTO type

Negotiation model	Stability definition	States								
		CC	CD	CE	DC	DD	DE	EC	ED	EE
(3a) No escalation	Nash	x	AB	–	AB	x	–	–	–	–
	Sequential	x	AB	–	AB	x	–	–	–	–
	Non-myopic	AB	B	–	A	x	–	–	–	–
(3b) A escalates	Nash	x	AB	–	B	x	–	A	B	–
	Sequential	x	AB	–	AB	B	–	A	B	–
	Non-myopic	B	B	–	A	x	–	A	B	–
(3c) B escalates	Nash	x	A	AB	A	x	B	–	–	–
	Sequential	A	A	AB	A	x	B	–	–	–
	Non-myopic	A	A	B	A	x	x	–	–	–
(3d) A and B escalate	Nash	x	A	AB	x	x	B	A	x	B
	Sequential	A	A	AB	A	x	B	A	x	B
	Non-myopic	A	A	B	A	x	x	A	x	x

maximum-demand state, ED or CD, if foresight is short; if foresight is greater than minimal, no state is stable for both parties. The implication of the analysis is that, in this case, state changes will continue indefinitely.

If both parties prefer to minimize conflict, but both have escalated, the situation is even more polarized, as shown in case (2d) of *Table 10.3*. The equilibria at low foresight (i.e., Nash and sequential stability) are the states in which one side has conceded to the other's maximum demand (CE and EC); the only other stable states are those in which a party concedes to the opponent's original demand (CD for A, DC for B). If foresight is high, each party's only stable state is total victory (EC for A and CE for B). In particular, there are no non-myopic equilibria, and instability is all that can be expected.

The compromise state, CC, is stable for each bargainer if and only if the horizon of foresight is an odd number not less than three; it is unstable otherwise and is consequently not a non-myopic equilibrium. In summary, when both sides are of the MinCon type, escalation is destabilizing, and counter-escalation is polarizing and does not re-establish stability.

The situation is even less promising when one side (A) is of the MinCon type and the other (B) is of the BTO type, as indicated by the four cases shown in *Table 10.4*. The analysis for case (3a), the no escalation model, is as above, and therefore is not repeated. There are three cases in addition to the no-escalation model: (3b) A escalates, (3c) B escalates, and (3d) A and B escalate.

When a MinCon bargainer (A) escalates and its BTO opponent (B) does not, the effects may be acceptable at low levels of foresight, but they are destabilizing at higher levels. After A has introduced an escalated demand, the only Nash equilibrium is CD, in which A concedes to B's demand. At the two sequential equilibria, CD and DC, one side concedes to the other's (original) demand. In these cases, the effects are predictable and mild, though it is rather surprising that, at the lowest level of foresight, A's escalation actually benefits B. The non-myopic stability criterion finds no equilibrium: the stable states for A are DC and EC (victories for A), and the stable states for B are CC, CD, and ED. It is difficult to make any clear prediction here, other than that there is no stability; A remains only at states where B concedes and A does not, but concession is not stable for B unless A concedes also.

The CC compromise state is non-myopically stable for B, although B's foresight must be at least five moves in order to achieve it (see *Table 10.5*). However, CC is not stable for any A whose foresight is five moves or more, so CC is not non-myopically stable for A and is not a non-myopic equilibrium. Thus, in case (3b), in which the side that most prefers to minimize conflict has escalated and the side that most prefers to maximize its concession differential has not, compromise is untenable for the escalating side.

In case (3c), a BTO bargainer (B) has escalated, but its MinCon opponent (A) has not. The escalation may be successful at low levels of foresight, but it is simply destabilizing at higher levels. After B has introduced an escalated demand, the only Nash or sequential equilibrium is CE, in which A concedes to B's escalated demand. This is a maximal victory for B and suggests that escalation may be an appealing course of action that enables a BTO bargainer to take advantage of a MinCon adversary – provided foresight is low. The effects of this escalation are predictable when foresight is low, but not when it is high. There are no non-myopic equilibria: the stable states for A are CC, CD, and DC, while the unique non-myopically stable state for B is CE. Again, the only reasonable prediction in this case is general instability.

The CC compromise state is non-myopically stable for A, whose horizon of foresight need be only two or more moves to achieve it. However, CC is never stable for B at any level of foresight. Again, compromise is untenable for the escalating side.

Case (3d) of *Table 10.4* refers to negotiation after escalation by both a MinCon bargainer (A) and a BTO bargainer (B). The analysis suggests that this case has much in common with case (3c), in which only the BTO bargainer has escalated. For the short-foresight equilibrium definitions, the unique equilibrium in (3d), as in (3c), is CE, a maximal victory for the escalating side. Also, there are no non-myopic equilibria at all in either (3c) or (3d): CE is the only non-myopically stable state for B, while the MinCon side is more accommodating with four stable states,

Table 10.5. Stability of compromise and non-myopic equilibria (NME) in negotiation models

Model	A	B	Escalation	Values of h for which CC is stable For A	For B	CC NME?	Another NME?
(1a)	BTO	BTO	Neither	$h \geq 3$	$h \geq 3$	Yes	No
(1b)	BTO	BTO	A	Never	$h \geq 2$	No	DC
(1d)	BTO	BTO	Both	$h \geq 7$	$h \geq 7$	Yes	No
(2a)	MinCon	MinCon	Neither	$h \geq 3$	$h \geq 3$	Yes	No
(2b)	MinCon	MinCon	A	$h = 3$ only	$h \geq 3$	No	No
(2d)	MinCon	MinCon	Both	$h \geq 3, h$ odd	$h \geq 3, h$ odd	No	No
(3a)	MinCon	BTO	Neither	$h \geq 3$	$h \geq 3$	Yes	No
(3b)	MinCon	BTO	A	$h = 3$ only	$h \geq 5$	No	No
(3c)	MinCon	BTO	B	$h \geq 2$	Never	No	No
(3d)	MinCon	BTO	Both	$h \geq 2$	Never	No	No

DC, CD, CC, and EC. The last is its most preferred state and is not available in (3c).

The long-term stability properties of the compromise state, CC, are also identical in models (3c) and (3d). CC is stable for the MinCon party (A) at any foresight level greater than or equal to two moves. However, CC is not stable for a BTO party with any foresight horizon.

The stability properties of the compromise state, CC, for simple departure games of horizon h (i.e., foresight of h moves) are summarized in *Table 10.5*. For each model, the types of A and B, and whether each has escalated, are given. The last two columns of *Table 10.5* simply record whether the compromise state, CC, is a non-myopic equilibrium and whether any state other than CC is a non-myopic equilibrium.

In summary, the analysis of the strategic value of escalation has been restricted to cases in which the bargainers are either of the BTO type (i.e., priorities are a low demand by the opponent and a high demand for itself) or of the MinCon type (i.e., priorities are minimization of the level of conflict, as well as demanding more than the opponent). If both bargainers are of the BTO type, the possibility of escalation does not seem to be a special problem provided the bargainers have enough foresight. If only one side escalates, it benefits from a stable state that favors it, though perhaps not excessively so. Clearly, there is a motivation to match escalation to escalation, but the net effect need not be destructive to the bargaining process.

If, however, either party is of the MinCon type, escalation as a bargaining tactic seems to destabilize the natural compromise without stabilizing any other state. A bargainer of the MinCon type facing a bargainer of the BTO type seems to be at a special disadvantage if the opponent escalates; as shown in *Table 10.5* with Models 3c and 3d, with minimal foresight this bargainer is willing to compromise, but its efforts are rejected by the escalating BTO bargainer. Surprisingly, perhaps, this same general conclusion holds if both bargainers are of the less aggressive MinCon type; if either party escalates, or if both do, the stability of the natural compromise is undermined and no other long-term stability arises. Perhaps the only aspect that is less benign when a BTO bargainer faces a MinCon bargainer rather than another BTO bargainer is that, facing a MinCon bargainer, the BTO bargainer aims strictly for its own most preferred state and refuses to accept anything else.

10.5   Conclusions

Is escalating during a negotiation like "jumping on a tiger's back," as George Ball suggested to Lyndon Johnson? The metaphor suggests that

- escalation leads inevitably to more escalation;
- the consequences of escalation are unpredictable and often unanticipated; and
- escalation is a risky strategy in that a party that escalates may end up worse off.

This theoretical study of escalation in bargaining, although limited to simple models and based on specific assumptions about preferences, has found qualified support for each of these statements.

- When parties are highly competitive, it is a disadvantage not to match the opponent's escalation; in this case, it is certainly reasonable to conclude that the consequence of escalation is more escalation. In other cases outcome prediction is more difficult, but not matching the opponent's escalation does not appear to bring positive benefits.
- When at least one bargainer is averse to conflict, escalation destabilizes a natural compromise, even for far-sighted bargainers, and does not produce any new stabilities. The analysis carried out here does not lead to any specific outcome prediction; several outcomes may be stable, and it is also possible that the conflict may not stabilize anywhere. Certainly, a bargainer who prefers to avoid conflict should not escalate against a more competitive opponent; but even more important is to dissuade or prevent the opponent from escalating.

- If decision making is conservative or horizons are short, the only stable outcomes after escalation may be decisive victories, for one side or the other. Thus, escalation may destabilize compromise, and the only stable endpoint may be better, or worse, for the escalating side.

Of course, this investigation is based on several assumptions that limit its generality, which makes these conclusions tentative. We now discuss these assumptions about how negotiations are structured and how they can be analyzed. First, real negotiations almost always allow each side a range of possible positions. The restriction that the outcome of the negotiation must be one of only a few possibilities is therefore unrealistic, an extreme instance of the so-called "small world" assumption. Consequently, this bargaining is not a search for compromise; the parties cannot structure their own "middle ground" and must work with a prespecified take-it-or-leave-it compromise. For many, the search for mutual benefit, or "negotiation dance" (Raiffa 1982, p. 128), is the essence of bargaining.

Second, the preference structures assumed in the analysis of these models may preclude some real possibilities. Assumptions (P1) to (P5) seem reasonable; the two representative types selected for analysis, BTO and MinCon, are easy to distinguish and, as the analysis shows, differ in their consequences. However, there may be many other equally different and interesting preference rankings consistent with (P1) to (P5).

As well, the analysis here is conducted on the assumption that each party is aware of the opponent's preferences. The use of GMCR II, which presumes only ordinal preferences, weakens this knowledge requirement – utilities or other cardinal measures of value play no role, and the parties are assumed to know only each other's preference rankings. Nonetheless, some aspects of a party's preference ordering, such as whether it prefers to beat the opponent or minimize conflict, are often treated as private information in negotiations. Behavior in negotiation, and therefore outcomes, may depend on mutual uncertainty about the other bargainer's type.

Uncertainty plays no role in our analysis, in fact. The methodology assumes that bargainers have no doubts about how choices determine the outcome, what the current status of the negotiation is, what moves the opponent is making, and, of course, what the opponent's preferences over the possible outcomes are.

Another assumption implicit in this analysis is that rational choice methods can provide insight into the choices of the parties. The graph model methodology used here makes rather weak assumptions about rational choice, but we have emphasized long-term stability, which presumes foresight, if not rationality.

Finally, another approach to escalation in bargaining might be that escalation should not be seen so much as an action that has or has not been performed, but rather as a threat. This view of escalation cannot be integrated easily into these models, so nothing is said about it here. For crisis models that involve escalation as a threat, see Brams and Kilgour (1988) and Zagare and Kilgour (1998, 2000).

In summary, our tentative conclusions about demand escalation as a bargaining tactic are as follows:

- Escalation may sometimes be a beneficial bargaining tactic, but only if the opponent does not reciprocate.
- Matching the opponent's escalation seems not to be harmful, though the best it can do is restore the situation that existed prior to the escalation.
- Escalation can destabilize a compromise, particularly when at least one bargainer prefers to avoid conflict.
- Escalation makes the outcome of bargaining harder to predict.
- If far-sighted, highly competitive bargainers mutually escalate, there is no net effect on the likely outcome of the bargaining.
- A bargainer who prefers to avoid conflict cannot gain by escalating and stands to lose if its opponent escalates.
- If both bargainers prefer to avoid conflict, both will be worse off after escalation.

References

Brams SJ (1994). *Theory of Moves*. Cambridge, UK: Cambridge University Press.

Brams SJ & Kilgour DM (1988). *Game Theory and National Security*. Oxford, UK: Basil Blackwell.

Fang L, Hipel KW & Kilgour DM (1993). *Interactive Decision Making: The Graph Model for Conflict Resolution*. New York, NY, USA: John Wiley and Sons.

Fang L, Hipel KW, Kilgour DM & Peng X (2003a). A decision support system for interactive decision making. Part 1: Model formulation. In *IEEE Transactions on Systems, Man and Cybernetics, Part C*, **33**:42–55.

Fang L, Hipel KW, Kilgour DM & Peng X (2003b). A decision support system for interactive decision making. Part 2: Analysis and output interpretation. *IEEE Transactions on Systems, Man and Cybernetics, Part C*, **33**:56–66.

Fisher R, Ury W & Patton B (1991). *Getting to Yes*, second edition. New York, NY, USA: Penguin.

Kilgour DM (1984). Equilibria for far-sighted players. *Theory and Decision* **16**:135–157.

Kilgour DM (2004). Prospects for conflict management: A game-theoretic analysis. In *Multiple Paths to Knowledge in International Relations*, ed. G Palmer, Z Maoz, A Mintz, C Morgan and RJ Stoll, pp. 73–94. Lanham, MD, USA: Lexington Press.

Kilgour DM & Zagare FC (1991). Credibility, uncertainty, and deterrence. *American Journal of Political Science* **35**:303–334.

O'Neill B (1991). Conflictual moves in bargaining: Warnings, threats, escalations, and ultimatums. In *Negotiation Analysis*, ed. Young HP, pp. 87–108. Ann Arbor, MI, USA: University of Michigan Press.

PBS (1983). *Vietnam: A Television History, LBJ Goes to War (1964–1965)*, video. Transcript available at http://www.pbs.org/amex/vietnam/104ts.html.

Peng X (1999). A decision support system for conflict resolution. PhD thesis. Waterloo, Canada: University of Waterloo.

Raiffa H (1982). *The Art and Science of Negotiation*. Cambridge, MA, USA: Harvard University Press.

Shubik M (1971). The dollar auction game: A paradox in noncooperative behavior and escalation. *Journal of Conflict Resolution* **15**:545–547.

Willson SJ (1998). Long-term behavior in the theory of moves. *Theory and Decision* **45**:201–240.

Zagare FC (1987). *The Dynamics of Deterrence*. Chicago, IL, USA: University of Chicago Press.

Zagare FC & Kilgour DM (1993). Asymmetric deterrence. *International Studies Quarterly* **37**:1–27.

Zagare FC & Kilgour DM (1998). Deterrence theory and the spiral model revisited. *Journal of Theoretical Politics* **10**:59–87.

Zagare FC & Kilgour DM (2000). *Perfect Deterrence*. Cambridge, UK: Cambridge University Press.

Chapter 11

Escalation, Readiness for Negotiation, and Third-Party Functions

Dean G. Pruitt

Conflict is said to escalate when one or both parties shift(s) to more extreme tactics – shouting instead of complaining softly, shooting instead of shouting, sending tanks instead of guerrillas. Escalation is the main reason why conflict has such a bad reputation. People are hurt and relationships are destroyed.

Escalation often develops through *conflict spirals*. Party A annoys party B, who retaliates, which provokes a more extreme tactic from A, and so on up the escalation ladder (Rubin *et al.* 1994; Pruitt and Kim 2003). Conflict spirals tend to take on a life of their own, in which the original issues may be all but forgotten.

Conflict often involves contentious behavior, in the sense of efforts to win, but this need not produce a conflict spiral. Conflict spirals occur when the parties engage in *negative reciprocity*, in which they respond to contentious behavior with more contentious behavior, fighting smoke with fire (Holmes and Murray 1996). Such spirals are avoided when the parties engage in *accommodation* and respond instead with yielding or problem solving (Rusbult *et al.* 1991).

Research on close interpersonal relationships shows that accommodation predominates in happy and committed relationships, while negative reciprocity predominates in distressed relationships (Sillars 1981; Rusbult *et al.* 1991; Bradbury

and Fincham 1992). This means that in distressed relationships, even trivial conflicts tend to escalate, with each partner retaliating in response to the other's retaliatory behavior (Pruitt 1998). One dynamic that underlies this escalation is distrust,
which produces a tendency to blame the partner for any annoyance. The partner
is seen as acting intentionally and with disregard for one's interests, and hence as
richly deserving to suffer (Sillars 1981; Fincham 1985; Manusov 1990). Since
blame and distrust are products as well as sources of escalation, it is clear that escalation tends to encourage more escalation and that a relationship that starts to
deteriorate often continues to do so on its own dynamic.

Dehumanization of the other party is another process that underlies escalation
(Kelman and Hamilton 1989). Dehumanization results from prior escalation or a
perception that the other party rejects values that are important to oneself (Struch
and Schwartz 1989; Robinson and Friedman 1995). An extreme form of dehumanization, which often encourages escalation, involves a view of the other as demonic
(Rouhana and Kelman 1994) or as a diabolical enemy (White 1984). Escalation is
also more likely when the other party is de-individuated, in the sense of not being
perceived as a unique individual (Worchel and Andreoli 1978). De-individuation
may explain why heavily escalated tactics are more likely to be used when the other
is at a physical (Milgram 1992) or social (Ransford 1968; Struch and Schwartz
1989) distance from the actor.

Conflict spirals are not the only dynamic of escalation. Escalation can also
develop as a *response to persistent annoyance*. For example, suppose that your
neighbors play loud music late at night. You might begin by mildly asking them
to stop. However, if that does not work, you may well shift your tactics in an
escalatory direction and demand that they stop, yell at them if they do not, and
eventually even call the police.

My students and I have found an orderly escalation sequence in a study of individual and group reactions to persistent annoyance (Mikolic *et al.* 1997). We produced annoyance by having confederates persistently withhold supplies that were
needed by the participants. The participants were allowed to call the confederates or the experimenter at any time, and most calls involved efforts to obtain the
needed supplies. Seven contentious tactics were identified in a content analysis of
these calls.

The contentious tactics were usually used in the order shown in *Table 11.1*.
All participants began with requests for return of the supplies. All but seven went
on to demands (statements that put pressure on the other party), all but eight of
these went from there to complaints (objecting to some aspect of the confederate's
behavior), and so on up to abuse (name calling or swearing). Some people reached
much higher levels of escalation than others. Those who reached a particular level
of escalation continued to perform at that level and all levels below it in the scale.

Table 11.1. Escalation in response to persistent annoyance (from Mikolic *et al.* 1997).

Scale level	Tactic	Number of individuals*	Number of groups*	Total number*
I	Requests	7	0	7
II	Demands	8	0	8
III	Complaints	21	5	26
IV	Angry statements	4	8	12
V	Threats	0	4	4
VI	Harassment	1	7	8
VII	Abuse	0	7	7
Total		41	31	72

*The entries in this table refer to the number of parties (individuals or groups) who escalated to the tactic shown on the left and no further.

The orderliness of these data suggests the existence of an escalation script that consists of standard steps, which either is a product of evolution or is culturally pre-scribed to cope with persistent annoyance. This script may help to understand why conflict spirals so often move toward harsher and harsher tactics rather than staying at the same level of escalation. Lacking insight into their own contribution to the conflict spiral, people often regard the situation as one of persistent annoyance from the other side. The other is seen as the aggressor and they as the victim. If their initial efforts fail to stop this aggression, they shift to more escalated tactics, as in the standard script. If this happens on both sides (e.g., Serbs and Kosovan Muslims both regard themselves as victims), escalation is likely to spiral out of sight.

11.1   Groups versus Individuals

Table 11.1 shows that groups escalated further in response to persistent annoyance than did individuals.[1] Other studies show that groups are more aggressive than individuals when the adversary is punitive and insulting (Jaffe and Yinon 1983) and that they use more threats (Betz and Fry 1995), react more harshly to norm violation (Rabbie and Lodewijkx 1995), and are more competitive in the Prisoner's Dilemma game (Schopler and Insko 1992). These findings have been explained variously as arising from defense of social identity, group polarization, group dynamism, de-individuation, diffusion of responsibility, anonymity, a sense of group power and invulnerability, or a tendency to distrust opposing groups more than opposing individuals (Schopler and Insko 1992; Mummendey and Otten 1993; Mikolic *et al.* 1997).

---

[1]The term "group," as used here, is a broad one that embraces organizations and states as well as smaller collectives.

One solution to the problem of intergroup escalation is crosscutting group memberships, where some members of group X and group Y are also members of group A (a crosscutting group). If additional members of X and Y are members of group B, the rivalry between groups A and B may further mitigate the X–Y conflict (Coleman 1957). The power of crosscutting has been demonstrated by Vanbeselaere (1991) in an experiment that involved perceived group membership, but no intergroup communication. The effect should be even stronger in real-life settings, where members of the crosscutting group(s) can urge restraint or mediate controversies. Thus, crosscutting was shown to diminish Hindu–Muslim escalation in Varshney's (2002) study of six Indian towns.

11.2 Routes to Negotiation in Highly Escalated Conflicts

Conflict escalation tends to disrupt communication between the parties, which makes it difficult or impossible for them to negotiate with each other and disturbs the chains of intermediaries that previously linked them. There are four main reasons for this. The first is that hostility makes it difficult for the parties to meet or reach agreement with each other. One should denounce the devil, not do business with him. Such attitudes were found in the Middle East before 1993, where it was illegal for Israelis to have contact with the Palestine Liberation Organization (PLO) and Arabs sometimes murdered other Arabs for having contact with Israelis. The second reason is that the two sides usually have such divergent goals and views of the situation that to reach an agreement seems hopeless. Why waste one's time? The third reason is fear that negotiation will weaken one's military capability by eroding one's image of toughness or reducing the militancy of one's fighting forces. The fourth reason is that escalation between two parties often polarizes the community within which they are situated (Rubin *et al.* 1994). Potential third parties join one side or the other, which makes it more difficult to solve the conflict.

There are two alternative routes to restoring communication and beginning to negotiate in highly escalated circumstances.

- The first is for the situation to become ripe, in Zartman's (1989) terminology – for both parties to begin to view the conflict as dysfunctional and to seek a possible nonviolent way out of it. This was the route that led to the 1993 Oslo negotiations that produced Yasser Arafat's Palestinian Authority (Pruitt 1997) and to the 1997–1998 Stormont negotiations that produced the agreement ratified by 70 percent of the residents of Northern Ireland (Pruitt 2000).
- The other is for third parties to force or cajole the disputants to the table by becoming directly involved in the conflict, using threats and promises, or encouraging a perception of possible solutions. This happened in the 1991 Madrid

Conference, which was attended by Israel because of US pressure and which accomplished very little. It also happened in the 1979 Lancaster House (London) negotiations, which led to the establishment of Zimbabwe. The combatants in the latter conflict were, on the one hand, two armies of African insurgents headquartered in Mozambique and Zambia, and, on the other hand, the Rhodesian settlers and an African government they had installed under Bishop Muzorewa. These parties did not view the conflict as dysfunctional in the sense of a mutually hurting stalemate. Indeed, Robert Mugabe, leader of the larger insurgent army, thought he was winning the war and many on the settler side were not convinced they were losing it (Stedman 1991). Negotiation was forced on Mugabe by his African allies (Mozambique and Zambia) and by the British, who threatened to recognize the Muzorewa government if Mugabe did not attend. The settlers and Muzorewa were cajoled to the table by the expectation that Britain would recognize the Muzorewa government if they attended (Davidow 1984; Stedman 1991).

11.3 Readiness Theory

To better understand the first of these routes, I have developed readiness theory (Pruitt 1997), a modification of Zartman's (1989, 1996, 1997) ripeness theory. Readiness for conflict resolution is viewed as a variable, rather than a state as in Zartman's theory, and it pertains to a single party, rather than to the situation between two parties as in Zartman's theory. The greater a party's readiness, the more likely it is to enter and stay in negotiation (or mediation), put human resources into the negotiation, make concessions, and take risks for peace.

Two states of mind contribute to readiness. One is the *motivation to escape the conflict*, which results from a perception that the conflict is dysfunctional or counterproductive.[2] A party sees that it is in a hurting (i.e., a costly) stalemate, or that the situation is moving toward some sort of catastrophe, or that it has a major problem that can only be solved by working with the other party. The other state of mind is *optimism*, a sense that it is possible to locate and move to a mutually acceptable agreement. Without optimism, a party is reluctant to take the risks and devote the resources necessary to move toward settlement, however motivated it is to escape the conflict. Early in a peace process, optimism often derives from what Kelman (1997) calls "working trust," a belief that the other side is also motivated to escape the conflict and hence make concessions. However, for optimism to be maintained, a party must eventually see the outlines of a possible agreement. It must have a sense that a formula can be devised that will bridge the two parties'

---

[2] When both parties are motivated to escape a conflict, we can speak of "motivational ripeness" (Pruitt 1997).

opposing positions – that they are not too far apart to reach agreement. This is what Zartman (1996) calls a perceived "way out."

These two states of mind have rather different sources. Motivation to escape the conflict derives from the circumstances the parties are in – the balance of military power, the extent of suffering on both sides, or the direction in which the situation seems to be moving. Optimism, if it develops, derives largely from events that occur after both sides have become motivated to escape. The parties themselves may engage in a *circular reassurance process* – a kind of courtship dance – in which they alternate making conciliatory gestures that send increasingly clear and compelling signals of this motivation to each other. The latter is like a conflict spiral in reverse. It is an exceedingly delicate process that can easily fail despite strong motivation to escape on both sides. There are two common sources of this failure:

- initial hostility and distrust because of the prior escalation, which make it hard to take a conciliatory move or to view the other party's actions as conciliatory; and
- actual hostilities (shooting, explosions) that so often continue during a period in which the prospects for settlement are being explored.

In addition, third parties, acting as *intermediaries*, often contribute to the development of disputant optimism, for at least four reasons:

- They are likely to be more aware than the disputants themselves that there is motivation to escape the conflict on both sides.
- They can tell each side of the other's motivation to escape.
- They can stimulate and coordinate the circular reassurance process – the courtship dance that improves optimism on both sides. For example, they can detect when the other side is ready to reciprocate a party's conciliatory moves and urge that party to make such moves; and they can interpret each side's conciliatory moves to the other side.
- They can grasp the two sides' needs and priorities and create integrative options in a way that is not possible for the highly biased disputants themselves.

In addition to encouraging optimism, third parties are themselves affected by this state of mind. The greater the chances of settling the dispute, the harder they will work.

The third parties in most peace processes occupy points along a *communication chain* that stretches from one side to the other (Pruitt 1994, 1995, 2000).[3] Such chains develop and are successful for several reasons:

- They provide a means of communication if the principals (i.e., the decision makers at the ends of the chains) refuse to talk with each other, as often happens in heavily escalated conflict.
- They provide political cover for the principals, who are usually reluctant to be seen as communicating directly with the adversary in the absence of assurances that the adversary will make substantial concessions. This is because communication in chains can be kept more secret and hence more deniable than direct communication. Political cover is particularly important in conflict that has escalated to the point of military operations. Direct negotiations are hard to justify in such an atmosphere, but negotiations through intermediaries can start and survive because leaders can deny that they are taking place.
- They provide a process for finding solutions. People who are adjacent to each other in a chain generally share more values, speak more of the same language, and trust each other more than those who are farther apart. This means that there will be better communication and problem solving at each point in the chain than could possibly occur between the principals at either end. Hence chains often find solutions that elude the principals.
- They provide trust to grease the process. Adjacent chain members are likely to be more trusting and have more influence over each other than those who are farther apart. In addition, principals are more likely to accept a proposal from an intermediary than from their adversary, because they trust the intermediary more and can more easily justify such concessions to their constituents. This makes agreement more likely.

Chains usually start out as a short segment (or segments) that includes only one of the principals. If this segment performs well, optimism and its components increase throughout the conflict system, which allows the chain to *grow at the ends* and eventually include both principals.

Optimism also causes chains to *shorten in the middle*, which allows people at a distance from each other to talk more directly. The eventual result of this shortening may be negotiation between the principals or those close to them. When chains shorten, the people who drop out of the middle usually do not disappear. Rather,

---

[3]Communication chains are sometimes called "channels." However, the term "chain" is more descriptive of this phenomenon and hence a better vehicle with which to analyze it.

they stay on as advisors to the remaining chain members and help them to talk across the chasms that still divide them. Furthermore, portions of the chain may continue to operate as back channels that move the negotiations ahead at points of impasse. The initial chains in highly escalated conflicts often involve unofficial intermediaries and hence Track 2 diplomacy. When these chains shorten, the process usually moves from Track 2 to Track 1 diplomacy.[4]

Several communication chains may operate at the same time, with different sets of intermediaries linking the principals. However, if the conflict is moving toward agreement, one of these channels usually becomes the main locus of negotiation, greatly eclipsing the others.

11.4 The Oslo Negotiations

The theory just presented helps to explain the peace process between the Israelis and the Palestinians. After years of heavily escalated conflict, negotiations took place in and around Oslo in 1993.[5] They consisted of 12 highly secret meetings between representatives of Israel and the PLO, which were assisted by Norwegian scholars and diplomats. The result was a Declaration of Principles signed by Israeli Prime Minister Yitzhak Rabin and PLO Chairman Yasser Arafat, which formed the basis for establishment of the Palestinian Authority.

Before the talks started, both sides were highly motivated to escape the seemingly intractable conflict between them. This was largely because of changed circumstances. The situation was clearly a stalemate – the Israelis could not defeat the Palestinians or vice versa. Furthermore, it was a *hurting* stalemate for Israel because of the cost of maintaining high military readiness and of containing the intifada. Israel was also concerned about support from the USA, which had put it on the margins during the Gulf War. Like Ehud Barak in the 1999 election, Rabin had won the 1992 election with a promise to negotiate peace with the Palestinians, which gave urgency to the Israeli motivation to escape the conflict. Arafat faced an impending catastrophe in the rapid rise of the Hamas movement, which threatened to supplant the PLO as leader of the Palestinians. Rabin was also worried about the rise of Hamas and another possible catastrophe: that Iran or a revitalized Iraq would make common cause with a fundamentalist Palestinian leadership, and so produce a larger military threat to Israel. It took Rabin a while after his election to

---

[4]Track 1 diplomacy involves formal negotiations between diplomats, while Track 2 diplomacy involves informal talks between citizens on either side of a conflict.

[5]Information about the Oslo negotiations can be found in Corbin (1994), Abbas (1995), Makovsky (1996), Pruitt *et al.* (1997), and Savir (1998).

realize that the PLO was the only valid representative of the Palestinians and that he had to rely on Arafat to solve the Palestinian problem. However, once he did so, he became highly motivated to negotiate a settlement with Arafat.

Though both parties were motivated to escape the conflict, they could not easily move to a negotiated agreement because of residues from the past escalation. Fortunately, a circular reassurance process took place during the seven months at Oslo, which resulted in a tremendous growth in optimism. At first, this growth was mainly at a personal level. The delegates developed camaraderie and a faith in one another's seriousness of purpose. Then optimism began to grow back home, as both sides made concession after concession and it became clear that these concessions emanated from the top levels in the PLO and the government of Israel. The result was a growing infusion of human resources into the process. Israel increased its level of representation at the talks, and Rabin and Arafat began to pay ever-closer attention to what was happening. There were several tense moments at which the talks seemed on the verge of collapse, but some really major concessions were eventually made, and agreement was reached.

Third parties were crucial to this circular process. Most important was Terje Larsen, a Norwegian social scientist who was collecting data in Gaza and became aware of the motivation to escape the conflict on both sides. He and his wife, a Norwegian diplomat, set up the meetings and provided substantial good offices at every turn. It is clear from how they handled the negotiations that they were aware of the need for a circular reassurance process. Also important were two Israeli professors who represented Israel in the first five meetings and provided reports that led the Israeli government to send actual diplomats to the remaining seven meetings. These professors can be thought of as intermediaries between the PLO and the Israeli government.

In line with readiness theory, the communication chain got longer at one end and shorter in the middle as optimism grew. Four stages of the chain are shown in *Figure 11.1.*

Stage I represents the chain before the start of the talks, as Larsen arranged for both sides to participate. Stage II represents the situation that obtained during the first five sessions. The Israeli foreign minister (Shimon Peres) was added at one end of the chain and the mediator was dropped in the middle, in the sense that Larsen sat outside the meeting room ready to provide assistance, but without becoming involved in the discussions. (The chain was somewhat longer between meetings, in that Larsen passed messages from one side to the other because of the fear that direct telephone contact between the two sides would be detected by someone in the outside world.) Stage III represents the situation that obtained in the final seven sessions, when Israeli diplomats took over from the professors, who stayed on as

	Arafat	PLO delegates	Mediator (Larsen)	Israeli professors	Israeli diplomats	Israeli foreign minister	Rabin
Stage I	Arafat	←→ PLO delegates	←→ Mediator (Larsen)	←→ Israeli professors	←→ Israeli diplomats		
Stage II	Arafat	←→ PLO delegates	←	↑ Israeli professors	←→ Israeli diplomats	←→ Israeli foreign minister (Peres)	
Stage III	Arafat	←→ PLO delegates	←		↑ Israeli diplomats	←→ Israeli foreign minister	←→ Rabin
Stage IV	Arafat	←				↑ Israeli foreign minister	←→ Rabin

Figure 11.1. Four stages of the communication chain between the PLO and the Israeli government.

advisors.[6] Stage IV represents a final telephone conversation between Arafat and Peres, in which the final details of the agreement were hammered out. The two of them did not talk directly, but what they said was repeated into the phone by another person in the room with them, so that it was essentially a direct conversation. The progression from Stage II to Stage IV shows how intermediaries drop out of a chain as optimism grows. The progression from Stages I and II to Stage III shows how Track 2 diplomacy, which involved Larsen and the Israeli professors, was replaced by Track 1 diplomacy, which involved diplomats on both sides.

There were other channels between the PLO and the Israeli government during this period, but none of these came close to the Oslo channel in importance. The most significant of these involved President Hosni Mubarak of Egypt as the intermediary. This reinforced the Oslo channel, for example, by allowing Arafat to check whether Rabin was committed to proposals being made in the Oslo channel, but it does not appear to have been a locus of true negotiation (Savir 1998).

11.5   The Northern Ireland Peace Process

Readiness theory also helps understand the Northern Ireland peace process.[7] Superficially this process looks quite different from the Oslo negotiations in that it took place over a period of 13 years rather than nine months and the intermediaries were major political actors rather than researchers and professors. Nevertheless, the same basic processes can be seen.

The adversaries fighting each other consisted of the Irish Republican Army (IRA; a Catholic paramilitary organization), on the one hand, and the British army, Northern Ireland police, and some Protestant paramilitary organizations, on the other. Again, the peace process began with the development of motivation to escape the conflict on both sides. There is reason to believe that, from the early 1980s onward, both the IRA leadership and the British government saw the situation as a stalemate in which neither side could defeat the other. It was a severely *hurting* stalemate for Britain because the conflict was enormously costly, in terms of soldiers to maintain in Northern Ireland, grants to prop up the Northern Ireland economy, criticism from abroad about human rights violations, and eventually bombs exploding in Britain. The conflict also became increasingly costly and risky for the IRA and Sinn Fein, the IRA's political arm. In 1985, Britain and Ireland signed a pact called the Anglo–Irish Agreement. This posed a military threat because it pledged the Republic of Ireland to work harder to stop IRA operations from their

---

[6]Negotiators (e.g., the PLO delegates and the Israeli diplomats) are viewed as intermediaries in this theory, because they have much the same functions as third parties in the chain (Pruitt 2000).

[7]Information about the Northern Ireland peace process can be found in Aughey and Morrow (1996), Bew and Gillespie (1996), Mallie and McKittrick (1996), Taylor (1997), and Mitchell (1999).

soil. It also posed a political threat because it gave the Irish government a voice in some of the affairs of Northern Ireland, which allowed Catholic concerns to be pursued nonviolently and thus eroded some of Sinn Fein's appeal to Catholic voters. In addition, the continued violence produced increasing criticism of the IRA from a war-weary Catholic population. The result was that Gerry Adams, president of Sinn Fein, and others in his organization made some conciliatory statements in 1986 and 1987.

This led to the formation of several informal communication chains that linked the IRA to the British government. The most important of these stretched from the leaders of the IRA to Gerry Adams (leader of Sinn Fein), to John Hume (leader of the Social Democratic and Labour Party [SDLP], the moderate Catholic party in Northern Ireland), to the Irish taoiseach[8] (Charles Haughey, then Albert Reynolds), and finally to the British prime minister (John Major, then Tony Blair).

Two parts of this chain were already in existence in 1987. The leaders of the IRA and Sinn Fein had always been close, and regular consultations took place between the British and Irish governments from 1985 onward. The situation in 1987 looked like this:

Stage I   IRA $\leftarrow \rightarrow$ Sinn Fein   Irish $\leftarrow \rightarrow$ British
                    (Adams)   government   government
                                              (Haughey)   (Major)

These partial chains were then linked together by John Hume, who contacted Gerry Adams to see what lay behind his conciliatory statements. The two men had several informal talks in 1988, which are known as the Hume–Adams dialogue; and then Hume met with the Irish taoiseach, completing the chain as follows:

Stage II   IRA $\leftarrow \rightarrow$ Sinn Fein $\leftarrow \rightarrow$ SDLP $\rightarrow \leftarrow$ Irish $\leftarrow \rightarrow$ British
                    (Adams)   (Hume)   government   government
                                                (Haughey,   (Major)
                                                Reynolds)

This chain operated intermittently, but effectively, over the next few years despite a stepped-up IRA military campaign, which heavily targeted Britain itself (Mallie and McKittrick 1996). Not only was the chain unpublicized, but the links to Sinn Fein were vigorously denied by the British government because of the IRA violence. Nevertheless, the chain produced, in 1993, a conciliatory joint statement by the prime minister of Britain and the Irish taoiseach, the Downing Street Declaration. Despite British denials, Sinn Fein and the SDLP heavily influenced this

---

[8]Taoiseach is the Irish term for prime minister.

declaration.[9] The declaration paved the way for an IRA cease-fire in 1994 and the official peace negotiations, which Sinn Fein joined in 1997. As mentioned earlier, a chain like this works because parties adjacent in the chain communicate better and have more influence over each other than parties at a distance from each other and because the principals at either end can deny that they are communicating with each other.

Between 1988 and 1994, we can see, in addition, a circular reassurance process between Britain and Sinn Fein, which led to the IRA cease-fire. One must peer through the haze of gunpowder and explosions to see these rays of light, but they were nevertheless there. Parts of this courtship dance were initiated by the principal parties, while other parts were orchestrated by the intermediaries, John Hume and Irish officials. A few highlights of this dance are as follows:

- In 1988, Sinn Fein sent signals that it was re-examining its policies, most notably by engaging in the Hume–Adams dialogue.
- In 1989 and 1990, the British secretary of state for Northern Ireland, Peter Brooke, made conciliatory speeches in which he said that Britain had no selfish economic or strategic interest in Northern Ireland and would respond with "imaginative steps" if the IRA abandoned violence. Hume had urged him to make these statements, which spoke to IRA and Sinn Fein concerns.
- At Christmas time in 1990, the IRA declared a three-day cease-fire, and in 1992 Sinn Fein published a conciliatory statement, "Towards a lasting peace in Ireland."
- October 1993 produced the Downing Street Declaration, in which Britain indicated, at the behest of the Irish Republic, that "new doors could open" if the IRA would renounce violence. Shortly thereafter, British Prime Minister John Major indicated that he would talk with Sinn Fein if they would stop their violence.
- In August 1994, the IRA declared a cease-fire and called for negotiation.

This reassurance process was circular in that each action reciprocated a prior action by the other party. A close examination of these events reveals another possible principle, that delay in reciprocating a party's conciliatory action diminishes that party's optimism. Thus, there was consternation in Britain because it took the IRA 10 months to respond to the Downing Street Declaration. In addition, Britain took so long to respond to the August 1994 cease-fire in starting negotiations that the IRA resumed hostilities in February 1996. (Fortunately, Britain quickly relented

---

[9]There is a striking similarity between parts of the Downing Street Declaration and documents attributed to Hume and Adams that appear in a book by Mallie and McKittrick (1996). Other parts of this declaration were designed to mollify the Northern Ireland Protestant community, which had been contacted by both the British and the Irish governments.

and the negotiations commenced, which prompted a new cease-fire that allowed Sinn Fein to take a seat at the table in September 1997.)

After the first IRA cease-fire, the chain began to shorten. Conversations took place between the Irish taoiseach and Gerry Adams, with Hume in attendance:

Stage III   IRA ← → Sinn Fein ←   →   Irish   ← → British
             (Adams)   government   government
                                          (Reynolds)   (Major)

The chain became even shorter in the final Stormont negotiations, in which Sinn Fein talked directly with the British government. As hypothesized by readiness theory, all the parties from the original chain were present in these negotiations.

Stage IV   IRA ← → Sinn Fein ←   →   British
             (Adams)   government
                                                  (Blair & staff)

During part of the period just described, there was another communication chain that went from Sinn Fein to a mysterious figure called "the contact," to British intelligence officers in Northern Ireland, and thence to the government in London. This back channel, which had been used in the 1970s and early 1980s, was most active in the period between 1990 and 1993. However, a Sinn Fein (1994) chronology of events in this channel indicates that it was not a negotiation site. Instead, it transmitted advance notice of developments on the British side and tried, without success, to set up direct negotiation between Sinn Fein and the British government. Mallie and McKittrick (1996, p. 254) say of this channel, "The real negotiations throughout this period actually involved Adams, Hume and Dublin, resulting in draft declarations which were later forwarded to London. But quite a few of the messages through the back channels concerned Hume–Adams, and at one stage the British appear to have passed back to the republicans, presumably for verification, a document which had been conveyed to them by Dublin." Thus, like the Mubarak channel discussed above, this secondary channel served to check the authenticity of communications over the primary channel.

11.6   The Lancaster House Talks – A Contrasting Case

In the cases just described, the third parties who presided over the negotiations (Larsen at Oslo and George Mitchell at Stormont) were mainly non-directive and let the disputants work things out on their own (see Mitchell 1999). A sharply contrasting third-party effort can be seen in the 1979 Lancaster House (London) talks that settled the civil war in Zimbabwe (see Stedman 1991).[10] The third party was

---

[10] Information about the Lancaster House talks and events preceding them can be found in Davidow (1984) and Stedman (1991).

Lord Carrington, Margaret Thatcher's foreign secretary. In addition to coercing the disputants to attend, Carrington kept these meetings on a tight leash and used heavy, coercive tactics. The delegations could not talk privately to each other, but only to the mediator. The mediator set the agenda and imposed a single text procedure in which only he could put proposals on the table. He altered these proposals occasionally in response to substantive objections from the delegates, but was rather sticky about doing so. He arranged for the insurgents to meet with their allies (the presidents of Mozambique and Zambia), who urged them to accept the mediator's proposals and threatened to abandon them if they failed to do so. He kept both sides at the table by means of threats and promises and set periodic deadlines for the acceptance of his proposals. The result was a new constitution that reduced the power of the white minority and a new election that was supervised by the British in a continuing effort to control the situation. Mugabe won this election and is still in office.

Why the huge difference in style of third-party intervention between the Lancaster House talks and those in Oslo and Stormont? My answer is that the disputants in the Middle East and Northern Ireland were ready for agreement – in the sense of being highly motivated for settlement – before the talks began, but this was not the case for Zimbabwe. Instead of a mutually hurting stalemate, Mugabe believed that his army was winning and only went to London because of pressure by Britain and his allies. The situation somewhat resembled that encountered in the 1991 Madrid Conference, which was attended by Israel only because of US pressure and which had minimal success. The difference between Lancaster House and Madrid is that Britain kept up the pressure and insisted on a substantive agreement that provided a solution to the conflict. This sort of behavior is necessary when the parties are extrinsically motivated by pressure from others rather than intrinsically motivated by a view of their conflict as dysfunctional. Otherwise the parties simply go through the motions.

What I am proposing is that light, facilitative tactics were appropriate for third-party intervention in Oslo and (to a somewhat lesser extent) Stormont because the parties were intrinsically motivated to escape the conflict, but heavy, directive tactics were appropriate in London because the parties there were not. This means, of course, that there had to be a difference in the type of third party involved. Light tactics can be used by any kind of third party, whether strong or weak, but heavy tactics require a strong third party. A weak nation like Norway or a prestigious individual like Mitchell could be useful in the Oslo and Stormont talks because their main job was to help with communication. A strong nation like Britain, under a leader who was the toughest since Churchill, was needed for the Lancaster House talks because the delegates had to be pushed around. The success of the latter talks also teaches us that heavy, directive tactics require a highly knowledgeable third party who understands the disputants well enough to predict their reactions and forge a settlement that is minimally acceptable to all of them. Otherwise, such tactics may well provoke a walkout even if the mediator is strong.

11.7   Summary and Conclusions

I started by talking about the nature of escalation and some of its dynamics. Escalation usually results from a conflict spiral – a vicious circle of hostile action and reaction – but the actors involved in such a spiral typically view themselves as reacting to persistent annoyance. Humans have a script to deal with persistent annoyance, which involves a steadily escalating progression of actions. Groups tend to follow this script to higher levels of escalation than do individuals, which is one possible explanation for the many severe intergroup and international conflicts in the world.

When a conflict is only mildly escalated and the disputants' positions are not far apart, it is easy to persuade them to negotiate, and third-party functions can be mainly facilitative. However, when a conflict is heavily escalated, peace depends on the deployment of more powerful forces. Either powerful third parties must employ heavy directive tactics, as in the Zimbabwe conflict, or the disputants must become thoroughly convinced that their conflict is dysfunctional, as in the Israeli–Palestinian and Northern Ireland conflicts. When both sides take the latter view, the role of third parties is to encourage enough optimism to initiate negotiations and keep the disputants talking.

One component of optimism is trust. Broad trust cannot be engineered easily after years of heavily escalated conflict, but it is sometimes possible for third parties to foster working trust – a belief that the other side wants to escape the conflict badly enough to make meaningful concessions. One way to accomplish this is to encourage a circular reassurance process – a courtship dance – in which the disputants make and reciprocate conciliatory statements and actions. Third parties can also encourage optimism by reassuring the parties about one another's interest in settlement and by devising solutions and partial solutions to the issues.

Several third parties are often involved in the resolution of intergroup conflict, and they are typically organized into communication chains that reach from decision makers on one side to those on the other. As optimism grows, chains tend to lengthen at the ends and shorten in the middle, which produces conversations between people at greater and greater distances from each other. Such conversations are usually necessary to develop a finely tuned agreement, but they tend to come late in processes that resolve highly escalated conflicts. Intermediaries who are dropped from a chain when it shortens usually remain to facilitate these conversations.

When heavily escalated conflicts are moving toward a solution, several communication chains are often in action. The more important of these are the locus of problem solving and idea development, while the less important provide an opportunity to transmit messages and check the authenticity of proposals conveyed over the more important chains.

It is interesting to note that of the three cases discussed in this chapter, the only one that produced a clearly lasting solution was the Lancaster House talks that led to the elections in Zimbabwe. Yet, paradoxically, this was the case in which the conferees were least ready for agreement and the third party was the most manipulative. One possible explanation for the differential success at Lancaster House is that the third party managed to gather virtually all the significant forces in the region[11] and point them in the same direction. The Oslo and Stormont negotiations, on the other hand, left out some major players. Missing at Oslo were Hamas and Likud, who became formidable opponents of the agreement, which eventually failed. Missing at Stormont were Ian Paisley's Democratic Unionist Party and its allies on the Protestant side. In the end, only about half the Protestant voters approved the agreement reached at Stormont, and Protestant leaders subsequently threatened to withdraw from the government, which forced the British to take over once again.

What this suggests is that the principle of a *minimal winning coalition*, a useful one for understanding parliamentary voting, needs to be rethought in ethnopolitical conflicts in which extremists tend to be powerful and frequently are armed. While seeming to win at first, such a coalition may eventually be overwhelmed by extremists (spoilers) who block the execution of the agreement. A favorite extremist tactic is to provoke retaliation from the other side, and thereby produce a conflict spiral that discredits the peace process. To achieve a lasting solution, what is needed instead is a *maximally viable coalition*, which contains the broadest spectrum of forces that can possibly reach agreement. If that coalition is broad enough, the remaining extremists become so isolated that they are likely to give up. Hopefully, such coalitions will eventually triumph in the Middle East and Northern Ireland.

Acknowledgment

An earlier version of this chapter was presented at the IIASA PIN Project's conference on "Escalation and Negotiation" in Stockholm, June 1999. I wish to thank Karin Aggestam, Daniel Druckman, Guy Olivier Faure, I. William Zartman, and others at the conference for their helpful comments. Suggestions by Christopher Mitchell were also quite useful.

---

[11] South Africa was the only major player omitted from the Lancaster House talks. Though the final agreement was probably not ideal in the South African view, it promised the kind of regional stability they were seeking.

References

Abbas M (1995). *Through Secret Channels*. Reading, UK: Garnet.

Aughey A & Morrow D (1996). *Northern Ireland Politics*. London, UK: Longman.

Betz B & Fry WR (1995). The role of group schema in the selection of influence attempts. *Basic and Applied Social Psychology* **16**:351–365.

Bew P & Gillespie G (1996). *The Northern Ireland Peace Process 1993–1996: A Chronology*. London, UK: Serif.

Bradbury TN & Fincham FD (1992). Attributions and behavior in marital interaction. *Journal of Personality and Social Psychology* **63**:613–628.

Coleman JS (1957). *Community Conflict*. New York, NY, USA: Free Press.

Corbin J (1994). *Gaza First: The Secret Norway Channel to Peace between Israel and the PLO*. London, UK: Bloomsbury; and New York, NY, USA: Atlantic Monthly Press.

Davidow J (1984). *A Peace in Southern Africa: The Lancaster House Conference on Rhodesia, 1979*. Boulder, CO, USA: Westview.

Fincham FD (1985). Attribution processes in distressed and nondistressed couples: Responsibility for marital problems. *Journal of Abnormal Psychology* **94**:183–190.

Holmes JG & Murray SL (1996). Conflict in close relationships. In *Social Psychology: Handbook of Basic Mechanisms and Processes*, eds. Higgins ET & Kruglanski A, pp. 622–654. New York, NY, USA: Guilford.

Jaffe Y & Yinon Y (1983). Collective aggression: The group-individual paradigm in the study of collective antisocial behavior. In *Small Groups and Social Interaction*, Vol. 1., eds. Blumberg HH, Hare AP, Kent V & Davies M, pp. 267–275. New York, NY, USA: Wiley.

Kelman HC (1997). Some determinants of the Oslo breakthrough. *International Negotiation* **2**:183–194.

Kelman HC & Hamilton VL (1989). *Crimes of Obedience: Toward a Social Psychology of Authority and Responsibility*. New Haven, CT, USA: Yale University Press.

Makovsky D (1996). *Making Peace with the PLO: The Rabin Government's Road to the Oslo Accord*. Boulder, CO, USA: Westview.

Mallie E & McKittrick D (1996). *The Fight for Peace: The Secret Story behind the Irish Peace Process*. London, UK: Heinemann.

Manusov V (1990). An application of attribution principles to nonverbal behavior in romantic dyads. *Communication Monographs* **57**:104–118.

Mikolic JM, Parker JC & Pruitt DG (1997). Escalation in response to persistent annoyance: Groups vs. individuals and gender effects. *Journal of Personality and Social Psychology* **72**:151–163.

Milgram S (1992). *The Individual in a Social World: Essays and Experiments*, second edition. New York, NY, USA: McGraw-Hill.

Mitchell GJ (1999). *Making Peace: The Behind-the-Scenes Story of the Negotiations that Culminated in the Signing of the Northern Ireland Peace Accord*. New York, NY, USA: Knopf.

Mummendey A & Otten S (1993). Aggression: Interaction between individuals and social groups. In *Aggression and Violence: Social Interactionist Perspectives*, eds. Felson R & Tedeschi JT, pp. 145–167. Washington, DC, USA: American Psychological Association.

Pruitt DG (1994). Negotiation between organizations: A branching chain model. *Negotiation Journal* **10**:217–230.

Pruitt DG (1995). Networks and collective scripts: Paying attention to structure in bargaining theory. In *Negotiation as a Social Process*, eds. Kramer RM & Messick DM, pp. 37–47. Newbury Park, CA, USA: Sage.

Pruitt DG (1997). Ripeness theory and the Oslo talks. *International Negotiation* **2**:177–182.

Pruitt DG (1998). Social conflict. In *Handbook of Social Psychology*, Vol. 2, fourth edition, eds. Gilbert DT, Fiske ST & Lindzey G, pp. 470–503. New York, NY, USA: McGraw-Hill.

Pruitt DG (2000). The role of third parties in ethnopolitical conflict. *Orbis* **44**:245–254.

Pruitt DG & Kim SH (2003). *Social Conflict: Escalation, Stalemate, and Settlement*, third edition. New York, NY, USA: Random House.

Pruitt DG, Bercovitch J & Zartman IW (1997). A brief history of the Oslo talks. *International Negotiation* **2**:177–182.

Rabbie JM & Lodewijkx HFM (1995). Aggressive reactions to social injustice by individuals and groups as a function of social norms, gender, and anonymity. *Social Justice Research* **8**:7–40.

Ransford HE (1968). Isolation, powerlessness and violence: A study of attitudes and participation in the Watts riot. *American Journal of Sociology* **73**:581–591.

Robinson RJ & Friedman RA (1995). Mistrust and misconstrual in union–management relationship: Causal accounts in adversarial contexts. *International Journal of Conflict Management* **6**:312–327.

Rouhana NN & Kelman HC (1994). Promoting joint thinking in international conflicts: An Israeli–Palestinian continuing workshop. *Journal of Social Issues* **50**:157–178.

Rubin JZ, Pruitt DG & Kim SH (1994). *Social Conflict: Escalation, Stalemate, and Settlement*, second edition. New York, NY, USA: McGraw-Hill.

Rusbult CE, Verette J, Whitney GA, Slovik LF & Lipkus GA (1991). Accommodation processes in close relationships: Theory and preliminary empirical evidence. *Journal of Personality and Social Psychology* **60**:53–78.

Savir U (1998). *The Process: 1100 Days that Changed the Middle East*. New York, NY, USA: Random House.

Schopler J & Insko CA (1992). The discontinuity effect in interpersonal and intergroup relations: Generality and mediation. In *European Review of Social Psychology*, Vol. 3, eds. Stroebe W & Hewstone M, pp. 121–151. Chichester, UK: Wiley.

Sillars AL (1981). Attributions and interpersonal conflict resolution. In *New Directions in Attribution Research*, Vol. 3, eds. Harvey JH, Ickes W & Kidd RF, pp. 279–305. Hillsdale, NJ, USA: Erlbaum.

Sinn Fein (1994). Setting the record straight: A record of communications between Sinn Fein and the British government, October 1990–November 1993. Unpublished document.

Stedman SJ (1991). *Peacemaking in Civil War: International Mediation in Zimbabwe, 1974–1980.* Boulder, CO, USA: Lynne Rienner.

Struch N & Schwartz SH (1989). Intergroup aggression: Its predictors and distinctness from in-group bias. *Journal of Personality and Social Psychology* **56**:364–373.

Taylor P (1997). *Behind the Mask: The IRA and Sinn Fein.* New York, NY, USA: TV Books.

Vanbeselaere N (1991). The different effects of simple and crossed categorization: A result of the category differentiation process or of differential category salience? In *European Review of Social Psychology*, Vol. 3, eds. Stroebe W & Hewstone M, pp. 247–279. Chichester, UK: Wiley.

Varshney A (2002). *Ethnic Conflict and Civic Life: Hindus and Muslims in India.* New Haven, CT, USA: Yale University Press.

White RK (1984). *Fearful Warriors: A Psychological Profile of US–Soviet Relations.* New York, NY, USA: Free Press.

Worchel S & Andreoli VA (1978). Facilitation of social interaction through deindividuation of the target. *Journal of Personality and Social Psychology* **36**:549–556.

Zartman IW (1989). *Ripe for Resolution: Conflict Resolution in Africa*, second edition. New York, NY, USA: Oxford.

Zartman IW (1996). Bargaining and conflict resolution. In *Coping with Conflict after the Cold War*, eds. Kolodziej EA & Kanet RE. Baltimore, MD, USA: Johns Hopkins University Press.

Zartman IW (1997). Explaining Oslo. *International Negotiation* **2**:195–215.

Chapter 12

Enhancing Ripeness: Transition from Conflict to Negotiation

Karin Aggestam

12.1 Introduction

This chapter originates in a basic puzzle about escalation and de-escalation in conflict and strategies to resolve it. The aim is to elucidate the *problematique* of how adversaries in a seemingly intractable conflict reach a point where they seek to resolve conflict through negotiations. How are we to explain and conceptualize the transition from conflict escalation to de-escalation? Why do adversaries come to embrace negotiations at a specific time, despite uncertainties and risks of failure? Which strategies may be used to enhance the prospect for a negotiated settlement?

One theoretical way to approach these questions is to utilize ripeness theory (Zartman 1989a). Ripeness theory illuminates the linkage between conflict escalation and negotiation through its emphasis on a specific situation, a ripe moment, that is favorable for timing de-escalation strategies. Diplomatic history, however, reveals several accounts in which such opportunities have been lost because of an inability of political leaders to act upon ripe moments. Such moments need to be seized, as argued by several scholars, if they are to be transformed into a negotiation process (Rubin 1991; Hampson 1996a; Zartman 2001). Hence, the critical phase between a ripe moment and the initial stages of negotiations requires a more thorough analysis.

This chapter aims to enlarge the notion of ripeness through a process-oriented perspective that strives to highlight the transition between escalation and negotiation. Which strategies can be utilized? How can ripeness be sustained and enhanced? For the analysis of this transitional period, a theoretical framework is presented that emphasizes the motivation of and opportunity for political leaders to negotiate, and the identification of focal points that may constitute the basis for coordinated expectations about negotiations. The theoretical framework advanced in this chapter is illustrated using a brief analysis of the Israeli–Palestinian pre-negotiations prior to the Madrid Conference in 1991.[1]

12.2   Ripe Conflict

Ripeness theory was introduced and developed by I. William Zartman with the aim of providing a general description of the most favorable moment to initiate negotiations. In this theory, a ripe moment is depicted as a "mutually hurting stalemate" (MHS), which is characterized by a deadlock. The parties are locked into a situation because of an impending catastrophe. In this situation, the disputing parties come to recognize, through a cost–benefit calculation, the sharp increase in costs of further escalation, which limits the use of unilateral strategies and enhances the prospect of a negotiated settlement as the only way out of an escalating situation (Zartman 1986, pp. 218–219). It is important to stress that an MHS consists of a *perceptual* event, which is formed on the basis of an intolerable and escalating situation. Unilateral escalation is no longer seen as an option because of the increasing costs and pains of conflict. A negotiated settlement therefore becomes more likely. In short, ripeness theory aims to depict a specific crisis situation, a plateau, that causes conflict to mature and turn ripe for resolution (Zartman 1989a).

Another way to conceptualize a ripe moment is as a mutually enticing opportunity (MEO), which is distinguished from an MHS by its emphasis on future gains rather than on costs. During a ripe moment, the parties begin to negotiate because they expect to achieve certain goals using alternative strategies instead of conflict (Mitchell 1995, pp. 44–45). Hence, the difference between an MHS and an MEO is based on divergent assumptions about what motivates the parties to engage in de-escalation. Is it negative experiences, such as increasing costs of escalation, or positive expectations of future gains? In other words, is the dominant frame of political actors characterized by a prospective time frame, which focuses on gains, or a retrospective time frame based on loss avoidance? Both accounts of a ripe moment may be useful in the analysis of ripeness, but as prospect theory underlines, political actors tend to focus more on loss avoidance than on absolute or relative gains (Stein 1993; Levy 1996).

[1]Parts of the theoretical and empirical analysis come from Aggestam (1999).

Several scholars have been inspired by Zartman's notion of ripeness and have attempted to refine ripeness theory through an identification of various favorable conditions for a negotiated settlement (see, e.g., Haass 1988; Stedman 1991; Kleiboer 1994). However, in their endeavors to refine ripeness theory, they tend to focus on factors that favor successful negotiations rather than to clearly delineate what constitutes a ripe moment. The basic question is whether successful negotiations indicate the existence of ripeness or if a ripe moment may be distinguished from the outcome of negotiations. According to Zartman (2001), ripeness theory strives to highlight a common situation prior to negotiation, that is, an MHS. It motivates conflicting parties to begin de-escalation, but it does not completely determine the success of a negotiation process. So, the question is whether ripeness theory serves as a predictive tool, providing practitioners with knowledge about when to initiate negotiations, or whether the theory primarily aims at a scientific theory that can explain the success or failure of negotiations. The distinction between prediction and explanation illuminates different aims of research and what ultimately is considered a ripe moment and good timing for negotiations. Ripeness theory may therefore risk conceptual stretching because of the different theoretical ambitions.

Still, the basic understanding of the theory is that some kind of appropriate moment exists when the parties converge in their perceptions that unilateral strategies are no longer effective. Again, this favors, but does not determine, the success of de-escalation strategies. Most importantly, political actors must act upon a ripe moment in conflict before the "season" is over. In this way, the theory points to a sequential time frame and an "organic" understanding of conflict (Lewitt 1994; Zartman 2001). Thus, a ripe moment needs to be turned from a passive situation into an active process for de-escalation and negotiation to occur. A relevant question is therefore how a ripe moment may be linked to efforts to resolve conflict. To address this question, we need to move beyond a situation-specific to a process-oriented understanding of ripeness. First, a ripe moment is, as stated, a perceptual event based on the values and preferences of the political leaders making the assessments (Kriesberg 1991, p. 2; Zartman 2001). Second, the challenge lies in *how* to act upon it. How can ripeness be enhanced and sustained in such ways that the conflicting parties come to accept negotiations?

To make an analysis of this precarious phase between escalation and negotiation, a theoretical framework is constructed that focuses on the following concepts:

- *Motivation* of political actors to initiate negotiations
- *Opportunity* and domestic legitimacy of political leaders to negotiate
- Identification and/or construction of *focal points* for negotiations

These three concepts comprise psychological, strategic, and functional processes that illuminate the parties' positions on negotiation and the strategies required to sustain and enhance ripeness.

12.3   Motivation to Negotiate

Motivation refers to the degree of ripeness of a given moment and its effects on political actors and their willingness to search for a mutually satisfying settlement (Pruitt 1997, p. 239). As Kriesberg (1991, p. 4) states, "These characteristics [of a ripe moment] may appear to have a reality independent of the adversaries. However, in a fundamental sense, they do not. What is the natural sequence and what is or is not reversible depend on subjective beliefs of adversaries and intermediaries." The time frame determines both how continuity and change in the conflict are viewed as well as what may be considered appropriate strategies to resolve the conflict. For instance, a retrospective time frame tends to have a conservative outlook and emphasizes the antecedence and recurrence of events within a given order. Consequently, a retrospective time frame interprets the near future and changes in a pessimistic and fatalistic way. In comparison, a person with a prospective time frame tends to encounter the future with a voluntaristic orientation and actively construct and shape change (Sztompka 1993, pp. 47–49). These examples indicate how the future might be perceived and the plausible implications of various time frames for efforts to resolve conflict. The understanding of the appropriate pace of a negotiation process may, for instance, differ precisely because of the different time frames of the political actors.

To conceptualize the motivation to negotiate, I have found Pruitt's adaptation of ripeness theory particularly useful. In his critique of ripeness theory, Pruitt highlights how the theory implicitly assumes that an MHS simultaneously affects all the conflicting parties. He therefore makes an adaptation of the theory by emphasizing "motivational ripeness," which refers to the willingness of the adversaries to search for a mutually satisfying settlement of the conflict. Moreover, he suggests that an analysis of motivational ripeness should contain a separate assessment of each party. "Full readiness for conflict resolution" exists when all the parties are motivated to prevent further escalation and are optimistic about reaching an agreement (Pruitt 1997, p. 239).

At the same time, we should not underestimate the perseverance of enemy images, which can undermine attempts to start a negotiation process. Well-established stereotypical enemy images tend to resist change. The other side may reject de-escalatory and confidence-building moves because they create dissonance in the image of the "other." Stedman (1996, p. 351) rightly states that "perceptions about the battlefield can change quickly, but perceptions about the trustworthiness of an opponent change slowly." As cognitive theory also underlines, political actors tend to interpret political events from "theory-driven" perceptions and pre-existing knowledge structures, seeking reassurances in familiar experiences and analogical reasoning (Larson 1985, pp. 29–34; Jönsson 1990, p. 52). Moreover, attribution theory illuminates the double standard that political actors frequently use when interpreting their own as well as other parties' behavior. For example, a distinction between dispositional and situational factors is often made in which dispositional factors are understood as enduring and internal characteristics of an actor, whereas situational features are external, contextual, and transient. As a consequence, political actors have a tendency to overemphasize dispositional factors when explaining the behavior of the adversary, whereas situational factors are accentuated when interpreting their own behavior. Thus, there is a tendency to have negative expectations about the behavior of the enemy and positive expectations about one's own actions. In theory this is labeled the "fundamental attribution error" (Heradstveit 1979, pp. 22–26). These attributional biases are often coupled with, and reinforced by, overconfidence in one's own assessment, while simplifying the cognition of the other, who often is viewed as a unitary actor (Bazerman and Sondak 1988, pp. 305–311; Larson 1988).

Hence, a number of psychological barriers prevent perceptual change. Yet, image change may take place after a period of trial and error, and failing unilateral strategies. Consequently, an opportunity to negotiate may open up, which makes political actors more receptive to learning, persuasion, and alternative cooperative strategies (Stein 1996, pp. 102–105; Aggestam and Jönsson 1997, p. 784).

12.4   Opportunity to Negotiate

Opportunity to negotiate refers to domestic legitimacy to change the pattern of conflict from escalation toward de-escalation and negotiation. Several empirical cases have demonstrated that major shifts in policies from conflict to cooperation need sufficient domestic consensus from a considerable part of the public (Bar-Siman-Tov 1994; Haass 1988). Negotiating conflict settlement highlights domestic constraints and the problematic nature of concession making. As Iklé (1991, p. 59) underlines, "nothing is more divisive for a government than having to make peace at the price of major concessions."

Stedman, in his attempt to refine ripeness theory, highlights the importance of interparty negotiations and the need to build domestic coalitions for peace. According to him, political leaders who pursue radical shifts in policy from escalation to negotiation require domestic support as well as a cohesive leadership that speaks with one voice (Stedman 1991, p. 211). A united leadership that enjoys domestic legitimacy provides a political leader with the opportunity and strength to negotiate and make concessions, without taking the risk of being called a traitor who is selling out national interests (Haass 1988, pp. 244–246; Iklé 1991, pp. 59–61). However, in politically divided societies it is particularly difficult to gain unequivocal legitimacy and consensus to pursue de-escalation strategies. As Kriesberg (1991, p. 7) points out, active domestic interest groups rarely raise demands in favor of more accommodative strategies, but rather against further concessions and compromises. These groups may try to prevent concession making and seek to undermine any attempts at de-escalation. Hence, a strong political leader with credibility and the ability to persuade the population at large of the significance of reaching peace may be required (see Aggestam and Jönsson 1997, p. 778). Double-edged diplomacy, as illustrated in Putnam's two-level game approach, highlights precisely this *problematique* of how political leaders are Janus-faced in that they are constrained by both what the other party will accept and what the domestic constituencies will agree to. This strategic interaction determines the opportunities and constraints that political leaders may have when pursuing negotiations (Putnam 1993, p. 71).

12.5   Focal Points for Negotiations

Resolving conflict ultimately relates to the coordination of expectations with regard to a negotiated settlement. As stated above, the effects of an MHS may not be simultaneous, and the understanding of the perceived way out of escalation may therefore differ among adversaries. For instance, do the parties seek the same type of conflict settlement? Hence, the parties' expectations of de-escalation and their perceptions of the timing and tempo of negotiations need to be coordinated and synchronized (see also Cohen 1996, p. 119). Schelling's concept of "focal point" may be useful here, since the notion highlights coordination efforts and how focal points may serve as a "road map" in a highly uncertain situation (see also Goldstein and Keohane 1993, pp. 16–17):

> People can often concert their intentions or expectations with others if each knows that the other is trying to do the same ... provide some clue for coordinating behavior, some focal point for each person's expectation of what the other expects him to expect to be expected to do. Finding the key, or rather finding a key – any key that is mutually recognized as the key becomes the key – may depend on imagination more than on logic ... A prime characteristic of most of these "solutions" to the problems, that is, of the clues or coordinators or focal points, is some kind of prominence or conspicuousness. But it is a prominence that depends on time and place and who the people are. (Schelling 1960, p. 57)

Also, other scholars emphasize the need for focal points and expectations with regard to negotiations. "Requitement" expresses an optimistic belief that the other party will reciprocate positively on de-escalation moves (Zartman and Aurik 1991, p. 156; Pruitt 1997, pp. 239–241). The identification of focal points may come to constitute a mutually agreed agenda on de-escalation, which enhances the prospect for successful negotiations and the possibility of developing trust and partnership between adversaries.

12.6   Enhancing Ripeness

An analysis of motivation, opportunity, and focal point in conflict may determine the degree of ripeness as well as explain the transition phase from escalation to negotiation. Yet, the question remains how to enhance and sustain ripeness, since the transition from a ripe moment in conflict to the initiation of a negotiation process is precarious. As Yossi Beilin (1999, p. 2), the Israeli architect behind the Oslo channel in 1993, recalls, "I was haunted by the many opportunities for peace that had been missed in the past. I had learned about them, taught about them, written about them and sworn to myself that I would never let such an opportunity slip through my hands, should I ever be in a position of influence." This quote describes a ripe moment as a dynamic process that needs to be sustained and transformed into a negotiation process. As Hampson (1996a, p. 210) rightly points out, "ripeness is a cultivated, not inherited condition."

Two strategies of negotiation that may enhance and sustain ripeness are given particular attention, namely, pre-negotiation strategies and third-party intervention.

How can risks and uncertainties be minimized during a transition period from escalation to de-escalation? How can the motivation and opportunity for political leaders to negotiate be enhanced? In what ways may third parties coordinate the adversaries' expectations of a negotiation process?

12.6.1   Pre-negotiation strategies

The concept of pre-negotiation has been used in a variety of ways, depending on the analysts' view as to the decisive element for initiating negotiations. Some scholars emphasize psychological processes over time (Kelman 1982; Rothman 1988), while others view pre-negotiation primarily in functional terms that are limited in time and space (Zartman 1989b). Adopting a broad and encompassing understanding of pre-negotiation, it is here understood as a purposive period with the objectives of exploring, preparing, and transforming the pattern of conflict toward successful negotiations (Stein 1989; Zartman 1989b). Enhancing and sustaining ripeness includes temporal, psychological, strategic, and functional processes. A ripe moment underlines the temporal dimension by highlighting a specific time when the parties come to recognize their interdependence and willingness to view negotiations as a viable option to an escalation of conflict. The psychology of negotiations concerns various strategies to sustain ripeness, such as increasing trust between the disputants and the motivation of political leaders to negotiate. The strategic dimension of negotiations relates to the opportunity of political leaders to negotiate, whereas the functional dimension concerns the identification of focal points to construct a joint formula for resolving conflict.

Increasing motivation

Moving away from escalation toward a negotiation process involves great risks and uncertainties about the outcome of such a process. For instance, political leaders may have doubts about the extent of concession making and willingness of the other party to reciprocate on de-escalation moves. The question is therefore how pre-negotiation strategies may assist and sustain this process. The advantage of a pre-negotiation process is that the parties have the possibility to explore and respond without any formal or official commitment to different ideas about de-escalation and negotiation. During such exploratory talks, the parties may come to identify common ground and assess gains and losses more accurately. Thus, uncertainties about the outcome of negotiations in general and compromises in particular may decrease. Informal face-to-face meetings between adversaries may also break psychological barriers and result in a revision of enemy images. The parties may, for instance, exchange assurances about their intentions and sincerity about pursuing de-escalation in general. This type of meeting may also constitute the first step toward building trust, confidence, and a sense of partnership, which increase the motivation to negotiate.

Creating opportunity

A pre-negotiation phase may also enhance the opportunity for political leaders to negotiate and initiate de-escalation. Since pre-negotiations frequently are informal and private, the constraints and negative impacts of hawkish domestic interest groups may be minimized. As several scholars (Colosi 1986; Klieman 1988) stress, secrecy can be required as a way to avoid domestic interest groups who may try to undermine the de-escalation process by criticizing their government for any conciliatory moves toward the enemy. Armstrong, for example, in his analysis of three cases in which adversaries pursued the path of de-escalation and concilia-tion,[2] concludes that negotiations that successfully reached a settlement were con-ducted away from the public, on a high political level, and with few participants involved (Armstrong 1993, pp. 138–140). Particularly when the first contacts are established between adversaries, informal and private meetings may be essential. In a more private context, the parties are able to communicate more directly and elaborate without any media attention or speculation about various agendas for ne-gotiations. Yoel Singer (1994), one of the Israeli negotiators in the Oslo channel, with extensive experience negotiating with Syria, Lebanon, and Egypt, emphasizes that "all the important, all the significant breakthroughs in the relationship between Israel and its neighbors took place as the results of secret negotiations."

Pre-negotiations may therefore provide time to prepare, build, and consolidate domestic support for negotiations and concession making. Pre-negotiations can provide political leaders with relevant information about the extent and contents of compromises and so improve their position to frame de-escalation and negoti-ation in a convincing and reasonable way for the public. This is particularly im-portant since de-escalation in general is a highly uncertain process that frequently produces fear and insecurity among domestic publics. During pre-negotiations, po-litical leaders may also use "trial balloons," for example, by leaking to the media specific ideas on negotiations as a way to test or measure the domestic support (Berridge 1995).

Identifying shared focal points

During pre-negotiations, the parties are able to explore, in a more flexible and in-formal way, various ideas regarding an agenda for negotiations, which may result in the identification of shared focal points. Moreover, through the experience of interacting in a nonviolent way, new norms and "rules of the game" may be estab-lished, which may further facilitate a de-escalation process. Another form of pre-negotiation that underlines the unofficial setting is "Track 2" diplomacy. Track 2 diplomacy is defined as "a process designed to assist official leaders to resolve or, in the first instance, to manage conflicts by exploring possible solutions out of public view and without the requirements to formally negotiate or bargain for advantage"

---

[2]The three cases are Willy Brandt's Ostpolitik initiative, which resulted in the 1972 Basic Treaty between West Germany and East Germany; Richard Nixon's and Jimmy Carter's negotia-tions with Mao Zedong and Deng Xiaoping, respectively, for normalization of relations between the United States and China, which was finalized in 1979; and the negotiations between Anwar Sadat, Menachem Begin, and Jimmy Carter that resulted in the Israeli–Egyptian Peace Treaty in 1979.

(Montville 1987, p. 7). This type of diplomacy may include a variety of actors, such as private individuals, nongovernmental organizations (NGOs), scholars, journalists, bureaucrats, politicians, etc. Interactive problem-solving workshops are a more controlled and specific form of pre-negotiation. With the assistance of skilled and experienced scholars, the parties are encouraged to promote various ideas of conflict resolution (Kelman 2002).

12.6.2   Third-party intervention

Third-party intervention is here limited to various mediation efforts by external actors who attempt to influence and strengthen the conflicting parties' conviction and perception of a ripe moment and the necessity of a negotiated settlement of conflict. Since the transition from escalation to de-escalation involves risks, third parties may, for example, act as risk managers and assist the parties to gain confidence in a negotiation process. Moreover, since a ripe moment is a perceptual event, mediators may come to play an important role at times when the adversaries themselves are not able to recognize or act upon it. Third parties may, in this regard, attempt to convince the parties to accept a negotiation formula by the use of either power or communication (see Aggestam 2002a, 2002b; Bercovitch 2002).

Persuasion with power

Some mediators view leverage and coercive power as useful instruments to enhance ripeness. A powerful mediator, frequently a superpower or a great power with political, military, and economic resources, may help the parties to minimize risks and uncertainties by assuming a credible role as a guarantor and sponsor of a negotiation process. Particularly for an intractable conflict in which enemy images are strongly held, a mediator may try to bridge and generate trust or even become a temporary trustee, or surrogate in the absence of trust (Aggestam and Jönsson 1997, p. 788; King 1997). Third parties who use power attempt to influence the parties' preferences and perceptions of de-escalation and negotiation. Consequently, third parties may, through coercive bargaining, alter and affect the structure and distribution of power. As a result, the adversaries may come to change their expectations about concession making and the outcomes of negotiations (Princen 1992). To persuade the antagonists to accept a negotiated formula, third parties may choose to offer or withhold rewards or to issue various kinds of threats. As Rubin (1992, p. 252) underlines, it is often "the whip of external pressure and the pain of unacceptable alternatives that drives disputants to the bargaining table." If third parties are successful in changing the cost–benefit calculation of adversaries, the perception of a ripe moment is strengthened and the transition from escalation to de-escalation becomes increasingly attractive. Thus, by affecting the balance of power between the disputants, third parties are "sharpening the stalemate and sweetening the proposed outcome" (Zartman 1995, p. 21). However, this type of leverage is not easily applied and includes serious risks, which may lead to counterproductive results. Some scholars even warn that too much coercion in combination with a low political willingness to de-escalate a conflict may produce badly designed agreements that are inclined to fail (Haass 1990; Hampson 1996b). Some disputants may, for instance, use the period of negotiations to improve their military positions and later return to unilateral escalation strategies (Webb *et al.* 1996).

Persuasion with communication

The majority of third parties are not able to exercise the kind of leverage discussed above. Mediation in a non-coercive form, such as communication and facilitation, is therefore more common. Third parties may in this capacity attempt to improve communication and the quality of interaction between the adversaries by conveying messages, facilitating, and arranging a suitable milieu for exploratory talks or alternative tracks of communication to the official channels. During such meetings, third parties strive to persuade and coordinate the parties' expectations of a negotiation process by highlighting mutual interests, focal points, and various formulas of how to reach a settlement. Rubin (1992, p. 266) argues that small states, in particular, are suited to play a constructive role during these efforts, since adversaries frequently perceive small states as non-threatening and trustworthy. Thus, similar endeavors by third parties may increase the motivation of adversaries to negotiate, build trust, and strengthen optimism that a settlement is achievable. Especially useful may be an interactive problem-solving workshop, as mentioned above, that focuses on non-coercive efforts to reframe the conflict and to transform enemy images. In this context, scholars assume the role of impartial and analytical facilitators who help the adversaries to reframe disputed issues, such as identity, security, etc. (see Kelman 2002).

12.7   Getting to the Madrid Conference: A Ripe Moment?

A brief analysis of the Israeli–Palestinian conflict from 1988 to 1991 is used here to illustrate empirically some of the theoretical arguments discussed above. In 1991, Israelis and Palestinians met, for the first time ever, at the negotiation table. The question is why the Israelis and Palestinians came to accept negotiations. An analysis of the parties' motivation and opportunity to de-escalate, as well as the existence of focal points for negotiations, reveals a contradictory picture of events leading up to the Madrid Conference. On the one hand, there was no distinct ripe moment or readiness to negotiate among Israeli and Palestinian leaders. Consequently, the US mediators found it very difficult to coordinate and construct a "road map" that could serve as an agenda for negotiations. This came to have several negative implications for the ensuing negotiations. On the other hand, since the Palestinian uprising in 1987, there were growing domestic demands among both the Palestinian and Israeli publics to resolve the conflict through negotiations.

12.7.1   Motivation to de-escalate?

During the period analyzed here, the Israeli political leadership consisted mostly of national unity governments, with two parties, the Likud and Labor, united in a platform of rejecting a Palestinian state and negotiations with the Palestine Liberation Organization (PLO). Yet, on other political issues the two parties had distinct interpretations of the conflict.

The dominant frame of the Likud disclosed a perseverance of self- and enemy images. The Likud reasoned and categorized political events, particularly the intifada, within a retrospective time frame, which was characterized by a pessimistic and fatalistic worldview that was suspicious of peace proposals. For instance, the rejection of an international conference was based on an understanding that it was a dangerous trap that might impose solutions on Israel. The Palestinian uprising was, in the Likud's understanding, exposing the true character of the Palestinians and the PLO in particular. The intifada proved, it was argued, the enduring inclination of the Palestinians toward violence and terrorism. The Algiers Declaration of 1988 (the PLO's acceptance of a two-state solution) was explained in situational terms as being based on tactics and hiding the true intentions of the PLO. Any suggestions of a two-state solution that would entail trading territories for peace, as stipulated in United Nations Security Council Resolution 242, and a freeze on building Jewish settlements were completely rejected as contradicting the self-images of the Likud and the ideology of a "Greater Israel" that originated from revisionist Zionism. Having to respond and adapt to pressures to resolve the intifada, Yitzhak Shamir came up with the suggestion of autonomy for the "Arabs in Eretz Yisrael," in line with the Camp David accords (Shamir 1989, pp. 176–179).

By comparison, Labor had a more prospective and optimistic time frame, which was characterized by active attempts to shape political events. Despite the international condemnation of Israel's brutal handling of the Palestinian uprising, the Labor Party was much less fearful and suspicious of proposals presented by third parties. Labor endorsed most of the proposals from the USA and Egypt, including the idea of an international conference. Labor also had a more diversified perception of the Arab world and recognized the moves toward moderation taking place in the region. Egypt and Jordan, in particular, were seen as important partners in the process. Moreover, the Palestinian uprising and the subsequent critical world opinion of Israeli behavior had a substantial effect on the Labor leadership. Less attention was given to an interstate settlement of the conflict, such as the Jordanian option, whereas a new and stronger emphasis was placed on a political solution to the Palestinian problem. For example, the Labor Party deemed it necessary to construct its own formula in response to US and Egyptian diplomatic pressures. In January 1989, Defense Minister Yitzhak Rabin presented a plan that focused primarily on the Palestinian elections to provide a partner with whom to negotiate a transitional period of self-rule (Flamhaft 1996, p. 65; Rolef 1997, pp. 262–264). As Rabin was part of the national unity government, Shamir initially stated that these were Rabin's private ideas; however, in May 1989 the national unity government presented its own formula, primarily based on Rabin's previous proposal. The document stated that negotiations should be based on the framework of the Camp David accords and free elections among the Palestinians. These changes, however, were incremental in that there were to be no negotiations with the PLO and no change in the status of the West Bank.[3] According to Rabin, "the 15 May 1989 peace initiative . . . was a historic turning point in viewing the Palestinians as a partner, separate from Jordan" (quoted in Ben-Yehuda 1997, p. 211). The local Palestinian leaders, however, viewed the elections plan as a "non-starter" and as an attempt to create an alternative Palestinian leadership to the PLO (*New Outlook* 1989).

The Likud Party was apprehensive about most of the formulas presented by third parties, fearing that the Israeli government might end up negotiating with the PLO on a Palestinian state (Flamhaft 1996, p. 66). James Baker, the US secretary of state, tried to find a bridging formula. The US proposal was, however, rejected by Shamir, who was under great pressure from the right not to make any concessions (Flamhaft 1996, pp. 69–73).[4] As a consequence of the Likud's rejection, the national unity government was dissolved in March 1990, just a few months before the Gulf crisis. A new Israeli government was formed with the support of small parties on the extreme right, the most right-wing government since the establishment of Israeli statehood.

The formation of a new Israeli government and the impending Gulf crisis meant the diplomatic momentum was lost. After the war, several diplomats, including US Secretary of State James Baker, identified a "window of opportunity," based on the view that the PLO was isolated and weakened while the Arab world was showing several signs of moderation. This presented an opportunity for new diplomatic

---

[3]The document distinguished two stages, a five-year transitional period to be followed by a permanent solution, with negotiations on a permanent status to be commenced no later than the third year of the transitional period. Additional parties invited to negotiate in the first stage were Jordan and Egypt (see Flamhaft 1996, pp. 228–229). Note the striking similarity to the "Declaration of Principles" signed in 1993 between Israel and the PLO.

[4]The Baker plan focused on Palestinian elections and tried to promote talks in Cairo between Israel, Egypt, and the USA (see Flamhaft 1996, p. 229).

initiatives. Shamir was still reluctant to accept most proposals, and not until the USA exerted great pressure did he agree to attend the Madrid Conference.

The frames of the PLO leadership on negotiations were similarly mixed, because of a combination of prospective and retrospective time frames. For instance, the Amman accord of 1985 (a joint Jordanian–Palestinian agreement on an international conference) and the PLO's subsequent withdrawal from the agreement are illustrations of the ambiguity and ambivalence of the PLO, since it feared that the accord might cause disunity among the Palestinian people. Yet the intifada moved the time frame of the PLO leadership in a prospective direction in that decisive diplomatic steps were taken, such as the official acceptance of a two-state solution and recognition of Israel. The disengagement of Jordan from the West Bank in July 1988 became an extra triggering event, as it left a political vacuum in the occupied territories. In November 1988, the PLO declared a Palestinian state based on the UN Partition Plan from 1947 and adopted a new political program in Algiers.

However, the overriding and continual concern of the PLO leadership of maintaining unity among the Palestinian people has frequently led to ambiguous, contradictory, and at times disastrous policies. An illustration is provided by the failure of the PLO to condemn the terrorist attack in Tel Aviv in 1989, which led to the termination of the US–PLO dialogue. Another example is the stance taken by the PLO leadership during the Gulf War, which exposed its relapse to a retrospective time frame of pan-Arab nostalgia fused with frustration over the lack of diplomatic progress toward a two-state solution.

To conclude, it is difficult to identify any real motivation for efforts to resolve the conflict in 1991. After the fall of the national unity government, the Israeli government was defensive and suspicious of every peace proposal that was put forth. The PLO, on the other hand, which before the Gulf War had expectations of becoming a partner in the peace process, was now severely weakened and preoccupied with its political and economic survival. Instead, the local Palestinian leaders in the West Bank and the Gaza Strip found themselves in the awkward position of being pressured into participating in a peace process, while continually restating that the PLO is the sole and legitimate representative of the Palestinian people.

12.7.2   Opportunity to de-escalate?

Since the intifada in 1987, the Palestinians in the occupied territories have expressed and articulated an active approach to ending the Israeli occupation and promoting a two-state solution. Hence, the Palestinian uprising broke away from the more passive and past-oriented approach of "steadfastness," that is, simply remaining on the land as an act of resistance. "Steadfastness" was increasingly seen as a failure to gain control in as many areas of Palestinian life as possible (McDowall

1989, p. 110; Robinson 1997, pp. 19–37). The mobilization was combined with explicit demands from several Palestinian organizations and parties from the occupied territories, which called for a moderation of the PLO and a decisive statement that accepted a two-state solution to the conflict to end the Israeli occupation. Palestinians on the West Bank and in the Gaza Strip had become increasingly frustrated by the lack of progress in diplomacy and concrete steps on the part of the PLO leadership, while the Israeli occupation continued with intensified settlement activities, expropriation of land, and deportations (Abu-Amr 1996; Muslih 1997, p. 46).

Still, during the Gulf crisis in 1990–1991, many Palestinians turned to a fatalistic approach, which viewed Iraqi leader Saddam Hussein as the one person who could end the Israeli occupation, something neither the PLO nor the intifada had been able to do. At the same time, Hamas gained in popularity and advocated a different understanding of the conflict that emphasized the return to an Islamic society and a rejection of any recognition of Israel.

Similarly, the Israeli domestic arena displayed a mixture of opinions. The intifada reinforced the "green line" (i.e., the international borders of 4 June 1967) in the minds of the Israeli public and strengthened the pre-existing divide in Israeli society regarding the future of the occupied territories. The political parties on the left, such as Mapam, Shinui, and Ratz, clearly stated, particularly after the Algiers Declaration of 1988, their willingness to talk to the PLO as well as their support of a demilitarized Palestinian state. Within the Labor Party as well, several members called for some type of negotiations with the PLO. However, for the parties on the right, the Palestinian uprising only strengthened the enemy images of violent Palestinians and the PLO as a terrorist organization.

Concurrently with the ongoing intifada, Israel was receiving thousands of Jewish immigrants each month from the former Soviet Union, which created a tremendous financial burden that affected several social sectors. For instance, there was an acute lack of housing for new immigrants and underprivileged Israelis. At the same time, the Israeli government, particularly then-Housing Minister Ariel Sharon, was actively encouraging Israelis and new immigrants, with financial incentives, to settle in the occupied territories. However, not many Israelis or new immigrants wanted to reside in the territories. Thus, this policy of subsidizing houses in the territories at a time when Israel was facing a major socioeconomic crisis created a heated debate over what the national priorities in Israel should be. The Shamir government requested loan guarantees from the USA to settle new immigrants, but the Bush administration required a freeze on building Jewish settlements in the territories – a precondition that was unacceptable to a government that believed in the notion of a "Greater Israel" (Baker and DeFrank 1995, pp. 541–543).

To sum up, the intifada had several effects in that the focus shifted back to the Palestine problem and shattered what for many Israelis had been an acceptable status quo of the conflict. However, the opportunities to resolve the conflict were mixed and contradictory. On the one hand, there were apparent signs in the international arena that promoted and supported negotiations, but in the Palestinian and Israeli domestic arenas the publics were split in their interpretations of what constituted the appropriate moment to begin negotiations. The Palestinians had been relatively united in 1988–1990, but with the increasing stronghold of Hamas and widespread disillusionment over the lack of concrete diplomatic results from the intifada, the Palestinian public became more reluctant and suspicious of a peace process. In Israel, the intifada caused an even deeper rift between the hawks and doves with regard to the advantages of negotiation and how to end the Palestinian uprising. At the same time, there was growing discontent among the Israeli public about the new Jewish settlements in the occupied territories at a time when Israel was facing financial difficulties in settling the great influx of immigrants.

12.7.3   In search of focal points for negotiations: US attempts to enhance ripeness

Notwithstanding the denial of any linkage of the Iraqi annexation of Kuwait to the Israeli occupation, shortly after the Gulf War the US administration revived the peace effort. It recognized that the war had created a "window of opportunity" to begin negotiations (Baker and DeFrank 1995, p. 412). However, the conflicting parties did not immediately share the Americans' optimism. The PLO was excluded from the process, and the "inside" Palestinian leadership was disinclined to participate in a Jordanian–Palestinian delegation without the official inclusion of the PLO. The Israeli government was reluctant to participate in the process and suspicious of the suggested structure for the negotiations (i.e., the two tracks of bilateral and multilateral negotiations) and of a Jordanian–Palestinian delegation in particular.

It is difficult to identify any obvious focal point for negotiations that was shared by the conflicting parties; consequently, the Americans had many difficulties in coordinating the parties' expectations of negotiation. Both sides tried to convince the Americans of their interpretations of fairness in the conflict, but in Baker's point of view that was "fighting symbols over substance" (Baker and DeFrank 1995, p. 496). The US mediation, in the pre-negotiation phase leading up to the Madrid Conference, therefore, was concerned primarily with procedural matters. Baker introduced a compromise formula to coordinate the parties' expectations regarding negotiation. The "two-track" approach that was suggested consisted of bilateral and multilateral negotiations. The multilateral track was intended to meet the Arab states' requirement for an international conference, while the bilateral track was an Israeli precondition to participation (Baker and DeFrank 1995, pp. 415–417).

The "inside" Palestinian leadership, however, continued to insist on a delegation of its own and PLO representation. The Israeli government was suspicious of the Jordanian–Palestinian delegation, fearing that the PLO might be represented. The invitation to an international conference was therefore not approved until the USA exerted pressure and provided the parties with letters of assurances.[5] The Americans used "constructive ambiguity" to transform politically contested issues into procedural matters. This strategy was based on the assumption that once the Palestinians and Israelis started to negotiate "there will be no turning back" (Baker and DeFrank 1995, pp. 420, 491). In conclusion, because of the lack of any substantial focal point for negotiations, the US mediation avoided constructing an agenda for negotiation. Instead, efforts were made to solve procedural questions and to coordinate a shared acceptance of bilateral and multilateral negotiations. Notwithstanding the US success in convening the Madrid Conference in 1991, the problem of Palestinian representation and the distinct understandings of the purpose of the peace process reappeared immediately in the first session of the official negotiations.

12.8   Conclusion

In this chapter, I elaborate upon a theoretical framework for the analysis of the precarious transition from escalation to negotiation. Utilizing ripeness theory as a starting point, with its identification of an appropriate moment to initiate negotiations, I move beyond the ripe moment to highlight the transformative and active processes toward de-escalation. First, the theoretical framework advances three key concepts: motivation, opportunity, and focal points. The motivation and opportunity for political leaders to negotiate and the existence of shared focal points for negotiations determine the degree of ripeness and the parties' readiness for de-escalation and negotiation.

Second, the theoretical framework also addresses the puzzle of how to enhance and sustain ripeness. Various active strategies, such as pre-negotiations and third-party intervention, are discussed. Pre-negotiations may function as a process of managing risks and uncertainties during which adversaries may assess concessions, gains, and losses, and identify common ground and focal points. Hence, during a

---

[5]Important points in these letters were, for the Palestinians, a recognition of the legitimate political rights of the Palestinian people; an opposition to Israeli occupation, including the annexation of East Jerusalem and the expansion of Jewish settlements; and a recognition of the rights of the Palestinians to select their own delegation (US Letter of Assurances to the Palestinians 18 October 1991 [1994]). In the letter to Israel, the USA underlined the special relations between the two countries, including an American commitment to Israel's security; the right of Israel to have secure and defensible borders; the opposition to an independent Palestinian state; the promise that the conference would have no mandate to impose a solution and no linkage between the various tracks of the negotiations; and representation of the Palestinians in a joint Jordanian–Palestinian delegation (US Letter of Assurances to Israel 18 October 1991 [1994]).

pre-negotiation phase, the parties can enhance a sense of trust and motivation to negotiate. Moreover, pre-negotiations may provide political leaders with the opportunity to build and mobilize domestic legitimacy and support for a shift toward de-escalation of conflict. Through third-party intervention, ripe conditions for negotiations can also be enhanced and sustained. Third parties have different kinds of leverage to make use of in their efforts to persuade adversaries of the necessity to de-escalate conflict. The use of power, such as offering rewards or threats of punishment, may come to influence the parties' preferences and cost–benefit calculations and eventually strengthen the alternative option of negotiations to conflict escalation. Strategies more commonly used by third parties are the non-coercive forms of communication and facilitation. A third party may, for instance, act as a go-between to facilitate improved communication and informal talks, or as a formulator to coordinate the parties' expectations of negotiations by suggesting various bridging formulas. As a result, third parties may come to break the psychological barriers against negotiations and enhance ripeness by reducing fears and uncertainties about the repercussions of de-escalation.

In sum, the transition from conflict escalation to negotiation is, as the theoretical framework shows, complex and multifaceted. The empirical illustration from the Israeli–Palestinian conflict also demonstrates that the transition is not a linear, but a cyclical process.

References

Abu-Amr Z (1996). Emerging trends in Palestine strategic political thinking and practice. Jerusalem: Passia.

Aggestam K (1999). *Reframing and Resolving Conflict: Israeli–Palestinian Negotiations 1988–1998*. Lund, Sweden: Lund University Press.

Aggestam K (2002a). Quasi-informal mediation in the Oslo channel: Larsen and Holst as individual mediators. In *Studies in International Mediation*, ed. Bercovitch J. London, UK: Palgrave Macmillan, pp. 57–79.

Aggestam K (2002b). Mediating asymmetrical conflict. *Mediterranean Politics* **7**:69–91.

Aggestam K & Jönsson C (1997). (Un)Ending conflict: Challenges in post-war bargaining. *Millennium: Journal of International Studies* **26**:771–793.

Armstrong T (1993). *Breaking the Ice: Rapprochement between East and West Germany, the United States and China, and Israel and Egypt*. Washington, DC, USA: United States Institute for Peace Press.

Baker JA & DeFrank TM (1995). *The Politics of Diplomacy: Revolution, War, and Peace, 1989–1992*. New York, NY, USA: GP Putnam and Sons.

Bar-Siman-Tov Y (1994). *Israel and the Peace Process 1977–1982: In Search of Legitimacy for Peace*. Albany, NY, USA: State University of New York.

Bazerman MH & Sondak H (1988). Judgmental limitations in diplomatic negotiations. *Negotiation Journal* **4**:303–317.

Beilin Y (1999). *Touching Peace: From the Oslo Accord to a Final Agreement*. London, UK: Weidenfeld & Nicolson.

Ben-Yehuda H (1997). Attitude change and policy transformation: Yitzhak Rabin and the Palestinian question, 1967–95. In *From Rabin to Netanyahu: Israel's Troubled Agenda*, ed. Karsh E, pp. 201–224. London, UK: Frank Cass.

Bercovitch J (2002). Introduction: Putting mediation in context. In *Studies in International Mediation*, ed. Bercovitch J, pp. 3–24. London, UK: Palgrave Macmillan.

Berridge GR (1995). *Diplomacy: Theory and Practice*. London, UK: Prentice-Hall/Harvester Wheatsheaf.

Cohen R (1996). Cultural aspects of international mediation. In *Resolving International Conflicts: The Theory and Practice of Mediation*, ed. Bercovitch J, pp. 107–128. Boulder, CO, USA; and London, UK: Lynne Rienner Publishers.

Colosi TR (1986). The iceberg principle: Secrecy in negotiation. In *Perspectives on Negotiation: Four Case Studies and Interpretations*, eds. Bendahmane D & McDonald J. Washington, DC, USA: Center for the Study of Foreign Affairs, pp. 243–260.

Flamhaft Z (1996). *Israel on the Road to Peace: Accepting the Unacceptable*. Boulder, CO, USA; and Oxford, UK: Westview Press.

Goldstein J & Keohane RO (1993). *Ideas and Foreign Policy: Beliefs, Institutions, and Political Change*. Ithaca, NY, USA; and London, UK: Cornell University Press.

Haass R (1988). Ripeness and the settlement of international disputes. *Survival* **30**: 232–251.

Haass R (1990). *Conflict Unending*. New Haven, CT, USA: Yale University Press.

Hampson FO (1996a). *Nurturing Peace: Why Peace Settlements Succeed or Fail*. Washington, DC, USA: United States Institute of Peace Press.

Hampson FO (1996b). Why orphaned peace settlements are more prone to failure. In *Managing Global Chaos: Sources of and Responses to International Conflict*, eds. Crocker CA, Hampson FO & Aall P, pp. 533–550. Washington, DC, USA: United States Institute of Peace Press.

Heradstveit D (1979). *The Arab–Israeli Conflict: Psychological Obstacles to Peace*. Oslo, Norway: Universitetsforlaget.

Iklé FC (1991). *Every War Must End*. New York, NY, USA: Columbia University Press.

Jönsson C (1990). *Communication in International Bargaining*. London, UK: Pinter Publishers.

Kelman H (1982). Creating the conditions for Israeli–Palestinian negotiations. *Journal of Conflict Resolution* **26**:39–75.

Kelman H (2002) Interactive problem-solving: Informal mediation by the scholar–practitioner. In *Studies in International Mediation*, ed. Bercovitch J, pp. 167–193. London, UK: Palgrave Macmillan.

King C (1997). *Ending Civil Wars*. Adelphi Paper 308, International Institute for Strategic Studies. London, UK: Oxford University Press.

Kleiboer M (1994). Ripeness of conflict? A fruitful notion? *Journal of Peace Research* **31**:109–166.

Klieman A (1988). *Statecraft in the Dark: Israel's Practice of Quiet Diplomacy*. Tel Aviv, Israel: Jafee Center for Strategic Studies.

Kriesberg L (1991). Introduction: Timing conditions, strategies, and errors. In *Timing the De-Escalation of International Conflicts*, eds. Kriesberg L & Thorson SJ, pp. 1–24. Syracuse, NY, USA: Syracuse University Press.

Larson DW (1985). *Origins of Containment: A Psychological Explanation*. Princeton, NJ, USA: Princeton University Press.

Larson DW (1988). The psychology of reciprocity in international relations. *Negotiation Journal* **4**(3):281–301.

Levy JS (1996). Loss aversion, framing, and bargaining: The implications of prospect theory for international conflict. *International Political Science Review* **17**:179–195.

Lewitt M (1994). *Let Them Eat the Figs: An Analysis of the Negotiation Process Leading to the Madrid Conference*. Working Paper Series 94-4, The Program on Negotiation. Cambridge, MA, USA: Harvard University Press.

McDowall D (1989). *Palestine and Israel: The Uprising and Beyond*. London, UK: I.B. Tauris & Co.

Mitchell C (1995). The right moment: Notes on four models of "ripeness." *Paradigms: The Kent Journal of International Relations* **9**:35–52.

Montville JV (1987). The arrow and the olive branch: A case for track two diplomacy. In *Conflict Resolution: Track Two Diplomacy*, eds. McDonald JW & Bendahmane DB, pp. 5–20. Washington, DC, USA: Foreign Service Institute, US Department of State.

Muslih M (1997). A study of PLO peace initiatives, 1974–1988. In *The PLO and Israel: From Armed Conflict to Political Solution, 1964–1994*, eds. Sela A & Ma'oz M, pp. 37–54. New York, NY, USA: St. Martin's Press.

New Outlook (1989). The election plan is a non-starter. An interview with Faisal Husseini, **33** (8 [August]).

Princen T (1992). *Intermediaries in International Conflict*. Princeton, NJ, USA: Princeton University Press.

Pruitt D (1997). Ripeness theory and the Oslo talks. *International Negotiation: A Journal of Theory and Practice* **2**:237–250.

Putnam RD (1993). Two-level games: The impact of domestic politics on transatlantic bargaining. In *America and Europe in an Era of Change*, eds. Haftendorn H & Tuschoff C. Boulder, CO, USA: Westview Press.

Robinson GE (1997). *Building a Palestinian State: The Incomplete Revolution*. Bloomington and Indianapolis, IN, USA: Indiana University Press.

Rolef SH (1997). Israel's policy toward the PLO. In *The PLO and Israel: From Armed Conflict to Political Solution, 1964–1994*, eds. Sela A & Ma'oz M, pp. 253–272. New York, NY, USA: St. Martin's Press.

Rothman J (1988). Negotiation as consolidation: Prenegotiation in the Israeli–Palestinian conflict. *The Jerusalem Journal of International Relations*, **13**:22–44.

Rubin JZ (1991). The timing of ripeness and the ripeness of timing. In *Timing the De-Escalation of International Conflicts*, eds. Kriesberg L & Thorson SJ, pp. 237–246. Syracuse, NY, USA: Syracuse University Press.

Rubin JZ (1992). Conclusion: International mediation in context. In *Mediation in International Relations: Multiple Approaches to Conflict Management*, eds. Bercovitch J & Rubin JZ, pp. 249–272. New York, NY, USA: St. Martin's Press.

Schelling TC (1960). *The Strategy of Conflict* (1980 edition). Cambridge, MA, USA: Harvard University Press.

Shamir Y (1989). Address to the American Enterprise Institute, Washington, DC, 6 April. *Journal of Palestine Studies* **18**:176–179.

Singer Y (1994). Interview with Karin Aggestam, Jerusalem, 30 June 1994.

Stedman S (1991). *Peacemaking in Civil War: International Mediation in Zimbabwe 1974–1980*. London, UK: Lynne Rienner.

Stedman SJ (1996). Negotiation and mediation in internal conflict. In *The International Dimensions of Internal Conflict*, ed. Brown ME, pp. 341–376. Cambridge, MA, USA: The MIT Press.

Stein JG (1989). *Getting to the Table: The Processes of International Prenegotiation*. Baltimore, MD, USA; and London, UK: The John Hopkins University Press.

Stein JG (1993). International co-operation and loss avoidance: Framing the problem. In *Choosing to Co-operate: How States Avoid Loss*, eds. Stein JG & Pauly LW, pp. 2–34. Baltimore, MD, USA; and London, UK: The John Hopkins University Press.

Stein JG (1996). Image, identity, and conflict resolution. In *Managing Global Chaos: Sources of and Responses to International Conflict*, eds. Crocker CA, Hampson FO & Aall P, pp. 93–111. Washington, DC, USA: United States Institute of Peace Press.

Sztompka P (1993). *The Sociology of Social Change*. Oxford, UK: Blackwell.

US Letter of Assurances to Israel 18 October 1991 (1994). In *The Palestinian–Israeli Peace Agreement: A Documentary Record*, ed. Institute for Palestine Studies, pp. 9–11. Washington, DC, USA: Institute for Palestine Studies.

US Letter of Assurances to the Palestinians 18 October 1991 (1994). In *The Palestinian–Israeli Peace Agreement: A Documentary Record*, ed. Institute for Palestine Studies, pp. 5–8. Washington, DC, USA: Institute for Palestine Studies.

Webb K, Koutrakou V & Walters M (1996). The Yugoslavian conflict, European mediation, and the contingency model: A critical perspective. In *Resolving International Conflicts: The Theory and Practice of Mediation*, ed. Bercovitch J, pp. 171–189. Boulder, CO, USA; and London, UK: Lynne Rienner.

Zartman IW (1986). Ripening conflict, ripe moment, formula, and mediation. In *Perspectives on Negotiation*, eds. Bendahmane D & McDonald J. Washington, DC, USA: Center for the Study of Foreign Affairs.

Zartman IW (1989a). *Ripe for Resolution*. New York, NY, USA: Oxford University Press.

Zartman IW (1989b). Prenegotiation: Phases and functions. In *Getting to the Table: The Processes of International Prenegotiation*, ed. Stein JG, pp. 87–108. Baltimore, MD, USA; and London, UK: The John Hopkins University Press.

Zartman IW (1995). Dynamics and constraints in negotiations in internal conflicts. In *Elusive Peace: Negotiating an End to Civil Wars*, ed. Zartman IW, pp. 3–29. Washington, DC, USA: The Brookings Institution.

Zartman IW (2001). The timing of peace initiatives: Hurting stalemates and ripe moments. *The Global Review of Ethnopolitics* **1**:8–18.

Zartman IW & Aurik J (1991). Power strategies in de-escalation. In *Timing the De-Escalation of International Conflicts*, eds. Kriesberg L & Thorson SJ, pp. 152–181. Syracuse, NY, USA: Syracuse University Press.

Part IV
Conclusion

Chapter 13

Lessons for Research

I. William Zartman and Guy Olivier Faure

Escalation is the other side of settlement, and negotiation links them together. To escalate means to increase by steps, referring to the dynamics of conflict. A party escalates – thus transitively – to hurt the opponent and make it change its behavior, either entirely (to give in) or partially (to negotiate). It may also escalate, less instrumentally, simply to retaliate or to punish, without any particular purpose in terms of making the opponent do something. In either case, it raises the opponent's cost of holding out or of seeking to win. In the process, it probably also raises the cost for itself, since escalations are generally not cost free to the escalator. It may continue to escalate on its own in this way, "turning the screws" on the opponent (to change the metaphor) until the latter changes its behavior in the conflict. In the simplest case, the party continues to escalate until it can go no further, either until the costs (or the depletion of resources) of escalation outweigh the benefits it seeks to obtain or until the opponent changes its behavior.

More likely than one-party escalation is for the opponent not to simply hunker down and resist, but to escalate in reaction, for a double purpose – to retaliate or halt the first party's escalation and to make the first party change its behavior in turn and give in or negotiate. Then escalation becomes a two-dimensional spiral – one is tempted to say "a double helix" – and the parties' calculation becomes more complicated. Parties may push the extent of their escalation in the hope that just one more step will produce the desired change in behavior, only to find that the step has become a round as the other party makes the same calculation. Conflict escalates – thus intransitively – and drags the parties' actions along.

If escalation were simply a matter of cold calculating policy making with full information, it could be practiced until it reached one of its possible outcomes: inflection of the other party's policies to either give in or negotiate, exhaustion of resources, or disappearance of the issue in conflict. If a party knew just how much it would take to make the other party move (change its behavior in the conflict), it might well escalate just that amount to produce the desired result. Furthermore, the analyst could also calculate the limits of each party's resources (or, more specifically, available resources at the level of importance of the issue in conflict) to see who would change policies first and then calculate the gap between the two parties' limits to see whether change would mean surrender (large gap) or negotiation (small gap). In this view, escalation would be a purely calculably transitive operation.

Unfortunately, such calculations are not reliable. It may suffice to call the disturbing element "uncertainty," but this is only accurate as a descriptive (not an analytic) term, and a broadly descriptive one at that. Information is incomplete (uncertain) because it is not present, and it is not present because the key terms – limits, costs, importance, gap – have no fixed meanings. Such limits and gaps are simply unknowable; but even if they were, the parties could also reckon that the mere intimation (an uncertainty) that it will escalate, presumably as much as necessary (another uncertainty), would produce the same result more cheaply. Many studies (Bueno de Mesquita *et al.* 1997) assume a strong and a weak party and investigate the paradox of asymmetry, but this is a caricature. Weak parties in conflict, like weak parties in negotiation (Paul 1994; Zartman and Rubin 2000), may have appropriate tactics and sources of action that allow them to escalate short of total war, just as they may be able to bargain short of total victory.

Escalation, like negotiation, follows a norm of reciprocity, in which an equivalent response is expected (Gouldner 1960; Keohane 1986; Larson 1988; Leng 1993; Zartman *et al.* 1996; Shell 1999). Breaking out of the exchange imposed by escalation and into the exchange imposed by negotiation is the challenge of conflict resolution. The interesting question is, How and when in this process of conflict can and do parties move from escalation or dynamic conflict into negotiation or dynamic conflict resolution, both as their own policy and as a move to entice the other into negotiations, or (epistemologically) as both an independent and a dependent variable? As in any good analysis, the process is more complex than a simple question suggests, and the answer depends on the terms of analysis on which it is based. To begin, it is important to examine the forms that an escalation can take, as analyzed in Section 13.1, to see the obstacles and opportunities that they present to the development of negotiation. Thereafter, the basic question can be faced in all its forms: How can and do parties move out of escalation into negotiation? How does escalation produce negotiation? The "can and do" needs emphasis: the analyses have examined the behavioral patterns of conflicting parties ("do") as well as the possibilities for goal-oriented action to break out of the grip of those customary behaviors ("can"). There needs to be a creative interrelation between description and analysis, and between prescription and synthesis, some of which is pursued in the final chapter, Chapter 14.

13.1 Forms and Outcomes

The policies of escalation (transitive) are part of a reciprocating process of escalation (intransitive) that has a mind of its own and can drag its participants along beyond the courses determined by rational policy. These intransitive aspects can be identified as deadlock, deterrence, races, entrapment, and vengeance, all forms of the escalation process that constrain and impose policies of the parties, both in regard to further escalation and in regard to the possibility of negotiation.

Deadlock, as analyzed in Chapter 2 by Guy Olivier Faure, refers to a condition or an outcome of the escalation process, an impasse with no way out and with even the alternative of further escalation blocked by definition. This common characteristic can result from an array of causes: cognitive, relational, contextual, structural, or processual. It can even occur in the de-escalation process, when the parties are objectively too far apart, have no bargaining zone, and are unable to make further concessions, bereft of resources to pay for trade-offs, reduced to their security point, and unwilling to go below it to buy in the other party. Thus, full deadlock is a condition in which the parties are hung in limbo between conflict and negotiation, unable to escalate out of the conflict or to concede into negotiation. The escalatory dynamics of conflict have brought them to this point, from which there seems to be no exit. The deadlock encapsulates the dilemma of conflict: its costly escalatory dynamics in search of victory lead to a costlier impasse, if not defeat.

Yet deadlock also has its purpose, for it keeps the other party as well as the first party in check. My deadlock is your deadlock, and so it keeps you from winning (even if it keeps me from winning). That realization can open both parties' thinking to "lowering the deadlock," either by reducing the cost of maintaining the deadlock or by seeking an even-handed solution to the conflict in which the parties are locked; that is, into payoffs rather than into payouts. However, the trap that hovers over this change is the "Alphonse–Gaston paradox," in which no party dares move first lest that action break the deadlock in favor of the other party. And so the parties return to the conflictual deadlock, unless a way is found for Alphonse and Gaston to cross the threshold at the same time.

On the international scene, the negotiations over the independence of Namibia, to which the question of Cuban troops in Angola was then added, is a good example of deadlock (Zartman 1989, Chapter 5; Crocker 1992). Negotiations made no headway because both parties nurtured the hope of being able to escalate their way to victory and neither could make concessions for fear of being overcome. When the natural linkage between the two conflicts was admitted, terms of trade were available (paired withdrawal of South African troops from Namibia and of Cuban troops from Angola, the presence of each set of troops serving as the excuse for the other). However, it was not until a mutually hurting stalemate (MHS) became established in the parties' minds (produced by a failed escalation to raise that was met with an escalation to call and a threatened escalation to raise) and a formula for simultaneous withdrawals was produced by the mediator that an agreement was possible.

Deterrence, as analyzed by Patrick Morgan (Chapter 3), is the purposeful use of projected escalation into deadlock, with escalation threatened to prevent the other party from escalating. It is deadlock once removed, since the parties are (at least) one step back from their conflict limits and are holding each other at arm's length to prevent direct contact in conflict. The problem with deterrence is the problem with any threat and hinges more specifically on uncertainty, since the reality of the threatened escalation is not certain and only becomes more certain when demonstrated, at which point it is no longer a threat but an escalation and a failed deterrent. Thus, the surest way to deter escalation is to remove its cause and to settle the conflict; the arm's-length deadlock can be the prelude to lowering the costly and dangerous conflict posture. However, the trap hanging over this move is that it disarms the very instruments that produced it. And so the parties return to their hair-trigger posture, ready to escalate to deter escalation, unless a way is found to assure the deterrence while at the same time pulling away from it.

Strategic arms relations during the Cold War are the classic example of deterrence, in which technical improvements in armaments constituted and imposed a continuing escalation between the parties, who at the same time negotiated limitations on their escalation that maintained the deterrent equivalence at an acceptable cost level (until cost broke the back of one of the parties). Thus, deterrence was both the condition of negotiation and the producer of limits on the parties' options and leverage. These negotiations, in turn, imposed a minimal but growing level of confidence building, which reinforced both deterrence itself and the possibilities of negotiation.

Arms races, as analyzed by Rudolf Avenhaus, Juergen Beetz, and D. Marc Kilgour (Chapter 4), are also purposeful uses of escalation, but the outcome, as originally presented by Richardson (1951, 1960), is not deadlock or deterrence, but war. The analysis shows that parties committed to their conflict will continue to escalate, and even if they prefer the current deadlock and/or deterrence, they will proceed to escalation if provoked. What began as purposeful transitive escalation is swept away in an automatic intransitive process. The inevitability of the original scenario has been somewhat tempered by the introduction of decelerating elements, such as fear and fatigue, intransitive brakes that make the parties rethink their mad race in terms of cost and consequences. However, the escalation effect then becomes a race between the parties' attributed constants, unless the race winds down at the same rate that it scaled up.

Arms races fit within the logic of the security dilemma, in which a party's efforts to assure its own security in the face of a perceived threat only increase the insecurity of the putative threatener, who makes similar efforts to increase its own security, which decreases the first party's security, and so on. Security dilemmas are often cited as the dynamic element in international politics, but in current times they are even more dramatic in the inter-ethnic relations of intranational politics. Fear here acts as the motor of the escalation, rather than its brake, as seen around the world from Afghanistan to Zaire. The examples show how difficult it is to turn these races into negotiations, with perhaps fatigue serving as the only remaining element to dampen the escalating effects.

Entrapment, as analyzed by Paul Meerts (Chapter 5), is escalation gone awry, illustrating the illusion of reliable calculation pointed out above. Parties become entrapped because they lose a sense of their limits and they seek to cover their losses rather than attain their gains. Escalation continues until the parties (to reverse the image) dig a hole for themselves from which they cannot escape alive. Entrapment is often presented in the business literature as an escalation against oneself, an attempt to retrieve sunk costs in a losing venture. It can just as well apply to two losing parties entrapped in their conflict with each other, and not only to one party caught in a conflict against a winner. Entrapment thrives on uncertainty, a lack of information as to what it would take to overcome the other party in conflict and as to one's own limits in goals and resources. Thus, the best way to avoid sinking into the hole is through improved decisional elements, such as planning, information, communication, and control. However, the trap that underlies entrapment is the intrinsic role of imperfect information in negotiation as well as in conflict. It is in each party's interest to dissimulate and bluff to gain an advantage, even in trying to deter the other from making the investments that may entrap it. And so the parties continue to dig their hole deeper, unless they are provided with a face-saving way out of their own escalation.

In international relations, Vietnam is the standard US case of entrapment, joined by Afghanistan for Russia, Algeria for France, all the way down to Congo for Zimbabwe, and Yemen for Egypt. The prevalence of the problem explains the current fixation on an exit strategy as a precondition to involvement. All the (completed) instances lead to the same conclusion: it takes a firm change of policy, at the hands of a changed leadership, to extract the entrapped escalator, and it takes negotiations to do so. This is because the trapped needs the help of the trapper to climb out of the hole as gracefully as possible. Of course, the entrapped could always pack up and go home, but in international relations that would entail further losses on the beach, from attacks during withdrawal, and on the home front, from public outcry. So – unlike in the examples from business – negotiation is the way to cut losses and prepare new relations. But it is also important to note that there are positive cases of entrapment, in which the parties must go through with negotiations because of deadlines and public promises they have imposed on themselves. The engagement of both Israelis and Palestinians, first in the Madrid Conference in 1991 and then in a search for the Oslo agreement in 1993, is an important example (Pruitt 1997; Baker 1999).

Vengeance, as analyzed by Sung Hee Kim (Chapter 6), is the motor and result of escalation, the ultimate mechanism behind the intransitive process, the aggressive equivalent of the defensive motor of fear. It feeds on the uncertainty of motives and establishes its own certainties of interest, which call for further retaliatory escalation. Vengeance is itself an escalation of motives and images, as identified in the introduction to this book, and fuels an escalation of actions, and it is this layered escalation that makes the process so difficult to control (Parks 1997; Tripp and Bies 1997). Unlike deadlock and deterrence (the logic of which also opens the process of conflict to resolution), vengeance, like arms races and entrapment, is the result of a closed and worsening logic that excludes negotiation. Hence, again unlike deadlock and deterrence, it is the process itself that needs to be addressed in arms races, entrapment, and vengeance, by countermeasures that break its logic and open the conflict to negotiation. Thus, the best way to avoid the effects of vengeance is to introduce apology and forgiveness. The problem with such measures is that they cannot be applied until vengeance has been vanquished, at least on one side, and until an initial settlement has been achieved or until negotiation deliberately deals with the causes of the conflict and creates mechanisms to build new relationships.

Yet vengeance has been tamed in a whole range of traditional societies from Ethiopia to Italy as a means of ending conflict and of opening the way to the negotiation of renormalized relations. The firmly established institution of blood money provides a single-step "escalation to call" as a mechanism of vengeance that stops further escalation cold. "Cold" and "mechanism" are appropriate terms, for underneath the elaborate rituals of grief and enmity lies a commercial calculation of the "worth" of a life in fixed terms of money or cattle among these groups in the Horn of Africa, which allows neither debate nor further conflict (Michaelson 2000). Thereafter, negotiation begins, over the details of the reconciliation, with apology and forgiveness either formally prescribed or assumed (Zartman 2000). The "civilized" world could take notice of these rituals as a way of turning vengeance into negotiation.

These five different forms or outcomes of escalation have their own logic of conflict that precludes negotiation. They also contain elements that either can turn that same logic into negotiation, in the case of deadlock and deterrence, or can at least point to the requirements for a contrary effect to overcome their logic of escalation, in the case of arms races, entrapment, and vengeance. These elements turn out to be standard components of the negotiation process – mediators to overcome the Alphonse–Gaston paradox, confidence-building measures (CBMs) to assure the effect of deterrence as it is being lowered, positive-sum outcomes to provide a face-saving way out of sunk costs, and forward-looking outcomes that address both deeper causes and new relationships. These elements appear again as the structures of escalation are examined in the search for answers to the basic questions, but more research is needed into their effects and potentialities.

13.2   Structures and Processes

The core of the analysis is found in addressing the question of how to get from escalation to negotiation. A review of the various forms and outcomes of escalation shows that escalation can lead to or even be the precondition for negotiation, but under what conditions? At this point the discussion turns to transitive escalation or, more precisely, to transitive actions to counter both transitive and intransitive escalation. Escalation can take off on its own (intransitive effect), but it takes specific efforts to stop it and wind it down.[1] The different approaches presented in Part II of this book provide different answers.

Both to begin and to conduct negotiations, a party concedes when the costs of producing and/or enduring further escalation outweigh the benefits achieved by it (Zeuthen 1930; Carlson 1995). Conceptually (although the effect is hard to calculate in reality outside of wage negotiations), a party concedes just to the point where it throws the burden of the calculation on the other party, forcing it to make the concession. This type of analysis has been used on the basis of fixed costs to indicate when a party concedes and where the final point of agreement – that is, the meeting point of respective concessions – lies. However, it can also indicate the amount of escalation that is necessary to make the other begin the concessions and then calculate the moves (amount of power) necessary to produce that escalation.

---

[1]This may not be completely true. The Richardson effect has been analyzed as containing its own brakes, through the dual effects of fear and fatigue (Smoker 1964), and the conclusion on arms races is that "some ... lead to war and some do not" (Siverson and Diehl 1989, p. 214; also, Vasquez and Heneham 1992, pp. 103–108). However, it is not clear whether even these effects are inherent in the process (intransitive) or are merely counters that operate on the decision makers who pursue arms races (transitive). In any case, even if they existed as fully autonomous intransitive effects, it would not change the need for specific policies to move to negotiation.

The tactical question about escalation, whether it is more effective to start with a large escalation right off the bat or to escalate only gradually to keep the burden of calculation and concession on the shoulders of the other party, has received much (inconclusive) attention. But the tactical question about negotiation, whether it is more effective to concede late or early, has not, as yet. The effects of large versus small escalations on negotiation, and the effects of definitive versus gradual concessions, need more work (Bartos 1978).

An examination of escalation between narrowing structural guideposts supports the role of certain types of gradual escalation as a catalyst for the initiation of negotiation. Escalations can be divided into two intentional types – escalations to call or match the level of power actions of the opponent,[2] and escalations to raise or exceed the opponent's power level; the latter are further divided into those that surpass, match, or fall short of the other's level. Escalations to raise that succeed, in the sense of overcoming the opponent, obviously do not lead to negotiation, unless it be a negotiation to define the terms of surrender. However, the three other types of "failed" escalation lead the parties to negotiation through a mixture of investment and invitation: they have put enough effort into the issue to want to recoup something through an agreed outcome, and they have signaled to each other their inability to achieve an outcome unilaterally. All impose or confirm an approximate stalemate, either by meeting the level of power of the opponent, on purpose or by default, or by returning to a previous impasse. But the escalation not only seals the stalemate at a given level of roughly matched power, which (re)affirms a static relation, it also indicates a burst of effort and commitment by a party to try to change that relation and to jolt the other into a search for a new outcome, and a similar burst of effort and commitment by the other to hold the first in check, which (re)affirms a dynamic relation. Interestingly, past escalations, even shortfalls, are much more propitious for negotiation than are threats of escalation in the future, since the investment level and the pain to the recipient are higher and more tangible (less uncertain). However, the caveat given in Chapter 7 by I. William Zartman about the ambiguity of the communicated distinction between the two types in reality needs to be reiterated.

An attempt to find an answer to the sudden-versus-gradual escalation question using different structural variables finds no significant difference based on symmetry or asymmetry of power sources, but reinforces the importance of escalation outcomes (notably stalemate) rather than escalation magnitude when conflict strategies are added to the explanation. Although a negotiated agreement is the least-frequent outcome of escalation to violence, whether through sudden violent

---

[2]Power here is defined as "an action designed to move the other party in an intended direction," not as simply the possession of resources (see Zartman and Rubin 2000).

initiation or through low-level hostility graduating to violence, escalation into violence is a nearly necessary condition for settlement. When conflict is initiated with violence, and the opponent is strong enough to reciprocate and does so, an impasse and a negotiated settlement are more likely outcomes than when the violence is not reciprocated. Unreciprocated escalation produces no stalemates and so tends not to produce negotiated settlements.

Once negotiation has begun, the same impact appears, visible through the empirical analysis of turning points or departures in the process. Generally "process departures," created by either internal or external precipitants, lead to improvements in the negotiation process and progress toward their successful conclusion. However, in a number of cases of deep-seated conflict, in either security or political negotiations growing out of value conflicts, escalation produced by internal changes (of leadership or policy) within one or more parties disrupts the negotiations and creates a negative turning point. In these cases, it generally takes an external intervention to bring the negotiations back on track. Turning points of any kind are stocktaking moments, and like escalation as pre-negotiation behavior they can move the process along. Yet conflict escalations during the negotiations tend to be beyond the capacity of the parties themselves to overcome and require third-party assistance.

The consequences of conflict escalation under negotiation produced by personality and/or policy types that focus on relative versus absolute gains, or distributive versus integrative approaches to negotiation, can be analyzed using the logical lens of game theory. These findings replicate socio-psychological analyses based on negotiators' interpersonal and motivational orientations (Rubin and Brown 1975). While warriors (hardliners), in Nicolson's (1963) terms, should not fail to reciprocate each other's escalation, lest they find themselves at a disadvantage in the negotiation, when one of the parties is a shopkeeper (softliner), escalation can be destabilizing, and when both are shopkeepers, escalation makes them both worse off. Again, the importance of stalemate is underscored: there is no evidence that it can be beneficial not to match escalation, and it never appears to be harmful to match escalation, even though it may only restore the previous balance. Conflict escalation during negotiation can be a useful bargaining tactic only if the other party does not reciprocate, and since the other can be expected to do so if it can, the tactic is only useful if such matching is impossible. On the other hand, when negotiations have reached or come within sight of salient compromise, conflict escalation destabilizes and does not produce new stabilities.

Coming from many analytical approaches, the works discussed repeatedly emphasize the importance of stalemate to the initiation of negotiations, which reinforces the findings of ripeness theory (Zartman 2000). Ripeness is a necessary but not sufficient condition for the initiation of negotiations, bilateral or mediated. If

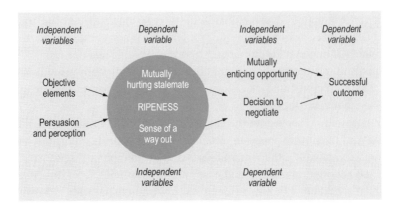

Figure 13.1. Ripeness.

the (two) parties to a conflict (i) perceive themselves to be in an MHS and (ii) perceive the possibility of a negotiated solution (way out), then the situation is "ripe for resolution" (i.e., for negotiations toward resolution to begin). In other words, when both parties escalate their conflict to the point where they run out of the capability to escalate further, when as a result they both feel stalemated, and when that stalemate hurts them, they are ready to initiate negotiations. It is important to note that "perceive," "feel," and "hurt" are subjective or perceptional elements; they may be related to objective conditions, but unless they are perceived, the effect is not present. This situation can be expressed as a model, in which ripeness is located as both a dependent and then an independent variable (*Figure 13.1*).

Alternatives that propose willingness or other synonyms as an explanatory variable miss the point, for they ignore the importance of the stalemate and do not explain what it is that causes the willingness (Haass 1990; Kleiboer 1994). On the other hand, there may be variations on the implied simultaneity and equality of the MHS, for example, the staggered stalemate in which one side alone feels stalemated and cannot escalate its way out, makes some concessions, and thereby draws the other into a cost calculation of concessions versus escalation, as discussed above. Another example is the revisionist blockade in which only the revisionist, or warrior, needs to be stalemated since the status quo party, or shopkeeper, is ready to negotiate anyway, as discussed above. However, the previous chapters all reaffirm the importance of a stalemate in escalation for the initiation of negotiation, and all also expand MHS thinking into other types of stalemates and appropriate tactics, by adding other explanatory elements, such as concession rates and personality types.

Readiness thinking brings in other elements that are useful when ripening is needed (i.e., when a sufficient sense of a stalemate is not present). These include the use of a third-party mediator, the activation of chains of communication, and the identification of focal points in the search for a formula for agreement. When only objective elements of ripeness exist, but the MHS is not perceived, specific tactics by mediators can bring the conflicting parties to understand the ripeness of their situation and turn to negotiations. The discussion of various forms and outcomes of escalation highlights the need for such devices to turn escalation into negotiation.

Yet if the stalemate produced by escalation is the necessary, even if insufficient, precondition to the opening of negotiation, it follows that negotiation is not the in-evitable result of stalemate. Not only does the opportunity offered by checked esca-lation have to be seized by the parties directly, or through the effects of a mediator, but also the rising escalation can produce other types of results. Righteousness for the true believer and implacable hostility for the embittered enemies are frequent emotional responses to escalation frustrated by mutual blockage, and the expended investment, rising costs, heightened commitment, and accumulated scars that esca-lation occasions only increase the obdurate reactions. Escalation can, indeed, make negotiation harder rather than easier. But that we know, and the possibility of esca-lation leading to negotiation, and the conditions of that outcome, are eventualities less intuitive and so are emphasized in this study.

13.3   Escalation and Negotiation

There is an enormous literature on escalation, which delves into multiple aspects of the phenomenon, but treats it as if it had no end. This work was given a major impetus by the Cold War, which was indeed considered as if it had no end. The link with negotiation, one of the three possible outcomes of escalation, was simply not made. This lacuna, too, was in large part the product of the Cold War, in which negotiation with the adversary to actually end the stalemate produced by escalation, rather than merely to keep escalation from running out of control (Kanet and Kolodziej 1991), was also not considered.

The present work makes that linkage and shows conditions under which esca-lation can, does, and should lead to negotiations when

- conflict costs accumulate and become too heavy to bear;
- stalemates occur from escalations to call, shortfalls in escalations to raise, or inabilities of either party to escalate further;
- threatened escalations are persuasive;
- third parties operate in communications chains to interrupt escalation reci-procity;
- alternative focal points and positive outcomes are waved at the parties to attract their attention; or
- a competitive adversary has escalated.

The study shows that escalation does not always preclude, but often actually invites negotiation, and that therefore parties should look for negotiation opportunities despite or because of recent escalations. This conclusion should by no means be taken to suggest that all escalation leads to negotiation; many of the preceding analyses, as well as other empirical studies (Bercovitch 2003), show that some types of escalation inhibit negotiation, although the present study also suggests that there may be more opportunities for negotiation out of escalation than actually practiced. To help analyze this problem, this study has been able to produce creative analysis by bringing together several different methodologies, involving a number of different disciplines and concepts, from the personal introspection of psychology through the structural frames of political analysis to the formal logic of game theory, and using several different collections of data.

However, it has not exhausted the subject. All of the analyses presented here invite further work to test the tentative conclusions reached. It is shown from several angles of analysis that escalation can lead to negotiation, not automatically by any means, but by providing an opportunity for parties to seize. However, the conditions under which that shift occurs or can occur are still not clearly identified. Under what conditions do negotiations follow the various types of escalations (rather than taking place under the threat of future escalation)? Under what conditions do calculations of the costs of escalation lead to concessions (rather than to further escalations)? Under what conditions do turning points produce a break-off of negotiation (rather than a return to the table)? Under what conditions is escalation stabilizing to negotiations (rather than producing rupture or renewing a race to victory)? These are all questions for which we only have parts of the answers, and which beg for more answers.

References

Baker J (1999). The road to Madrid. In *Herding Cats*, eds. Crocker C, Hampson FO & Aall P. Washington, DC, USA: US Institute of Peace.

Bartos O (1978). Simple model of negotiation. In *The Negotiation Process*, ed. Zartman IW. Newbury Park, CA, USA: Sage.

Bercovitch J (2003). Mediation. In *Peacemaking in International Conflict*, ed. Zartman IW. Washington, DC, USA: US Institute of Peace.

Bueno de Mesquita B, Morrow JD & Zorick E (1997). Capabilities, perception and escalation. *American Political Science Review* **91**:15–27.

Carlson L (1995). A theory of escalation and international conflict. *Journal of Conflict Resolution* **39**:511–534.

Crocker C (1992). *High Noon in Southern Africa*. New York, NY, USA: Norton.

Gouldner A (1960). The norm of reciprocity. *American Sociological Review* **15**:161–178.

Haass R (1990). *Conflicts Unending*. New Haven, CT, USA: Yale University Press.

Kanet R & Kolodziej E, eds. (1991). *The Cold War as Cooperation*. Baltimore, MD, USA: The Johns Hopkins University Press.

Keohane R (1986). Reciprocity in international relations. *International Organization* **40**:1–27.

Kleiboer M (1994). Ripeness at conflict: A fruitful notion? *Journal of Peace Research* **31**:109–116.

Larson D (1988). The psychology of reciprocity in international relations. *Negotiation Journal* **4**:281–302.

Leng R (1993). Reciprocating influence strategies in interstate crisis bargaining. *Journal of Conflict Resolution* **37**:3–41.

Michaelson M (2000). *Afar-Issa Conflict Management*, ICWA Letters MM-18, January. Hanover, Germany: Institute for Current World Affairs.

Nicolson H (1963). *Diplomacy*. New York, NY, USA: Oxford University Press.

Parks JM (1997). The fourth arm of justice: The art and science of revenge. In *Research on Negotiations in Organizations*, eds. Lewicki R, Bies R & Sheppard B. Greenwich, NY, USA: JAI Press.

Paul TV (1994). *Asymmetric Conflicts: War Initiation by Weaker Powers*. New York, NY, USA: Cambridge University Press.

Pruitt DG, ed. (1997). Ripeness theory and the Oslo talks. *International Negotiation* **2**(2):91–104.

Richardson LF (1951). Could an arms race end without fighting? *Nature* **168**(29 Sept):567.

Richardson LF (1960). *Arms and Insecurity*. London, UK: Stevens & Sons.

Rubin JZ & Brown B (1975). *The Social Psychology of Bargaining and Negotiation*. New York, NY, USA: Academic.

Shell GR (1999). *Bargaining for Advantage*. Baltimore, MD, USA: Penguin.

Siverson R & Diehl P (1989). Arms races, the conflict spiral and the onset of war. In *Handbook of War Studies*, ed. Midlarsky M. Boston, MA, USA: Unwin-Hyman.

Smoker P (1964). Fear in the arms race. *Journal of Peace Research* **1**:55–63.

Tripp T & Bies R (1997). What's good about revenge? In *Research on Negotiations in Organizations*, eds. Lewicki R, Bies R & Sheppard B. Greenwich, NY, USA: JAI Press.

Vasquez J & Heneham M (1992). *The Scientific Study of Peace and War*. New York, NY, USA: Lexington.

Zartman IW (1989). *Ripe for Resolution*. New York, NY, USA: Oxford University Press.

Zartman IW, ed. (2000). *Traditional Cures for Modern Conflicts: African Conflict Medicine*. Boulder, CO, USA: Lynne Rienner.

Zartman IW & Rubin JZ, eds. (2000). *Power and Negotiation*. Ann Arbor, MI, USA: University of Michigan Press.

Zartman IW, Druckman D, Jensen L, Pruitt DG & Young HP (1996). Negotiation as a search for justice. *International Negotiation* **1**:79–98.

Zeuthen F (1930). *Problems of Monopoly and Economic Welfare*. London, UK: Rout-
    ledge and Kegan Paul [reprinted in Young O (1975). *Bargaining*. Urbana, IL, USA:
    University of Illinois Press].

Chapter 14

Strategies for Action

Guy Olivier Faure and I. William Zartman

Confronted with the possibility of an escalation or caught in the gears of an escalation process, the practitioner, whether statesman, diplomat, politician, lawyer, or businessperson, has to react in real time. He or she must understand the situation, but also has to act and to do this within a set of constraints. Henry Kissinger, having been both an analyst and a statesman, provides an extremely instrumental description of the particulars of the task of each one:

> The analyst can choose which problem he wishes to study, whereas the statesman's problems are imposed on him. The analyst can allot whatever time is necessary to come to a clear conclusion; the overwhelming challenge to the statesman is the pressure of time. The analyst runs no risk. If his conclusions prove wrong, he can write another treatise. The statesman is permitted only one guess; his mistakes are irretrievable. The analyst has available to him all the facts; he will be judged on his intellectual power. The statesman must act on his assessments that cannot be proved at the time that he is making them; he will be judged by history. (Kissinger 1995, pp. 27–28)

What makes this book especially relevant in terms of added value is that it offers to practitioners something more than they can draw from their own experiences. The point is to induce from research, which is based on real-world cases, effective actions. These actions, whose use has been validated through experiences, are a way to bring a considerable amount of knowledge to serve other actors.

Facing escalation, several questions may enter the negotiator's mind. When the escalation appears as a possible event, what are the available actions that would *prevent* entering this mutually coercive process? When such a process is engaged, if the will of the actor is to make his or her own demands prevail by means of a confrontational logic, what is the most useful advice that could be given to enable these objectives to be achieved, in other words to *manage* the escalation? Finally, if he or she wishes to interrupt the escalation process to *shift to negotiation*, or to relaunch the negotiation process, what are the means that could be implemented?

Before dealing with these issues, several preliminary observations must be made. The first one concerns the nature of the problem at hand. When the possibility of escalation appears, it becomes essential to be able to diagnose it. Escalation itself is relatively easy to identify because it is expressed through quite specific features, but foreseeing the occurrence of escalation is far more difficult. The set of signals that announces a possible escalation may be just a tactical maneuver from the other party, a bluff. The prediction that an escalation process must be entered may also result from a misunderstanding of the signals sent by the other side.

As in any social interaction, escalation has a life of its own, a specific rationale that escapes, to some extent, the control of the various parties to the conflict. One has to assess how far one can go without playing the "sorcerer's apprentice" and so setting in action a mechanism that will not be controllable and will end with counterproductive effects.

The degree of expectation of each of the parties also plays an important role. For instance, the North Atlantic Treaty Organization (NATO) ideology of the "death toll zero" led to types of action extremely different from those produced with regard to the concept the Vietminh had about their own human losses during the Vietnam War.

Power distribution is an essential component in a conflict situation. Thus, one has to assess the relative strength – the degree and direction of asymmetry – of the parties and the reliability and stability of their sources of power. These conditions need to be fulfilled to increase the probability of reaching a successful outcome. What about the positional power, as with in the case of a negotiation over pollution or use of water (e.g., building a dam); is the party upstream or downstream, as with countries riparian to the Danube? What are the possible coalitions on both sides? What about their degree of cohesiveness, coherence, and stability? World Wars I and II provide a number of illustrations of coalition-building processes, coalitions that shifted as countries changed sides.

Finally, any action included in an escalation process has to be thought of within a time frame. A negotiator must be alert to identify the ripe moment for action and, more specifically, for which type of action. Strategies only make sense within a context. The Japanese attack on Pearl Harbor and the launching of the submarine war in the Atlantic Ocean by the Germans during World War II demonstrate the crucial role of the time frame, which is a decisive explanatory element of the failure of both actions. Considering the asymmetry in resources, neither of these powers could win in the long run.

14.1 Preventing Escalation

Most events cast their shadow ahead of them. If a forecast of the outcome of a conflict is uncertain, it is up to the strategist to recognize the possibility of it escalating. To this end, a variety of indicators can be taken into account, such as the existence of precedents, the resources available, the other party's motivation, the degree of cohesion, culture, and values, the context, the importance of the stakes, and the existence of alternative solutions. When an analysis of such indicators reveals the possibility of an escalation trigger, two options remain: to prevent the escalation or to manage it.

In the case of an emerging conflict, deterrence may be an effective tool, but it can in no way be a substitute for negotiation. In a full-blown conflict, following Morgan (see Chapter 3), deterrence encourages negotiation if it is highly burdensome, with the prospect of worsening, or if it appears to be adequate to protect against exploitation when parties are willing to start negotiation. Otherwise, deterrence is considered antithetical to negotiation.

The point for the actor is to reduce the risks of escalation and to avoid finding himself "a son corps défendant," caught in a process over which he no longer has control. Several basic principles drawn from the cases analyzed in the previous chapters can be put forward.

Principle 1: Consider the history of the other party

One of the basic skills required in conflict management is the ability to anticipate the behavior of one's counterpart. To this end, one must learn about the other party's past, culture, psychology, and former experiences, and the vision of the problem it might have generated. Strategic thinking is restricted to the level of conflicts of interests, but the individual also needs other inputs, such as meaning and coherence between past and present. This is why it is, if rational, still difficult for an actor to consider the current situation with no reference to past events. The search for congruence, humanity, and the need for structuring elements are basic requirements that cannot be ignored.

What we know about the way the other views a situation is what makes it possible to establish a forecast. In such a case, if the other has, for instance, a highly conflicting vision and exibits defensive antagonistic behavior, a clear propensity for escalation may be diagnosed. It is essential to consider this possibility before making any move. Collecting the necessary information can be done through a great variety of channels, such as interviewing former counterparts of the other party and resorting to informal information channels.

Principle 2: Resort to professional negotiators

A number of experimental works shows that professional negotiators are less prone to escalate than are other people. Their experience, their values, and their ability to anticipate enable them to better control the situational logic in which they are involved. The sheer fact that professional negotiators are not personally parties to the dispute, and thus are not emotionally involved, gives them the ability to stand at some distance from the problem and exercise restraint when required.

A professional negotiator is not simply someone who makes a living through the act of negotiating; he must have been trained in negotiation techniques and have acquired through specific training or through his own practice a satisfying control over himself, his emotions, and his intellectual approach to the problems. When possible, it is advisable to resort to professional negotiators in situations in which a risk of escalation, and all the negative consequences attached to it, can be foreseen.

Principle 3: Consider time and resources already invested as non-recoverable costs

One of the most common strategic mistakes made in negotiation situations is simply trying not only to optimize one's outcome, but also to compensate previous losses. This is typically the case when the involvement is so strong that it becomes extremely difficult not to include the past and the liabilities in the construction of the problem (Rubin *et al.* 1994). One is caught in a mechanism of contentious behavior that tends to be self-reinforcing. The Vietnam War provides an illustration of such a mechanism: the US government considered that the many lives that had already been sacrificed should not have been lost in vain. Making the costs salient has a paradoxical effect. It may deter a party from getting into an escalation process, but it may also incite a party to escalate in order to recover its losses. Such an attempt combines two contradictory logics and introduces additional values, such as justice, retaliation, and revenge, which bring some complexity, if not inconsistency, to the decisions to be made. It may thus give birth to quite unrealistic goals. In fact, the most realistic and reasonable attitude is to act as though the current situation were the start of the process and to forget about the past, at least in the definition of the objectives.

Principle 4: Set limits to your own involvement beforehand

In an auction, which is a typical case of escalation, the wise buyer sets a limit to his or her offer before the start of the sale. In a casino, a well-advised gambler decides upon a bet limit before starting to gamble. In the same way, in order not to be caught in an escalation spiral that is impossible to control and that could lead to entrapment and mutual disaster, the party to the conflict must set, prior to any action, a limit to the resources that will be put into play. To avoid being caught up in such a mesh, the player must plan an overall strategy with adequate means of action, in which setting limits and deadlines is just basic wisdom.

Retaliation is a classic response to an aggressive move from the other party. It is often used to neutralize the counterpart, to contain his or her initiatives, or to re-establish a kind of comparative fairness in the way each party treats the other. However, in order not to trigger an escalation process, a retaliatory action has to appear proportional to the action that prompted it. This is a basic condition if the norm of fairness is to play a mitigating role. An excessive reaction, a punishment that is too severe, instead of getting the system back to a balanced state, would feed escalation dynamics and thus lead parties to go where they never wanted to be.

Principle 5: Consider the decision to escalate from the other's perspective

Deciding on escalation presupposes that the other party will not do the same and ultimately will submit. In this sense, the decision is the result of a strategic calculation. It is essential to apply the same method from the other party's perspective. If the conclusion is similar – that is, if the escalation option is equally attractive for both sides – there is a quasi-certainty that the other party will adopt this course of behavior. In such a case, it becomes reasonable not to engage in such a process, for it does not offer any benefits in the short-term perspective. Also, it is necessary to make sure that your own escalating scale and that of the other party are identical, which is not always the case. In fact, in studying US–Soviet relationships during the Cold War, Kahn (1965) showed that the two scales did not coincide at all.

Principle 6: Disseminate information on some of the possible consequences

One reason a party may engage in an escalation process is its failure to recognize the negative aspects, especially in the long run. This is why, for instance, in the dollar auction game, in which participants try to get a dollar (or the equivalent in the local currency) at the lowest cost, knowing that the second bidder also has to pay without getting anything in return, some people end up buying a bank note for as much as 10 times its value. Providing information on the possible consequences of the escalation thus has a deterrent function for the other party. NATO's strategy in the mutually assured destruction version of deterrence made public the rationale of its defensive system. In the same way, as pointed out by Patrick Morgan (see Chapter 3), Soviet spokesmen openly stated that if a serious war were to break out, escalation to the all-out level would be inevitable. Thus, making possible consequences of an escalation known may have a deterrent effect, especially if the counterpart did not originally have a clear view of these consequences.

Principle 7: Assess the process as well as the outcome

The form is not a secondary element in a negotiation process compared with the substance. The form conditions the outcome. At the same time, the form expresses values, because there are moves that are desirable, others that are acceptable, and others that are not acceptable. Moves made should not contradict the values linked to the content. The process must not be, at the origin, a dynamics that, once launched, escapes from the actors' will and so risks leading to worse. Thus, at each stage of the negotiation or of the conflict, it is important to assess the process in order to avoid such a risk.

Concern about saving face may play an important role as a party may be preoccupied with not showing a sign of weakness and consequently giving a firm or even a tough expression to its conduct. In doing so, it imperils the reputation of the other and induces a temptation for him or her to escalate in tone and in form.

14.2   Managing Escalation

In principle, escalating by reference to the position of the other is an initiative that should lead the other to adopt a behavior that it otherwise would not have adopted. Such a result should be more favorable to the interests of the escalating party. This is the *raison d'être* of the whole approach. When the escalating option has been chosen, what basic requirements should be taken into account to make it as productive as possible for oneself? In broad cost–benefit terms for the attainment of one's own objectives, such as inducing fear on the other side, making it feel hopeless, and persuading it to give in, several recommendations can be put forward.

Recommendation 1: Make sure that the other party has an accurate understanding of the signals you are sending

Engaging in a gradual escalation often starts with warnings or threats being issued. The sender must always make sure that they are really understood as such.

Misunderstandings abound in this domain. Some threats may be taken as jokes, as slips of the tongue, or as excessive language due to current circumstances with the mistaken belief that they bear no consequences.

The absence of anger in the expression of a threat may be misinterpreted as a sign of appeasement. The Gulf War of 1991 might have been avoided had the USA ensured that its threats were taken as such. US Secretary of State James Baker's meeting with Iraq's foreign minister, Tariq Aziz, in Geneva for a last-chance negotiation to prevent the coming war was meant to clearly indicate that the USA would intervene militarily if Iraq did not quit Kuwait. The calm and steady tone of the threat was meant to show that it was not a reaction out of anger; instead it generated a huge misunderstanding on the Iraqi side, which interpreted it as a sign that the USA was not that upset by the current situation (Triandis 1994, p. 29).

Recommendation 2: Ensure the credibility of your commitment in the eyes of the other

If a party issues a threat or wants to show how committed it is, it has to make its message credible. There are a number of ways to ensure credibility, among which are technical knowledge, strict respect of an ethical or religious principle, and high emotion. Building up a threshold that leaves very little room for escalation before an open conflict erupts can also be an effective device. As shown by Morgan (see Chapter 3), negotiation is not a reliable tool for preventing escalation. Deterrence equalizes the capabilities of both sides if each party is able to hurt the other seriously. Equality in psychological terms may translate into political weight. The French nuclear strategy decided by French President Charles de Gaulle typifies this approach.

Recommendation 3: Check carefully that the other party has the resources and ability to make the concessions you request

Once you have shown your determination to escalate if necessary, and assuming that your message is absolutely credible, there is still another condition to meet. The other party may not have the power to abide by your demands or may not have the resources to make the required concessions. In such cases, escalation becomes a useless move. For instance, a terrorist group can make exorbitant demands but cannot expect a seat at the United Nations. In a number of countries, social conflicts can only be solved within the official legal framework. In the case of hostage taking, some governments meet extreme difficulties to circumvent the law when trying to meet out-of-norm demands.

Recommendation 4: Make sure that there is a fair chance that the other party will give in

Deciding to escalate means that you assume there is a reasonable chance that the other party will not continue with the escalation. You must find some clues or indications that enable you to think so. These could be the result of a logical process provided that the other side can be considered as fully rational. These clues could also be drawn from past experiences, from similar cases that happened in comparable conditions.

A clear illustration of the importance of that requirement is the Israeli–Palestinian case, in which each party still believes that it can solve the conflict on its own terms and impose on the other its own solution. Every time, each party has found a way to escalate one more step in deciding a new action, such as resorting to suicide bombers or the construction of a wall to separate the Israeli and Palestinian zones of settlement.

The Falkland Islands / Islas Malvinas invasion launched by the Argentine governments went wrong for them because they made an inaccurate assumption about the response of the British government, who, far from giving in, struck back and reconquered the islands.

Recommendation 5: Consider the possible long-term consequences

People tend to apply a little blindly the old saying "a bird in the hand is worth two in the bush." In the same way, they look for small immediate advantages, which in the long run may appear paltry, either because they could have gained much more in the longer term or because this immediate gain will be counterproductive in the long run (i.e., if the other party resents it and seeks revenge).

A decision with negligible consequences in the short run may have dramatic effects in the longer term, especially on the structure of the game, and thus modify the whole rationale of the system. The point is then to anticipate the long-term consequences and see if they are truly favorable before making the initial move. Feeding an escalation process may thus involuntarily give the adversary more credibility or greater visibility, or give rise to sympathy for it, or even create new allies. Thus, a small dictator challenging a world power may gradually gain the stature of a hero, a quasi-mythical figure, or even a martyr.

Getting into an entrapment process is a major risk in terms of consequences. As underlined by Brockner and Rubin (1985), entrapment is a process in which one party expends more of its resources than seems justifiable by external standards. A desire to protect the "investment" or to avoid an expense leads it to persist in this behavior, with a possible consequence being an increase in the actual cost. Thus, it is essential to foresee if there is a risk of getting entrapped before making any escalatory move.

14.3 Shifting from Escalation to Negotiation

The mechanism of intransitive escalation makes it particularly difficult for any voluntary action by an actor to affect the final outcome. The escalation process is such that conflict dynamics can take over the outcome and lead all parties into a situation in which, in the end, there are only losers. A number of works point out that, to avoid this process, one has to go through an intermediate stage that first matches the other side's escalation before any attempt is made to escape this mutually coercive mechanism. The most likely outcome is a deadlock, which is already a much better situation than escalation because it corresponds to a stabilized state. Although the new situation is still embedded in a lose–lose dynamics (a minimum-payoff equilibrium in game-theoretical terms), it has the advantage of being a balanced relationship, a springboard toward another state.

Unless a party uses escalation to avoid negotiation, as pointed out by Morgan (Chapter 3), at some stage the process has to come to a standstill, which leaves room for new initiatives.

Deadlock is a turning point in a conflict, the end of escalation if not yet the beginning of negotiation. Once the parties have left the arena of violence, a number of effective strategies to start or to restart the negotiation process may be used. In all cases, it is essential to act at the "ripe moment" to avoid resources and energy being totally wasted or the actions taken becoming counterproductive. Turned into practical advice, these strategies are as follows:

Strategy 1: Step back from the action

Make use of the helicopter effect to take a higher view of the problem and to include more elements in the picture. Then, offer this broader view of the overall situation to the other party. Issues that seem essential, and that have become real bones of contention, may no longer look so harmful. The global picture may reveal more factors that intervene, and consequently help the parties to better understand the complexity of the situation. In this case, what works for one side may also work for the other. So, whenever possible, share these perceptions.

A display of the broader picture may help convince the other party that, for instance, external audiences do not necessarily view him as a defender but as an aggressor. This new consideration may be effective in modifying his attitude, especially if the counterpart cares about his image and reputation. Inducing the other to take some distance regarding a sensitive issue, offering him another way to look at a situation, may thus contribute to reducing the level of conflict, to diluting it in a broader set of components of the overall situation and in doing so to facilitate the resumption of discussions.

Strategy 2: Reframe the parties' perception of the issue's value

"The future lasts long," de Gaulle used to say when taking a historical perspective. Applying this to the search for a possible shift from escalation to negotiation would mean integrating the present in a long-term time frame to help the other party adopt a more far-sighted perspective of the problem. This could also encourage everyone to consider the situation from where they now stand instead of recalling (and more or less unconsciously including) sad events from the past and grievances from history in the possible deal.

One should try to help the other give up the idea of recuperating sunk costs through negotiation. After having invested a considerable amount of energy, time, and resources, a party does not want to lose these contributions and thus seeks to compensate for them by increasing the level of its objectives. If such a view satisfies a sense of fairness, it makes the relaunch of a negotiation process more difficult as demands increase. The only rational way to handle this problem is to forget about one's ego and start from the new situation as if no losses had ever been incurred. These initiatives may considerably change the value of the stakes and ease the de-freezing process.

Escalation is usually costly and painful for both parties, not just for the one considering the problem. Thus, another effective initiative related to issue valuation consists in avoiding a focus only on cost reduction, and instead combines it with "gains analysis," telling the counterparts about what their potential gains could be if an end were put to escalation. The multiplier effect produced by such combination may constitute a driving force toward the resumption of talks.

Strategy 3: Work on the context of the deadlock

One way to work on the context of the deadlock is, for instance, to build up a coalition to gain leverage on the overall situation. This can be what Dean Pruitt (see Chapter 11) calls a "maximally viable coalition." If a balance is restored in the relation, it may become easier to persuade the other that she will not be able to impose her own solution and thus bring her to the negotiation table. Another way is to create some favorable event in the broader context or introduce new information that may help the other party to reconsider her position. Another is to suggest the possibility of a radical change in the external conditions such as a modification in the strategic balance of forces by an alliance reversal or a technological discovery.

A new threat, linked to the current evolution of the context, may also produce the same effect. A credible threat may also help to unlock a stalemated situation, such as the threat of dropping a third atomic bomb on Japan issued by US President Harry Truman. Until then, it had not been possible, regardless of the human costs, to modify the attitude of the Japanese government. In reality, there was no third bomb available, but the fact that two bombs had already been dropped and the large number of resulting casualties had been enough to make the threat credible in Japanese eyes, deterring them from carrying on with the war.

Restating bonds of commonality and invoking overarching values may also contribute to improved communication and secure better conditions for opportunities to negotiate. This procedure is often used in the resolution of disputes in traditional societies (Gulliver 1979; Faure 2000, 2003; Zartman 2000). A traditional chief must not only be a leader, but must also be capable of achieving a consensus among disputants, of restoring harmony, of repairing the broken social fabric. For instance, calling people by terms of kinship and emphasizing common values are ways to restore conditions for a relaunching of the negotiation process. Such a method is especially effective in a group that already perceives itself to be a community. The task is considerably more difficult in the case of a nation, a region, or the whole international community.

Strategy 4: Resort to a third party

A mediator may do a very effective job, especially if the level of trust between the protagonists and the credibility of their exposed intentions are both low. Words from a reliable mediator can be far more effective than moves made by the parties to the conflict, because often the latter would be interpreted as "tactical," conceived to fool the other side. Using Track 2 diplomacy or resorting to informal channels belongs to the same category.

A variation of third-party intervention is the emergence of a figure with enough political stature and historical credibility to be unchallenged as a person. This often charismatic figure may stop the escalation process, even if the point is no longer to secure gains but to cut losses, as General de Gaulle did with the war in Algeria, which led to the independence of that country.

Expressions of escalation can be very different according to cultures and stakes, which may result in a great variety of techniques or measures to cope with them. Thus, status competition between groups of the same society led to a phenomenon of economic exchanges that put on stage an extremely destructive logic of escalation in the social life of a tribe of the northwest coast of North America: the Kwakiutl engaged in a "luxury" competition, the potlatch, by exchanging gifts. The goods offered were blankets, fish oil, canoes, money, household goods, copper shields, or other items of value (Barnett 1938). Chiefs of groups challenged one another in a ceremony in which each had to return with interest what he had received from the other. Everyone also destroyed part of what he had to show his status and avoid being considered inferior to his counterpart. Thus, the Kwakiutl did not hesitate to break into pieces their most precious goods, the copper shields, and throw them into the sea. This escalation process was ended by Canadian law, which included jail sentences for the trespassers. In this case, a powerful third party was able to restore harmony in the group and preserve the interests of all parties by imposing a new value, such as peace instead of competition.

Similarly, in Europe at the end of World War II, the real winner, the USA, instead of punishing the culprit as every European nation who suffered German or Italian invasion would have liked, decided to change the nature of the game and create the conditions to avoid the endless repetition of an endemic conflict with Germany.

Strategy 5: Induce a focal point

In many situations there is a kind of obvious or seemingly "natural" solution, a prominent figure or aspect that ensures fairness in the deal to come. For example, it can be a river or a mountain if the point is to define a border. If what is at stake is reaching a negotiated agreement on numbers, splitting the difference is often viewed as a balanced solution, for each party produces an equal contribution to this purpose. This is the application of a general, widely accepted principle. Round numbers, symbolic figures, often provide focal points.

In a negotiation in China to set up a joint venture between a foreign and a local company, a deadlock that was turning into a quite hurting stalemate was unlocked by a statement made by the multinational company to the Chinese party that it was going to be the 68th joint venture of the group. In Chinese culture, the number 6 suggests harmony and the number 8 stands for prosperity. The local company did not want to lose the opportunity of starting the project under such favorable auspices and immediately restarted the negotiation process.

In such a case, the ideal strategy is to suggest a focal point that has some clear advantage for oneself and no obvious disadvantages for the other side. As emphasized by Schelling (1960), bringing a focal point to the fore introduces a new dynamics activated by the symbolic or the cultural value of that point. This subtle power of attraction may help to relaunch the rational process aimed at reaching this focal point and thus help to escape from the escalation mechanism.

Strategy 6: Invent a "decommitting formula"

A "decommitting formula" calls on motives external to the conflict. The idea is to create a new situation, totally disconnected from the former one. Thus, former grievances may no longer apply, new criteria for evaluation may apply, and the deadlock may be over. Inventing such a formula is different from reframing and the helicopter effect in that a move toward the other has to be made, a concrete action has to be performed. Eradicating the need for vengeance by expressing repentance, as Germany did after World War II, can be an effective way to decommit. Otherwise, as observed by Kim (Chapter 6), negotiation has a very limited capacity to cope with human passions, such as the desire for revenge. Peace has a price that must be paid. There is no real settlement unless all of the parties renounce seeking compensation. The point is not to forget, but to forgive as the basic condition for reconciliation. This is often done through a process of mourning with pilgrimages, commemorations, and symbolic actions. The huge resentment remaining in China toward the Japanese after their devastating occupation of parts of China is considerably fed by the protracted absence of repentance. None of the successive governments of Japan has really tried to resort to such a decommitting formula.

Strategy 7: Redesign a solution based on an acceptable concept of fairness

Redesigning a solution based on an acceptable concept of fairness can be achieved through issues aggregation that builds up a new formula for agreement. Introducing fairness through a principle of justice to counter bald power relations may help parties to reconsider the overall situation and to meet at the negotiation table within the framework of a new value. Equality concerning contributions or losses (concessions), meeting the specific needs of each party, or allocation according to the respective contributions may be acceptable principles. Regardless of the principle of fairness considered, the point is to reconstruct a formula of agreement, a new architecture for a solution based on a shared norm of fairness that will operate as moral cement.

Finding a precedent that has stood the test of time may be quite instrumental. Resorting to a precedent reassures the parties, gives more legitimacy to the project, and alleviates the suspicion that may exist with regard to a formula whose final consequences, once it has been implemented, are as yet unclear. If such a formula has already been applied to the satisfaction of both parties, this precedent will work as a warrant of a mode of fairness providing a solid ground for the agreement to last.

14.4   Conclusion

In an escalation situation, nothing is ever desperate. Both history and daily life provide a number of examples of ways out that can be acceptable by the parties involved in the conflict. Ultimately, the parties caught (or close to being caught) in an escalation process should not consider themselves to be victims of circumstances over which they have no control. They remain in charge if they are able to take initiatives or to make moves to influence the escalation process. When the escalation takes on a life of its own because of the inexperience or the awkwardness of the parties, it still can be reintegrated within their sphere of control by the various means indicated above.

The methods and techniques drawn from this book are immediate means of action to unlock a situation that is often dramatic and costly for all parties involved. Parties may thus take actions that impact the various components of the situation, such as the actors, the background, the values and interests of each party, the strategic dimension, and the level of the perceptions and problem framing. In all cases, these actions have to be selected according to contextual characteristics. In this very exercise, as in that of their implementation, the personal judgment and skill of the negotiator are decisive factors in the success or failure of a negotiation. Thus, negotiation is still a science and an art, as Raiffa (1982) defined it when speaking about "interpersonal skills, the ability to convince and to be convinced, the ability to employ a basketful of bargaining ploys, and the wisdom to know when and how to use them."

Seven principles to prevent escalation, five recommendations for managing it effectively when such an option has been chosen, and seven strategies to get back to negotiation are like a symphony of possible actions available to all those who do not want to submit themselves to a destiny that escapes their own control.

References

Barnett HC (1938). The nature of potlatch. *American Anthropologist*, **40**:349–358.

Brockner J & Rubin JZ (1985). *The Social Psychology of Conflict Escalation and Entrapment*. New York, NY, USA: Springer-Verlag.

Faure GO (2000). Traditional conflict management in Africa and China. In *Traditional Cures for Modern Conflicts*, ed. Zartman IW, pp. 153–165. Boulder, CO, USA: Lynne Rienner Publishers.

Faure GO (2003). *How People Negotiate*. Dordrecht, The Netherlands: Kluwer Academic Publishers.

Gulliver PH (1979). *Disputes and Negotiations: A Cross-Cultural Perspective*. New York, NY, USA: Academic Press.

Kahn H (1965). *On Escalation: Metaphors and Scenarios*. New York, NY, USA: Praeger.

Kissinger H (1995). *Diplomacy*. New York, NY, USA: Touchstone Books.

Raiffa H (1982). *The Art and Science of Negotiation*. Cambridge, MA, USA: Belknap/Harvard University Press.

Rubin JZ, Pruitt DG & Kim SH (1994). *Social Conflict*. New York, NY, USA: McGraw-Hill.

Schelling TC (1960). *The Strategy of Conflict*. Cambridge, MA, USA: Harvard University Press.

Triandis HC (1994). *Culture and Social Behavior*. New York, NY, USA: McGraw-Hill.

Zartman IW (2000). *Traditional Cures for Modern Conflicts*. Boulder, CO, USA: Lynne Rienner Publishers.

Index

About the Processes of International Negotiation (PIN) Network at the International Institute for Applied Systems Analysis (IIASA)

Since 1988, the PIN Network at IIASA in Laxenburg, Austria, has been conducted by an international Steering Committee of scholars, meeting three times a year to develop and propagate new knowledge about the processes of negotiation. The Committee conducts one to two workshops every year devoted to the current collective publication project and involving scholars from a wide spectrum of countries, in order to tap a broad range of international expertise and to support scholarship on aspects of negotiation. It also offers mini-conferences on international negotiations in order to disseminate and encourage research on the subject. Such "Road Shows" have been held at the Argentine Council for International Relations, Buenos Aires; Beida University, Beijing; the Center for Conflict Resolution, Haifa; the Center for the Study of Contemporary Japanese Culture, Kyoto; the Diplomatic Academy, Tehran; the Netherlands Institute of International Relations, Clingendael, The Hague; the Swedish Institute of International Affairs, Stockholm; the University of Cairo; University Hassan II, Casablanca; the University of Helsinki; and the UN University for Peace, San José, Costa Rica, among others. The PIN Network publishes a semiannual newsletter, *PINPoints*, and sponsors a network of over 4,000 researchers and practitioners in negotiation. The Network has been supported by the William and Flora Hewlett Foundation and the US Institute of Peace. Contact: pin@iiasa.ac.at.

Members of the PIN Steering Committee

Rudolf Avenhaus
The German Armed Forces
   University, Munich

Franz Cede
Austrian Ambassador to Belgium
   and NATO

Guy Olivier Faure
University of Paris V–Sorbonne

Victor Kremenyuk
The Russian Academy of Sciences

Paul Meerts
The Netherlands Institute of
   International Relations, Clingendael

Gunnar Sjöstedt
The Swedish Institute of
   International Affairs

I. William Zartman
The Johns Hopkins University

Selected Publications of the PIN Program

Peace versus Justice: Negotiating Backward- and Forward-Looking Outcomes, I.W. Zartman, V. Kremenyuk, editors, 2005, Rowman & Littlefield Publishers, Inc., Lanham, MD, USA.

Negotiating European Union, P.W. Meerts, F. Cede, editors, 2004, Palgrave Macmillan, Basingstoke, UK.

Getting It Done: Post-Agreement Negotiations and International Regimes, B.I. Spector, I.W. Zartman, editors, 2003, United States Institute of Peace Press, Washington DC, USA.

How People Negotiate: Resolving Disputes in Different Cultures, G.O. Faure, editor, 2003, Kluwer Academic Publishers, Dordrecht, Netherlands.

Professional Cultures in International Negotiation: Bridge or Rift?, G. Sjöstedt, editor, 2003, Lexington Books, Lanham, MD, USA.

Containing the Atom: International Negotiations on Nuclear Security and Safety, R. Avenhaus, V.A. Kremenyuk, G. Sjöstedt, editors, 2002, Lexington Books, Lanham, MD, USA.

International Negotiation: Analysis, Approaches, Issues, 2nd Edition, V.A. Kremenyuk, editor, 2002 Jossey-Bass Inc. Publishers, San Francisco, CA, USA.

Preventive Negotiation: Avoiding Conflict Escalation, I.W. Zartman, editor, 2001, Rowman and Littlefield Publishers, Inc., Lanham, MD, USA.

Power and Negotiation, I.W. Zartman, J.Z. Rubin, editors, 2000, The University of Michigan Press, Ann Arbor, MI, USA.

International Economic Negotiation. Models versus Reality, V.A. Kremenyuk, G. Sjöstedt, editors, 2000, Edward Elgar Publishing Limited, Cheltenham, UK.

Negotiating International Regimes: Lessons Learned from the United Nations Conference on Environment and Development (UNCED), B.I. Spector, G. Sjöstedt, I.W. Zartman, editors, 1994, Graham & Trotman Limited, London, UK.

International Multilateral Negotiation: Approaches to the Management of Complexity, I.W. Zartman, editor, 1994, Jossey-Bass Inc. Publishers, San Francisco, CA, USA.

International Multilateral Negotiation: Approaches to the Management of Complexity, I.W. Zartman, editor, 1994, Jossey-Bass Inc. Publishers, San Francisco, CA, USA.

International Environmental Negotiation, G. Sjöstedt, editor, 1993, Sage Publications, Newbury Park, CA, USA.

Culture and Negotiation. The Resolution of Water Disputes, G.O. Faure, J.Z. Rubin, editors, 1993, Sage Publications, Inc., Newbury Park, CA, USA.

Processes of International Negotiations, F. Mautner-Markhof, editor, 1989, Westview Press Inc., Boulder, CO, USA.